FUN WITH THE FAMILY™

Connecticut

Hundreds OF Ideas FOR Day Trips WITH THE Kids

SEVENTH EDITION

Doe Boyle

gpp

travel

Guilford, Connecticut

The prices, rates, and hours listed in this guidebook were confirmed at press time. We recommend, however, that you call establishments to obtain current information before traveling.

To buy books in quantity for corporate use or incentives, call **(800) 962-0973** or e-mail **premiums@GlobePequot.com**.

Text design by Nancy Freeborn and Linda R. Loiewski
Maps by Rusty Nelson © Morris Book Publishing, LLC
Spot photography throughout © Photodisc and © RubberBall Productions

ISSN 1540-2169
ISBN 978-0-7627-4776-4

Printed in the United States of America
10 9 8 7 6 5 4 3 2 1

For Tee, who still believes it can be done.

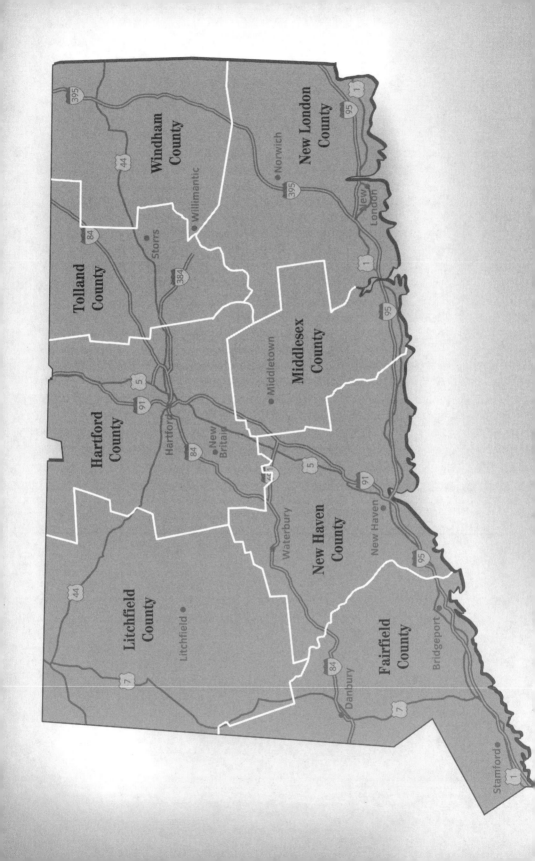

Contents

Preface

In Noah Webster's 1828 *American Dictionary of the English Language,* the word *adventure* is defined, in part, as follows: "an enterprise of hazard; a bold undertaking in which hazards are to be encountered and the issue is staked upon unforeseen events." What better description exists of the social phenomenon known as the family day trip, where two or fewer adults headily depart for an outing with an assemblage of one or more children, a map, a travel guide, maybe a camera, a jugful of lemonade, a six-pack of sandwiches, and an abundance of high expectations for fun?

In most families, a variety of ages, interests, and tastes need to be considered at the outset, or the family day trip will threaten to collapse under the weight of varying expectations even before the family car has left the driveway. On some days, simple variables like weather and traffic conspire against the best-laid plans for an enjoyable day.

Perhaps no certain way exists to predict the hazards that may beset your family adventures, but *Fun with the Family Connecticut* will at least reduce them. Basically, this is a presifted collection of destinations selected by a team of family-fun experts. All the treasures of Connecticut are, in fact, too numerous to be covered in a book this size—even in this thoroughly updated seventh edition. Some categories—annual fairs and festivals, for instance—could fill a book of their own. The selection process, therefore, was both objective and subjective. In some cases, inclusion represents a unique or outstanding attraction, superior facilities, or a broad range of appeal. Exclusion usually represents a decision to limit similar attractions within a certain radius or to reduce what might otherwise result in an overemphasis on one category in the book as a whole. Nearly every town in Connecticut, for example, has a wonderful historical society or historic home. Nearly every county has more than one nature center, bird sanctuary, or wildlife preserve. Christmas tree farms and pick-your-own farms are everywhere, as are toy shops, amusement arcades, and family-friendly eateries. The selection process has resulted in a final list of more than 400 attractions and events, nearly all of which were recently visited by the author and her team of experts. In addition to these are more than 300 suggestions for lodgings and restaurants. Your team of experts should peruse the options and pick those that suit you and your family best.

Even a cursory look through the pages of this book will reveal an obvious emphasis on the state of Connecticut itself and on its varied attractions. Don't be deceived, however. Less obviously, the spirit of the book resides in the heart of its title—it is a celebration of family and a celebration of fun within the context of that unit. How lucky you are that Connecticut is the tool you will use for insight into yourselves as a family. Not only will you learn much about science, nature, and history as you travel the picturesque byways of this pretty New England state, but you will also learn much about each other.

As you read this guide, be assured that I have made every effort to be clear in my descriptions and evaluations of the attractions, restaurants, and accommodations selected for inclusion in these pages. I've made it my business to explore this state thoroughly and thoughtfully with the interests of children in mind. The task of writing this guide has been approached with both enthusiasm and integrity, and I've written the reviews of each entry as positively and fairly as I am able. No matter how appealing or interesting the reviews may seem, you alone as the user of this guide are best equipped to consider the ages, interests, dispositions, and physical and intellectual development of your children. You alone can decide whether a certain attraction may enchant and delight your children or frustrate and disappoint them. *Fun with the Family Connecticut* will, I hope, help you make happy choices, but be sure to trust your own instincts and knowledge of your family.

Scientist and naturalist Rachel Carson wrote, "If a child is to keep alive his inborn sense of wonder, he needs the companionship of at least one adult who can share it, rediscovering with him the joy, the excitement, and the mystery of the world we live in." In that vein, I invite you to use this travel guide to your own advantage. Urge each other toward new experiences. Challenge yourselves to explore what you have not yet discovered. Learn about a topic you have never been taught. Open your eyes to sights you have never before paused to consider. Most important, use this guide to nurture the curiosity, the playfulness, and the imagination of every member of your family. These are the gifts that will sustain you.

Enjoy the journey.

Acknowledgments

M any thanks are owed to the scores of people associated with the attractions listed in these pages. Space restraints prevent a listing of their names, but all—from executive director to publicity manager to docent—provided a gracious welcome, much information, and the opportunity to enjoy their facilities as "ordinary" families would.

Thanks are also due the folks at the tourism districts throughout the state, who graciously accept my phone calls and keep me on their mailing lists and Web updates. All of them are prompt, encouraging, and professional in providing cheerful and generous assistance.

Special thanks this time around to Pat Palombi and Cathy Sidor of Coastal Fairfield County Convention & Visitor Bureau; Diane Moore of the Central Regional Tourism District; Janet Serra of the Northwest Connecticut Convention & Visitors Bureau; Bill Reed of the Last Green Valley/Quinebaug and Shetucket Heritage Corridor; and Eliza Cole of the Eastern Regional Tourism District.

Credit must also be given to the dedicated rangers of the Connecticut State Park and Forest System. With each edition of this guide they have renewed my faith in the possibility that we can preserve and protect our land and educate and entertain our citizens at the same time. Each one of these knowledgeable individuals was friendly, enthusiastic, and committed to maintaining the parks for family use.

The folks at The Globe Pequot Press are owed thanks as well. The work of its editors and designers is in truth as important as my own. I am grateful for their attention to the bones and spirit of this work.

For their great leads, advice, and opinions, I thank the legions of friends and other folks who tell me their adventures, clip articles and reviews, and send me scurrying to see what they have seen. For their unflagging optimism and affection, I thank my husband and my daughters. Their loving support is essential to the happy completion of my work, and as I have written before, I cannot think of finer traveling companions through this book, this world, this life.

Introduction

Connecticut's Bounty

You're already a step ahead of many travelers if you've chosen to tour Connecticut. The rich history of the region has woven a tapestry of attractions that range from typically Yankee to uniquely sophisticated. Among these are boat, train, and trolley rides; science centers and planetariums; canoe trips and river raft races; amusement parks and carousels; art museums; zoos; beaches; skiing and skating centers; and performing arts.

Many attractions reflect Connecticut's remarkable multicultural populations and their histories. Once home to dinosaurs and mastodons, the prehistoric fertile valleys were later roamed by the nomadic ancestors of the Algonkian people. The Mohegan tribe of the Algonkian nation called the region Quinnehtukqut, meaning "along the long tidal estuary." The area's indigenous population is represented in many exhibits and festivals throughout the state.

The arrival of the Dutch in 1614 and the establishment of the Hartford Colony by Thomas Hooker in 1636 led to the founding of the Connecticut Colony in 1639 and the subsequent decimation of the native population. Despite the shameful nature of that transition, much of value about the European influence can be learned today. Wave after wave of immigrants enriched the development of the state. Scholars, inventors, artists, industrialists, and others whose deeds made American history have left their mark. So, along with miniature golf courses and water slides, museums and historic sites appear with regularity on the list of attractions families will enjoy. In fact, you may have trouble deciding where to visit first.

Using This Book

Arranged by county in a roughly west-to-east progression and then by geographic proximity of towns within each of the eight county chapters, each entry includes basic information such as addresses, telephone numbers, Web sites, hours, and admission rates. Then there is a brief but detailed review of what families can expect to see (or learn or explore). Bear in mind that the age recommendations are somewhat subjective based on the author's experience or suggested guidelines.

The maps at the beginning of each chapter are a quick reference to the towns covered in each county. Not intended to replace a good highway map or to provide routes for driving tours, the maps should help you gain a general sense of the area.

At the end of each chapter are listings of additional sources of information.

Rates

Throughout this book dollar signs provide a sense of the price range at various establishments. For meals, prices are per individual dinner entrees. Keep in mind that meal prices generally do not change seasonally but that lunch may be less expensive than dinner. For lodging, rates are for a double room, European Plan (no meals), unless otherwise noted. In addition, guests are charged state sales tax, not included in the room rate. Lodging rates usually are seasonal, with higher rates prevailing during the warm months, at holiday and school vacation times, or in winter near ski centers. Be sure to inquire about special rates. Camping rates are listed under individual attractions and reflect nightly campsite fees. Rates for attractions represent the range per person for both adults and

Connecticut's State Parks and Historic Sites

The rangers at Connecticut's state parks and historic sites are some of the most dedicated professionals employed by the State of Connecticut, committed to preserving safe public access to 200,000 acres of state-owned lands. Stewards of 2,000 miles of rivers and streams, 800 miles of hiking trails, 1,300 campsites, and 100 public boat launches, they are dedicated to implementing Governor M. Jodi Rell's 2006 initiative called No Child Left Inside (check the Web site www.nochildleftinside.org). Designed to encourage families to enjoy the recreational resources of Connecticut's state parks, the Web site lists all of the parks and their features and services, with links to all special events in the parks throughout the year, a parks trivia quiz, and information on obtaining season passes ($50 per Connecticut vehicle for one-year admission to all parks). Before you set out on a trip to any of Connecticut's state parks or historic sites, be sure to check the Web site for current information on park hours and services. Always carry a heavy-duty plastic bag to pack out trash; bring along drinking water and toilet tissue. Do not allow children to swim when no lifeguards are present. Obey signs that indicate closed trails and restrooms. Look for news about closings or delayed openings on the No Child Left Inside Web site or the Connecticut State Parks Web site (http://dep.state.ct.us/stateparks).

children. Free admission for younger children, if offered, is noted separately. If a facility hopes for a donation, that too is noted. Keep in mind that many "free" facilities do indeed welcome the public at no charge but also depend on visitors' generosity. Remember also that rates change frequently, and the range reflects the prices charged in fall 2007.

Rates for Lodging

$	$51 to $75
$$	$76 to $99
$$$	$100 to $124
$$$$	$125 and up

Rates for Restaurants

$	most entrees under $10
$$	most $11 to $15
$$$	most $16 to $20
$$$$	most over $20

Rates for Attractions

$	$5.00 and under
$$	$6.00 to $10.00
$$$	$11 to $20
$$$$	over $20

If you are planning to stay at an inn or a bed-and-breakfast, call before your visit, and be honest about the number and ages of the children in your family. In hotel rooms with two double beds and perhaps a couch and plenty of floor space, families may be able to sleep three or four small children, for whom there may be no extra charge. In the smaller hostelries, however, space in guest rooms is often more modest; many rooms contain only one double or queen-size bed. Cribs and rollaway cots are available at all of the listings in this book, and a charge of $10 to $20 is usually added for each.

Please note that all restaurants in Connecticut are smoke-free.

Special Needs and Equipment

If your family has special needs, call before you depart. Families with infants and toddlers may also benefit from an inquiry about the use of strollers, knapsacks, child carriers, and so on. Inquiries about the use of cameras and audio and video equipment may also spare you any disappointment.

A Word to the Wise

Although the hours and prices listed in this guidebook were confirmed at press time, we strongly recommend that you call ahead to obtain current information before traveling. Exhibits and facilities change—even locations shift and, unfortunately, some places close down altogether. Restaurants and lodgings are especially changeable, and Web sites sometimes include outdated information. Don't hesitate to let us know if you discover changes you'd like to pass along for future editions.

Attractions Key

The following is a key to the icons found throughout the text.

SWIMMING		**FOOD**	
BOATING/BOAT TOUR		**LODGING**	
HISTORIC SITE		**CAMPING**	
HIKING/WALKING		**MUSEUMS**	
FISHING		**PERFORMING ARTS**	
BIKING		**SPORTS/ATHLETIC**	
AMUSEMENT PARK		**PICNICKING**	
HORSEBACK RIDING		**PLAYGROUND**	
SKIING/WINTER SPORTS		**SHOPPING**	
PARK		**PLANTS/GARDENS/NATURE TRAILS**	
ANIMAL VIEWING		**FARMS**	

Fairfield County
Gold Coast and Green Woods

Widely known as Connecticut's wealthiest, busiest, and most densely populated area, Fairfield County offers a distinctive mix of attractions that belies the stereotyped reputation that gave parts of it the nickname the Gold Coast. True, vast estates fight for space alongside sleek corporate headquarters and manicured suburban enclaves, but much more is also here along this coastal plain, the gateway to New England.

Out-of-state visitors looking for a taste of New England within 60 miles of Manhattan can stop here to sample the Yankee charms of industry, prosperity, and abundance so evident in Fairfield County. This part of the state has long been popular as a

TopPicks for fun in Fairfield County

1. Stepping Stones Museum for Children

2. Audubon Center of Greenwich

3. Stamford Museum and Nature Center

4. *SoundWaters* Eco-Cruises

5. The Maritime Aquarium at Norwalk

6. *G. W. Tyler* Cruises to Sheffield Island Lighthouse

7. Westport Country Playhouse Family Festivities

8. The Beardsley Zoological Gardens and Carousel

9. Devil's Den Nature Preserve

10. Squantz Pond State Park

FAIRFIELD COUNTY

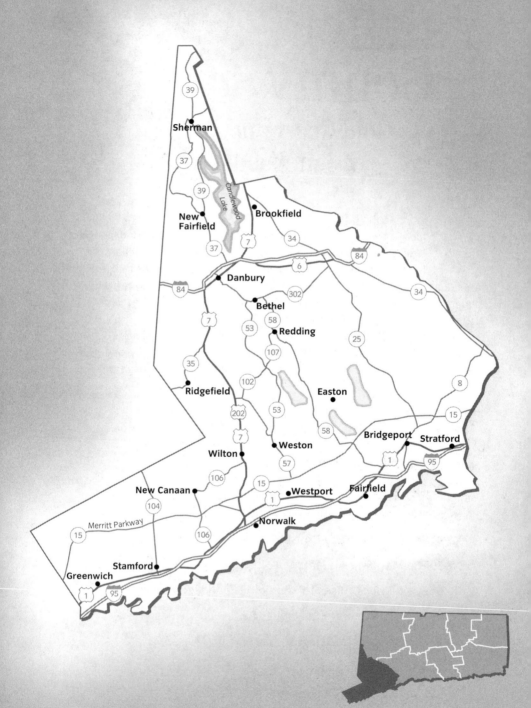

playground for those seeking the forest, fields, and flowers in spring; the sea and sun in summer; the glorious foliage and bounties of the harvest in autumn; and the snowy serenity of the lanes and pastures in winter. Throughout the seasons, the famed Gold Coast offers a multifaceted gestalt of glitz and glade to suit all tastes and ages.

Some families may wish to search for fun in the county's metropolitan areas. The urban movers and shakers of Stamford, Norwalk, and Bridgeport woo travelers wary of the city by providing state-of-the-art museums, aquariums, playgrounds, and performing-arts stages equal to those in Boston and New York. Families adventuring among the city-based destinations will find well-marked streets, good lighting, safe parking, and top-notch facilities to ensure worry-free enjoyment of the city.

Families on the lookout for activities centered on the aquatic and nautical delights of Long Island Sound will find myriad opportunities for fun on and in the waters off the Gold Coast. First-time visitors may want to get their feet wet, so to speak, aboard tour boats that range from an ecological research vessel to a steam-powered cross-Sound ferry or a replica three-masted schooner. Families with their own boats can enter the Sound at a score of docks, marinas, and public launching sites. Fishing charters, daylong and overnight cruises, and sailboat and kayak rentals can be arranged through many operators. Families content with simpler pleasures can take beach gear to any of several public areas for castle-building and beach-combing in the sand.

When the charms of life on the water no longer float your boat, trade your sea legs for a landlubberly stroll through attractions wholly or partly dedicated to the marine and tidal ecosystem. You'll gain Sound-related education at Greenwich's Bruce Museum and at Norwalk's Maritime Aquarium and the Stepping Stones Museum.

Care to leave behind the bustle of both city and seaside? Fairfield County has hidden pleasures north of the Interstate 95 and Route 1 highways. Nature centers, wildlife refuges, and bird sanctuaries also provide shelter for world-worn seekers of solitude.

If you can't go far, at least take the slow lane to the back roads of Greenwich, New Canaan, Stamford, Westport, and Fairfield. If you can, go farther—to Easton, Redding, Ridgefield, Bethel, Brookfield, and the roads that lace around Candlewood Lake in New Fairfield. A yearlong tribute to Mother Nature lies around each bend of these pretty-as-a-picture roadways. Perfect for hiking, bicycling, and cross-country skiing, these trails, paths, and byways meander through maple and conifer forests, farmlands, and orchards, and alongside rivers, streams, and waterfalls. Far from the clamor to the south, families who take these roads less traveled can savor the joys of outdoor recreation in the Eastern Woodlands.

A Heart-to-Heart Chat about Arteries

Lower Fairfield County has some interesting road signage on its main arteries, signage that may prove confusing to newcomers. The three main routes that run the length of the county from its New York border on the west throughout the remainder of the county as it extends east are Interstate 95 (also called the New England Thruway and the Connecticut Turnpike), the Merritt Parkway (State Route 15), and U.S. Route 1 (also known as the Boston Post Road, the Post Road, King's Highway, as East or West Main Street or Avenue, or as some other name altogether). All these roads run east–west, but they have signs that say they go north–south. This smacks of some twisted Yankee humor along the lines of "You can't get there from here," but it's not. The roads are labeled that way because in general they lead north from New York and south from Boston. To confuse matters further, in Fairfield County the entrance signs to both the Merritt Parkway and Interstate 95 usually read "North—New Haven" and "South—New York." Pull out a map and look at the names of the towns and cities along both routes. Be sure that you know whether you intend to travel east or west to or through these towns. Then, when you hop up on the highway or parkway, go north if you mean to go east and go south if you wish to go west. It's a perverse little system, ain't it?

A Word to the Driver

The main arteries for visitors traveling through Fairfield County are also the main arteries for commuters traveling from their jobs in New York and New Haven to their bedrooms in suburbia. Traffic, especially northbound, on I-95 and the Merritt Parkway (Route 15) is nearly always heavy from 4:00 to 7:00 p.m. on weekdays year-round. Heavy-but-steady becomes stop-and-go or even bumper-to-bumper even earlier on Fridays and before holidays from Memorial Day through Columbus Day as city dwellers hit the road in search of sun and fun in New England.

Whenever possible, avoid I-95 and the Merritt during these hours. Instead, stay busy in one place—dinnertime is a convenient excuse for staying put—or take Route 1 if you must head out at this time.

Should you become enmeshed in wall-to-wall machinery at some point, it is often best to stay on the road you have chosen—just rock steady with good tunes to pass the time. The other road is likely to be as crammed as the one you wish to exit, although switching can be effective if an accident has caused the delay. Tune the radio to a station with a traffic report and get the scoop. If you are near Stamford, Route 137 (Washington Boulevard to High Ridge Road) will take you between I-95 and the Merritt. In Norwalk, Route 7 or Route 53 will get you on a true north–south track between the two highways. In Fairfield, Route 58 (Black Rock Turnpike) connects the two roads, and in Bridgeport the Route 25 Connector at exit 27A is the route to take.

Greenwich

Visitors approaching Fairfield County from the New York border won't have far to drive for a full day of family-perfect activities. Home to corporate executives, artists, writers, athletes, and actors, the prestigious town of Greenwich is enriched by the varied interests and talents of its wealthy inhabitants.

Adding to Greenwich's riches are its most beautiful assets: rolling hills, verdant woodlands, and 32 miles of shoreline along Long Island Sound and its estuaries. Although much of the coast and woods is privately owned, there is plenty that visitors can share in this top-drawer community, especially now that Greenwich beaches have been legally opened to out-of-town visitors.

Bruce Museum of Arts and Science (ages 5 to 12)

1 Museum Drive; take I-95 exit 3 or Merritt exit 31; (203) 869-0376; www.brucemuseum .org. Open year-round, Tuesday to Saturday 10:00 a.m. to 5:00 p.m. and Sunday 1:00 to 5:00 p.m. Closed Monday and major holidays. $$; children under 5 free. Free to all on Tuesday.

One of the most sophisticated museums in the region, the Bruce houses approximately 15,000 objects in three categories: fine and decorative arts, cultural history, and environmental sciences. Pre-Columbian and Native American artifacts, American paintings, including Cos Cob Impressionist works, prints, and sculpture, French and American costumes, pottery, Tiffany glass, and more are in the art galleries. Changing exhibitions feature such diverse collections as textiles, dollhouses, photography, and mechanical banks.

The science galleries focus on the past 500 years of local history and ecology, taking visitors from ancient to modern times. Within this wing, the cavelike minerals gallery preserves a collection of ores, crystals, precious stones, and fluorescent minerals. An archaeological dig tucked into the coastal exhibit depicts the discovery of the Manakaway site on Greenwich Point and includes artifacts unearthed during the excavation. Interactive exhibits allow visitors to experience the evolution and ecology of Long Island Sound. These galleries also include a simulated wigwam of the Eastern Woodland Indians, a cross-section of a tidal marsh ecosystem, a marine touch tank, a diorama that takes audiences from dawn to dusk in a coastal woodland ecosystem, and an ecological awareness gallery focusing on tree and water communities.

The Bruce offers a museum store and a continuous schedule of festivals, workshops, concerts, and children's programs. The museum also runs a small nature center at the beach at Greenwich Point. Perfect for families with young children, the **Seaside Center** offers free educational activities about the environment for visitors of all ages. A touch tank is maintained at the site along with other modest displays on marine life, but the best parts of a visit here are the guided beach and

The Beaches **of Greenwich**

Responsible use and limited parking space have proven the best tools for protecting Greenwich's beautiful coastal parks. Residents are required to purchase seasonal passes; nonresidents willing to pay the day-use fees ($ admission per person, plus $$$ vehicle parking fee), charged only from May 1 through October 31, can enter the town beaches on any given day as long as parking spaces are available. Beach tickets and parking passes must be purchased at the town hall or the Eastern Greenwich Civic Center; they are not available at the beaches. Daily admission tickets are not required after 5:00 p.m., even in the summer season, but you will still need to have a prepurchased parking pass. The 147-acre park at **Greenwich Point** is a good bet for families. Excellent for fishing and bird-watching, it also features a large swimming beach with concessions, restrooms, and play areas; the **Seaside Center** (see Bruce Museum entry); ponds; a seaside garden; an arboretum; and biking paths. Open from 6:00 a.m. to sunset, the park is connected to the mainland by a strip of land known as Tod's Driftway. Take Sound Beach Avenue south 1.8 miles from Route 1 to a right turn on Shore Road, then onward to the park entrance. You can also go to Byram Park (Byram Shore Road) for the same fees. In addition to its beach, it has a freshwater pool and tennis courts. It opens at 9:00 a.m.

Great fun, too, are the beaches at **Great Captain's Island** and **Little Captain's Island.** The ferry service (mid-June to September; $) at the **Arch Street Dock** takes visitors to **Island Beach** on the three-acre island or to the more primitive seventeen-acre island, where families may enjoy swimming, picnicking, and walking the trail to the nineteenth-century lighthouse. One caveat: To board the ferry and debark at the beaches, you need to be the guest of a Greenwich resident who can show a beach card, and you pay a day-use fee ($$) plus the ferry fare ($). A concession operates on Little Captain's Island, but pack a picnic and beverages for a day on Great Captain's Island. If you would like to cruise the harbor and islands, you can take the ferry service's two-hour **Cruise to Nowhere,** offered from early June through early September; all passengers pay one low fee ($$); children under 5 are free. Tickets are available at the Arch Street Dock from 10:00 a.m. on the day of the cruise; be sure to come for tickets early in the day. For more cruise and ferry service information, call (203) 661-5957, or to see the schedule go to www.greenwichct.org/ParksAndRec/prFerryService.asp. For information on beach passes, call the Beach Card Office at (203) 622-7817 or the Park Pass Office Help Line at (203) 662-3788. To sort through all the details at your leisure, check www.greenwichct.org/ParksandRec/ParksandRec.asp.

marsh walks, sensory hikes, nature crafts, beach-seining activities, and environmental games. The Seaside Center is open from early July through late August on Wednesday through Sunday from 10:00 a.m. to 4:00 p.m. For information on its schedule of programs, check the Web site or call the museum. Nonresidents must pay the Greenwich Point Park day-use fees.

The Bruce Memorial Park and Playground (all ages)
Immediately adjacent to the Bruce is a great place to rest, run, or picnic. Views of a tidal marsh and Long Island Sound provide the backdrop. Leave your car at the museum or park on the street. **Free.**

Audubon Center of Greenwich (all ages)
613 Riversville Road at John Street, Merritt exit 28; (203) 869-5272; http://greenwich. audubon.org. Open year-round daily 9:00 a.m. to 5:00 p.m. Interpretive Building closed Easter, Thanksgiving, Christmas, and January 1. $, free to National Audubon Society members.

In Greenwich's northern reaches, 15 miles of trails lead through 686 acres of woodlands, meadows, ponds, and streams. The Interpretive Building houses an exhibit gallery, a demonstration beehive, a bird observation window, a model backyard wildlife habitat, and the excellent Nature Store.

Several loop trails provide options for varying schedules and hiking abilities. None of the trails are strenuous, but some are moderately difficult. The Discovery Trail leads past a pond replete in summer with bullfrogs, duckweed, and dragonflies. Stay on the trail long enough and you'll walk right across the top of a pretty waterfall at the edge of Mead Lake. The landscape here is extraordinarily pretty and restful, and the trees are among the most awesome specimens in Connecticut. Return in autumn for the spectacular foliage and for the annual hawk migration that can be observed from the Quaker Ridge Hawk Watch Site.

Audubon Center offers hikes, bird-watching activities, butterfly programs, aquatic studies, day camps, and workshops for children and adults. Call or check the Web site for a calendar of these events.

Connecticut Impressionist **Art Trail**

A nationally recognized art trail links fourteen Connecticut museums. Four sites are in Fairfield County, where some say the American Impressionism movement was born. All the sites are covered in this book: the Bruce Museum (Greenwich), Bush-Holley Historic Site (Greenwich), Aldrich Contemporary Art Museum (Ridgefield), Weir Farm National Historic Site (Wilton), Yale Center for British Art and Yale University Art Gallery (New Haven), Florence Griswold Museum (Old Lyme), Lyman Allyn Art Museum (New London), Wadsworth Atheneum (Hartford), Hill-Stead Museum (Farmington), William Benton Museum of Art (University of Connecticut/Storrs), Slater Memorial Museum (Norwich), Mattatuck Museum Arts and History Center (Waterbury), and the New Britain Museum of American Art (New Britain). A series of outdoor exhibits called Viewpoints features reproductions of American Impressionist paintings on large display panels at or near the sites where the artists actually worked. Look for these at Sherwood Island State Park in Westport, the Hadlyme Ferry Landing, Kent Falls State Park in Kent, and Windham Mills Heritage Park in Willimantic. For more information on the trail and special events, itineraries, and packages offered in association with each museum, check the Web site www.arttrail.org. For a free brochure on the trail, call the Coastal Fairfield County Convention & Visitor Bureau at (800) 866-7925 or any of the other state tourism bureaus.

Fairchild Connecticut Wildflower Garden (all ages)

North Porchuck Road. Open daily, dawn to dusk. Free. Audubon Center visitors are welcome to walk the trails of a second parcel just a mile away on North Porchuck Road.

This 127-acre tract offers 8 miles of trails through native flowering plants and ferns. Established by Benjamin Fairchild in the early 1900s as an example of naturalistic landscaping, Fairchild Garden is especially lovely in the spring. On the two properties, more than 900 species of plants, 35 species of mammals, and 160 species of birds have been recorded.

Bush-Holley Historic Site (ages 7 to 12)

39 Strickland Road in Cos Cob; (203) 869-6899; www.hstg.org. Gallery, visitor center, and house museum open year-round Tuesday through Sunday, noon to 4:00 p.m. Bush-Holley House tours at 12:15, 1:15, 2:15, and 3:15 p.m. Tuesday through Sunday from March through December and on weekends only in January and February. Closed Easter, July 4, Thanksgiving, Christmas, and January 1. $$; children under 6 free. Free to all on Tuesday.

If the visual arts or pre-Revolutionary history and colonial lifestyles interest you, visit this National Historic Landmark. Owned and operated by the Greenwich Historical Society, whose mission is to interpret the house and its uses through the past three centuries, the 1732 structure is a classic central-chimney saltbox. Once home to farmer and mill owner David Bush and later a boardinghouse operated by the Holley family, the house is also the site of one of the first American Impressionist art colonies. Childe Hassam and J. Alden Weir, among others, painted here from 1890 to 1925. Examples of their works are displayed, along with an authentic re-creation of Elmer MacRae's studio and a fine collection of household implements, tools, furniture, and textiles. A charming visitor center orients families to the house as well as to the art colony and local history. Three tableaus feature life-size figures in light and sound presentations describing the history of the site, and five interactive stations offer hands-on displays about local history and arts. Changing exhibitions such as 2007's *Once Upon a Page: Illustrations by Cos Cob Artists* are also launched annually. Check the Web site to see if the current exhibit seems well suited to your family's interests. If you tour the house, be sure to ask for the Colonial Fun Pack cards that help youngsters get the most out of a visit here. From September through May, the Vanderbilt Education Center offers drop-in Family Fun Days (one Saturday each month; noon to 2:00 p.m.; $–$$) , in which you and your children learn about history and art through craft workshops, singalongs, storytelling, and dramatic presentations. Check the Web site for the schedule of programs.

Children may also attend the two-week Summer History Camp to learn about eighteenth-century colonial life, history, and art. Designed for kids in grades two, three, and four, each session is divided into a Colonial American Week and an Art Colony Week. Hearth cooking, painting, drawing, printing, fishing, ice cream–making, and other art may be among the activities. In the Young Artist Camp, designed for kids in grades five, six, seven, and eight, campers study drawing, painting, and print-making and learn how to present their work. A **free** Candlelight Open House in mid-December offers costumed guides, refreshments, and entertainment from 4:00 to 7:00 p.m.; check the Web site for this year's date.

Putnam Cottage (ages 7 to 12)

243 East Putnam Avenue (Route 1); (203) 869-9697; www.putnamcottage.org. Tours from April through December on Sunday from 1:00 to 4:00 p.m., or by appointment anytime. $, children under 12 free.

Built circa 1692, Putnam Cottage was used during the Revolution as a meeting place of military leaders, including former resident General Israel Putnam, second in command to George Washington. Restored to appear as they might have in 1700, its unusual fish-scale shingles, fieldstone fireplaces, and eighteenth-century herb garden are among the cottage's special features. The collection includes Putnam's desk, Bible, and glasses, the mirror through which he supposedly saw the British coming, and his military uniform.

Children may enjoy visiting on the last Sunday in February for the reenactment of Putnam's famous ride down the steep stone cliff east of the cottage; they will be delighted to see redcoats and rebels—in full regalia—skirmish on the grounds.

Where to Eat

Meli-Melo. 362 Greenwich Avenue; (203) 629-6153. This very French, very friendly creperie is great fun for kids and incredibly delicious. Try the ham and swiss cheese crepe or the fabulous banana and Nutella wheat crepe. *Magnifique*. Fresh-made soups, salads, sorbets. Very festive juice bar. Open daily from 10:00 a.m. to 10:00 p.m. $

Pasta Vera. 48 Greenwich Avenue; (203) 661-9705. Open daily for lunch (except on Sunday) and dinner, this is the best place for pasta and pizza. Adults will enjoy favorites with excellent sauces. Paninis, salads, soups, tons of takeout. $–$$

Penang Grill. 55 Lewis Street; (203) 861-1988. This popular and inexpensive Malaysian restaurant will suit any food explorers with a taste for spicy Thai/Indonesian/Chinese favorites. Lunch and dinner daily. $–$$

Quattro Figli. 280 Railroad Avenue; (203) 869-4443; www.quattrofigli.com. This cheerful, casual tiny gem has a chic ambience and great dishes for adult palates, but also offers specially made and -priced children's entrees, great little "pizzettes," and very fun build-your-own sundaes. Lunch and dinner Tuesday through Sunday. $$–$$$

Where to Stay

Harbor House Inn. 165 Shore Road, Old Greenwich; (203) 637-0145; www .hhinn.com. 23 rooms, including 3 suites in Victorian mansion near the beach. Private baths, some with whirlpool, complimentary breakfast. Nonsmoking; no pets. Bicycles available. $$$$

Howard Johnson Greenwich Hotel. 1114 Boston Post Road, in the Riverside section; (203) 637-3691 or (800) 654-2000. Standard best bet for families. 104 units, restaurant, outdoor swimming pool. Kids stay **free.** Complimentary continental breakfast. $$

Hyatt Regency Greenwich. 1800 East Putnam Avenue, Old Greenwich; (203) 637-1234 or (800) 233-1234. Luxurious, tasteful, convenient to everything. 373 rooms (13 suites), restaurants, health club, indoor pool, day spa. Complimentary continental breakfast. $$$$

Stanton House Inn. 76 Maple Avenue; (203) 869-2110. 22 rooms, plus 2 suites, in vintage mansion close to town. Breakfast included. Private baths, outdoor pool, beach passes. No smoking. $$$$

Stamford

The glitziest city in Fairfield County, Stamford offers excellent opportunities for family fun in both its southern and northern extremes, along with a handful of lesser-known choices in between. The museums, galleries, performing arts centers, shops, and restaurants sprinkled among the downtown office towers that rise just 5 miles east of Greenwich make the city's center sparkle with a sophisticated vitality. Its shoreline urges visitors to tarry awhile near the marinas and beaches and on the waves of the Sound. Lastly, its northern hills lure families to the hidden pleasures of Stamford's surprising woodlands. In every season, there's a reason to visit Stamford.

Stamford Center for the Arts (all ages)

The Rich Forum, 307 Atlantic Street; The Palace Theatre, 61 Atlantic Street; box office (203) 325-4466 or offices (203) 358-2305; www.scalive.org. $$$–$$$$

The Rich Forum and the Palace Theatre add a dash of panache to Stamford's cultural attractions. From September through June, the Rich Forum's lush performing arts complex hosts highly acclaimed theater productions featuring top performers from around the world. Many of these full-stage performances from Broadway and London are suitable for the whole family. In 2007, for instance, George Balanchine's production of *The Nutcracker* was staged here, as was *High School Musical*.

The Palace Theatre is a fully restored architectural masterpiece with incredible acoustics. Permanent home to the Stamford Symphony Orchestra, the Connecticut Grand Opera, the New England Lyric Operetta Company, the Stamford City Ballet, and the Connecticut Ballet, the Palace offers single-night or short-run performances of music, dance, drama, and other family entertainment such as circuses, magic shows, and musical comedies. The 2007 Family Series included the Flying Karamozov Brothers and the *Adventures of Flat Stanley*. In 2007, the Palace launched a **free** Summer Children's Theatre for groups of ten or more children ages four through twelve and their families. Six productions were staged on Tuesdays and Thursdays in July and August in the inaugural year. Check the Education page of the Web site for a list of the current productions and the show times; call to make the required advance reservations.

Stamford Theatre Works and the Purple Cow Children's Theatre (ages 3 to 12)

200 Strawberry Hill Avenue; (203) 359-4414; www.stamfordtheatreworks.org. September through May. Tuesday through Saturday evenings and Saturday and Sunday matinees. $$–$$$$ ($ for lap-sitters at Purple Cow)

Not-for-profit professional productions often lauded as innovative, experimental, thought-provoking, and socially relevant are of primary interest at Stamford Theatre Works, a historic, 150-seat barn theater. Most of the full productions staged here are best for adults and children older than twelve. Budding thespians, however, may want to participate in the classes offered at STW School for the Performing Arts; children in kindergarten through sixth grade can sign up for acting classes; children in grades two through seven can take singing and musical theatre classes.

Purple Cow productions are wonderful for children ages three to eight. Affordable and fun, they are typically offered at 10:00 a.m. and at noon on selected Saturdays in May, June, and July, and sometimes during the December holiday season. Puppet shows, magic, fairy tales, and dramatizations of children's literature are the usual fare; call ahead or check the Web site to be sure the lights are going up on the Purple Cow this year.

Curtain Call Theater at the Sterling Farms Theatre Complex
(ages 8 to 12)   (♫)
1349 Newfield Avenue; (203) 329-8207; www.curtaincallinc.com. Open year-round. $$$–$$$$

Specializing in theater for the lighthearted, Curtain Call does four main-stage productions each year, along with musicals and interactive murder mysteries. Ticket prices may be the best theater bargain in the state; subscriptions are even better deals; students pay just $12 per show. Both stages have been renovated and enlarged, with comfortable seating and improved sightlines. In 2007–08, the cabaret-style Dressing Room Theatre staged such classics as *12 Angry Men* and *A Man for All Seasons*. Bring your own dinner or snacks and beverages and enjoy the show. In the Kweskin Theatre, full-scale musical productions such as *Miracle on 34th Street*, *Guys and Dolls*, and *Thoroughly Modern Millie* entertained audiences of all ages in 2007–08. Ask about the appropriateness of individual shows if you'd like to take young children.

SoundWaters Eco-Cruises and Community Center for Environmental Education (all ages)   (△) (⬡)
Schooner: 4 Brewers Yacht Haven Marina, at the foot of Washington Boulevard; education center: Holly House in Cove Island Park; (203) 323-1978; www.soundwaters .org. Open Tuesday through Saturday, 10:00 a.m. to 5:00 p.m. Eco-cruises, $$$–$$$$; sunset and fireworks cruises $$$$. (Note: No children under the age of 5 are allowed aboard the *SoundWaters*.) Reservations and advance payment are required; call (203) 406-3335. For weather and sail updates, call the Schooner hotline at (203) 406-3333. Private charters available. Two-hour guided canoe trips ($$$$) around Holly Pond are on the second Saturday of each month, June through September, from 1:00 to 3:00 p.m.

If the smell of the salt breeze draws you toward the water, try to catch a ride on the 80-foot *SoundWaters,* a replica of a three-masted sharpie schooner that offers two-hour eco-cruises from early June to mid-October. Led by trained naturalists, the cruises focus on the ecology, history, culture, and future of Long Island Sound. You can help raise the sails, haul in the trawl net, and examine the catch in four stations that focus on various aspects of marine life and ecology. Public sails on this floating classroom are offered three to five times monthly during the warm season. Special sails, such as a Fireworks Sail in early July, are also open to the public.

The **SoundWaters Community Center for Environmental Education** is located at Cove Island Park (see Cove Island Park sidebar) in the restored historic Holly House. History, natural science, and marine and maritime exhibits are among the displays here. Aquarium tanks showcase freshwater and saltwater creatures; come to see the fish get fed every Saturday at 1:00 p.m. Check the Web site for the yearlong calendar of programs and events for preschoolers through undergraduates and for information on the array of summer day and overnight camps. In spring and fall, special family arts and ecology days are scheduled. These interactive events are perfect for children ages four to twelve. Concerts and canoe trips are frequent. Reservations are strongly encouraged. From Labor Day to Memorial Day, parking at Cove Island is **free** both to Stamford residents and nonresidents. In season, day visitors must pay a parking fee to enter Cove Island; registrants for camps and multi-session programs receive parking passes.

Stamford Museum and Nature Center (all ages)

39 Scofieldtown Road; (203) 322-1646; www.stamfordmuseum.org. Open year-round. Museum and galleries: Monday through Saturday and holidays, 9:00 a.m. to 5:00 p.m.; Sunday 11:00 a.m. to 5:00 p.m. Heckscher Farm and Nature's Playground: daily 9:00 a.m. to 5:00 p.m. Closed Thanksgiving, Christmas, and New Year's Day. Planetarium shows on the second Sunday of each month year-round at 3:00 p.m.; $, plus museum entrance fee. Observatory hours, weather permitting, are 8:00 to 10:00 p.m. on Friday from September through April; 8:30 to 10:30 p.m. from May 1 to Labor Day; $ with no entrance fee. Museum and Nature Center, $$; children 4 to 17, $; children 3 and under free.

This 118-acre property has features like no other Connecticut park. You might begin at the Overbrook Nature Center, an information hub with exhibits that orient visitors to the site and serves as a starting point for programs, guided walks, and self-guided hikes. Outside the center you can trace a brick walkway that edges a garden of native plants, and beyond that you might walk the 3 miles of woodland trails. These include a pond habitat with an adjacent picnic area, a streamside boardwalk with benches, handrails, braille signs, and sensory stations, and the quarter-mile universally acces-sible Wheels in the Woods trail. The center's trails also connect to those of the adja-cent Bartlett Arboretum.

Next be sure to visit Heckscher Farm, a working nineteenth-century farm re-creation that includes a 1750 barn on hillside pastureland, a working garden, and fifty animals, including cows, horses, pigs, goats, chickens, geese, and sheep. In its midst is a country store and a tiny gem of an exhibit dedicated to eighteenth- and nineteenth-century farm life and tools.

The complex also includes Nature's Playground, a wooded one-acre children's play area. An 8-foot-high hollow log leading to a 3-foot hollow branch opens onto a sandpit where kids can dig for fossil and dinosaur bone replicas. A 6-foot-high hollow stump features copies of insect galleries and honeycombs. Among other features are two 7-foot-wide hawks' nests in which to climb, a large-scale chipmunk burrow in which to rest, and a 30-foot-long otters' slide on which, of course, to slide. A water environment area includes play possibilities such as dam construction or boat racing. A tree house, beaver lodge replica, and rope spider's web complete the scene.

That's not all, though: Move on to Animal Embassy, an environmental education "home" for fifteen live exotic animals; demonstrations are commonplace when the exhibit is open Tuesday through Sunday from 10:00 a.m. to 2:00 p.m. After that, check out the Stamford Museum in the Bendel Mansion. Here are changing fine art exhibitions, Americana, and nature exhibits. Several dioramas are the highlight of the Native American gallery, which includes artifacts from four major North American Indian groups. All exhibitions include a children's corner that makes each topic understandable to youngsters. The museum has one of the largest collections in the country of the work of Gutzon Borglum, the sculptor who carved Mount Rushmore. Of those, two sculptures are on permanent display. *Eagle and Serpent* is at the museum's entrance and *Centaur* is in the mansion's sun room. The museum is also home to a planetarium and an observatory, with the largest telescope east of the Mississippi.

Held among all these areas are annual events such as Spring on the Farm Day, a Harvest Festival, and Maple Sugar Sunday. Along with monthly Outdoor Adventures programs and summer camps, these events are all listed on the Web site calendar.

Bartlett Arboretum (all ages)

151 Brookdale Road; (203) 322-6971; www.bartlettarboretum.org. Open year-round, daily, 8:30 a.m. to sunset. The visitor center is open 8:30 a.m. to 4:30 p.m. Monday through Friday, except on holidays. The greenhouse is open weekdays only from 9:30 to 11:00 a.m. Suggested donation for adults, $. Leashed pets are welcome. Access for people with mobility impairments is somewhat limited; call ahead to arrange accommodation to any special needs.

Just down the road from the Stamford Nature Center is this sanctuary of natural-growth oak, maple, and hickory trees interspersed with evergreens, ash, birch, beech, and yellow poplar. Perennial borders, a conifer garden, a native wildflower garden, and a nut tree collection are among the major areas of this gorgeous state-owned arboretum.

Recently improved in beautiful and inventive ways, the arboretum offers 5 miles of trails through its lush gardens, woodlands, and wetlands. A shallow reflecting pond at the end of the Woodland Trail is a perfect destination for young children, as is the boardwalk that leads through the red maple Swamp Trail. The self-guided Ecology Trail combines portions of each of these trails. Pick up a guidebook at the visitor center so you can enjoy the descriptions of twenty-seven stations along the trail. "Bee" sure to check out the arboretum's honeybee hives in the wildflower meadow and the glass-walled observation hive in the education building. The arboretum's

Cove Island **Park**

Located at Cove Road and Weed Street on the eastern end of Stamford, Cove Island Park is an eighty-three-acre recreation area right on the Sound. The largest public park in the city, it is open year-round and offers a wide beach with a pavilion and concessions, picnic areas, horseshoe pits, tennis courts, basketball courts, a softball field, a playground, a path for walkers and joggers, a separate path for in-line skaters and bicyclists, and an ice rink.

From Memorial Day weekend through Labor Day, nonresident visitors must purchase a one-day parking pass; the fee in 2007 was $20 per vehicle. Call the Stamford Parks and Recreation Department (203-977-5214) or the Terry Connors Ice Rink (203-977-4514) for details on purchasing the passes. Passes cannot be purchased at the Cove Island gate. You can also check the Web site www.stamfordrecreation.com. Even in season, nonresident walkers or bikers can enter the park at any time at no charge. Nonresident visitors to the SoundWaters Environmental Center must also purchase a parking pass. Off-season, nonresident vehicles can enter daily at no charge.

Try to stay for one of the guided beach walks sponsored by Save the Sound Inc. throughout the summer. Midday and evening walks offer a study of the shoreline animals and plants. Ask the park attendant for a schedule.

Public sessions (roughly two hours long) are offered at the skating rink year-round. Summer sessions are Friday night and Saturday and Sunday afternoons. Winter sessions are more frequent. Call for the current schedule. Admission $$, rental $.

trails also connect to the Stamford Nature Center's trails, so visits to both areas can be combined.

If your group includes children under twelve, you might want to borrow a nature activity backpack from the visitor center before you set out on a walk. Crayons, scratch pads, a magnifying glass, and a wonderful set of cards with games, questions, activity suggestions, and educational information enhance the experience for the whole family.

Take a stroll through the greenhouse for a look at the incredible cacti and succulents among the tropical and temperate plants in the collection. Lastly, stop again at the visitor center, which contains a gallery with rotating art exhibitions, a plant clinic, and a horticulture resource library.

The arboretum offers one-hour guided walks suitable for the whole family throughout the year, typically on Sunday at 11:15 a.m. and sometimes at twilight on Thursday. A donation is suggested. Check the Web site for a schedule of these walks and for information on the excellent drop-in day and after-school programs ($$$$) for children ages five to ten. Several such programs are offered each month; registration is recommended. An annual plant sale and Garden Fair is offered in early May, and two concert series ($) suitable for the whole family are held every Sunday in July and August. Pack a picnic and come for Morning Music from 10:00 to 11:00 or Evening Music from 5:00 to 7:00. Check the Web site for concert dates and event details.

Where to Eat

Brasitas. 954 East Main Street; (203) 323-3176. This friendly, welcoming establishment is casual enough for families and delicious enough for anyone. The Caribbean/Latin American fare includes child-friendly quesadillas, empanaditas, wraps, corn cakes, tacos, soups, and salads. Fresh, wholesome, and delightful at lunch and dinner daily, inside the cozy dining room or outside in warm weather. $$–$$$

City Limits Diner. 135 Harvard Avenue; (203) 348-7000. Delightfully retro and refreshingly contemporary choices are on the huge menu at this absolutely sparkling 1950s-style establishment attached to the La Quinta Inn. Perfect for families, it seats 220 for casual snacks, breakfasts, lunches, and dinners at typically modest diner prices. Open 7:00 a.m. to 11:00 p.m. Sunday through Thursday and until midnight on weekends. $–$$$

Quattro Regali. 245 Hope Street; (203) 964-1801. Cozy, convenient, and confusing—how can we choose between thirty-two equally wonderful pasta dishes? Lunch Monday to Friday only, 11:30 a.m. to 3:00 p.m.; dinner daily from 5:00 p.m. Patio in warm weather. $$

Tat's on Summer. 184 Summer Street; (203) 325-2222. This busy, cheerful all-you-can-eat Chinese buffet right downtown provides lunch daily from 11:30 a.m. to 4:30 p.m. and dinner daily from 4:30 p.m. Children's meals are discounted 25 percent to 50 percent, depending on their age. $

Where to Stay

La Quinta Inn & Suites. 135 Harvard Avenue; (203) 357-7100. 158 rooms; 30 suites. Restaurant, fitness center, indoor pool. Continental breakfast. $$$$

Holiday Inn Select. 700 Main Street; (203) 358-8400. 383 rooms, 3 suites, restaurant, coffee shop, fitness center, sauna, indoor pool. Coffeemakers, hair dryers, irons. $$$$

Stamford Marriott. 243 Tresser Boulevard; (203) 357-9555. 508 units, including 6 suites, health club and spa, sauna, indoor and outdoor pools. Lower weekend rates. $$$$

Stamford Suites Hotel. 720 Bedford Street; (203) 359-7300. 45 units with full kitchen, health club privileges with indoor and outdoor pools, tennis, continental breakfast. $$$– $$$$

Hampton Inn & Suites. 26 Mill River Street; (203) 353-9855. 99 units, including suites. Restaurant; complimentary hot breakfast. $$$$

New Canaan

Exquisite in nearly every way is the gracious and affluent suburb of New Canaan, just 8 miles northeast of downtown Stamford via Route 137 or 106. Its busy village center is chock-full of boutiques, restaurants, bakeries, and bookstores, many of which are specially designed to fulfill the whims of children. If you hate malls but love to shop, spend a day in New Canaan. Two of the best downtown places are luckily paired: Be sure to browse at **Elm Street Books** (35 Elm Street; 203-966-4545) and take whatever you buy to **Rosie** (27 Elm Street; 203-966-8998), just next door. Pull up a few chairs to the window-seat banquettes to read while you eat. When you are rested and refreshed, stash your books in a backpack and explore two of Fairfield County's treasures.

New Canaan Nature Center (all ages)

144 Oenoke Ridge; (203) 966-9577; www.newcanaannature.org. Discovery Center and gift shop open year-round, Monday through Saturday from 9:00 a.m. to 4:00 p.m. Closed on major holidays. Trails and grounds open daily, dawn to dusk. Free; donations accepted.

A respite from the thrust and parry of lower Fairfield County's version of civilization, the Nature Center's forty acres of diverse habitats include 2 miles of trails and boardwalk through meadow, woods, and marsh. Its compact size makes the center accessible to small children while remaining of interest to older visitors.

A bird-watching platform, two ponds, a wildflower garden, a butterfly field, a maple syrup shed, an orchard, a cider house, and an herb garden are all on the property. The excellent Discovery Room, located in the visitor center, houses exhibits and activities in the natural sciences. See a living bee colony, crawl through a "burrow," make leaf rubbings, handle animal homes and hides, or make animal tracks with rubber stamps and ink. Learn about soil, seeds, minerals, geology, migration, and animal defense mechanisms; check out snakes, newts, turtles, and fish in several habitat tanks.

Back outside is the live birds of prey exhibit, the Animal Care Building for the rehabilitation of injured creatures, and a solar greenhouse. The Education Building and Annex house the center's nature program for children ages three to five and are used for natural-science birthday parties, after-school activity programs, and parent-child programs. The Nature Center hosts such annual events as the Halloween Owl Prowl, Fall Fair, and Holiday Market and offers a full slate of walks, day camps, live animal demonstrations, and canoeing, hiking, and bicycle trips.

New Canaan Historical Society (ages 7 to 12)

13 Oenoke Ridge; (203) 966-1776; www.nchistory.org. The Town House is open to the public year-round, Tuesday through Saturday from 9:30 a.m. to 4:30 p.m. On Saturday only, the building closes from 12:30 to 2:00 p.m. The other buildings are open for docent-led tours by appointment. Donation.

This complex includes five buildings housing seven museums and a library. The 1764 Hanford-Silliman House, furnished in the style of its eighteenth- and nineteenth-century inhabitants, includes a beautiful collection of dolls, toys, and quilts. The Tool Museum houses the tools of the housewright, cabinetmaker, wheelwright, wainwright, tanner, farmer, cooper, farrier, and shoemaker. The fully operational New Canaan Hand Press is a re-creation of a nineteenth-century printing office; the 1878 John Rogers Studio and Museum, dedicated to the famed "people's sculptor" of the same name, houses a fine collection of Rogers's work actually sculpted in the studio. The 1799 Rock School is an original, fully furnished New Canaan one-room schoolhouse.

The Town House includes a library and exhibition room, a Costume Museum, and the Cody Drug Store. The Costume Museum spans 200 years of American life; the Cody Drug Store contains fixtures, salves, ointments, scrip books, patent medicines, and even the ice cream parlor from the original 1845 store, once on New Canaan's Main Street.

The society offers living-history reenactments and encampments, after-school workshops, and special event days (such as an annual ice cream social) when all buildings are open to the public. Call ahead to arrange a family tour of all the buildings.

Where to Eat

Rosie. 27 Elm Street; (203) 966-8998. Stop at this merry place for breakfast, lunch, or carrot cake, which can certainly count as a nutritious meal all by itself. A classic American children's menu includes scrumptious house-made mac and cheese; lunches include three fresh soups a day, paninis on great bread, and wonderful and whimsical cupcakes. Don't miss it—and buy a book next door on your way out or in. Open Tuesday through Sunday. $–$$

JP's Country Cupboard. 17 Elm Street; (203) 966-6163. This old-fashioned malt shop/cafe has been serving American comfort food for more than fifty years. A charming blast from the past, with jukebox oldies, real milkshakes, even curbside take-

out service. Soups, salads, sandwiches, omelets. Children's menu. Breakfast and lunch daily; dinner Tuesday through Sunday. $

Garelick and Herbs. 97 Main Street; (203) 972-8200. Great eat-here or take-out sandwiches, soups, baked goods, salads. Open Monday through Saturday, 8:00 a.m. to 7:00 p.m.; 9:00 a.m. to 5:00 p.m. on Sunday. $

Gates. 10 Forest Street; (203) 966-8666. Just outside the village, this place is colorful and noisy, the food is excellent and original, and a children's menu keeps youngsters happy. Lunch Monday through Saturday; dinner daily; Sunday brunch. $–$$$

Taste of Asia. 73 Elm Street; (203) 966-8830. This spotless eatery offers Szechuan-style cuisine, a handmade-noodle bar, and usually on weekends only, Shang-hai dim sum. Open daily for lunch and dinner. $–$$. If it's SRO here, try Plum Tree (70 Main Street) or Ching's Table (64 Main Street).

Where to Stay

The Maples Inn. 179 Oenoke Ridge; (203) 966-2927.

The Roger Sherman Inn. 195 Oenoke Ridge; (203) 966-4541.

Both of these venerable classic country inns offer deluxe accommodations in standard rooms and suites welcoming to families; rollaway beds and cribs are available. Complimentary continental breakfasts are offered at both establishments. The Roger Sherman also offers fine dining daily in its award-winning restaurant. $$$$

Norwalk

Even were the city not chock-full of terrific attractions, Norwalk's interesting history and charming coastline would make it a perfect family destination. As it is jam-packed with all these qualities, however, there is no doubt that Norwalk is one of Connecticut's most popular cities with tourists. This guide includes only the top attractions and events in town. The city's center is 7 miles east of downtown Stamford and 5 miles south of the center of New Canaan.

The Maritime Aquarium at Norwalk (all ages)

10 North Water Street; (203) 852-0700; www.maritimeaquarium.org. Open daily except Thanksgiving and Christmas Day. Regular hours are 10:00 a.m. to 5:00 p.m.; from July 1 to Labor Day open until 6:00 p.m. Environmental Education Center; cafeteria; museum store. Seal feedings: 11:45 a.m. and 1:45 and 3:45 p.m. daily; shark feedings: 12:40 p.m. on Sunday. IMAX films: 11:00 a.m. and 1:00 and 3:00 p.m. daily, and at 7:30 p.m. on Friday, Saturday, and Sunday. Admission charged to the aquarium alone, to the IMAX alone, or to both together. $$–$$$, children under 2 are free. Parking available at adjacent municipal lots at additional cost.

The flagship of the artsy SoNo neighborhood, this aquarium/theater/maritime museum is a celebration of the fragile ecosystems of Long Island Sound and its estuaries. Overlooking Norwalk Harbor, this attraction includes twenty-two aquariums with more than 125 species of marine life.

Stroll from one habitat re-creation to another, beginning at the salt marsh and culminating at a 110,000-gallon tank with sharks, stingrays, and other creatures of the open ocean. Watch harbor seals swim in a pool and river otters tumble and slide in a simulated woodland and shoreline habitat. View the underwater ballet of loggerhead sea turtles, and handle sea stars, horseshoe crabs, and other tidal pool inhabitants in a touch tank.

All Aboard the *Oceanic*

The Maritime Aquarium offers two-and-a-half-hour public marine-life study cruises on its research vessel, the 40-foot trawler *Oceanic*. On winter weekends from December through March, see the seals that inhabit the Sound during the coldest months. In summer, learn about the ecology of the Sound as you collect water samples, haul a trawl net, and examine the catch in the shipboard touch tank. Summer cruises leave daily at 1:00 p.m. from July 1 through Labor Day and on Saturday and Sunday only in May, June, September, and October. Board the *Oceanic* at the aquarium's dock on the Norwalk River near the IMAX theater entrance. Call (203) 852-0700, extension 2206 for reservations. $$$$

In the maritime museum area, watch crafters build wooden boats in the centuries-old tradition of New England boatbuilders. Discover the names and uses of boats such as the dory, sandbagger, and sharpie as you learn about marine navigation and Norwalk's oyster industry.

Before you go home, watch an IMAX film in the six-story-high theater. An 80-foot-wide screen creates a you-are-there effect, and the 24,000-watt sound system keeps you on the edge of your seat.

Changing exhibitions and related programs are frequent and wonderful. Birthday parties and overnight visits can also be arranged. Special events, lectures, camps, and workshops are commonplace at the aquarium, and many are tailored to children of specific or all ages.

G. W. Tyler Cruises to Sheffield Island (all ages)

Seaport Dock, just south of the Maritime Aquarium at the corner of Washington and Water Streets; call the Norwalk Seaport Association (203-838-9444) for schedule, information, and reservations, which are highly recommended, or check www.seaport.org. On weekends and holidays, from early May through September 30, cruises depart at 11:00 a.m., 2:00 p.m., and 3:30 p.m.; on weekdays from mid-June through Labor Day, cruises depart at 11:00 a.m. and 3:00 p.m. Check the Web site or call ahead for exceptions to this schedule and for current-season updates. Seating is first come, first served. Arrive a half-hour early to allow time for parking in the nearby Maritime lot. $$–$$$

This clean, comfortable, forty-passenger, single-deck covered pontoon offers a forty-five-minute cruise to the outermost of the Norwalk Islands, where one can disembark for an hour and a half of beachcombing, bird-watching, picnicking, or touring the 1868 stone lighthouse.

The knowledgeable *G.W. Tyler* crew and captain offer a lively narration on the trip to the island. Stories about the wildlife areas of Norwalk Harbor are mixed with explanations of various buoys, historical details on landmark structures, and legends of the islands.

Once on dry land at Sheffield Island, passengers can spend time as they choose. Most folks take the tour of the lighthouse. Several of its ten rooms are open to the public, and four flights of stairs lead to the lovely black-capped light tower. Decommissioned in 1902, when a new light was built a quarter-mile inshore, the original light is no longer in the tower. If you prefer to relax in the tranquility of an island idyll, bring along a picnic and spread a blanket in the three-acre picnic grove for a leisurely lunch or brunch. Limited refreshments (beverages, trail mix, and such) are sold on the island, but you might want bring your own snacks. You can also swim (at your own risk—no lifeguards are here) or comb the beach. An environmentally friendly restroom is on the island.

The sixty-acre island also includes the **Stewart B. McKinney National Wildlife Refuge.** Within its boundaries is a 2,000-foot nature trail with observation deck, or

SoNo Historic District and
SoNo Arts Celebration

Like the Sheffield Island lighthouse, this waterfront area is listed on the National Register of Historic Places, and its comeback from decay is a tribute to the city of Norwalk. Centered on Washington, Water, and South Main Streets, SoNo is a picturesque neighborhood of boutiques, restaurants, galleries, and interesting attractions. The **Railroad Switch Tower Museum,** on Washington Street tucked high above the roadway at the railroad overpass, is an interesting slice of history. For more information on this historic structure, call its visitor center at (203) 246-6958. It is open weekends from noon to 5:00 p.m., May through October. The Web site is www.westctnrhs.org/tower.htm. **Free.**

If you like the arts, come to SoNo during August for the **free** three-day **SoNo Arts Celebration.** Hundreds of juried fine artists exhibit their work in a sidewalk show spanning several blocks. Live-music performances, an antique auto parade, storytelling, dance exhibitions, a film fest, and a giant puppet parade are all part of the festivities. The children's area has hands-on projects designed for young artists. Food is abundant, and area attractions and merchants plan special events. Similar events and festivities occur at the **Splash! Festival** held annually in June for **free;** a real treat among the many water-related harborfront activities is the Hong Kong–style dragon boat race. For information on the neighborhood and its events, call (203) 866-7916 or visit www.southnorwalk.com.

you can encircle the refuge by walking the perimeter of the island. Don't forget to note the time your cruise will depart if you set out on such an excursion: The last cruise departs the island at 5:15 p.m. on weekdays and 5:45 p.m. on weekends and holidays. The seating area on the *G. W. Tyler* is covered to protect you from sun, wind, or inclement weather. A bathroom and a snack-and-drinks bar add to your comfort.

Lockwood-Mathews Mansion Museum (ages 6 and up)

295 West Avenue, in Mathews Park, near the junction of I-95 (exit 14 North or exit 15 South) and Route 7; (203) 838-9799; www.lockwoodmathewsmansion.com. Open April 1 through January 1, Wednesday through Sunday from noon to 4:00 p.m., with tours at noon, 1:00, 2:00, and 3:00 p.m. Closed on major holidays. Gift shop. $$, children 8 and under free.

If any child in your family would like to see a castle, come here. A National Historic Landmark, this remarkable four-story stone chateau redefines splendor and elegance. Originally built in 1864 for Legrand Lockwood, Wall Street investment banker and railroad magnate, the lavish Victorian mansion features the craftsmanship of the finest American and European artisans of the time. Incredibly fine inlaid woodwork, marble floors, frescoed walls, gold-leaf ceilings, crystal chandeliers, and fine decorative arts (such as charming music boxes the tour guides will play for you) are found throughout the sixty-two rooms that surround the mansion's magnificent skylit octagonal rotunda. Future special tours will even include the servants' quarters and the astonishing basement, with its brick ovens, wine cellar, vault, and bowling alley.

Hourlong guided tours of the most impressive of all these rooms are preceded by a short film describing the house's ongoing restoration. Annual events include a charming Victorian ice cream social in early summer. Other exhibitions, festivals, and special tours are held each year; check the Web site for current information.

Stepping Stones Museum for Children (ages 1 to 10)

303 West Avenue, in Mathews Park; (203) 899-0606; www.steppingstonesmuseum .org. Open year-round 10:00 a.m. to 5:00 p.m. daily from Memorial Day through Labor Day; from the day after Labor Day to the Sunday before Memorial Day, open Tuesday from 1:00 to 5:00 p.m. and Wednesday through Sunday from 10:00 a.m. to 5:00 p.m. Also open on most Monday holidays. Closed on January 1, Easter, Thanksgiving, and Christmas. $$, children under age 1 are free.

One of the most popular attractions in the state for families with young children is this marvelous interactive learning center. Designed to meet the intellectual, physical, and emotional needs of young children and based on the idea that children learn best through hands-on investigation and discovery, this museum is a "please touch" fantasyland. Firmly rooted in down-to-earth philosophies regarding a child's sense of wonder and curiosity, Stepping Stones branches upward and outward from the point of view that kids love to and need to use all their senses as they learn.

In diverse exhibits that explore the arts, science and technology, and culture and heritage, children can immerse themselves in sensory-rich environments guaranteed to educate as well as entertain. The museum's only permanent exhibit is its entrancing Color Coaster, a 27-foot-tall kinetic sculpture in constant motion near the entrance to this wonderland. Beyond it, in a variety of learning labs, galleries, theaters, and outdoor areas, are such exhibits as Infant Oasis, Toddler Terrain, Waterscape, In the Works, and Rainforest Adventure.

The youngest visitors entering the tot-friendly Toddler Terrain can crawl into a giant tree, cross a carpeted "pond"—on stepping stones, of course—or check out the Busy Wall, composed of mirrors, gears, doors, and noisemakers. In Waterscape, with model streambeds, dams, and waterwheels, children learn about flotation and current under a giant see-through umbrella that protects them from an overhead rainstorm. In the Works presents concepts of motion, energy, gravity, and electricity; Rainforest Adventure focuses on tropical forests around the world. Children can use binoculars, magnifying lenses, and field guides to make discoveries in this and four other interactive environments. Indoor and outdoor activities, theater performances, concerts, workshops, and a parent-teacher resource center are among the unique aspects of this museum. The Age of Reason museum store is beyond excellent, and the Stepping Stones Cafe provides inexpensive, child-friendly snacks and light meals. One of the best such learning environments in the country, Stepping Stones is a sure bet for families.

The Norwalk Museum (ages 8 and up)

41 North Main Street at Marshall; (203) 866-0202; www.norwalkct.org/norwalkmuseum. Open year-round Wednesday through Sunday from 1:00 to 5:00 p.m. (closed Monday, Tuesday, and holidays). Gift shop; reference library. Free.

The small but innovative Norwalk Museum seeks to educate and entertain visitors by presenting the past hundred or so years of Norwalk history from a commercial and artistic point of view. Located in a historic building just a block from the Maritime Aquarium, the museum celebrates the great number of goods invented or manufactured in Norwalk. The Merchants' Court gallery includes items that added to the city's

Aw, Shucks! Oysters!

Another of Norwalk's famed festivals is the **Norwalk Oyster Festival,** held annually the weekend after Labor Day. Celebrating Long Island Sound and its seafaring past, the waterfront events include an arts and crafts show, tall ship tours, an oyster shucking contest, and the typical foods and hoopla of summer festivals. Call (203) 838-9444. $–$$, children under 5 are free.

economy. From hats to scales to high-powered binoculars to light fixtures, each display brings to mind the glory days of authentic local artisans and industries. The Dunne's Hardware exhibit re-creates the authentic interior of a store that existed in the city from 1912 to 2003. The Lockwood Gallery of changing exhibitions has more of an artistic focus, typically with Norwalk or Connecticut themes.

Where to Eat

Chocopologie. 12 South Main Street; (203) 838-3131. Made for families who like to eat, drink, and be merry, this lively cafe proves that chocolate is a food group. It serves breakfast (all day), lunch (soups, sandwiches on great crusty bread, salads, quiche), and dinners (the same as lunch), but the best part of all are the handmade chocolates to swoon for. Come watch the process that takes place in the chocolate workshop. $–$$

Lime. 168 Main Avenue; (203) 846-9240. Come here for delicious natural foods and vegetarian specials from the simple to the gourmet. Soups, salads, excellent breads, and Middle Eastern and Mediterranean specialties, plus seafood, steak, chicken, and grilled cheese and nachos. Lunch and dinner Monday through Saturday; dinner only on Sunday. $–$$$

Strada 18. 18 Washington Street; (203) 853-4546. For pizza and calzones that are a little more gourmet in a setting that is a *little* more adult, come here for thin crusts and inventive toppings, good salad combos, great gelato, house-made sorbets, and biscotti. Lunch and dinner daily, noon to 9:30 p.m. (later on weekends). $–$$$

Fat Cat Joe. 5 Wall Street; (203) 523-0389. Breakfast and lunch are served daily from 7:30 a.m. Try the breakfast pie (scrambled eggs on pizza crust—yum) and house-made banana and other breads. Great soups, too. Oh—and coffees of all sorts. $

Silvermine Tavern. 194 Perry Avenue; (203) 847-4558. For a special, old-fashioned treat, dine in a colonial inn overlooking a waterfall and pond. Families are warmly welcomed for New England–style country cuisine. Lunch, Wednesday through Saturday; dinner, Wednesday through Sunday; Sunday brunch. Live jazz Thursday through Sunday. Outdoor deck. Children's menu. $$$–$$$$

Where to Stay

Courtyard by Marriott-Norwalk. 474 Main Avenue; (203) 849-9111 or (800) 647-7578. 145 units, restaurant, health club, indoor pool. $$$$

DoubleTree Hotel. 789 Connecticut Avenue; (203) 853-3477. 268 rooms, restaurant, fitness room, indoor pool. $$$$

Norwalk Inn & Conference Center. 99 East Avenue; (203) 838-5531 or (800) 303-0808. 71 units, restaurant, fitness center, coffee shop, outdoor pool. Full breakfast. $$$$

Silvermine Tavern. 194 Perry Avenue; (203) 847-4558. 11 rooms in 1785 country inn in sylvan setting. Antiques and fireplaces add to the old-fashioned ambience. Continental breakfast. $$$$

Westport

Bordering Norwalk on the west and Fairfield on the east, shore-hugging Westport usually needs no introduction. Long famous as a haven for writers, actors, artists, and other glitterati, it is well known as the suburb of suburbs with a dash of panache rivaled only by its imitators. Families are attracted to the beaches and the woodlands as much as to the entertainment, the shops, and the restaurants. Year-round and seasonal activities ensure that there's always fun for the family in Westport.

Earthplace: The Nature Discovery Center (all ages)

10 Woodside Lane; (203) 227-7253; www.earthplace.org. Open year-round. Grounds, 7:00 a.m. to dusk daily. Building, Monday through Saturday from 9:00 a.m. to 5:00 p.m. and Sunday from 1:00 to 4:00 p.m. Closed on major holidays. Building admission, $$; children 1 to 12, $; admission to grounds is free for all.

Open 365 days a year from dawn to dusk, the sixty-two-acre wildlife sanctuary at this unique facility includes 2 miles of trails for all ages, especially the very young. A Swamp Loop Trail, an open field habitat, and a universal-access trail called Wheels in the Woods are among the six trail options outside. A lovely wildflower courtyard and a bird and butterfly garden showcase both native and introduced plants. An outdoor Birds of Prey area features two bald eagles, several owls, hawks, vultures, and other species.

Inside Earthplace's 20,000-square-foot museum is an exhibit hall with such interactive areas as the Tiny Treehouse and the Explorer's Clubhouse. A live-animal hall with many species of indigenous creatures offers frequent special demonstrations. Changing displays focus on ecology and animal biology. A working water-quality lab, a wildlife rehab center, and a gift shop are also here.

Best of all, though, are the workshops, guided walks, outdoor classes, and summer camp programs. Beachwalks, family campfires, maple-sugaring, birdbanding, a holiday fair, and more are open to all visitors. If none of those options appeal, still come to this little slice of wilderness—wild turkeys, pheasants, red foxes, deer, hawks, songbirds, and more await you.

Sherwood Island State Park (all ages)

Off I-95 exit 18. Turn south at the end of the ramp to enter the park; (203) 226-6983. Open daily year-round, 8:00 a.m. to sunset. Day-use fees, $$–$$$ per vehicle. Off-season parking is free, except on weekends in May and September, when the charge is again $$–$$$.

This park's 1½-mile beach is preceded by 234 acres of open space, two picnic groves, and several drives, footpaths, and walkways. Swimming, fishing, and scuba diving or snorkeling are permitted in the Sound (scuba divers must register with the rangers); on dry land you can enjoy kite flying, volleyball, badminton, horseshoes, bocce, and bicycling. A softball field can be used on a first come, first play basis. Bring your own equipment for all of the above.

The park's appeal to families is enhanced by a self-guided interpretive nature trail that points out flora, fauna, and special areas of importance to Long Island Sound and its estuaries. Just ½-mile long, it is perfect for families with young children and is informative for all ages. In the park's east pavilion, a nature center, linked to the trail, celebrates the marine environment. Among the indoor displays are a marine aquarium, marsh tank, and touch tank with local species of marine life. Outdoors, a bird observation deck provides an overview of the shore habitat. Tree and bird guides and maps are available at the pavilion to help visitors enjoy the flora and fauna, and naturalist-guided walks and talks are scheduled each season. A memorial dedicated to Connecticut citizens who lost their lives on September 11, 2001, is located near the park's landmark black cherry tree.

The park provides public restrooms, changing rooms, outdoor showers, a first-aid station, and lifeguards (from Memorial Day through Labor Day). Only the restrooms are available in the winter. A concession stand operates in summer. Folks are welcome to picnic or barbecue.

Westport Country Playhouse (ages 4 and up)

25 Powers Court, off Route 1; Box office: (203) 227-4177 or (888) 927-7529; www .westportplayhouse.org. Family Flex Passes are $260 each. Groups of 10 or more save up to 30 percent off the regular ticket price. For group sales information, call (203) 227-5137, extension 120. For a Family Festivities brochure, call the box office. $$$

For more than seventy-five years, this wonderful, old-time summer-stock playhouse has offered professional productions starring such legends as Henry Fonda, Helen Hayes, Jessica Tandy, Gene Kelly, Liza Minnelli, and Cicely Tyson, among many others. First located in a cow barn–turned–tanning factory and then a rustic theater with post-and-beam construction and bench-style seating, the playhouse was completely renovated and expanded in 2005.

Actress Joanne Woodward and other theater supporters have worked tirelessly to bring the theater to new heights. Now the playhouse is a year-round venue with state-of-the-art technology paired with its traditional country-roots charm. Theater lovers can enjoy the usual bill of fare: musicals, comedies, and dramas, and a slate of Family Festivities with a special focus on theater-goers ages four to twelve. Fairy-tale productions, puppet theaters, magic shows, and concerts are often among those entertainments. Among the Family Festivities of the 2007–08 season were a puppet-presented medley of *Aesop's Fables; Pinkalicious*, based on the book by Elizabeth Kann and Victoria Kann; Katie Couric's musical *The Brand-New Kid;* and Roald Dahl's *James and the Giant Peach,* performed by Signstage Theatre in American Sign Language and spoken English. Tickets to 2007–08 Family Festivities were $12 per ticket for four shows, $14 per ticket for three shows, and $16 per ticket for one or two shows. Everyone in the audience requires a ticket. A Family Flex Pass is available for ten tickets to any performance during the season, including the all-ages production of *A Christmas Carol* and other major theatrical productions as well as the Family Festivities shows. Tickets to the playhouse's Halloween Spooktacular are **free**, by reservation. Check the Web site for details about this special annual event.

Levitt Pavilion for the Performing Arts (all ages)

Jesup Road, behind the Westport Public Library; (203) 226-7600 for a calendar or (203) 221-4422 for recorded information on the concert hotline; www.levittpavilion.com. Free.

If theater ticket prices are too high for your budget (and even if they're not), don't miss the festival atmosphere at the Levitt. Another sort of summer theater, it is one of the most ambitious undertakings of its kind.

On the banks of the Saugatuck River, this open-air series offers more than fifty evenings of entertainment from late June through late August. Bring a blanket, chairs, and a picnic to the lawn in front of the band shell and enjoy the **free** performances suitable for the whole family.

Tuesday is Potpourri Night—maybe swing, maybe the community band, maybe stories for children. Wednesday is Family Night (mime, puppetry, magic, storytelling). Thursday is classical/cabaret/theater, Friday is Party Time (folk, reggae, bluegrass, or rock 'n' roll), Saturday is pop/rock/blues, and Sunday is big band/blues/jazz. On Monday there is no show. Occasional special events—one or two—do charge admission. Call for a calendar. Showtimes vary slightly, but Wednesday and Sunday performances are usually at 7:00 p.m. and most others are at 8:00 p.m. Friday and Saturday are designated as alcohol-free evenings. A food or ice cream concession operates on some nights, but most folks bring pizza or other picnic fare.

Park in the municipal lots in back of the public library on Jesup Road off the Post Road East (Route 1) and walk up the gravel path toward the band shell at the side of the river.

Where to Eat

Bertucci's. 833 Post Road East; (203) 454-1559. Tasty pasta, fresh salads, and crusty rolls, among other family-pleasing dishes and pizzas of all sorts. Open Monday through Saturday from 11:00 a.m. to 10:00 p.m. and Sunday from noon to 10:00 p.m. $$

DeRosa's. 577 Riverside Avenue; (203) 227-7596. Great pastas, superb pizza, great folks here, doing everything right for more than twenty years. Open daily from 11:00 a.m. for lunch and dinner. $$

Katzenberg Kafe. 22 Main Street; (203) 221-1321. Wraps and deli sandwiches are the main fare here, along with soups, chilis, and a kosher hot dog bar. Great hot cocoa specials. Breakfast and lunch from 8:00 a.m. on weekdays and 9:00 a.m. on weekends. $

Where to Stay

The Inn at Longshore. 260 Compo Road South; (203) 226-3316. Twelve rooms (3 suites) in this lovely country inn overlooking the Sound. Playground, pool, tennis, golf, boating, beach swimming. Complimentary breakfast buffet. $$$$

The Westport Inn. 1595 Post Road East; (203) 259-5236 or (800) 446-8997. Full-service hotel with 115 units, indoor pool, sauna, fitness center, restaurant. Complimentary continental breakfast. Weekend packages. $$$–$$$$

Fairfield

Settled in 1639, Fairfield is one of Connecticut's oldest towns, so it's not surprising to find beautiful historic homes and still-quaint village centers within its boundaries. Populated mostly by farmers, tradespeople, sailors, and shipbuilders through much of the eighteenth century, the town was burned by the British in 1779. Rebuilding was slow but determined, and soon the community had rallied as Southport and Black Rock Harbors helped to reestablish Fairfield's place as an important port of entry. Two centuries later, Fairfield's shoreline location still influences life in this thriving, comfortable community.

Ogden House and Gardens (ages 7 to 12)
1520 Bronson Road; (203) 259-6356 or (203) 259-1598; www.fairfieldhs.org. Public tours from May through September on Sunday from 1:00 to 4:00 p.m. $

A meticulously restored historic site for those interested in pre-Revolution life, Ogden House, owned and operated by the Fairfield Museum and History Center, is a 1750 saltbox farmhouse furnished to portray the lives of its first inhabitants, Jane and David Ogden. An eighteenth-century kitchen garden and a native wildflower garden are also on the picturesque property overlooking Brown's Brook near Mill River.

In addition to annual events celebrating the gardens and the seasons, Ogden House offers an annual Hands-On History Camp during the second week in July. Designed to take children (ages eight to eleven) back to the time of Jane Ogden, the program offers cooking, tin lantern piercing, taffy pulling, and eighteenth-century games. Birthday parties include a guided tour with a docent portraying Mrs. Ogden, hoop-rolling lessons, and a choice of crafts such as candle dipping, wood carving, or corn-husk doll making. High school students can make reservations to participate in the archaeological dig taking place on the property, and an ongoing schedule of hands-on workshops for children has included teddy bear repair, gravestone study, and principles of archaeology.

Fairfield Museum and History Center (ages 7 to 12)
370 Beach Road; (203) 259-1598; www.fairfieldhs.org. Open Monday through Friday from 10:00 a.m. to 4:00 p.m., Thursday from 10:00 a.m. to 6:00 p.m., and Saturday and Sunday from noon to 4:00 p.m. Closed on major holidays. $; children under 5 are free. Separate fees for some programs and workshops.

Take to **the Sea**

For great lessons on physical, spiritual, and environmental fitness, get the family out on Connecticut's waterways in a traditional, fossil-fuel-free vessel of one sort or another. Kayaks, canoes, rowboats, sailboards, and small sailboats are offered as rentals throughout the state. Below are some of the best outfitters in Fairfield County. Some also offer lessons, camp programs, and guided tours. A few offer winter as well as warm-weather opportunities. All are well worth the fees and reservations that may be required.

Below Deck. 157 Rowayton Avenue, Rowayton; (203) 852-0011.
Darien Windsurfing. Nearwater Lane, Weed Beach, Darien; (203) 655-6757.
Gone with the Wind Surf Club. Nearwater Lane, Weed Beach, Darien; (203) 852-1857.
Kayak Adventure, LLC. 24 Poplar Street, Norwalk; (203) 852-7294.
Longshore Sailing School. 260 Compo Road South, Longshore Club Park, Westport; (203) 226-4646 .
Norwalk Sailing School. Calf Pasture Beach Road, Norwalk; (203) 852-1857.
Outdoor Recreation Services. 244 Melody Lane, Fairfield; (203) 610-3717.
Outdoor Sports Center. 80 Danbury Road, Wilton; (203) 762-8797.
Sailaway Sailing School. Captain's Cove Seaport, 1 Bostwick Avenue, Bridgeport; (203) 332-SAIL.
Small Boat Shop. 144 Water Street, Norwalk; (203) 854-5223.
Sound Sailing Center. 54A Calf Pasture Beach Road, Norwalk; (203) 838-1110.
SoundWaters Coastal Education Center for Environmental Education. 1281 Cove Road, Cove Island Park, Stamford; (203) 323-1978.

In its brand-new 13,000-square-foot home behind the Fairfield Town Hall, this "small" museum has undergone huge changes since the last edition of this volume. Spacious new exhibition galleries, a classroom for education programs, an extensive library and genealogy research center, and a lovely gift shop are all within the striking post-and-beam building now incorporated into a cultural and historical campus that includes the Sun Tavern, Burr Mansion, and town hall, among other important Fairfield landmarks. The museum holds an important permanent collection of 15,000 objects from pre-Revolutionary days to the present, including costumes, furnishings, and decorative arts.

The library continues to open its doors to those interested in Connecticut history and genealogy, but the big change here is the capability to offer many more workshops, educational programs, musical entertainments, story hours, and such special events as encampments and reenactments. Check the museum Web site for the latest information on the excellent new programming and activities for families.

Birdcraft Museum and Sanctuary (all ages)

314 Unquowa Road; (203) 259-0416; www.ctaudubon.org/visit/birdcraft.htm. Open year-round Tuesday to Friday from 10:00 a.m. to 5:00 p.m. and Saturday and Sunday from noon to 4:00 p.m. $

Just south of I-95, this six-acre enclave was founded in 1914 as the first songbird sanctuary in the United States. More than 120 species of birds have been documented here. Huge maples hung with vines, century-old rhododendrons, sassafras, and highbush cranberry are along the trail through the woodlands and across a beautiful wooden boardwalk above a shallow pond. Sit awhile at the gazebo and listen to the birds and frogs. Look for the nesting night herons.

Inside the turn-of-the-twentieth-century museum, designated a National Historic Landmark, the venerable history of the museum is preserved in classic exhibit areas. Four galleries feature birds and mammals of New England, grouped in diorama displays by habitat and seasons. The murals here are exceptional, as is the gallery of African animals. These exhibits fulfill the dream of Mabel Osgood Wright, founder of the Connecticut Audubon Society and founding member of the American Conservation Movement. It is in the property's vintage cottage, reincarnated as a visitor center, that guests are introduced to Ms. Wright's important contributions to conservation and are oriented to the varied attractions. The cottage's Nature Observatory space includes a hands-on classroom for activities and workshops, a library, an observation deck, and a nature gift shop and bookstore.

A variety of hands-on children's programs, story hours, summer camps, and natural history and crafts workshops fills the needs of young naturalists, but you can also stroll around on your own or take a one-hour guided tour, arranged by appointment. Come the second Saturday of May for International Migrating Bird Day, a festival of bird-watching, crafts, a book sale, and lessons on how to attract birds to your own yard.

Roy and Margot Larsen Bird Sanctuary and Connecticut Audubon Center at Fairfield (all ages) 🚻 💺 🍁

2325 Burr Street; (203) 259-6305. The nature center is open year-round, Tuesday through Saturday, from 9:00 a.m. to 4:30 p.m. Admission to the center is free. The sanctuary is open daily, year-round, from dawn to dusk. $

Located in the Greenfield Hill neighborhood in the north end of town, the beautiful 160-acre tract of New England woodland was created on reclaimed farm property. Juxtaposing habitats and trails to allow people maximum opportunity to experience the diversity without disturbing the refuge, this model wildlife sanctuary features 6 miles of trails, including a Walk for the Disabled, that lead visitors to marshes, ponds, streams, vernal pools, meadows, and coniferous and hardwood forests.

In addition, you can visit the Connecticut Audubon Center at Fairfield (with natural science exhibits, a discovery room, live animal displays, and a gift shop/bookstore) and the Educational Animal Compound of nonreleasable animals. See a peregrine falcon, a red-tailed hawk, and several owls.

Summer camps, workshops, naturalist-guided walks, junior naturalist programs, and field trips are frequent. You can even have your birthday party here.

The Dogwood **Festival**

Graced by beautiful vintage homes as well as modern mansions, the winding roads of northern Fairfield take you through lightly populated residential enclaves and into a perfect antique village center punctuated by one of the nation's most stately and classic Congregational churches. Known as Greenfield Hill, the area is heavily planted with dogwoods and is famed for its annual **Dogwood Festival** in mid-May. A great outing for Mother's Day or any other reason, it provides opportunities to enjoy the beauty of springtime in Connecticut.

To celebrate the gorgeous pink-and-white blossoms of more than 30,000 dogwoods, the Greenfield Hill Congregational Church (1045 Old Academy Road; www.greenfieldhillchurch.com) plans a four-day schedule of festivities that includes an arts-and-crafts show, a plant sale, walking tours and luncheons, musical programs, children's games, and a white elephant sale. Buy food here or bring a picnic. Bring along a camera to capture the day forever. For information, call the church (203-259-5596) and ask for the Festival Committee telephone number. Admission and parking are free.

Beachin' It

Long attractive for its 8 miles of shoreline, Fairfield has five public beaches that allow residents and visitors to enjoy the Sound. Call the Fairfield Parks and Recreation department at (203) 256-3144 for current parking policies and prices. $$$–$$$$

Penfield Beach (Fairfield Beach Road) and **Jennings Beach** (South Benson Road) offer pavilions, concessions, restrooms and showers, playgrounds, and convenient parking. **Southport Beach** (Pequot Avenue) is quieter, less crowded, and has great sandbars for young children, plus restrooms and a concession. It's also just past the historic village center of Southport—a pleasant place to stroll and pick up some picnic goodies at the **Spic and Span Market** (203-259-1688; open Monday through Saturday), also on Pequot Avenue.

Where to Eat

Centro Ristorante. 1435 Post Road; (203) 255-1210. Located downtown (near Sherman Green) is this casual but elegant Italian restaurant that offers a bit of panache combined with a down-home feeling that is accommodating to families. Homemade pastas, great caesar salad, good seafood, thin-crust pizzas, and much more. Patio in warm weather. Open Monday through Saturday for lunch and daily for dinner. $$–$$$

Firehouse Deli. 22 Reef Road; (203) 255-5527. Open daily, Monday through Saturday 7:00 a.m. to 5:00 p.m. and Sunday 8:00 a.m. to 4:00 p.m. Sandwiches, tacos, salads. Takeout or sit-down self-service. Outside seating in warm weather. $

Southport Brewing Company. 2600 Post Road; (203) 256-2337. Views of the microbrewery are clear from every table in the house, but you're here for the soups, sandwiches, salads, thin-crust pizzas, and chicken, seafood, and pasta dishes. Patio in season. Open for lunch daily from 11:30 a.m. and dinner from 5:00 p.m. $$

Frank Pepe Pizzeria Napoletana. 238 Commerce Drive; (203) 333-7373. Finally, another chance of getting a flavorful slice or two of famed Frank Pepe's crisp New Haven pizza. Way beyond good, this is pizza at its finest. Lunch and dinner daily. $–$$

Where to Stay

Fairfield Inn. 417 Post Road; (203) 255-0491 or (800) 347-0414. Clean, cream-of-the-crop, independently owned motor inn. 80 units, outdoor pool. Complimentary continental breakfast. In-room fridges. Circle Diner on the premises. $$–$$$$

Merritt Parkway Motor Inn. 4180 Black Rock Turnpike; (203) 259-5264 or (888) 242-4742. Perched atop a hill at the north end of town. 40 units, restaurant. Complimentary continental breakfast. $$$

The Inn at Fairfield Beach. 1160 Reef Road; (203) 255-6808. 14 suites with kitchenettes in immaculately renovated Fairfield landmark near Penfield Point. Daily, weekly, and monthly rates. Rooms are stocked with coffee, tea, fresh cream, and paper products. Open year-round. $$$$

Best Western Black Rock Inn. 100 King's Highway Cut-Off; (203) 659-2200. Brand-new 100 percent nonsmoking motel convenient to Fairfield, Bridgeport, and Stratford attractions, beaches, transportation. 60 rooms; complimentary continental breakfast; fitness room. In-room fridges. $$$$

Bridgeport

The wealth of activities offered to tourists in Bridgeport is suited to no one better than children. In recent years each of the best attractions has expanded or improved in some way, and the blue street signs help usher visitors to the good, clean fun that can still be found here despite the political scandal that has tarnished this shoreline city.

Unknown to most folks who skirt the city on I-95 and the Merritt Parkway are the facts that Bridgeport has the longest public waterfront in the state, more protected historic districts than any other Connecticut municipality, and two expansive parks designed by famed landscape artist Frederick Law Olmsted. It's not too early to celebrate the renaissance of Bridgeport as its devoted entrepreneurs and investors and its diverse ethnic communities infuse the city's culture with energy and vitality. The center of the city is a mere 4 miles from downtown Fairfield.

Discovery Museum and Planetarium (all ages)

4450 Park Avenue, exit 47, Merritt Parkway; (203) 372-3521; www.discoverymuseum .org. Open year-round Tuesday to Saturday 10:00 a.m. to 5:00 p.m. and Sunday noon to 5:00 p.m.; also Monday 10:00 a.m. to 5:00 p.m. in July and August. Closed on major holidays. $$; children under 5 free.

Hands-on in nearly every way, this museum contains interactive exhibits in the areas of science and art, all designed with a special focus on visitors ages four to twelve. Children and other visitors of all ages can make discoveries about space science, physical sciences, electronics, electricity, magnetism, and light, for instance, through changing exhibitions that are installed three times a year. Come often—something new is likely to be here.

The lowest floor includes Moon Base Discovery, a learning play space for kids under five, with simplified hands-on science for the youngest visitors. The realistic twenty-first-century lunar base includes computer space programs, a lunar periscope, a hydroponic garden, a lunar greenhouse, a lunar rover, and a lunar school bus. It is also home to the **Henry B. DuPont III Planetarium.** Daily shows offer a dramatic look at the heavens; programs change throughout the year. Cinemuse high-definition movies play frequently in a small auditorium; these films are often matched in theme to the current exhibitions, as are the fine arts exhibits hung in the Balcony Gallery. The museum is also the site of one of the nation's sixteen **Challenger Learning Centers,** a computer-simulated mission control and space station where participants perform experiments and collect data as astronauts would. Afternoon mini-missions are offered here to groups and birthday parties, and curriculum-related Wonder Science Parties are also frequent; call for reservations for both of these programs.

Inside the museum is a small gift shop and a cafeteria space where you may bring in your own picnic lunch or snacks; vending machines in this area offer limited snacks and beverages of minimal nutritional benefit. Outside are some easy and short nature trails that may help you burn off some empty calories; plans are afoot in this area for a solar-system planetary trail, which may be in place by the time you visit. Check the museum Web site for daily events, movie times, and the most up-to-date information on changing exhibitions.

Captain's Cove Seaport (all ages)

1 Bostwick Avenue; (203) 335-1433; www.captainscoveseaport.com. Seaport stores and restaurant open roughly May 1 to September 30 from 11:00 a.m. Closing time varies with the weather. Free admission to Seaport. Boat rides and charters, $–$$; Dundon House, $.

One of the friendliest examples of Bridgeport's gradual recovery from blighted pockmark to merry dimple in the cheek of the Sound is this busy place at the edge of historic Black Rock Harbor. Part marina, part museum, and part shopping arcade, Captain's Cove is the baby of Kaye Williams, an imaginative Black Rock native and lobsterman who began the cleanup of this derelict area in the 1980s. Along with the

Harbor Yard **Ballpark and Arena**

Thousands of kids have already cheered through the first several seasons of baseball in Bridgeport's **Harbor Yard ballpark,** constructed near the waterfront for the city's Class A, Atlantic League team, the **Bluefish.** The 5,300-seat stadium features box seats, club seats, and skyboxes, a supervised play area, a barbecue picnic area, food concessions, restrooms, and on-site parking. Also in this sports complex is the **Arena at Harbor Yard,** where the **Bridgeport Sound Tigers** of the American Hockey League take to the ice as the premier affiliate of the New York Islanders. Their forty-game season runs from October through April. For baseball tickets, call the Bluefish Ticket Office at (203) 345-4800; for hockey tickets, call the Sound Tigers box office at (203) 334-GOAL. The sports complex is located at 500 Main Street, off exit 27 on I-95. $$–$$$$

marina and a boat repair shop are a 500-seat restaurant, the Sailaway sailing school (see www.teamsailaway.com or call 203-209-3407), harbor cruises, and a charming boardwalk filled with twenty-five tiny boutiques, including a candy store, an ice cream shop, and all sorts of purveyors of nautical gear, toys, clothing, crafts, and other classic summer-at-the-shore gifts.

The surprises that await you at Captain's Cove are as variable as the New England weather. Special events are planned nearly daily in the summer months. Whenever you come, stroll, shop, have a look at the restaurant's 40-foot model of the *Titanic*, or put a quarter in the player piano while you wait for your excellent fish and chips. The boardwalk offers live entertainment every weekend. Before or after a meal, you may want to watch the boats in the marina or, better yet, take a harbor cruise. Most notable of the many vessels at Captain's Cove is the **STV *Unicorn,*** a double-masted gaff-rigged schooner built in 1947 with metal salvaged from captured German U-boats after World War II. It's not always in port because it is a sail training vessel—and the only tall ship in the world with an all-female, all college-educated professional crew. On special occasions the *Unicorn* may be open for deck tours at no charge, but even if no special event is going on, the friendly crew will be happy to answer your questions, and, of course, you can admire the ship from dockside. If you happen to have preteen or teenage daughters, you may want to take a closer look at the *Unicorn* when it is in Bridgeport and learn about the weeklong Sisters Under Sail leadership expeditions, which are quite remarkable (check www.tallshipunicorn.com for details). The laudable mission of the *Unicorn* and its owners, Dawn and Jay Santamaria, is to develop young women's confidence and decision-making skills; that they choose to do so often on the gentle waters of Long Island Sound is Connecticut's good fortune. The ship is also available for private day-sail charters and overnight cruises.

If you'd like to get out on the water, you can take a harbor tour on ***Chief,*** a thirty-five-passenger vessel that offers forty-five-minute cruises ($–$$) on the weekends for folks six years of age and older. You'll learn harbor lore while exploring the waters of historic Burr Creek.

The Seaport also includes a small maritime museum in the restored Victorian **Dundon House.** Once the home of a Bridgeport coalyard operator, the house contains exhibits on the maritime history of Black Rock Harbor as well as Long Island Sound's environment, economy, fisheries, and oyster beds. Photographs depict the history of three local lighthouses that guided sailors and fisherfolk, and a collection of interesting items salvaged from nearby waters provides an eye-opening look at nautical litter. It is open for guided tours ($) by appointment only.

The city's Aquaculture high school for regional youth wanting to learn marine skills and sciences is also on the property, as is the **Gustave Whitehead hangar** at the end of the Seaport's main dock. Inside the latter is a replica of the glider built and flown by Bridgeport native and aviation pioneer Whitehead, supposedly before the Wright brothers took their famed flight at Kitty Hawk, North Carolina. Both the school and the hangar can be toured; call the Seaport for more information.

The Beardsley Zoological Gardens (all ages)

1875 Noble Avenue; (203) 394-6565; www.beardsleyzoo.org. Open from 9:00 a.m. to 4:00 p.m. daily, except for Thanksgiving, Christmas, and New Year's Day. Rain forest building open 10:30 a.m. to 3:30 p.m. $$, children under 3 free. Zoo-only visitors do not have to pay the parking fee ($ for Connecticut vehicles, $$ for out-of-state vehicles) charged to users of Beardsley Park.

Continually improving, especially in the past five years, this facility has marvelous new exhibits throughout its fifty-two-acre site inside Beardsley Park. Dedicated to wildlife research, conservation, and education, Connecticut's only zoo participates in an international program called the Species Survival Plan. Rare or endangered species such as Amur tigers from Russia's Far East, along with North American red wolves, scarlet ibises, and sandhill cranes, live here with 120 other species. Inside the rain forest building, for instance, is an outstanding South American re-creation. Toucans, saki monkeys, tortoises, ocelots, golden lion tamarins, and adorable marmosets live with tropical birds in this open-aviary exhibit. In the amazing Wolf Observation Learning Facility, floor-to-ceiling windows in the Wolf Cabin in the center of the zoo's wolf habitat provide close-up views of red wolves and timber wolves.

Elsewhere on the site, explore the Alligator Alley wetlands trail to see river otters, alligators, and a beautiful new free-flight aviary. Hike the Predator Walk, which features hunter species, and the Hoofstock Trail, which borders the habitat of llamas, bison, deer, and antelope. The New England Farmyard enclosure is a petting zoo that features bunnies, goats, geese, and sheep. In the warm months, the delightful Bug House features native insects.

Pony rides, an outdoor classroom, a gift shop, the Peacock Cafe, and a handicapped-accessible terraced picnic grove are also on the grounds, as is the Hanson Exploration Station, often used for the zoo's greatly expanded public outreach and educational programming Check the Web site for news of lectures, demonstrations, drop-in programs, and such fee-based programs as Zoo Tots and Zoo Crew.

Not to be missed here is the pavilion that houses exhibits from the beautiful antique **Pleasure Beach carousel** as well as its operating modern replica. Admire magnificently restored examples of the graceful animals of the original ride, saved from the wrecking ball, then hop onto the reproduction for a wonderful whirl ($). It is open seasonally from 10:30 a.m. to 4:00 p.m.

Be sure to visit more than once. Plans are also under way for such new exhibit themes as an Asian plateau and an Arctic tundra. You can sign up on the Web site for e-mail delivery of the *CTZooTimes,* a monthly newsletter.

Barnum Museum (all ages)

820 Main Street; (203) 331-1104; www.barnum-museum.org. Open year-round 10:00 a.m. to 4:30 p.m. Tuesday through Saturday and noon to 4:30 p.m. on Sunday. Also open on many Monday holidays. $, children under 3 free.

Prepare to enter the "Greatest Show on Earth" and one of New England's best themed museums. If you have only one day to spend in Bridgeport, make sure you

The Barnum Festival

If you are charmed by Barnum's hoopla, return to the city for its annual **Barnum Festival,** a multifaceted celebration that includes the Great Street Parade on or near each Fourth of July. Among parades held across the nation, this event has historically been second in size only to Macy's Thanksgiving Day extravaganza. Road races, a fabulous marching band competition called Champions on Parade, a Jenny Lind voice competition, a children's Wing-Ding parade and carnival at the Beardsley Zoo, and fireworks are on the calendar of events. Check the Web site for the complete list of events and details on obtaining tickets for events that require them. For information, call the Barnum Festival Society at (203) 367-8495 or visit www.barnumfestival.com.

make this museum one of your stops. Designed to immerse the visitor in the experience of its exhibits, the Barnum creates the effect of a journey back in time.

Dedicated to the life and times of P. T. (Phineas Taylor) Barnum, the museum also celebrates the remarkable industrial heritage of Bridgeport and the culture of the circus in general. The first floor concentrates on Barnum the showman, entrepreneur, politician, and journalist. The successful juggler of half a dozen careers during his eighty-one years, Barnum started the circus when he was sixty! According to Barnum, his circus was "the most expensive and marvellous combination of the world's wonders ever brought together." You'll be easily drawn in to his magic from the minute you step inside the museum.

A real elephant right in the lobby and a display of Barnum's famed Feejee Mermaid set the tone, and it only gets better from there. Make sure the kids watch the excellent short clip from the A&E biography of Barnum so they get a fix on who P. T. really was. On the second floor you'll get a sense of the once-great city of Bridgeport in its heyday. A fabulous exhibit of all the products invented here will surprise visitors of all ages. On the third floor, enter the circus. See a real Egyptian mummy, Tom Thumb and Lavinia Warren's clothing and furniture, memorabilia of Jenny Lind, and the incredible 1,000-square-foot Brinley's circus, a hand-carved five-ring extravaganza, done completely to scale and massive even in miniature.

Completely renovated since its reopening in the late 1980s, the new Barnum Museum has become better than ever. Be sure to step right up and see its new interactive exhibits and intriguing changing exhibitions, usually in keeping with Barnum's fascination with popular culture. Check the Web site for public programming events that are perfect for families or are designed specially for children.

Lights Up **at the Klein**

Bridgeport's beautifully restored Art Deco–style **Klein Memorial Auditorium** (910 Fairfield Avenue; 203-366-4647; www.theklein.org; $$–$$$$), long the home of the Bridgeport Symphony Orchestra, is enjoying a jubilant renaissance. Single-night or short-run productions here include musical, theatrical, and dance performances. At least one winter holiday spectacular or concert is offered each season, and a production especially for children typically is staged by a well-known traveling company. In 2007, the New England Ballet performed *The Nutcracker*, the Manhattan Transfer staged a holiday concert, and the wacky and wonderful Paper Bag Players brought a bundle of laughs to the stage with their joyfully silly *On Top of Spaghetti*. Check the Web site for details of the current season; tickets can be purchased through the box office or in some cases online. Unless they are sold out, tickets for all shows can also be purchased at the door ninety minutes before show times. **Free** parking is available.

Downtown Cabaret Theater (all ages)

263 Golden Hill Street; (203) 576-1636; www.dtcab.com. Open year-round, Friday through Sunday; children's series October to May. Performances Saturday and Sunday at noon and 2:30 p.m. $$$, subscriptions also available. Call the box office from Tuesday through Sunday, 10:00 a.m. to 4:00 p.m., or buy tickets online. Secure parking ($) is located in the City Hall lot across the street.

This theater produces shows, from Broadway hits to musical revues, nearly every weekend of the year. Matinee and evening performances are given cabaret-style; patrons sit at tables and bring their own picnics and refreshments. Many performances are suitable for children older than eight, and a special 5:30 performance is staged for families. You can bring your dinner here, enjoy the show, and still have everyone at home and in pajamas at a reasonable bedtime.

The most popular pull for families, though, is the Cabaret's award-winning Children's Company. For more than a quarter century, this troupe of adult actors has offered an enormously successful slate of musical matinees for children ages four to twelve. Nearly every weekend from mid-October through mid-May, you can enjoy exceptional original and classic productions. Bring lunch, snacks, beverages—or birthday cake—and enjoy the merriment.

Playhouse on the Green (all ages)

177 State Street; tickets: (203) 345-4800, extension 150; www.playhouseonthegreen .org. $$$–$$$$, subscriptions also available.

Located in an amazingly revitalized historic district in the heart of downtown, the Playhouse on the Green is a 225-seat theater created inside a 1911 bank building across from the beautiful McLevy Green. The playhouse is a year-round venue, offering affordably priced dramas and comedies suitable for adults and teens. In addition, performances specifically aimed at families with young children are offered occasionally during the year. In 2007, the playhouse offered such productions as *The Brothers Grimm Fairy Tales* for children six to thirteen and *Home for the Holidays,* which portrayed seasonal celebrations, traditional carols, and popular songs from 1940 to the present.

The Bridgeport to Port Jefferson Steamboat Company
(all ages)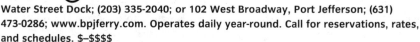
Water Street Dock; (203) 335-2040; or 102 West Broadway, Port Jefferson; (631) 473-0286; www.bpjferry.com. Operates daily year-round. Call for reservations, rates, and schedules. $–$$$$

The huge white boats at the pier just a block from the downtown transportation terminal offer ferry service across Long Island Sound. Used for both excursions and commuter transportation, the ferry functions as both pleasure cruiser and as a means of getting by car to the prettier parts of Long Island more quickly than you'd go via New York City or the Throgs Neck Bridge. Three ferries run thirty-two round trips between Bridgeport and Port Jefferson each day. From Bridgeport, the boats usually depart every hour on the half-hour between 6:30 a.m. and 9:30 p.m. Each ferry has enclosed passenger decks, topside sun decks, restrooms, and food service in onboard restaurants and bars.

Travel on foot, with bicycles, or with your car to Port Jefferson, a small village of shops and restaurants that caters to day-tripping crowds. Call the numbers above to

Seaside Park

At Bridgeport's southernmost tip lies **Seaside Park,** a 325-acre expanse designed by Frederick Law Olmsted and Calvert Vaux and donated to the city by P. T. Barnum. The park is reached through the magnificent Perry Memorial Arch over Park Avenue. Designed by Henry Bacon in 1916, the same year he designed the Lincoln Memorial in Washington, the arch is the gateway to the 2.5-mile peninsula that features a shoreline drive, a wide, white-sand beach, playing fields, concessions, and walking paths. Nonresidents wishing to drive through or spend a day at the park must stop at a checkpoint to purchase a day-use pass ($$ for CT vehicles, $$$ for out-of-state vehicles from Memorial Day weekend through Labor Day weekend. Be sure to find the beautifully restored bronze P. T. Barnum statue along the shoreline drive. Swimming is sometimes prohibited due to pollution, but the park is widely used year-round, from dawn to sunset. Call the Bridgeport Parks Department (203-576-7233) for more information.

obtain a brochure describing the Port Jeff attractions. Theatre Three (516-928-9100) presents reasonably priced ($$$–$$$$) well-known hits suitable for almost the whole family (children under age six are not permitted at Main Stage productions). Children's matinee productions ($$) are offered in July and August for the entire family. Go to shop and stroll, have some dinner, see a show, and sail home by starlight. It makes a sensational day trip.

The sailing time on the ferry is about an hour and fifteen minutes each way. Charters, moonlight cruises, and dance cruises are available.

Where to Eat

Taco Loco. 3170 Fairfield Avenue; (203) 335-8228. In the historic Black Rock neighborhood, come to this casual, colorful place for authentic Mexican classics: tacos, enchiladas, fajitas, tortilla soup, and excellent paella. Outdoor terrace. Lunch and dinner, Tuesday through Sunday. $–$$

Take Time Cafe. 211 State Street; (203) 335-7255. Open from 6:30 a.m. to 3:30 p.m. on weekdays, this downtown coffeehouse/bakery is close to the museums, theaters, and ballpark. Outstanding bagels, sandwiches, muffins, and other kid-friendly fare, perfect for breakfast, lunch, and picnics. $

Vazzy's. 513 Broadbridge Road; (203) 371-8046. This down-home, family-owned Bridgeport fixture has some of the city's best pasta and hands-down best pizza. Lunch and dinner Monday through Saturday from 11:00 a.m. and Sunday from 1:00 p.m. $$

Joseph's Steakhouse. 360 Fairfield Avenue; (203) 337-9944. Just two blocks from the corner of Main Street, this old-fashioned, elegant steakhouse gets rave reviews from all directions. Friendly father-of-five owner encourages steak-sharing between parents and kids; famed home fries and crisp salads can complete a meal that makes the whole clan happy. Lunch on weekdays; dinner daily. $$$–$$$$

Where to Stay

Bridgeport Holiday Inn. 1070 Main Street; (203) 334-1234 or (800) HOLIDAY. Convenient downtown location. 228 rooms, 6 suites, health club, indoor pool, restaurant, coffee shop. Kids **free;** weekend packages with tickets to attractions. $$$

Trumbull Marriott. 180 Hawley Lane, Trumbull; (203) 378-1400. Convenient to parkway, Route 8, and Bridgeport attractions. Health club, indoor and outdoor pools, 320 rooms; kids **free;** weekend packages. $$$–$$$$

Stratford

This small municipality on the easternmost border of Fairfield County often gets lost in the shuffle as travelers rush past it on I-95 in an effort to beat the traffic in or out of New Haven and Bridgeport. Despite its long history as one of Connecticut's oldest shoreline communities, it has not recently enjoyed a reputation as a hot spot for tourism, but a couple of projects under development may soon change that situation. Perhaps the most exciting of these works-in-progress is the long-awaited reopening of the American Stratford Festival Theater, a re-creation of the Bard's famed Globe Theatre in London. The Town of Stratford recently dedicated $2.5 million to the redevelopment of the theater and its beautiful lawns overlooking the lower Housatonic River. With some luck and lots of hard work, the relighting of that stage may occur before the next edition of this book appears. Look for news on the Web sites www.stratfordfestival.com or www.townofstratford.com.

In keeping with Stratford's long association with the aviation industry is a second developing project to watch for in the near future: The Connecticut Air and Space Center is under organization at the former site of the Vought-Sikorsky plant, where Connecticut's official state aircraft—the World War II fighter plane, the F4U Corsair—was made from 1939 to 1948. Check the Web site http://ctairandspace .org for the latest information on this museum, which promises to feature Connecticut's contributions to the science of aviation. Until the completion of those endeavors, families can still enjoy other interesting destinations in this pleasant town.

Children's Garbage Museum (ages 5 to 12)

1410 Honeyspot Road Extension, I-95 exit 30; (203) 381-9571 or (800) 455-9571; www .crra.org/education. Open to school groups daily in the academic year; open to families from noon to 4:00 p.m. Wednesday through Friday (September through June) and 10:00 a.m. to 4:00 p.m. Tuesday through Friday (July and August), plus Family Fun Days on selected Saturdays and December holiday openings. Free.

This museum features twenty-two interactive exhibits that teach children about the importance of recycling and the responsible treatment of garbage. One of the exhibits is a soft-sculpture compost pile in which children can crawl into a simulated worm tunnel to see how organic matter decomposes into soil. The museum's mascot is Trash-o-saurus, a 24-foot-long dinosaur constructed from trash.

Visitors generally spend about an hour at the hands-on exhibit area, then take a tour of the next-door Southwest Connecticut Regional Recycling Plant, where recyclables are sorted and prepared for sale to remanufacturers. Most visitors then return to the museum to create a craft or buy a gift made from recycled or reusable material.

Stratford's **Best-Kept Secrets**

The sand spit at **Long Beach** offers one of Fairfield County's best beach-combing opportunities. Park at the base of Washington Parkway among the restaurants near Marnick's Rodeway Inn and walk from Point No Point, at the eastern end of the seawall, toward the west, where Stratford's Long Beach stretches toward Bridgeport's Pleasure Beach. Except for the occasional interruption of an airplane returning to or leaving the nearby airport, you'll be alone with the wind, surf, and wildlife in this secluded spot.

As you return from a weekend beach walk, the music from **Long Beach Skateland** (55 Washington Parkway; 203-378-9033; $$) may tempt visitors both young and old to add wheels to their feet and take a few turns around this old-fashioned roller-skating rink. To protect their specially coated wooden floor, the owners allow only traditional quad skates, which are available for you to borrow at no extra charge. Most skate sessions feature contemporary Top Forty hits; Sunday evenings offer the charming lilts of organ music. Year-round, sessions are Friday 7:00 to 9:30 p.m., Saturday 2:00 to 4:00 p.m. and 7:30 to 10:00 p.m., and Sunday 2:00 to 4:00 p.m. and 7:00 to 9:00 p.m.

On the east-facing cove that cups the mouth of the Housatonic River, Stratford's **Short Beach Park** (Park and Recreation Department: 203-385-4052) offers families the best day-tripping bargain of all the public beaches along the Connecticut shore. Nonresidents pay a modest day fee per vehicle ($) to use the beach and the park's ballfields, tennis courts, basketball courts, and playground. Picnic tables and grills are also available, and a concession operates in the summer months. For an extra charge, visitors can use the park's nine-hole golf course or its miniature golf course. The park is open year-round, dawn to dusk. Lifeguards are on duty mid-June through Labor Day; during this time the restrooms and outdoor showers are also operational.

A quirkier new place to consider for history and transportation buffs is Stratford's **Merritt Parkway Museum,** operated by the Merritt Parkway Conservancy. This "lobby museum" is located in the Ryder's Landing shopping area at 6850 Main Street. A 10-foot guide to the parkway is mounted on the wall there, and a thirty-minute video tells the story of the parkway's construction, its engineering challenges, its famed bridges, and its preservation. For more information, call (203) 661-3255 or check www.merrittparkway.org. The museum, by the way, is just a short walk from the new **bike and pedestrian path** that leads from Ryder's Lane across the new **Sikorsky Bridge,** which spans the Housatonic River between Stratford and Milford.

Boothe Memorial Park and Museum (all ages)

5774 Main Street, Putney, a northern section of town; (203) 381-2046 for tours and museum information, or (203) 381-2068 for Stratford parks department. Park grounds open year-round daily from approximately 8:00 a.m. to dusk. Buildings open for guided or self-guided tours May 1 through November 1; Tuesday through Friday 11:00 a.m. to 1:00 p.m. and on weekends from 1:00 to 4:00 p.m. Free.

This thirty-two-acre park overlooking the Housatonic River was once the site of an estate owned by two wealthy, and apparently eccentric, brothers whose family had successfully farmed the site for more than 300 years. Today this National Historic Landmark includes two of the original Boothe homesteads, plus a trolley station, a tollbooth plaza, a model lighthouse, a miniature windmill, an icehouse, an outdoor basilica with an organ house, an 1844 chapel, a barn with a weaving loom and other objects related to nineteenth-century farm life, a working blacksmith shop, a clocktower museum, and an amazing redwood monument called the Technocratic Cathedral! An observatory hosts the Boothe Memorial Astronomical Society's meetings and public open houses. Check the society's calendar for open-house nights, when young and beginner astronomers are invited to observe stars and comets or whatever else the night skies reveal. Check www.bmas.org for more information. Programs are free.

Surrounding this intriguing conglomeration are acres of parkland offering gardens; walking paths; picnic groves with tables, barbecue grills, and shelters; a playground; ballplaying areas; and restrooms. The buildings and restrooms close in November, but ice-skating and sledding are allowed in the winter, weather permitting.

National Helicopter Museum (all ages)

2840 Main Street, at the eastbound side of the tracks at the old Stratford Railroad Depot; (203) 375-5766 or (203) 767-1123. Open Memorial Day through October 15, Wednesday through Sunday, 1:00 to 4:00 p.m. Donation requested.

If you have aircraft buffs in your clan, an hour at this small museum, located in the old red Stratford Railroad Depot, will be enjoyable if you can't make it up to the New England Air Museum in Windsor Locks. Exhibits trace the development of the helicopter and the life of aviation pioneer Igor Sikorsky, founder of Stratford's famed Sikorsky Aircraft industries. Museum displays include the cockpit of the V-22 Osprey (an airplane that hovers like a helicopter), several helicopter engines, and miniature models of Sikorsky's helicopters. Also on display are drawings of early helicopter prototypes (such as da Vinci's Helix) and photographs of helicopters used in various military operations.

Where to Eat

Knapp's Landing. 520 Sniffens Lane; (203) 378-5999. At the mouth of the Housatonic River at Sniffens Point, just north of Short Beach, this establishment offers continental cuisine year-round. Seafood, pasta, chicken, steaks, soups, sandwiches, and salads. Open-air deck in warm weather. Lunch and dinner Tuesday through Sunday. $$

Marnick's Restaurant. 10 Washington Parkway; (203) 377-6288. Owned by the same family for more than fifty years, this right-on-the-water favorite serves perfect family fare, reasonably priced. Steaks, seafood, sandwiches, salads, and burgers. Ask for a window table overlooking the Sound or eat on the waterfront patio in warm weather. Open daily. $–$$

The Peppermill Steak and Fish House. 225 Longshore Boulevard; (203) 870-8445. A Westport fixture for forty years, this steak and seafood house has relocated to the Stratford Ramada Inn. As usual, it offers tasty meats and seafood and other familiar American fare, including children's entrees. Open daily for lunch ($–$$) from 11:00 a.m. to 3:00 p.m. and dinner ($$$–$$$$) from 5:00 to 10:00 p.m.

White Lilac Tearoom. 2410 Main Street; (203) 378-7160. For a slightly fancy and fanciful setting for a mother-daughter outing or other special occasion, regardless of your gender, try this charming place for lunch, tea (both served Tuesday through Saturday), and dinner (Wednesday and Friday only). Tea is served the proper British way, complete with wee sandwiches, scones, and clotted cream; lunch offers salads, sandwiches, and quiches. Reservations recommended. $–$$

Where to Stay

Rodeway Inn. 10 Washington Parkway; (203) 377-6288. In the interest of travelers shopping by brand-name recognition, Marnick's family-owned motel on the Sound has changed its name, but it's still the same old-fashioned (but fully renovated) waterfront hostelry, as it has been for half a century. 29 rooms, restaurant. Waterfront rooms have balconies, microwaves, and refrigerators. Guests welcome to use the motel's private beach for swimming and shore fishing. $$

Stratford Ramada. 225 Lordship Boulevard; (203) 375-8866 or (800) 2RAMADA. 145 rooms, restaurant, indoor pool. Continental breakfast. $$–$$$

Shelton

In another of Fairfield County's bucolic corners lies the growing town—a small city, really—of Shelton, easily accessible from the Merritt Parkway and Routes 8 and 110. North of Stratford and west of Trumbull and Monroe, the city is also bounded by the Housatonic River, which is among its greatest natural resources. Suburban developments and shopping areas encroach on land that was once—not too long ago—woodland and farmland, but efforts like those of the Shelton Land Trust (www .sheltonlandtrust.org) and the City of Shelton Open Space Plan (sheltonopenspace .googlepages.com) do protect some of the earlier ambience of its hilly countryside.

Freshly **Pressed**

Any cider you drink in Shelton may have come from **Beardsley's Cider Mill and Orchard** at 278 Leavenworth Road (Route 110). The Beardsley clan has run this operation since 1849, so they have had plenty of practice pressing cider at their mill, as well as baking delicious pies. You can pick (weekends only) more than thirty different varieties of heirloom and other apples in the orchards here—or just buy a bagful in the shop. While you munch a crisp apple or try your free sample of unpasteurized cider, you can watch the pressing operation in the mill. Learn about the method they employ to protect you from bacteria (it's all in the lighting system, you might say). You'll be hard-pressed to leave without stocking up on locally made honey, maple syrup, jams, jellies, and applesauce. Excellent cookies, pies, cheesecake, and cider doughnuts are good accompaniments to your jugful of cider, too. Open from September through December, Monday through Friday noon to 6:00 p.m. and weekends from 10:00 a.m. to 6:00 p.m. For more information, call (203) 926-1098 or check the Web site, www.beardsleyscidermill.com.

Check the Web sites of these organizations for insights into the area's beauty and additional ideas for fun with the family on its remaining farms and trails. For a sense of Shelton's early history and culture, you might also visit the **Shelton History Center** (203-925-1803), a lovely one-acre enclave comprising the 1872 Trap Falls Schoolhouse, the 1822 Marks-Brownson House, and the nineteenth-century Wilson Barn. Excellent educational programs and summer camps are offered there for families and children.

Jones Family Farms

Main farm: 606 Walnut Tree Hill Road; Pumpkinseed Hill farm: 130 Beardsley Road; (203) 929-8425; www.jonesfamilyfarms.com. Free admission; pay per pound for the produce you buy; all trees, $50 in 2007. Strawberries, early June through mid-July; blueberries, mid-July to late August; call for picking hours and conditions; pumpkins, late September through Halloween; Christmas trees, mid-November through December 24. Please leave pets at home during pumpkin season; leashed pets are allowed on the tree farm but not in the historic barnyard, winery, or gift shop.

During the growing season, this family-fun place is one of the most popular outdoor attractions in the state. From June through December, come here to enjoy the great outdoors and connect with the farmers who work so hard to bring food to our tables. You can help them out by picking your own strawberries and blueberries on the main farm in the summer season, and then come to Pumpkinseed Hill to pick pumpkins in the fall. During the winter holidays, return for one of the state's largest selections of perfect Christmas trees. The Jones family has been farming these parcels since the mid-1800s, when Welsh-Irish immigrant Philip Jones staked a claim here. Now his great-great-grandson Terry and Terry's son, Jamie, have taken on the stewardship of this 400-acre Century farm.

You may learn something valuable about sustainable agriculture while you're here having fun. "Be good to the land, and the land will be good to you" is the farm motto, and it shows in the family's approach to pest management, crop rotation, and preservation of soil structure. You may check out the fine soil of Shelton's White Hills on a ramble through 200 acres of Christmas trees, fifteen each of berries, or the twenty-five acres of pumpkin patches, or you might prefer to take a hayride ($) or walk the corn maze ($) in the autumn. A UNICEF Children's Festival the last weekend in October offers fun activities such as gourd tosses, pumpkin decorating, sing-alongs, and wagon rides; in winter, stop at the old dairy barn to browse in the Holiday Gatherings gift shop and have a cup of hot mulled cider at the Christmas canteen.

Indian Well State Park

Howe Avenue (Route 110); (203) 735-4311; www.ct.gov/dep; open daily year-round from 8:00 a.m. to sunset. Weekend and weekday per-vehicle parking fees ($$) from Memorial Day through Labor Day.

This state park with 153 acres along the Housatonic River gets its name from the waterfall and splash pool at its base. According to legend, an ill-fated romance between two young Native Americans met its end at this site, but local native inhabitants never actually used this water place as a well. Likely they enjoyed the same activities you might enjoy here today: picnicking near the cascades; boating, fishing, and swimming in the river; and hiking on the Paugussett Trail through the woodlands. (A 2.5-mile section of the 8-mile trail, which ends in the town of Monroe, is accessible near the entrance to the park; no fee is charged for access to the trail.) A volleyball court and a picnic shelter with grills and tables are also here, along with restrooms. The swimming area has lifeguards in the summer months. No camping is allowed.

SportsCenter of Connecticut

784 River Road (Route 110); (203) 929-6500; www.sportscenterct.com. Open 365 days a year; hours vary for each sport and activity; call or check the Web site. Each individual activity fee is generally $–$$$.

This enormous recreation complex is a long way from the more pastoral settings of Shelton. In a bright-lights, big-city style, it offers glitzy pay-as-you-play opportunities year-round, sunup to sundown, for active families with a yen for physical challenges. The world's only double-decker ice rink is here, and it's a doozy. Both indoor rinks, stacked one over the other, are NHL-sized and offer public skating hours six days a week, year-round, plus pickup hockey games several times each month. Eighteen holes of miniature golf are available day and night year-round, weather permitting; the outdoor course features a waterway and falls and lots of pretty landscaping. If it rains on your game, you can ask for a poncho or a free game token. If you prefer real golf to the mini variety, you can hit a bucket of balls at the driving range or take lessons at the Junior Golf Academy. At Fun Bowl, in the Golf Center building, even small children feel successful when they roll the three-pound balls down the lane: Automated bumpers block the gutters for beginners, and automated scoring makes it easy to keep track of all the fun the kids are having. Eight outdoor batting cages can pitch you balls at your choice of 28 to 91 miles per hour; you rent the opportunity to swing at these for a half-hour or an hour at a time. If jungle games are more your style, head straight to the Rinks building for Lazer Tag. The indoor forest here is 5,000 square feet—plenty of room to act out whatever drama you can invent as you battle your way through the tree-lined, rock-walled pathways to base camp. If all this is not enough for whatever energy your team has, SportsCenter also has two full-size basketball courts for rent, and they melt the ice on one of the rinks in the springtime for in-line hockey leagues.

You can have birthday parties here as well, and meals of the fast-food sort are available at the Rinks Food Court. A Planet Fitness also operates here, as do a golf shop and a pro shop for many kinds of sports gear. What, no pool, rock-climbing wall, or go-karts? Those are the only fun missing here, so if your own backyard is letting you down and the woods and ponds don't beckon, come here, where everything is go-go-go!

Where to Eat

Sassafras Restaurant & Ice Cream Parlor. 13 Huntington Plaza; (203) 929-3249. For breakfast and lunch and J. J. Lawson's gourmet ice cream, there's no better place for families than this independently owned eatery serving casual American fare. Breakfast and lunch, daily from 7:00 a.m.; dinner, Monday through Saturday. $–$$

Trattoria Roma. 232 Leavenworth Road; (203) 929-5177. In the White Hills Shopping Center, this family-owned trattoria offers pizza as well as authentic family-style Italian cuisine in a casual setting perfect for, well . . . families. Lunch, Tuesday through Friday; dinner from 4:00 p.m. Tuesday through Sunday. $$

Where to Stay

AmeriSuites Shelton Corporate Towers. 695 Bridgeport Avenue; (203) 925-5900. 128 suites with refrigerator, microwave; indoor pool, fitness center. $$$–$$$$

Courtyard by Marriott. 780 Bridgeport Avenue; (203) 929-1500. 161 units (12 suites), restaurant, lounge, fitness room, indoor pool. $$$–$$$$

Hilton Garden Inn Shelton. 25 Old Stratford Road; (203) 447-1000. 142 units (3 suites), refrigerator, microwave; restaurant, health club, whirlpool, indoor pool. $$$$

Easton/Redding/Weston

The area between Fairfield in the south and Danbury in the north is sliced vertically in two by Route 58, a great road through lovely countryside. Routes 53 and 57 north from Westport also lead you toward the quiet pleasures of life north of the rat race. If you have spent a few days in the cities on the Sound, give yourselves a break and head for the farthest reaches of the county. Meander awhile—along green-canopied lanes in summer, beside snow-capped fences and stone walls in winter.

Going north from Fairfield on Route 58, you'll pass through the stately conifer forests surrounding the Hemlock and Aspetuck reservoirs. Stop in Easton at the casual Bluebird Inn Restaurant (203-452-0697) at the junction of Route 58 and Route 136 for some home-cooked vittles. If you start out early, have one of their great breakfasts; they open daily at 7:00 a.m. and close at 2:00 p.m. except on Sunday (8:00 a.m. to 1:00 p.m.). Once you're back in the car, pause again just a hair up the road at the aeration fountain spouting high into the air at the edge of the Hemlock reservoir. Let its music soothe your soul, then return to the car and stop just a few miles onward at the **Aspetuck Valley Orchards** (203-268-9033) produce stand. In three seasons, there's something special here—fresh fruits and vegetables, locally made honey,

Down on **Silverman's Farm**

Young children may especially enjoy a visit to **Silverman's Farm** in Easton, where an animal farm, a seasonal cider mill, and sixty acres of pick-your-own fruit await those who favor fun in the outdoors. Located at 451 Sport Hill Road (Route 59), 2.5 miles north of exit 46 of the Merritt Parkway, the farm is open daily year-round, except Thanksgiving, Christmas, and New Year's Day. Come here from July 15 to pick peaches, plums, nectarines, sunflowers, and apples, in approximately that order, and later in the growing season, to choose pumpkins, gourds, and Christmas trees. From early September to mid-November, see fresh apple cider pressed right before your eyes. In the fall, take a tractor-drawn wagon ride through the fields and orchards. At the animal farm ($), see goats, sheep, pigs, fallow deer, buffalo, llamas, long-horned cattle, emus, and other exotic birds. Picnic tables, washing stations, and restrooms are available in this area. Shop for farm-fresh produce, house-made pies, scones, and cookies, plus jams, salsas, honey, and syrup in the rambling farm market; check out the florist shop for flowers, mums, wreaths, and poinsettias in season. Call ahead (203-261-3306) for the pick-your-own schedule or to arrange birthday parties here. You can check the Web site at www.silvermansfarm.com.

maple sugar candies—in case someone needs just a little something. Pick up some trail food for later.

Continue north on Route 58 until you reach the junction of Route 107 at Redding Ridge. Take a left and drive east on 107—so, so pretty. Continue on Route 107 (about 5 miles) until you reach Route 57, then go south on Route 57. Drive 2.7 miles and take a left on Godfrey Road, then another left on Pent Road for a walk through southwestern Connecticut's largest nature preserve.

The Nature Conservancy's Devil's Den Nature Preserve
(all ages) 🕷

33 Pent Road, Weston; (203) 226-4991; www.nature.org/wherewework/northamerica/ states/connecticut. Trails open dawn to dusk daily; preserve office open 9:00 a.m. to 5:00 p.m. Monday to Friday. Free.

This beautiful refuge includes 1,746 acres of woodlands, wetlands, and rock ledges separated by valleys with swamps and streams that sustain nearly 200 species of birds and mammals and nearly 500 species of trees and wildflowers. The site of prehistoric native encampments and a seventeenth-century colonial settlement, the preserve has a mill pond, a lovely ravine with a tumbling cascade, and 21 miles of trails, including loop routes for every age, fitness level, and time schedule. Free guided walks are offered (call for the schedule), but if you prefer to walk unescorted, pick up a trail map in the parking lot at the registration center. Rangers ask that you register before entering the trails. No pets, bicycles, or mechanized vehicles are permitted here. There are no restrooms, and no camping is allowed.

Wilton

First settled by Europeans in 1651 and later established as a parish of Norwalk in 1726 by a group of forty families, Wilton remains, in the twenty-first century, a small town of twenty-seven square miles in the Norwalk River Valley. Mostly residential, it is a generally quiet place with some quintessentially New England features that visiting families may enjoy. Two such attractions are described in some detail in the following paragraphs, but for those who may spend a weekend or more in this vicinity, mention is due the **Wilton Historical Society's Heritage Museum** (224 Danbury Road; 203-762-7257). At this site are two historic homes that showcase an extensive collection of decorative arts and domestic implements from 1740 through 1900. Between them, the 1757 Raymond-Fitch House and the 1735 Betts-Sturges-Blackmar House contain twelve period rooms furnished to show the passage of time through Wilton's early history. Locally made stoneware and redware plus an extensive collection of costumes, textiles, dolls, toys, and dollhouses are also displayed. Both homes host special events and exhibitions throughout the year.

Weir Farm National Historic Site (ages 5 to 12)

735 Nod Hill Road; (203) 834-1896; www.nps.gov/wefa. Except for Thanksgiving, Christmas, and New Year's Day, the grounds are open daily year-round dawn to dusk. Visitor center open Wednesday through Sunday from 9:00 a.m. to 5:00 p.m. from May through October, and Thursday through Sunday from 10:00 a.m. to 4:00 p.m. from November through April. Studio tours May through October, Wednesday through Saturday at 11:00 a.m. and 1:00 and 3:00 p.m. and on Sunday at 1:00 and 3:00 p.m. Check the Web site for studio-tour schedule in colder months. On Sunday at 11:00 a.m., year-round, the guided Stone Walls Walking Tour is offered. Free.

The first and only national park in Connecticut and the only one in the country dedicated to a painter, Weir Farm is the former home of noted American Impressionist J. Alden Weir (1852–1919). One of the foremost painters of his time, Weir acquired the farm in 1882 in the area known as Branchville between Wilton and Ridgefield. His summer retreat from New York City, Weir Farm is the subject of many of his paintings.

On fifty-seven acres straddling the Wilton/Ridgefield border, the secluded site includes Weir's farmhouses, studios, and barns, all among the rocky meadows and rolling woodlands of the lower Danbury Hills. If you need a place to restore the soul, please do come here to visit the place where Weir also raised his three little girls.

A video introduction to Weir Farm's history and importance is offered at the Burlingham House visitor center, which also includes historic photographs of the farm and changing exhibitions of the work of visiting artists. Be sure to pick up a copy of **Passport to Weir Farm,** a kids' activity booklet designed especially for visitors ages eight to twelve, or ask for a *Junior Ranger* booklet that helps youngsters earn a National Park Service junior ranger badge during a two-hour visit here.

The property is open daily from dawn to dusk for strolling and bird-watching. Professional and amateur artists are welcome to bring easels and paints, for sketching on the public portions of the property. The Weir Farm Historic Painting Sites Trail features twelve sites identified as the original inspiration for works of art done at the farm. The self-guided trail is easy walking through woods, fields, and wetlands, past gardens and historic structures, and along old stone walls and fences. A trail guide with color reproductions of the paintings is available at the visitor center ($).

You can also sign up in advance for the very popular (and **free**) Stone Walls Walking Tours, given on Sundays at 11:00 a.m. While exploring the farm's landscape, you also learn about the various kinds of walls laid here between 1775 and the 1930s.

Bring a picnic if you want to spend the day. Wear socks and walking shoes, and bring insect repellent. The socks may be a must for some of you—we encountered poison ivy in many places. If you arrive without art supplies and your children are inspired to draw, ask at the visitor center for the loan of a sketch pad and crayons. You might also ask about art classes offered for children and adults periodically throughout the year.

Woodcock Nature Center (all ages)

56 Deer Run Road, Wilton; (203) 762-7280; www.woodcocknaturecenter.org. Trails open dawn to dusk daily. Visitor center open year-round Monday through Friday and, in the cooler months, on most Sundays, from 9:30 a.m. to 4:30 p.m. Donation requested.

Located in both Ridgefield and Wilton, this small preserve is great for young children. It has 2 miles of trail and swamp boardwalk, a pond, an interpretive center with exhibit areas, and a store with nature-related books, gifts, and supplies. Botany walks, bird-watching, geology and wildlife talks, and similar programs are among the usual activities. A junior naturalist program and summer day camp are offered for children.

Where to Eat

Soup Alley. 239 Danbury Road; (203) 761-9885. Soup is the word here, Monday through Friday, 10:30 a.m. to 6:00 p.m., and Saturday until 4:00 p.m. Along with nearly a dozen soups daily, you can buy salads, an entree or two, a sandwich or two, beverages, and desserts to take out or to eat in. $

The Schoolhouse at Cannondale. 34 Cannon Road at Cannondale Village; (203) 762-8810. Once a one-room schoolhouse built in 1871, this lovely and unique place on the Norwalk River has gussied itself up recently to serve a more adult clientele, but a Sunday brunch and an outdoor patio at waterside make it a family-friendly, if more elegant, place to dine for special occasions. Open for dinner Wednesday through Saturday from 5:00 p.m.; Sunday brunch ($$), 10:00 a.m. to 3:00 p.m. $$–$$$

Where to Stay

Four Points Hotel by Sheraton. 426 Main Avenue, which is Route 7, in Norwalk; (203) 849-9828 or (800) 325-3535. Located near exit 40 of the Merritt Parkway, this hotel has 127 units, including 5 suites. Restaurant, exercise room. $$$$

Ridgefield

While the northern sections of Fairfield County's coastal cities and towns become more rural as you leave the Route 1/I-95 corridor, it's not until you're inland 10 miles or so that you notice Fairfield County's split personality. From points north, Fairfield County is downright bucolic except for the city of Danbury. Small towns with pretty greens and white clapboard churches dot the countryside. The pace slows. The air is clean. You might even forget you are in the most densely populated county of the state.

Visitors with children will enjoy the pedestrian-friendly nature and size of Ridgefield's pretty town center, where most of its attractions, shops, and restaurants are clustered. Its Aldrich Museum enjoys national renown for its art as well as for its exceptional family education programs; its historic **Keeler Tavern Museum** is especially welcoming and accessible to children; and its many boutiques and restaurants, both sophisticated and simple, have friendly proprietors who clearly cater to a family-oriented clientele. Spend the day just strolling here on the lovely town green or in pretty **Ballard Park,** right in the center of the village. Have lunch, check out the toy store or even the terrific library, and be sure to leave time for both museums. If you live anywhere nearby, be sure to check out the incredible lineup of family-perfect performances at the nearly incomparable Ridgefield Playhouse (203-438-5795; 80 East Ridge; www.ridgefieldplayhouse.org).

The Aldrich Contemporary Art Museum (ages 6 to 12)
258 Main Street (Route 35); (203) 438-4519; www.aldrichart.org. Open year-round, Tuesday through Sunday, from noon to 5:00 p.m. $–$$, children under 18 free. Free to all on Tuesdays. Gallery tour, Sunday at 2:00 p.m.

Surprising to find in a residential suburb like Ridgefield is this sophisticated museum founded in 1964 by Larry Aldrich, an innovative connoisseur of fine art. Right in the center of town, the internationally renowned Aldrich focuses its attention on new talents and currents in art and culture. Originally located in a historic building, the Aldrich moved its exhibitions several years ago into a magnificent addition linked to the renovated older structure. Twelve galleries, a hundred-seat performance space, an education center, a screening room, a 22-foot-high project space, larger visitor education spaces, and a redesigned outdoor sculpture garden are among its features.

In addition to exhibitions of the work of emerging and midcareer artists, the Aldrich is dedicated to contemporary video artists and performing artists. These focuses are all accommodated in the redesigned complex. World-class concerts, performances, readings, and films are offered on a regular schedule. Children's art days, studio visits, and interactive family tours add to the museum's appeal to visitors of all ages.

Keeler Tavern Museum (ages 5 to 12)
132 Main Street; (203) 438-5485; www.keelertavernmuseum.org. Tours by costumed guides from February 1 through December. Open Wednesday, Saturday, and Sunday from 1:00 to 4:00 p.m. Closed on Easter Sunday, July 4, Thanksgiving, Christmas, and in January. Last tour at 3:30 p.m. $

Reputed as the most hospitable stop on the coach route between New York and Boston, Ridgefield's historic tavern was built about 1713 and operated as one of the most important inns in Connecticut for 130 years. A hub of community life in Ridgefield and a meeting place for patriots in Revolutionary War days, the tavern was fired on by British troops during the Battle of Ridgefield. A small cannonball remains imbedded in a corner post of the house. The tavern's taproom is a cheerful reminder of the comforts the inn offered to weary eighteenth-century travelers. Although the tavern was modified several times in its history (once by famed architect and former owner Cass Gilbert), its main rooms are furnished according to the period closest to its early days. Visitors can also see the ladies' parlor, the dining room, the bedchambers, and the kitchen. Woodenware, cooking implements, and other domestic utensils illustrate the colonial lifestyle. Be sure to stroll through the lovely walled garden Gilbert designed for his wife.

Where to Eat

Early Bird Cafe. 88 Danbury Road; (203) 438-1395. It's a little more out of the way of the main village, but it's just off Route 35, and some folks drive miles for the delicious French toast and omelets. Open Monday through Saturday from 5:30 a.m. to 3:00 p.m. and Sunday from 7:00 a.m. to 1:00 p.m. $

Gail's on the Common. 103 Danbury Road; (203) 438-9775. Patty Finnegan-Hughes's perfect family restaurant features award-winning pancakes, omelets, skillet specials, soups, salads, sandwiches, and more. This longtime local favorite is open for breakfast and lunch daily until 3:30 p.m. $–$$

Southwest Cafe. 109 Danbury Road; (203) 431-3398. For family dinners, this is the best bet in town. Kids under 12 have their own menu of southwestern and Tex-Mex favorites like flautas, fajitas, tacos, and such. Great salads, wraps, soups, and much more. Lunch and dinner daily; live music on Thursday and Saturday evening. $$–$$$

Deborah Ann's. 381 Main Street; (203) 438-0065. For the sweetest treats ever, go straight to this cheerful shop. Every kind of deliciousness is here, from bonbons, truffles, and turtles to gummies, jellies, and all flavors of beans. All of that plus locally famed and absolutely epicurean Mr. Shane's Homemade Ice Cream. Open daily, year-round. $

Where to Stay

Days Inn. 296 Ethan Allen Highway; (203) 438-3781. Convenient to I-84, 36 units with fridges and such, complimentary continental breakfast, restaurant. $$

West Lane Inn. 22 West Lane, Route 35; (203) 438-7323. Elegant four-diamond inn, 16 rooms (3 efficiencies) with private baths, continental breakfast. $$$$

Bethel

If you have spent the night in Ridgefield on the way toward the top of the county, you might want to take Route 102 south from Ridgefield's center to Route 7 in the village of Branchville, then take Route 107 north again to Route 58. Go north about 3 miles on 58, and you'll soon be in Bethel, a smallish community with an agricultural and manufacturing past. Before you reach town, though, visit Connecticut's Valley Forge.

Putnam Memorial State Park (ages 7 to 12)

Route 58 between Redding and Bethel near Route 107 junction; (203) 938-2285, or (866) 287-2757 for the State Parks Division. Park open daily 8:00 a.m. to dusk; museum open from Memorial Day to Columbus Day from 11:00 a.m. to 5:00 p.m. on weekends only. Pit toilets; picnic tables. **Free.**

Site of the 1778–79 winter encampment of General Israel Putnam's Northern Brigades of the Continental Army, the park includes a small museum built on the original picket post from which the sentries guarded the barracks and magazine. The museum contains exhibits related to the Revolutionary War and the encampment.

On a self-guided tour of the area, you can also see the remains of the gunpowder magazine, a reconstruction of the officers' barracks, a guardhouse reproduction, and the remains of the soldiers' huts. Reenactments of the Revolutionary War encampment, with artillery demonstrations and cavalry and infantry camp life activities, are presented during the annual Patriots' Weekend, usually in July. The park's 183 acres attract summer visitors for fishing, hiking, and picnicking. Winter brings cross-country skiers.

Blue Jay Orchards (all ages)

125 Plumtrees Road; (pick-your-own information) (203) 748-0119; www.bluejayorchards.com. Open daily from August through late December from 9:30 a.m. to 5:30 p.m. **Free,** except for whatever you buy.

Chockablock with good, better, and best New England foods, this farm grows apples, pears, and pumpkins. Its roadside market offers freshly made pies, jams, jellies, maple syrup, honey, sweet cider pressed in its mill, and cinnamon cider doughnuts.

A calendar of special events includes an Apple Festival in late September, hayrides to the pumpkins in October, and a Christmas tree sale in December. Let me be fair, though. Sometimes the joint is jumping—hayrides, painted pumpkins, hundreds of red-cheeked kids having a ball. Sometimes it's as sleepy as a dog in August, and the only thing moving is the dust on the road. You might like it better one way or the other—you be the judge. Either way, the apples are crisp and the pies are delicious.

Israel Putnam Statue

A magnificent bronze statue of "Old Put" shaking his fist at the British while atop his trusty steed stands at the entrance to Putnam Memorial State Park. Not surprisingly, the sculptor is notable herself. Anna Hyatt Huntington created the statue at the age of ninety-four.

Pick-Your-Own Pleasures

Blue Jay Orchards is one of the largest farms open to the public (see entry), but others in Fairfield County also offer pick-your-own crops or at least buy-it-right-from-the-farmer market stands:

Warrup's Farm. 51 John Read Road, West Redding; (203) 938-9403; www .warrupsfarm.com. Certified organic vegetables, flowers, pumpkins, maple syrup (demonstrations 10:00 a.m. to 5:00 p.m. the first three weekends in March), beautiful country lane, free-range poultry, and barnyard animals. Hayrides in pumpkin season. Farmstand open Tuesday through Sunday, July through October.

Holbrook Farm. 45 Turkey Plain Road (Route 53), Bethel; (203) 792-0561; www.holbrookfarm.net. Open March through November, Monday through Saturday 10:00 a.m. to 6:00 p.m. Closed Sundays. All kinds of produce fresh from their fields; bakery and farm market with locally made honey, meats, cheeses, flowers, jams, soaps, and much more.

Maple Row Tree Farm. 538 North Park Avenue, Easton; (203) 261-9577; www.mrfarm.com. Christmas trees, wreaths, garlands, oxen- or tractor-drawn wagon rides, hot cider. Open daily from the day after Thanksgiving to Christmas Eve, this 200-acre farm is the perfect setting for finding the perfect tree.

Free CT Farm Maps offer complete lists of berry farms, orchards, vegetable farms, tree farms, and sugarhouses. Call (860) 713-2503 to request a copy of the map from the Connecticut Department of Agriculture.

Where to Eat

Plain Jane's. 208 Greenwood Avenue; (203) 797-1515. Owned for nearly thirty years by two sisters who obviously know how to cook for families, this clean, fresh, unintimidating restaurant is a standout for homemade, unprocessed, healthy American cuisine. Original art for sale on the walls; traditional lunch and dinner served 11:00 a.m. to 9:00 p.m. Monday through Thursday and until 10:00 p.m. on Friday and Saturday. Early-bird specials 4:00 to 6:00 p.m. Monday through Saturday. $$

Dr. Mike's Ice Cream. 158 Greenwood Avenue; (203) 792-4388. Stop here for what the doctor recommends—Dr. Mike, that is—ice cream extraordinaire. If you love rich, creamy, coat-your-throat ice cream, you're going to love Dr. Mike's. The long list of flavors is sure to please everyone. Open from noon to 11:00 p.m. daily in summer. Winter hours are shorter. $

Bethel Cafe. 269 Greenwood Avenue; (203) 790-4433. Open daily right next door to the movie house, this snug place offers house-made soups, creative sandwiches and omelets, crisp salads, warm crepes, and more at lunch and dinner Wednesday through Sunday, breakfast on Saturday and Sunday, and dinner only (4:30 to 7:30 p.m.) on Monday and Tuesday. $

Where to Stay

Best Western Stony Hill Inn. 46 Stony Hill Road; (203) 743-5533 or (800) 528-1234. 36 units. Restaurant, outdoor pool, continental breakfast; forty acres with pond. $$$

Danbury

Take Route 53 out of Bethel for about 3 miles to Danbury, a small city famous for its nearly 200-year history of hat manufacturing. Now better recognized for the corporate headquarters that were drawn here by low real estate prices and a convenient location on Interstate 84, Danbury has some family destinations that reflect its interesting past.

Danbury Museum and Historical Society (ages 7 to 12)

43 Main Street; (203) 743-5200; www.danburyhistorical.org. Open in the summer for tours Tuesday, Thursday, and Saturday, 11:00 a.m. to 4:00 p.m. and at other times of the year by appointment for tours on Tuesday, Wednesday, and Thursday. Donation.

This interesting collection of buildings includes the 1785 John and Mary Rider House with seventeenth- and eighteenth-century furnishings and costumes. The John Dodd Hat Shop also has terrific exhibits explaining Danbury's world-famous hat-making industry, the impact hat-making had on the growth of related industries, and the history of hats from a fashion point of view. A Revolutionary War exhibit includes facts you never knew about the Daughters of the American Revolution, and a fascinating woodworking exhibit of carpentry and joinery tools offers lessons about time-honored handcrafts.

Among the most important buildings on the museum site is the restored Marian Anderson Studio, where the famed opera singer rehearsed for the fifty years in which she made Danbury her home. Exhibits in the studio tell about her magnificent contralto voice, her career, and her struggles and triumphs in her journey toward racial equality.

Danbury Railway Museum (all ages)

120 White Street; (203) 778-8337; www.danbury.org/drm. From April through October, open Tuesday through Saturday 10:00 a.m. to 5:00 p.m. and Sunday noon to 5:00 p.m. From November through March, open Wednesday through Saturday 10:00 a.m. to 4:00 p.m. and Sunday noon to 4:00 p.m. Hours expand in midsummer; call for schedule. $–$$, children 2 and under free. Special holiday excursions may be higher.

Who doesn't love trains? Whatever magic they have, it is something very attractive to most children and quite a few mature adults. Here in Danbury you can explore the restored Union Station, totally face-lifted to just about what it looked like when it was built in 1903 for the New York, New Haven & Hartford Railroad. Alfred Hitchcock's thriller *Strangers On a Train* was filmed in and near this station in 1950, when the station was still an important stop for the New Haven Railroad. By the 1980s, though, the city and its rail service were in decline, and the engine house and freight house here had been torn down. Listed on the National Register of Historic Places since 1995, when interest in its history and restoration was revived, the station is in business again.

Check out the nifty memorabilia in the station, and operate three model railroad layouts. Then, tour the six-acre railroad yard filled with seventy vintage railcars, boxcars, a locomotive, and other artifacts. A sleeping car and an observation car from the 20th Century Limited that ran between New York and Chicago are part of the collection. Train rides range from short rides in the yard, hourlong excursions out of the yard, and daylong trips that head for the Hudson River Valley. Thomas the Tank Engine rides, Easter Bunny rides, Halloween Pumpkin Patch train rides, and Santa trains decorated in the railyard are part of the special family fun here. Call or check the Web site for the current schedule.

Ives Concert Park (all ages)

Mill Plain Road, Westside Campus, Route 6; (203) 837-9226; www.ivesconcertpark .com. $$$$, children 3 to 12 $$–$$$, children 2 and under free.

Spread over thirty-nine acres of the campus of Western Connecticut State University, the center offers top-drawer entertainment in an open-air gazebo–covered stage throughout the summer months. In the colder months, other concerts, plays, and other musical productions take place at Western's Berkshire Theatre or at the Ives Concert Hall on the midtown campus. Named in honor of Pulitzer Prize–winning composer Charles Ives, considered the father of American music, the Ives center hosts symphonies, jazz, folk, blues, theater, dance, and popular artists on its summer stage. Ticket prices and performers vary, but you can always count on exceptional quality and value. A free Family Fair in September features community artists and musical performers as well as the Ives Festival Orchestra. You can bring lawn chairs and picnics to any concert, but no pets, grills, alcoholic beverages, or glass containers.

Where to Eat

Bangkok. 72 Newtown Road; (203) 791-0640. For an authentic Thai experience, you can't beat this colorful and cozy restaurant, which has served traditional favorites for twenty years. The staff dresses in traditional costumes, and the atmosphere is warmly convivial and welcoming to families. Lunch and dinner, Tuesday through Friday; dinner only on weekends. $$

Where to Stay

Quality Inn and Suites. 78 Federal Road; (203) 743-6701 or (800) 4-CHOICE. 72 units, restaurant, indoor pool, exercise room, continental breakfast. $$$–$$$$

Ethan Allen Hotel. 21 Lake Avenue, Danbury Extension; (800) 742-1776. 195 rooms and suites, restaurant, health club, sauna, outdoor pool. $$$$

Holiday Inn. 80 Newtown Road; (203) 792-4000. 114 units, including 11 executive rooms with king-size beds and sofas. Restaurant, outdoor pool. Kids stay **free.** Full hot buffet breakfast is complimentary. $$$$

Brookfield and New Fairfield/ Sherman

Six miles north of Danbury (taking Route 7 north), Brookfield town center has developed rapidly in the past ten years, especially along the Route 7 corridor. However, the Brookfield countryside remains rural, or at least suburban, in character, and the beauty of Candlewood Lake and Lake Lillinonah adds to the town's charm. Farther to the west and north are the two small towns of New Fairfield and Sherman. Although their centers, linked by Routes 37 and 39, have charms of their own, there is no doubt that their greatest attractions are Candlewood Lake and Squantz Pond State Park.

Candlewood's **Story**

Nearly 1,400 men created the lake in the woodlands and farmlands nestled between the rolling hills of Brookfield and New Fairfield. Five hundred lumberjacks hand-felled 4,500 acres of trees, burning the lumber in massive bonfires. Dams were constructed, and in 1928 the first pumping operation began bringing water from the Housatonic River. Soon the Connecticut Light and Power Company was able to generate electricity by letting the water pour down an enormous pipe called a penstock and into an immense turbine.

Almost immediately the incredible beauty of the newly formed lake lapping the wooded shoreline caused land prices to skyrocket. Development escalated rapidly as the area began drawing homeowners as well as vacationers to the pretty coves of the 60-plus miles of shoreline along the 11-mile-long lake. This valuable new landmark was christened **Candlewood** after the native candlewood trees whose sapling branches had sometimes been used as candles by early settlers.

Mother Earth Gallery and Mining Company (ages 6 to 12)
806 Federal Road, Route 7; (203) 775-6272; www.motherearthcrystals.com. Open Monday and Wednesday through Saturday from 10:00 a.m. to 6:00 p.m. and Sunday noon to 5:00 p.m. Closed Tuesday. The mine closes at 4:30 p.m. on Sunday and at 5:30 p.m. on the other days. $$$ (prospecting), $$$$ (birthday parties)

This looks like an ordinary storefront with an inventory of pretty neat stuff—crystals, minerals, shells, candles, wind chimes, nature-related toys, and environmentally friendly merchandise with a New Age touch. It's also something more.

It has a mine in it, full of crystals and minerals and semiprecious stones. And you can go prospecting with a bucket and a miner's hard hat complete with headlamp. A birthday celebration in the Miner's Shack party room buys you a Planet Earth cake and juice, a game of Rocko, a video trip around the world to learn about real mines and gem production, and a chance to go prospecting for amethysts, obsidian, calcites, fossil shark teeth, or other treasures. Not your birthday? Go prospecting anyway. Serious collectors and beginners alike will love the exceptional minerals and gemstones sold here, and, if you are tempted to really go prospecting in the

Fishing at Squantz Pond
and Candlewood Lake

Some fishers say you can't have a bad day fishing in the lakes in this neck of the woods. It's not unusual to land a ten-pound trout, so anglers young and old come to try their luck for one of these trophy fish. Bass also love these waters, and bass tournaments are common summer events as hundreds of boats crowd this vast waterway for both the sport and the great dinners that result from fishing in it. Pickerel, carp, catfish, bluegills, and white and yellow perch proliferate as well. Fish from your boat, the shoreline, or public piers and docks. Remember that Squantz Pond has a special pier for handicapped anglers.

Call the Candlewood Lake Authority (860-354-6928) for more information on either lake. The state Department of Environmental Protection Web site (www.ct.gov/dep) will steer you to both the *CT Boater's Guide* and *CT Angler's Guide,* which provide details for both bodies of water. On the DEP site you can also find state boat-launch sites and info on the marinas that provide fuel, boating goods, boat rentals, and boat services. The DEP online store also offers for sale its *Fisheries Guide to the Lakes and Ponds of Connecticut.* It's a great buy especially for anglers with plans to travel from place to place throughout the state.

Connecticut hills, Mother Earth also sells the materials you'd need to find or polish your own gems.

Candlewood Lake (all ages)

Built in 1926 to provide hydroelectric power to the region, Candlewood is the largest artificial lake in Connecticut. Now bordered by private residences, it's pretty as a picture in every season and popular with vacationers and day-trippers even in the quiet of winter. Use Route 39 to travel the length of the western side of the lake; smaller side roads branch off Route 7/202 on the eastern side.

Much of the lakefront is held in private hands, although house, cottage, and cabin rentals are common. Families interested in renting by the week or month can check local newspaper listings or contact the Northern Fairfield County Association of Realtors at (203) 744-7255. You can also check out www.candlewood lake.org.

The five towns (Danbury, New Milford, and Brookfield also touch the lakeshore) bordering the lake also have beaches. Some of these are opened to out-of-town visitors at a daily rate. Public boat launches are also available at some of the town beaches on the perimeter, and docks are on the east shore at Down the Hatch Restaurant and near the Candlewood Inn caterers.

Squantz Pond State Park (all ages)

Route 39; (203) 797-4165; www.ct.gov/dep. From Memorial Day weekend through Labor Day, day-use parking fee from 8:00 a.m. to 6:30 p.m., $$–$$$ (higher fees on weekends).

This pretty area of low hills and woodlands surrounds Squantz Pond, a 5-mile arm of Candlewood Lake. The park offers a public boat launch from which boaters can gain access to Candlewood by passing under the Route 39 causeway that crosses the narrowest connection of the two bodies of water. Other wonderful summer fun here includes Jet Skiing, waterskiing, fishing, swimming, scuba diving, hiking, and picnicking. In winter the park is perfect for ice-skating, ice fishing, and cross-country skiing. The main entrance to the park is off Route 39 in the town of New Fairfield. From the southern junction of Routes 37 and 39, take 39 north about 4 miles to the entrance. If you're at the north end of the loop, in Sherman, take 39 south about 6 miles.

Along the shore are picnic groves, barbecue areas, a guarded swimming area, and a bathhouse with changing rooms and restrooms (but no showers). A special pier allows handicapped visitors to fish. Easy to moderate hiking trails along the lakefront and into the beautiful Pootatuck Forest start at the north end of the picnic area on the pond's western shore.

A food concession provides typical fare such as burgers, dogs, and fries in the summer. They often stock necessities like foil and charcoal for those who want to barbecue.

Pedalboats and canoes rent for $10 an hour; canoes can also be rented for the day for $30. Squantz Pond is actually better for canoeists than is Candlewood. The high-speed powerboats on the larger lake create so much wake that canoeists have a safer, saner day with the smaller numbers of boats that remain on Squantz.

Sherman Playhouse (age 8 and up)
Junction of Routes 37 and 39; (860) 354-3622; www.geocities.com/~shermanplayers. $$$ (less for students)

From April through December this community theater presents new and classic plays and musicals. Curtain time is 8:00 p.m. on Friday and Saturday. Sunday matinees are at 3:00 p.m.

Where to Eat

The American Pie Company. Junction of Routes 37 and 39 in Sherman; (860) 350-0662. In the same building as the post office, this eatery has everything kids love at breakfast, lunch, and dinner. Chicken pot pie, shepherd's pie, homemade soups, salads, sandwiches, great desserts. Open daily from 7:00 a.m., no dinner on Monday. $–$$

Chris's Restaurant. 189 Federal Road, Brookfield; (203) 775-7072. For folks who'd prefer a slightly less casual ambience, this longtime favorite is newly designed and updated, but it features the same great chef and hearty American fare. Excellent seafood, pastas, chicken, steak, and veal dishes, plus an affordable children's menu and plenty of kid-friendly appetizers. Lunch and dinner daily. $$–$$$

Down the Hatch. 292 Candlewood Lake Road; (203) 775-6635. In northern Brookfield, this place offers great views of the lake and great food. Fresh fish, big burgers, and perfectly grilled chicken. Outside deck, often packed with families. Open daily for lunch and dinner in season. Closed Monday and Tuesday in early fall. Closed entirely November through March. $–$$

Rickyl's Brookfield Luncheonette. 800 Federal Road; (203) 775-6042. Freshly prepared and cooked-to-order American cuisine, including omelets, fresh-fruit pancakes, homemade soups, creative sandwiches, salads, and much more. Open Tuesday through Friday for breakfast and lunch. Breakfast only on Saturday and Sunday. $

Where to Stay

Newbury Inn. 1030 Federal Road, at Routes 7 and 202 in Brookfield; (203) 775-0220; www.newburyinn.com. Newly renovated in 2007, this hotel offers 46 units, including 6 suites/efficiencies and some rooms with whirlpool spas or private patios; complimentary deluxe continental breakfast served in breakfast lounge with fireplace. On 5-acre grounds, a mile from Candlewood Lake. $$$–$$$$

General Information

Coastal Fairfield County Convention and Visitors Bureau. Gate Lodge at Mathews Park, 297 West Avenue, Norwalk 06850; (203) 853-7770, (800) 866-7925, or (888) 289-3353; www.visitfairfieldcountyct.com.

Connecticut Welcome Centers in Fairfield County are located at I-84 Danbury (eastbound), I-95 Darien (northbound), Merritt Parkway Greenwich (northbound).

Litchfield County

Artful Pleasures and Historic Treasures

From its northwest corner where it meets the Berkshire Mountains of Massachusetts to the fertile valleys formed by the Housatonic and Farmington Rivers as they dissect the foothills, Litchfield County is famed for its beauty, history, and tranquility. Punctuated by charming colonial towns, picturesque lakes, and thousands upon thousands of acres of farms, forests, and parks, it is an intriguing mix of rural and affluent culture. Resorts, restaurants, antiques shops, and country inns draw visitors from all over to share in the wealth, while farm markets, country fairs, and nature preserves draw visitors eager to taste the salt of the earth.

Families have much to gain by exploring the Litchfield Hills. Leave behind your health clubs and home-based gymnasium equipment, and come here instead to keep

TopPicks for fun in Litchfield County

1. Appalachian Trail

2. Kent Falls State Park

3. Mohawk Mountain Ski Area

4. Mount Tom State Park

5. Quiet Sports in the Housatonic Valley—Breadloaf Lodge

6. Fishing at Twin Lakes—O'Hara's Landing

7. Local Farm's Old-Style Life Skills Workshops

8. Lee's Riding Stable

9. Tubing the Farmington River—Satan's Kingdom Recreation Area

10. Institute for American Indian Studies

LITCHFIELD COUNTY

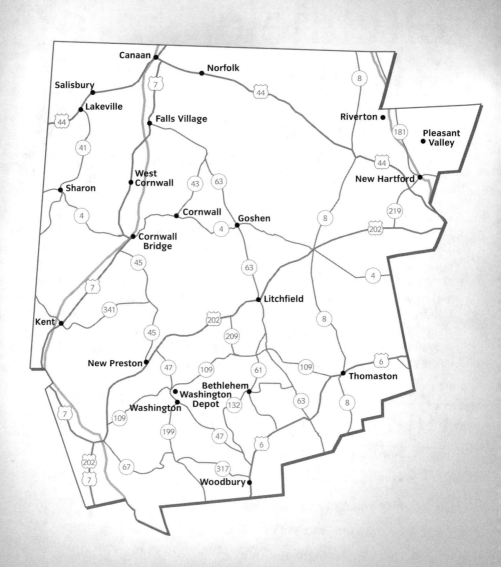

fit and trim in the fresh air. Outdoor recreation opportunities abound in every pristine corner of the county. Hiking, bicycling, canoeing, fishing, kayaking, whitewater rafting, tubing, downhill and cross-country skiing, horseback riding, swimming, and camping entice health-minded families to the Litchfield Hills.

Other families may be drawn to the spark of creative and spiritual energy that seems to reside in the nooks and crannies of the county. Fine artists, country crafters, writers, musicians, actors, and other folks driven by the Spirit and the Muses—even gardeners, vintners, chefs, and Benedictine sisters—have made their homes in these woodlands and have set up shop so that visitors might have the pleasure of enjoying their artistry. Potteries, stained-glass studios, woodcarving shops, glassworks, and galleries and boutiques showcasing all of their creations proliferate side by side with playhouses, concert halls, cooking schools, wineries, arboretums, and ornamental gardens. If your aim is to inspire the budding talents within your family, you will find no lack of opportunity to encourage one another to believe in the importance of creative careers and vocations. If you have no ulterior motive except to enjoy the displays and performances, a grand tour of the county's theaters, ateliers, and galleries will leave you awestruck.

Those of you excited by history, especially Native American lifeways, colonial settlement, and the American Revolution, will love Litchfield County. Historic homes, ruins and archaeological sites, excellent museums, and festivals celebrating the past are ubiquitous here. This book will cover only a select number of these sites and events. This volume's selection is intended to be what the author considers the best sites for families.

Lastly, Litchfield is the perfect place for wanderers. Dress in the casual garb of the vagabond and meander down the scenic highways and waterways that lead to places only more lovely at each bend in the road or river. The Northwest CT Convention & Visitors Bureau has created a booklet of tours suitable for car, foot, boat, and bike. Each of these adventures renews both body and soul. Do yourselves a favor and journey here.

Woodbury

Using Routes 25, 34, or 8 to get to I-84, you might make Woodbury your first stop in Litchfield County. Larger and more populated than many Litchfield County towns, Woodbury was settled in 1673 and was once known for its agriculture and its production of cutlery and cloth. Day-tripping families will discover that the town is now famed as the place to go for antiques.

Woodbury's Famous Antiques and Flea Market (all ages)
Held at the junction of Routes 6 and 64; (203) 263-2841; www.woodburyfleamarket .com. Open every Saturday mid-March through mid-December, weather permitting

(most vendors come from April through mid-December), from 7:00 a.m. to 3:00 p.m. **Free** admission and parking.

Families wary of entering crowded shops full of expensive goods may enjoy a trip to this child-friendly outdoor market of up to 150 vendors. Go early for the best selection or late for the best bargains. Antiques are well mixed with junk; new stuff is well mixed with authentic collectibles. Two food stands make it easy for you to come for breakfast or stay for lunch.

The Glebe House Museum and Gertrude Jekyll Garden
(ages 6 and up)

Hollow Road off Route 6; (203) 263-2855; www.theglebehouse.org. Open from 1:00 to 4:00 p.m. Wednesday through Sunday from May through October. Expanded hours on Saturday from 10:00 a.m. to 4:00 p.m. June through August. Open weekends only in November from 1:00 to 4:00 p.m. Open by appointment December through April. $

This 1745 minister's farmhouse, or glebe, is an exceptional example of eighteenth-century architecture and is especially welcoming to children. The mood inside the house is warm and inviting. Artifacts are laid out in positions of use, and children are enthusiastically addressed on tours tailored to the interests and schedules of visitors. Historically important as the site of the first election of an American bishop of the Episcopal Church in 1783, the house has many fine (and simple) furnishings and a charming gift shop/bookstore. Its beautiful perennial garden is the only one in the United States designed by renowned English landscape designer Gertrude Jekyll.

Most important for interested families, a History Camp for children ages eight to twelve is offered each summer. A weeklong program of colonial activities, it is an eye-opening experience of eighteenth-century daily life. Several sessions are often offered. Be sure to return on "All Hollow's Eve," a one-night extravaganza late in October. This special evening includes candlelight tours of the museum, other nearby sites, and the Old Burying Ground; storytellers; and refreshments. This is a spooky but delightful experience, suitable for younger children as well as older—but parents should be the judge of individual children's capacities for scary stories and ghostly happenings.

Woodbury Ski and Racquet Area (ages 3 and up)
785 Washington Road, Route 47; (203) 263-2203; www.woodburyskiarea.com. Open weekdays from 10:30 a.m. to 10:00 p.m., Saturday from 9:00 a.m. to 10:00 p.m., and Sunday from 9:00 a.m. to 4:30 p.m. $$$–$$$$

This year-round recreational facility attracts thousands of outdoor sports enthusiasts each year. In winter its fourteen alpine downhill trails are especially popular with children and with beginner and intermediate skiers. Lessons, rentals, and night skiing specials are offered, and a double chairlift, two rope tows, a handle tow, and snow-making equipment keep the pace active all season long. Two major half-pipes and a quarter-pipe provide excitement for snowboarders. A base lodge and ski shop flesh out the amenities that keep Woodbury on a par with other Connecticut ski areas. Ask about the Winter Carnival in January—a weeklong extreme extravaganza.

Three tubing and sledding courses with a dedicated lift are also available, from a gentle glide for beginners to a two-lane, bobsled-like run for thrill-seekers. Seven kilometers of groomed cross-country trails are also on the property; these improved trails are lighted and have snowmaking, tracking, and tilling.

A recently resurfaced and expanded year-round skateboarding park and an in-line skate course are also here. In the warm seasons, you can also camp, swim, picnic, and play tennis and paddle tennis. Concerts, from rock to reggae, are also offered from time to time in the summer. Check the Web site to see what's on the calendar.

Flanders Nature Center (all ages)

Church Hill and Flanders Road, off Route 6; (203) 263-3711; www.flandersnaturecenter .org. Trails open daily year-round, dawn to dusk. Free.

Nature lovers will enjoy this center's two sanctuaries at Van Vleck Farm and Whittemore, where trails lead through 1,000 acres of woodland, bog, a nut tree arboretum, and more. Bird and wildflower walks, a fall festival, and a variety of programs such as maple-sugaring in March are among the opportunities for discovery. The Trail House offers a nature shop and some small exhibits; it's open Saturday from 9:00 a.m. to 5:00 p.m.

Where to Eat

Carmen Anthony Fishhouse. 757 Main Street South; (203) 266-0011. As perfect for families as for discerning adult diners, this casually elegant establishment is open for lunch and dinner daily year-round. Fresh fish is the specialty here; soups, salads, pastas, and a special selection of kids' favorites are also available. $$–$$$

Elenni's. 40 Sherman Hill Road, Route 64 at Route 6 junction; (203) 263-2566. Greek pizza, pasta, chicken, salads, grinders, calzones. Open daily for lunch and dinner. $–$$

Where to Stay

Curtis House. 506 Main Street; (203) 263-2101. One of Connecticut's oldest hostelries, this rambling 1754 colonial inn and carriage house in the heart of Woodbury offers guest rooms that range from small with shared bath to huge or linked with private bath. Restaurant. $$–$$$$

Longwood Country Inn. 1204 Main Street South; (203) 266-0800; www.long woodcountryinn.com. Small families with children over age 10 looking for accommodations in a refined setting might ask for guest room number five in this restored 1789 colonial. More rooms to be offered in upcoming expansion. Full country breakfasts are included in the room rate. $$$$

Kent

I don't believe there's a family alive who won't find something to please every member in the beautiful town of Kent. About 12 miles north of New Milford on Route 7, the village center was once little more than a bump in the road. But it hums now with the activities generated by the shops, galleries, restaurants, bakeries, and natural and historical attractions that line Route 7 as it passes through one of northwest Connecticut's most interesting villages.

Bull's Bridge (all ages)

Officially in Gaylordsville, 3.8 miles south of Kent's center; just off Route 7 on Bull's Bridge Road. Free.

Originally built in 1760 by Isaac Bull to carry iron ore and charcoal over the Housatonic, the current bridge is one of two remaining covered bridges open to traffic in Connecticut. The view of the river and its beautiful whitewater cascades and ravines is perfect from the bridge. A small scenic loop trail leads to other views of the woodlands, rapids, still water, and wildlife in the area. A parking area on the western side of the bridge allows you to stop here safely and walk to several clearly marked sites and trails. A second hiker parking area is located a bit farther along Bull's Bridge Road at the entrance to the Appalachian Trail section (see sidebar), marked with white blazes.

Kent Village Center

On Route 7, also called Main Street, mostly north of the Route 341 intersection.

In the center of Kent, stroll through the shops and galleries. All lovely, some are especially suited to families. **Toys Galore and More** (860-927-4091) is self-explanatory.

It's **Revolutionary**

Historically important because of the integral role it played in the Revolutionary War, Kent supplied the Continental Army with iron ore, goods, and soldiers. It also offered a strategic location on a main waterway to Long Island Sound and on the marching road between Lebanon, the army's supply depot, and Washington's headquarters in New York. Now, nearby and along this same route, lies a sizable stretch of the **Appalachian Trail,** including the longest river walk on the whole 2,144-mile hiking path. You can enter this easy-to-moderate 7.8-mile portion of the trail near Bull's Bridge. You'll find the trailhead off of Route 341 west. Go to Skiff Mountain Road, and bear right at the fork to the Appalachian National Scenic Trail. The trail is marked with white blazes, and the area closes at sunset.

Sometimes they put bubble solution and giant bubble wands outside in the brick plaza—so fine for fun. Other favorites are **Foreign Cargo** (860-927-3900), which has great funky and exotic import clothing, unusual jewelry, and an upstairs gallery of American antiques and Asian, African, and Pacific Island art. If the kids enjoy them or can allow you to enjoy them, at least peek into the art galleries. Our favorite is the **Heron American Craft Gallery** (860-927-4804), which offers top-quality handcrafts in all price ranges. When the gallery gazing and boutique hopping leave you weary, head for the restaurants.

Sloane-Stanley Museum (ages 5 and up)

Route 7, north of Kent center; (860) 927-3849. The museum itself is open Wednesday through Sunday from 10:00 a.m. to 4:00 p.m. mid-May to October 31. The grounds remain open until 4:30 p.m. during that time. $

Just north of the village on the left side of the road where the railroad tracks border Route 7, stop for a look at one of the most surprisingly moving exhibits we've seen in the state. Gathered through the efforts of the late author/artist Eric Sloane, the collection includes tools made by colonial Americans as early as the seventeenth century.

Revealing much about the early settlers' experiences and their adaptation to their new home, the tools are fascinating in their diversity, their ingenuity, and in their beauty. Each object has been finely crafted, mostly by hand, primarily from the hardwoods of the Eastern Woodlands. The presence of each cabinetmaker, each farmer, each cook seems to fill the post-and-beam barn in which the collection is housed. A videotape featuring Sloane himself explains the philosophies behind the artist, his work, and the museum collection.

The museum also includes a complete re-creation of Eric Sloane's art studio along with some of his original works. Outside the museum is a small cabin Sloane built in 1974 with the use of notations found in a young boy's 1805 diary. The simple realities of frontier life are made obvious throughout the austere interior of this display.

A visit to the ruins of the **Kent Iron Furnace** (also on the property) may have some interest (see why in the next sidebar). Long important as a producer of pig iron, the blast furnace is partially restored. A diorama inside the museum explains the process of smelting pig iron and shows how the blast furnace would have worked.

Connecticut Antique Machinery Association Museum
(ages 5 and up)

Route 7, north of Kent center; enter property at Sloane-Stanley Museum; take driveway to right; (860) 927-0050; www.ctamachinery.com. Museum and grounds are open mid-May through October 31, Wednesday through Sunday 10:00 a.m. to 4:00 p.m. A donation ($) is gratefully accepted.

One of Connecticut's newest museums is a tiny village of sorts constructed on eight acres of wooded property adjacent to the Sloane-Stanley Museum. Visitors can tour

Hitting the **Iron Heritage Trail**

I assure you that none of my children would have said, "Hey, Mom, let's go check out Connecticut's Iron Heritage Trail! It sounds awesome!" But if you are of the No Child Left Inside philosophy, as I am, and you are yearning for an outdoor romp with a nifty educational/environmental element, then you might consider contacting Ronald D. Jones (860-435-9183), chairman of the **Upper Housatonic Valley National Heritage Area** (P.O. Box 1942, Lakeville, CT 06039; www.upperhousatonicheritage.org). Ask him to send you a trail guide to the Iron Heritage Trail through the Tri-State Salisbury Iron District, in which you and the kids can explore the remains and restorations of the forty-plus blast furnaces, lime kilns, forges, and iron mining and mill sites in northwestern Connecticut, southwestern Massachusetts, and eastern New York. These sites, all within the watershed of the Upper Housatonic River, were in operation from 1735 to 1923. In addition to the furnace in Kent at the Sloane-Stanley site, you can visit the 40-foot-high **Beckley Iron Furnace** on Lower Road in East Canaan, beautifully situated along the pretty Blackberry River. It used to produce eleven tons of pig iron each day and has a terrific "salamander" you'll want to learn about. Bring a picnic to this pretty spot, and be sure to choose a bit of iron slag from the pile to take back to school for show-and-tell. You can also hike to the **Mount Riga Furnace** and the **Lime Rock tower,** both in Salisbury. Mount Riga features spectacular views from Bald Peak; Lime Rock once produced thousands of railroad car wheels. The trail guide has a map and clear descriptions of the best sites. Whether you drive the suggested routes from place to place or just hike to specific points, it takes you through some mighty pretty country, not to mention to another era in Connecticut's history. All of the hikes to each site are easy to moderate and suitable for young family members; guided walks are also offered from time to time, so check the Web site for more information.

the eight new or restored buildings of the Connecticut Antique Machinery Association. The complex houses the state's largest display of steam and gas engines and tractors, as well as other antique agricultural and industrial machinery and mining equipment. Arranged on the site are such buildings as the Agricultural Hall (a tractor barn housing fifty tractors from the late 1800s to the 1950s), the Cream Hill Agricultural School (the state's first such school, moved here from Cornwall with its original desks, kitchen implements, library, and natural science and curiosities collection), and the Connecticut Museum of Mining and Mineral Science (the largest permanent display in the state of native minerals and rocks, historical bricks, and mining equipment). The last-mentioned includes amazing small dioramas depicting gold mining, brick making, and iron smelting, complete with miniature figures and signage that tells the story of the nation's mining heritage and industry. Among the other buildings are a blacksmith shop, engine halls, an engine house for the museum's operating narrow-gauge railway, and an oil pumping station from Pennsylvania.

Most displays are labeled, and educational signage is in place in some areas, but be sure to take the guided tours offered here. They generally last an hour, but volunteers will take into account the ages of your party and your areas of interest. Despite its apparent potential for lots of bells and whistles, this tends to be a quiet place. Demonstrations are given only at special events, such as the three-day Fall Festival (see sidebar). Check the Web site for upcoming events.

Kent Falls State Park (all ages)

Route 7 about 5 miles north of Kent's center; (860) 927-3238. Open year-round. A parking fee ($; $$ for out-of-state vehicles) is charged on weekends and holidays only from Memorial Day weekend through Labor Day weekend.

Wander northward from the Sloane-Stanley Museum until you reach this park on the right side of the road. Leave your car at the parking lot right off Route 7 at the base of the wide meadow that slopes down from the hills above. Beyond the meadow are the beautiful cascading waterfalls known as Kent Falls. Beginning in the town of Warren, the mountain stream known as Falls Brook reaches Kent through a series of drops, about 200 feet in total. Each drop is as pretty as the last as the falls descend through a dense forest of hemlocks, creating pools and potholes that openly invite visitors to dip a toe or two or even more into the cold, clear (but not potable) water.

Which Way Did He Go, **George?**

Local lore documents that George Washington may have nearly lost a trusty steed as he crossed Bull's Bridge one day in March 1781. It's uncertain how the accident happened or whether the horse was Washington's own mount, but it is clear that one of his horses fell into the roiling waters under the bridge as his company made the passage on the way to meet with the French to make plans for naval support against the British. Washington's diary for the day records that the cost of retrieving the horse from Bull's Bridge Falls was $215. The time spent on this rescue and the cost incurred lead some historians to guess that the animal may not have been just any ordinary horse.

Fall **Festival**

If you're ever in Kent the last Friday, Saturday, and Sunday in September, stay for the annual **Connecticut Antique Machinery Association's Fall Festival.** Sounds awful, right? It's not—at this three-day machinery extravaganza, you may see cider making, threshing, wood splitting, blacksmithing, broom making, or shingle making. Check out the draft animals, antique cars and trucks, homestead displays, and working exhibits of steam and gas engines, farm equipment, steam launches, and motor canoes. Enjoy a cup of the CAMA's famed Engineer's Vegetable Beef Soup or cruise the other food vendors from 10:00 a.m. to 4:00 p.m. Call (860) 927-0050. $; children 5 and under are **free.**

Two trails to take you to the top of the falls are cut through the forest on either side of the stream. We suggest you climb up the .25-mile south trail directly to the right of the falls as you face them from the meadow and descend on the north trail, which you reach by crossing the bridge at the top of the south trail. The trails are fairly steep at points, but not strenuous. Small children will manage well if they rest from time to time. Stairs and railings on the south trail will help those who haven't had a workout in a while. The slightly longer north trail angles off into the woods a bit away from the falls. You'll miss a pretty walk through the New England woodlands if you don't come down this way.

"Swimming" in the strictest sense is prohibited here, but wading or bathing (in bathing suits, please) in designated areas is absolutely allowed. Where else can you cavort directly under a waterfall? The deepest pool, depending on the water level in a particular year, will be waist- or even chest-high for adults, so don't take your eyes off small children if you're not going in with them. Wading, for them, may be very close to swimming in at least two of the pools in which wading is allowed.

After you cool off, try some fishing in the stream as it nears the meadow. The stream is stocked with trout, and no license is necessary for children under sixteen. Picnic tables are scattered throughout the meadow and under the trees near the parking lot. Grills and toilets are also available. You have to pack out your own trash, so be prepared. The falls tend to be most dramatic in the spring, by the way, when melting winter snow raises the water level; the forest, however, is most dramatic in fall. In winters when the water freezes, the falls form giant icicles. Maybe you'll just have to return in every season.

Macedonia State Park (all ages)

Four miles northwest of the village off Route 341; park office: (860) 927-3238; campground office: (860) 927-4100. Open year-round; seasonal camping. Free day-use; camping, $.

With 2,300 acres, this park has excellent trails offering spectacular views of the Catskill and Taconic Mountains. Camping (eighty sites, mid-April to September 30), hiking, stream fishing, picnicking, and cross-country skiing are all available here. Take the loop trail to Cobble Mountain (1,380 feet at the summit) for a view you won't forget. It's just a half-mile to the top, then a mile down on another trail, or you can retrace the way you came. Ask a ranger for a map.

Where to Eat

Belgique Patisserie. 1 Bridge Street at the junction of Routes 7 and 341; (860) 927-3631. The best place for tarts, Belgian pralines, chocolates, ice cream, hot chocolate, and coffees. Open year-round, Wednesday to Sunday. $

Fife 'n Drum Restaurant and Inn. Route 7; (860) 927-3509. Three-star restaurant in the style of an elegant but homey tavern, wonderful New England classic cuisine at lunch (11:30 a.m. to 3:00 p.m.), dinner (from 5:30 p.m.), and Sunday brunch. Piano music in the evening, played by the well-known owner/host. Adjacent inn offers lodging, and a lovely shop offers tempting gifts. Closed Tuesday. $$–$$$

Stroble Baking Company. Route 7; (860) 927-4073. Breads, pastries, cakes, cookies, and coffee are the highly rated take-out specialties here; soups, sand-wiches, and salads are the bonus. Open daily year-round 8:00 a.m. to 6:00 p.m. $

Where to Stay

Cooper Creek Bed and Breakfast. 230 Kent Cornwall Road; (860) 927-4334. This 1860 Greek Revival B&B offers a charming two-room suite with private bath as well as three to five guest rooms that have private or shared baths, all within the main house. Families with infants up to one year old are welcome to stay Sunday through Thursday; families with children ages six or older are welcome at any time. Full breakfast. Non-smoking. Two-and-one-half-acre property to play in. $$$–$$$$

Fife 'n Drum Inn. 59 North Main Street in the center of the village; (860) 927-3509. 8 large rooms with private baths, restaurant (see above). $$$

Sharon

If your last stop in Kent was Macedonia State Park, you might consider continuing north along Route 341 into New York State, then eastward again on Route 41 back to Connecticut and the town of Sharon. (As the crow flies, Sharon is about 10 miles north of Kent; the surface route is about 15 miles.) Charming and barely there, Sharon existed in the eighteenth century and has not developed much since. That's a tribute, not a criticism. The beauty of the place and the careful stewardship of the community are apparent in its lovely town green and the historic homes that surround it, but there's really just one special place here for families. If your kids are old enough, the show is appropriate, and if the time of your visit is summer-stock time, you might also enjoy a second treat: a performance at the **TriArts Sharon Playhouse** on Route 343 (49 Amenia Road; 860-364-7469; www.triarts.net). More than a few steps above the average community-theater offerings, these professional-quality productions are almost always family-friendly fare, and the tickets are very affordable. Look here too for a small slate of winter productions and staged readings in the theater's Bok Gallery, and if you live nearby, check out the many children's theater workshops for your young thespians.

Sharon Audubon Center (all ages)

Route 4; (860) 364-0520; www.audubon.org/local/sanctuary/sharon. Trails open dawn to dusk daily year-round; building open year-round from Tuesday through Saturday from 9:00 a.m. to 5:00 p.m. and on Sunday from 1:00 to 5:00 p.m. Closed major holidays. Access to the trails, $. No charge for center's main building.

Like all of the Audubon Society's facilities, the 684-acre Sharon Audubon Center is exceptionally well done, with 11 miles of carefully tended trails and boardwalks throughout several habitats. Pond, swamp, marsh, and woodland areas have clearly marked, self-guided interpretive nature walks. Naturalist-guided tours highlighting such topics as birds, trees, or mammals are also offered for families or groups.

The center's main building includes natural science exhibits, a noncirculating library, and an excellent gift and book shop. The children's Adventure Center has a feature we've not seen anywhere else: listening boxes to sit inside. Tapes triggered by children's weight play sounds of whales, rainstorms, and more. Kids can crawl through a simulated beaver's den, identify skulls, look at a real honeybee hive, and more.

Outdoors, a wildlife rehabilitation center provides temporary shelter for injured animals; turtles, snakes, and birds are the most common species found here. If you come in spring or summer near evening or early morning, you may see the beavers at Ford or Bog Meadow Ponds. Warblers tend to stop here on their annual fall and spring migrations, so bird-watchers (and listeners) might enjoy a visit at those times. The center also maintains an herb garden, a wildflower garden, and a butterfly and hummingbird garden.

Check the Web site for the dates of the wonderful annual Sharon Audubon Festival ($–$$), featuring hands-on crafts for children, demonstrations, workshops, music, pony rides, and food. It is held rain or shine. You might return in late October for the Audubon Kids Day ($). A costume parade, hayrides and a hay-bale maze, nature activities, and pumpkin carving are among the events. Look, too, on the Web site for the naturalist-led educational programs for parents and children, offered throughout the year.

Where to Eat

Little Brick House Pizza. 30 West Main Street; (860) 364-1321. For now, anyway, this terrific little spot is the only place in town to pick up a bite to eat. Great pizza, grinders, and salads are the fare. Cash and checks only. Lunch and dinner, 11:00 a.m. to 8:00 p.m. Tuesday through Saturday. $

Where to Stay

Sharon Motor Lodge. Route 41; (860) 364-0036. 22 large rooms, nonsmoking rooms available, outdoor pool, small restaurant across the street. AAA and Mobil approved. Nice grounds, set back from the main road. $$$

Cornwall Bridge

In a roughly elliptical shape drawn by Routes 7, 128S, and 4, you'll find the separate villages of Cornwall Bridge, Cornwall, and West Cornwall, with one of the three nearby state parks or forests shouldering each of them. Together this trio composes the town of Cornwall. Traveling north from Kent on Route 7, Cornwall Bridge is the first of the three. One of those villages you can easily pass through before you know you have reached it, Cornwall Bridge is a beautiful area with a couple of sites of interest to families.

Cornwall Bridge Pottery (ages 5 and up)

Route 7; (860) 672-6545 or (800) 501-6545; www.cbpots.com. Open daily from 9:00 a.m. to 5:00 p.m. year-round. Call ahead if you want to make sure someone is there to show you around, or feel free to poke around on your own—respectfully. Your best chance to see the potters at work is Monday through Friday. Call ahead to see where the potters are in their production cycle. Free.

On the east side of Route 7 a mile north of the Route 45 junction and a mile south of the junction with Route 4, visit the pottery workshop and see the potters and the 35-foot-long wood-fired kiln at work. I suspect your family will love to see this process.

Todd Piker is owner, potter, philosopher, and excellent businessman. His pots (and plates, bowls . . .) are exceptionally beautiful and eminently useful. Browse here or at the pottery's store (discussed in the West Cornwall section) for the pots you might find most usable for the needs of your family. Still-beautiful and useful seconds are available here; perfect pots are at the store.

Housatonic River Outfitters Inc.

24 Kent Road at the junction of Routes 4 and 7; (860) 672-1010; www.dryflies.com. Open Monday through Saturday from 9:00 a.m. to 5:00 p.m., Sunday from 9:00 a.m. to 4:00 p.m. Longer hours from May through fall.

Come here for top-quality fishing equipment, fly-tying materials, outerwear, fishing vests and other outdoor clothing, maps and books, camping equipment, and luggage. An amazing inventory of anglers' flies includes more than 50,000 in all. They will provide guide services for spin- or fly-fishing the river. All-day guided float trips in comfortable inflatable rafts can be arranged, complete with customized lunches. Licenses are available here. The staff can also arrange lodging and dinner reservations or point you toward activities in the Litchfield Hills.

Housatonic Meadows State Park (all ages)

One mile north of Cornwall Bridge on Route 7; park office: (860) 927-3238; camp office: (860) 672-6772. Open year-round; seasonal camping. Day use 8:00 a.m. to sunset. Alcohol prohibited. Free day use; camping $.

One of the state's best and most scenic campgrounds is right on the river and offers plenty of opportunities for hiking, fishing, and canoeing. Along one 2-mile stretch only fly fishers are allowed. You can watch them or be one of them (the latter only with a license). Cross-country skiing is popular here in winter. In warmer weather, ninety-five campsites are available from mid-April through December. Hikers may like knowing that the park's Pine Knob Loop Trail connects to the Appalachian Trail and passes lovely cascading waterfalls.

Housatonic Meadows Fly Shop and Tightline Adventures Guide Service (ages 8 and up)
Breadloaf Mountain Lodge and Cottages (all ages)

13 Route 7; (860) 672-6064; www.flyfishct.com. Shop open from 8:00 a.m. Monday through Thursday and from 7:00 a.m. Friday and weekends. Closings vary with the day and season. Breadloaf Mountain Lodge open year-round.

The folks who run the fly shop here say, "There's no tonic like the Housatonic," a phrase apparently borrowed from Oliver Wendell Holmes, who may indeed have been the first to say it. The folks here are happier than ever to help you find out how to enjoy yourselves on the river, and, in fact, they have invented a very clever and pleasant way to get families and others to stay happy longer: Their beautiful Breadloaf Mountain Lodge and Cottages were hugely popular in 2007, their first season. Located right across from the state park entrance and picnic area, the fly shop carries a bazillion flies and everything else you'd need for a lifetime of fishing. Equipment rentals are also available, along with licenses. Day-trippers in need of instruction or a guide will find all their needs met here. Full- and half-day float trips in drift rafts are expensive for most families, but if you have the do-re-mi, the guides here can sure sing that tune. Lunches are included on the full-day trips. Call well in advance to make your arrangements; you can't just show up at the door.

   The historic lodge and its adjacent five brand-new cottages are about as charming and as practically appointed as can be. These too come at somewhat of a dear price, at least for my family's budget, but they are totally terrific if you can spare the change, and so far, not one of the happy families who stayed here has balked at the tariff. Each of the cottages has a fully equipped kitchenette, gas fireplace, and queen-size bed or twin beds, or some combo thereof. All can also accommodate rollaway cots and such for families. Screened porches with built-in daybeds allow for more enjoyment of the beautiful setting within earshot of the river and wildlife. Personal barbecue grills at each cottage make meal prep fun and easy; coffee and homemade muffins are delivered fresh to your door each morning. Pair this lodging arrangement with a long weekend or even a week or more of quiet-sport fun in this pretty valley, and you're all set for happiness. The folks at the fly shop are pleased to set you up with all kinds of guided or self-guided outdoor recreation, from bird-watching and fishing to canoeing, kayaking, cycling, hiking, skiing, and more. The splurge may be well worth it. This place gets my vote for the best outdoor recreation destination in the Litchfield Hills.

Cornwall

In the area closest to the village center called Cornwall is one of Connecticut's best sites for family fun in winter as well as in warmer weather.

Mohawk Mountain State Park and Mohawk Mountain Ski Area
(all ages)
48 Great Hollow Road, Route 4; ski area: (860) 672-6100 or (800) 895-5222; www.mohawkmtn.com; park: (860) 424-3200; www.dep.state.ct.us. Open for skiing from Thanksgiving Day to early April. No day-use parking fee.

Connecticut's largest and oldest ski area, Mohawk has twenty-three trails and slopes, five lifts, and snowmaking equipment for 98 percent of the slopes. Families can enjoy day and night skiing, snowboarding, and 5 miles of cross-country ski trails in the Mohawk State Forest. Snowmobiling is allowed in designated areas of the park. Rental ski equipment is available, as are services like waxing and repairs. The PSIA Mohawk Learning Center provides lessons for all ages and skill levels; young children can participate in the SKIwee program.

The historic, renovated Pine Lodge offers skiers a place to rest and get warm; it has a ski-to restaurant and a sundeck. The base lodge has a retail ski shop and head-quarters for rentals, lessons, and food services.

In summer and fall, hiking, mountain biking, and picnicking draw thousands of visitors each year. Famous for its rare and fragile black spruce bog, Mohawk State Park and Forest are laced with trails, including a portion of the Mattatuck Trail and original segments of the Appalachian Trail. A climb to the wooden observation tower at Mohawk Mountain's 1,683-foot summit will leave you speechless, not from the exercise but from the view. The summer park rangers will give you a map and directions to the trailhead. A food concession, toilets, picnic tables, and a nature trail area make for great day-tripping.

Local Farm Old-Style Life Skills Workshops (ages 5 and up)

(860) 672-0229; www.motherhouse.com. See the calendar on the Web site for workshop dates, times, and locations. $35 per person; $50 for a family of four, with potluck lunch provided by the teacher and participants.

Priceless. Just perfectly priceless. This little corner of the world is a better place, that's for sure, because of the energy, effort, and mission of the remarkable Debra Tyler, who raises and milks Jersey cows, among her many other passions. Debra also offers a series of special classes in satisfying and simple lifeways that some of us might consider old-fashioned (but wish we knew how to do). Throughout the year, Debra and her like-minded colleagues offer workshops in bread-making, bee-keeping, goat-raising, wool-gathering, herbal crafts, and much more. Family Cow workshops, among her most popular offerings, teach the benefits and practicalities of cow ownership. All the workshops are open to families with kids of all ages, and all are hands-on and interactive in nearly every way. You'll breathe easier here in the company of the capable people who will coax you back in time in a real-world, real-simple way. Preregistration is required, and the workshop locations can vary. Debra has a lease arrangement on one of the prettiest farms in Cornwall, but not all workshops take place on this property.

West Cornwall

You have to visit West Cornwall if only to see Connecticut's finest and largest covered bridge. Built by Ithiel Town in 1837 of native oak, the **West Cornwall Bridge** is a beauty beyond a shadow of a doubt, and I don't think anyone is too jaded to feel its magic as it leads you across the river and back in time. I wish I could have heard the clip-clop of horses' hooves instead of the rumble of my car wheels as we made our crossings.

The village at West Cornwall is picturesque and very tiny, and for many travelers the bridge is in fact the main attraction. Traveling families may want to explore the bridge on foot, and you might also enjoy the small park and footpath along the waterway. Extended hikes on the Appalachian Trail are nearby. If you'd like to linger awhile in the village, there's Barbara Farnsworth's used- and rare-book store, a post office for you to drop a pretty picture postcard in the mail, the workshop of famed Shaker furniture maker Ian Ingersoll, a couple of gift and craft shops, such as the **Wish House** (413 Main Street; 860-672-2969) and the **Cornwall Bridge Pottery Store** (415 Main Street; 860-672-6545; www.cbpots.com), and a few lovely restaurants.

The spacious pottery store sells lead-free stoneware crafted by its owner, Todd Piker, and other local artisans. Handblown glassware, woodenware, leather goods, jewelry, furniture, clothing, and other quality crafts are also sold here.

Clarke **Outdoors**

The beautiful river that flows through the countryside and the Housatonic State Forest may appeal to your sense of adventure. If so, **Clarke Outdoors** can help you enjoy a 10-mile stretch through quiet water and easy white-water that is perfect for both knowledgeable and novice paddlers available from mid-March through early December. Drivers take you to the put-in point in Falls Village. You can choose to canoe, kayak, or raft. The halfway point is at the West Cornwall Bridge, where you can take out for a picnic on the banks. The pick-up and take-out point is at the Housatonic Meadows State Park. Hot showers are available back at the Clarke shop.

No more than three people are allowed in each canoe, and the minimum age allowed is seven. Single-paddler kayaks, sit-yaks, and inflated rafts that can hold four, six, or eight paddlers and passengers are also available. The minimum age allowed on the rafts is three. All rates include life vests and shuttle service that takes you to the put-in and picks you up at the take-out.

Offering one of the largest selections of canoe and kayak equipment in the Northeast, Clarke's retail store (860-672-6365; www.clarkeoutdoors .com) just south of West Cornwall on Route 7 is also the registration point where you begin this journey. Reservations are a must on weekends and many weekdays. Call at least a week in advance. American Canoe Association–certified instructors, including former national canoe champion Mark Clarke, provide lessons and guided trips. A kayaking school offers weekend lessons for adults and special groups for children ten to seventeen. Call (860) 672-6365 for information. Rates vary; $$$–$$$$

Where to Eat

The Wandering Moose Cafe. 421 Sharon Goshen Turnpike (Route 128, or Main Street); (860) 672-0178. Casual, diner-style cuisine perfect for families. Breakfast and lunch, Tuesday through Friday from 7:00 a.m. and weekends from 8:00 a.m. Dinner Wednesday through Sunday from 5:00 p.m. $–$$

Where to Stay

Cornwall Inn. 270 Kent Road (Route 7), in Cornwall Bridge; (860) 786-6884 or (800) 786-6884. The main building of this refurbished eighteenth-century inn has two options for families, including adjoining rooms connected by a private bath. Three rooms with two double beds in each are in the adjacent motel-style lodge. Outdoor pool and hot tub. Continental breakfast included. The inn's restaurant and tavern serves New American cuisine from 5:00 p.m. Thursday through Sunday. $$$

Salisbury/Lakeville

If you can, continue north on Route 7, swing left when you reach Route 112, following the signs for Salisbury and Lakeville. Route 112 leads to Route 44, where you'll take a right. Connecticut doesn't have a prettier town than Salisbury. They should place signs at the edge of the town that say "Please do not disturb." A quiet corner of pure sanity, Salisbury is home to beautiful Lake Wononscopomuc, on which is the Town Grove, an incomparable summer recreation spot. Here too is Mount Riga State Park and one of the state's most-hiked trails to Bear Mountain. Charming inns and lovely shops are in both village centers and tucked on their quiet country roads. The Appalachian Trail passes through town, as do several other trails. Call the Salisbury Town Hall for information on these trails and the Heritage Walks that are offered from time to time.

Mount Riga State Park (ages 8 and up)

From the intersection of Route 44 and Route 41 in the center of Salisbury, go north on Route 41 3.2 miles to the Undermountain Trail parking area on the left. No fees; no services. Open year-round dawn to dusk. Be sure to hike with a trail map or other written directions and safe footgear.

If you love the outdoors, you're in the right spot here. Basically this park exists pretty much entirely to provide access to the state's highest summits and most spectacular views. The iron industry had a real hold on this part of Connecticut a century ago, and you can still see the remains of the old charcoal roads, charcoal pits, and ore pits, some of which are now small ponds. This park is very well used by hikers, and trails are well marked, but no other amenities or services are here. Pack in everything you might need for your day. All the hiking here is moderately to truly strenuous, and there is no truly easy route to the summit. See the sidebar for one good option for hardy hikers.

Connecticut's **Agricultural Fairs**

Each year more than fifty agricultural fairs are held in Connecticut to celebrate the successful labor of the state's growers and their families. Nearly a score of these are classified as major fairs, and the towns of the Litchfield Hills host some of the state's largest and oldest fairs. Bethlehem, Bridgewater, Harwinton, Riverton, and Terryville are among these. My favorite is the Goshen Fair, which is always on Labor Day weekend. For more information and a complete guide to Connecticut's fairs, visit the Association of Connecticut Fairs Web site at www .ctfairs.org.

Bear Mountain and the
Appalachian Trail

Parts of Salisbury are traveled exclusively on foot by hikers walking Connecticut's 52 miles of the Appalachian Trail. Near the northernmost piece of the trail as it emerges from Massachusetts lies the peak of Bear Mountain, the highest full peak in the state at 2,316 feet. From its topmost point, you can see lots of Connecticut plus New York State and Massachusetts.

Pack a lunch and some water and, from the junction of Route 44 with Washnee Street near the Salisbury Town Hall, take Washnee Street west and drive .6 mile to Mount Riga Road. Follow Mount Riga Road 2.6 miles to Mount Washington Road, take a sharp right to the north and continue 2.8 miles to an old woods road on the right. Park carefully on the side of the road and walk onto the woods road, continuing for 1 mile until you reach the white-blazed Appalachian Trail. The ascent from here to the top of Bear Mountain is the easiest of all the challenging approaches to the summit, but young children may still need to take it slow over the rough trail. It can be tricky following wet weather. Proceed to the top of the mountain, where a stone monument rests, and share a lunch while you enjoy the vistas. Watch children carefully, since some overlooks skirt the mountain's sheer face. Some hikers may actually ascend by the toeholds in that vertical trail. Don't let your children attempt to descend that route. Retrace your path to the woods road and your parked car.

You can also access the peak from the longer Undermountain trail off Route 41, 3 miles north of Salisbury center, with a parking area on the left. You'll hike about 2 miles, pretty much straight up, then take a right when you see the marker for the Appalachian Trail. From that point, it's about a mile to the Bear Mountain summit.

O'Hara's Landing at Twin Lakes (all ages)

254 Twin Lakes Road; (860) 824-7583; www.oharaslanding.com. Open daily in season.

If you can't resist the idea of a day fishing lazily on a pretty-as-a-picture lake high in the hills, come to O'Hara's Marina on picturesque Twin Lakes. Launch your own boat or rent a canoe, a rowboat, or a small powerboat. Pontoon boats that hold eight to ten passengers are also available. You can fish, water-ski, or water-tube, but you need to bring your own equipment or purchase it here. Twin Lakes has some of the best fishing in the state, so a day on the water is bound to be exciting for young anglers. Bring your own gear or purchase bait and tackle at the shop here. If the trophy trout elude you or the sun gets to you, return to shore and have a bite to eat in the snack bar or cafe-style restaurant. The restaurant (open on weekends from April 15 to October 10 and daily in the three summer months) serves breakfast and lunch only, but you may not want to leave this pretty place until after sunset.

Town Grove (all ages)

Ethan Allen Street, in Lakeville, on Lake Wononscopomuc. Town Grove Manager available at the boathouse to the left of the park entrance. Purchase a season pass ($50 for residents; $300 for nonresidents) or a day pass ($$ per person) at the boathouse. Call the town offices (860-435-5170) for more information. Open from 7:00 a.m. to 8:00 p.m. daily in the summer season. Access to the park is limited in the winter season. No dogs allowed.

The Town of Salisbury welcomes nonresidents as well as residents to its lakefront park. You'll find a playground and a picnic area with barbecue grills; a small store offers ice cream and sundries. Boating and fishing are the most common activities here, of course; canoes and kayaks can be rented by the hour, half-day, or full day.

Separate lifeguarded swimming areas are available for small children and for older swimmers who might want to venture to the rafts in deeper water. Dressing rooms and restrooms are open in season.

Where to Eat

The Boathouse at Lakeville. 394 Main Street (Route 44), Lakeville; (860) 435-2111. This Adirondack-style restaurant is cheerful and welcoming to families. Great vegetarian dishes, plenty of seafood; soups and sandwiches at lunch. Open daily for lunch noon to 3:00 p.m.; dinner from 5:00 p.m. $$–$$$

The Woodland. Route 41, Lakeville; (860) 435-0578. Hearty American cuisine in a casual, country setting for lunch (noon to 2:30 p.m.) and dinner (from 5:30 p.m.), Tuesday through Saturday; Sunday, dinner only, from 4:00 p.m. $$–$$$

Where to Stay

Inn at Iron Masters. 229 Main Street (Route 44), Lakeville; (860) 435-9844; www.innatironmasters.com. 28 spacious rooms with sitting areas, private baths. Outdoor pool, continental breakfast, Hearth Room with fireplace. $$$$

Interlaken Inn, Resort, and Conference Center. 74 Interlaken Road (Route 112), off Route 7, in Lakeville; (860) 435-9878 or (800) 222-2909; www.interlakeninn. On 30 acres with two lakes, this resort offers an 82-unit contemporary building, a century-old B&B, and duplexes with fireplaces and kitchens. Restaurant, outdoor pool, sauna, tennis, golf, boating, lake swimming, fitness center. Great weekend packages, especially for families—you can even bring the dog! $$$–$$$$

The White Hart Inn. On the village green in Salisbury, Routes 41 and 44; (860) 435-0030 or (800) 832-0041; www.whitehartinn.com. Elegant country inn in restored vintage building. Canopy beds, veranda overlooking village. 26 charming rooms with private baths. 2 restaurants including a casual menu in the historic pub. Three meals available daily to guests as well as to the public. $$$$

Canaan/Falls Village

For those who live near the crowded New York–to-Boston corridor of I-95, visiting Canaan is like visiting another country—a very rural, quiet country. Somehow Canaan and the villages (Falls Village, South Canaan, East Canaan) surrounding it soothe the soul, restoring harmony to crowded lives. Fall foliage attracts tourists in droves, but it's pretty here in summer, too. If you live downstate or in the city, you're going to think these pristine hills and woodlands are out of this world. You can smell the green. Drop your plans for anything that smacks of rushing about in the fast lane. You won't find much here in the way of "attractions" really: It's not so much a place to come as it is a place to *be*. Reserve a campsite or a bed with a hearty breakfast and stay awhile. Hike the trails, take a bike ride, fish for trout, and make your way to the places where the hills come alive with the sound of music—and water.

Falls Village Station Nature Trail, Great Falls of the Housatonic, and Dean Ravine Falls (all ages)

An easy loop for young hikers is the Falls River Station Nature Trail, which can be reached from a parking area on Water Street, off Route 126. Linked to the Appalachian Trail, it's about three-quarters of a mile through fields and forest, with markers and a trail guide that explain the changing landscape from the days of the iron industry to the present reforestation. To see the Great Falls of the Housatonic, which is the state's second-largest river, take Route 126 North a third of a mile or so from its junction with Route 7, then bear left on Main Street; follow the road to Falls Village center, where you'll bear right and go down the hill. At the traffic island, turn left and go under the railroad bridge, pass the hydropower station, and cross the river. Turn right on Falls Mountain Road, and right on Housatonic River Road; park at the scenic overlook. This cascade is especially dramatic in the spring, when the dam above the falls has planned water releases. The water flows over a 60-foot ledge, and short hiking paths take you to an upper viewpoint and a lower observation point. In early springtime, this is nothing short of astonishing: Who would have thought Connecticut's wee mountains and quietwater rivers could produce such a sound? To get to Dean Ravine Falls, head to Music Mountain (see below), off Route 7, near the intersection of Music Mountain Road and Cream Hill Road. The trail begins to the left of the parking area near the music hall. Follow its blue blazes downhill; it's an easy ten-minute walk to the cascades, which also tumble down a 50-foot drop. There is a picnic area at Dean Ravine.

Music Mountain (ages 8 and up)

Gordon Hall, off Route 7 or 63; (860) 824-7126 on weekdays 9:00 a.m. to 5:00 p.m. or (860) 364-2084; www.musicmountain.org. Tickets may be purchased by mail in advance, by telephone for credit-card payments, or picked up at the box office on concert days. $$–$$$

This legendary and especially soothing compound in Falls Village is not a place exactly, but a festival. The nation's oldest continuous chamber music festival, it also features jazz, blues, baroque, and folk music on its picturesque grounds just off Route 7 near the Housatonic Valley Regional High School. You can also enter from Route 63 near the junction of Route 126.

Founded in 1930 as the permanent home of the Gordon String Quartet, Music Mountain's intimate and acoustically perfect wooden concert hall seats 335 on its softly cushioned pews; its 132 acres of lawn and grove are idyllic. The site is listed on the National Register of Historic Places. Picnic tables are provided for those who'd like to pack a boxed lunch or dinner to enjoy before the performances.

Offered from early June to mid-September, most of the chamber concerts are on Sunday at 3:00 p.m. Saturday performances are usually at 8:00 p.m., but some may begin a half hour earlier or later.

Where to Eat

Mountainside Cafe. 251 Route 7 South, Falls Village; (860) 824-7886. Perfectly casual and welcoming, this local favorite is a special place that serves up breakfast and lunch daily from 6:30 a.m. to 3:00 p.m. year-round. From April through October 31, come for dinner on Friday and weekends; November 1 to March 31, dinner is Friday only. Check the sandwich board outside for boxed lunches, perfect for picnicking. Open-mike poetry and music on Friday nights. A handful of simple rustic cabins are available here, too, for nightly rentals. $

Toymaker's Cafe. 85 Main Street, Falls Village; (860) 824-8168. The perfect casual establishment for snacks, soups, sandwiches, muffins, and more, all served up by good people. Open Thursday through Sunday for breakfast and lunch from 7:00 a.m. $

Freund's Farm Market. 324 Norfolk Road (Route 44), East Canaan; (860) 824-0650; www.freundsfarmmarket.com. Delicious, that's all, at least if you think pie makes a good breakfast and breads and cheese make great lunch. Muffins, breads, brownies, fresh local produce, and pick-your-own raspberries. There are even popcorn cobs available. Open year-round. $

Where to Stay

Inn at White Hollow Farm. 558 Lime Rock Road, Route 112, Lime Rock; (860) 435-8185. 4 "gracefully appointed" rooms, each with private bath, on the upper floor of a lovely white farmhouse. Fully equipped kitchen, dining area, and wrap-around porch on the lower floor. Very private. Coffee and baked goods each morning. On-site hiking and fly-fishing. Corn maze nearby. Smoke-free. $$$$

Locust Tree B&B. 131 East Canaan Road (Route 44), Canaan; (860) 824-7163; www .locust-tree-bed-and-breakfast.com. 7 rooms with private and shared baths in a gorgeous expanded 1700s farmhouse with double-story wraparound porches. Full country breakfast. Open year-round. $$$–$$$$

Lone Oak Campsites. Route 44, East Canaan; (860) 824-7051; www.loneoak campsites.com. Open April 15 to October 15, this large family campground has many tent and RV sites, but also rents 40-foot trailers with kitchen, bath, and bedroom, and a cabin with 2 rooms and a fridge. $

Norfolk

Norfolk is inarguably beautiful, nestled in the rolling shoulders and knolls of the Berkshire foothills, looking much the same as it might have a hundred years ago. There's not a lot of action here, but a full day or even a weekend, if you plan ahead, can be enjoyed in this sylvan village 7 miles east of Canaan. If you can, bring bicycles.

If ever a New England village could be fairly described as quaint, it is Norfolk. Beyond the few "attractions" described below, there is a most exquisite public library well worth a peek inside, the quintessential tall-spired, white Congregational church flanked by a lovely fieldstone chapel with Tiffany windows, and yet another state park, Haystack Mountain, just a mile or so up the road.

The Norfolk Chamber Music Festival (ages 6 and up)

Off the town green at the junction of Routes 44 and 272 on the Ellen Battell Stoeckel Estate; (860) 542-3000; www.yale.edu/norfolk. Concerts Thursday through Saturday in June, July, and August. Prices vary, free to children under 18.

Summer home of the Yale Music School, this magical enclave is the perfectly serene setting for a chamber music festival that invites nationally and internationally famed quartets and quintets of piano, woodwinds, and strings for Friday and Saturday evening concerts throughout July and August. Held rain or shine in the historic redwood and cedar Music Shed, these 8:00 p.m. concerts are affordable for adults, discounted for young adults, and, amazingly, completely free to children, all summer long, every concert. In addition, on Tuesday and Thursday nights at 7:30 and Saturday mornings at 10:30, Young Artists Recitals feature the Fellows of the Norfolk Summer School playing recognizable favorite standards and an eclectic mix of new and old pieces. Perfect for families, these concerts require no tickets, and there is a suggested donation ($). Call or check the Web site for a schedule.

Almost every summer a special family concert is planned especially for children ages six to twelve. Often, each family concert begins with a "musical conversation," an hourlong preconcert show that previews the featured music and draws children into the theme. No matter which concert you attend, bring along a picnic to enjoy before or after the program. The Pub (see Where to Eat) can provide terrific picnic choices.

Loon Meadow Farm Hayrides and
Carriage Rides

What could provide more old-fashioned good fun than a private hayride, carriage ride, or winter sleigh ride, complete with hot cider and antique lap robes? Loon Meadow arranges such outings (by reservation only) on Norfolk's village lanes and woodland trails. Four-person carriages, wagonettes, hay wagons, and sleighs are among the vehicles. Call the farm at (860) 542-6085 for the full scoop or check the Web site at www.loon meadowfarm.com. $$$$

Dennis Hill State Park (all ages)
2.5 miles south on Route 272 from center of village. Open year-round. Free.

Families will enjoy an easy loop-trail hike of 2 miles along an old lumber road through the woodlands to a fieldstone gazebo that provides a place to picnic and look out over the views of the hills. Along the way you'll pass through stands of oaks, maples, hemlocks, and mountain laurels and see the remains of a colonial hearth and chimney. When you have nearly returned to the point from which you started, you can walk or drive the paved path to the 1,627-foot summit of Dennis Hill, where, on clear days, an octagonal bungalow with a rooftop observation platform allows you to see three states, views of several towns and villages, and the surrounding mountains— Bear Mountain to the west and Haystack just north of Norfolk, Mount Everett and Mount Greylock in Massachusetts, and the Green Mountains of Vermont.

Both trails are easy to find without maps. The first trail is yellow blazed and begins just beyond a wooden gate; the second is paved, popular, and clearly marked.

Where to Eat

The Speckled Hen Pub. Across from the music festival grounds on Route 44; (860) 542-5716. Close to the town green, this historic setting offers English-style ambience but American food, perfect for families. Sandwiches, salads, soups, pizzas, chili; take-out dinners available for alfresco dining before the concerts. Lunch and dinner Tuesday through Sunday from 11:30 a.m. $$–$$$

Where to Stay

Blackberry River Inn. (860) 542-5100 or (800) 414-3636. For two and a half centuries this colonial inn has welcomed guests to its 27 acres with hiking trails 4–5 miles into the hills, trout fishing in its brook, tennis, outdoor pool, and apple orchard. 20 rooms, including pairs of rooms linked by a private bath, are perfect for families with children. Full country breakfast. $$$$

Goshen

Traveling south from Norfolk on Route 272 toward Torrington will take you through a slice of Goshen, which is a slice of heaven. You can follow 272 south to Route 4, which you'll then take west to the center of Goshen at its junction with Route 63. At this point, the scenery and the clean air may lead you to believe you're at the top of the world. A visit to Goshen's newest attraction may convince you that you've actually stumbled upon Eden.

Action Wildlife Foundation (all ages)

337 Torrington Road, which is Route 4; (860) 482-4465; www.actionwildlife.org. Open from 10:00 a.m. to 5:00 p.m., April through late October. In April, May, September, and October, open Thursday through Sunday. From late June to Labor Day, open daily. Weekend hayrides ($), intermittently, depending on the number of visitors. Closed on stormy days. $–$$

Located on a 116-acre former dairy farm on Route 4, just west of the Torrington border, this nonprofit game park is home to more than 200 exotic animals that roam relatively freely over about ninety acres currently open to the public. On the forty acres closest to the park entrance, several fenced or walled compounds provide enclosures for thirty-two species of such creatures as the scimitar oryx, red stags, Scottish Highlander cattle, fainting goats, zebras, fallow deer, aoudads, ostriches, bison, yaks, elks, reindeer, and Russian boar. Crisscrossed by stone walls, the park has a petting and feeding barn, a picnic area, and several ponds. A drive-through parcel of fifty additional acres features pygmy donkeys and miniature horses. Visitors can walk on pathways throughout the complex; on weekends, tractor-drawn wagon rides are offered.

Still under development here is a museum that is currently paired with the foundation's gift shop. Displayed now are about fifty mounted animal specimens in somewhat limited diorama-style natural environment settings. Park owner James Mazzarelli and other game hunters have collected these big-game mounts from throughout the world. While some animal lovers may take offense at this project, it is intended to educate and inform visitors about endangered habitats and species.

Where to Stay

Mary Stuart House B&B. Route 4, Goshen; (860) 491-2260; www.marystuart house.com. This 1798 country home offers 4 bedrooms, 2 private sitting rooms, and a two-bedroom cottage with kitchen, living room, private bath. Generous country-style continental breakfast. Volleyball and badminton in season. Hot tub. Screened porch. Children and pets welcome. $$–$$$$

Riverton/Pleasant Valley

The Riverton area (east of Route 8 and about 8 miles north of Winsted) is just a plain old nice place to be. Generally described for this book's purposes, the Riverton environs is the roughly rectangular area created by the roads linking Riverton, Pleasant Valley, Barkhamsted, and West Hartland—the perfect spot for a world-weary family to restore some equilibrium.

The village proper of Riverton is a rather small hamlet centered on Route 20 and West River Road. A restaurant and an old-time general store that sells fishing licenses, firewood, and camping supplies, along with great all-American lunch fare and breakfasts, are all within a spit of this corner. Nearby are a venerable old inn and Peter Greenwood's wonderful glassblowing studio in the historic former Union Episcopal Church. It's all worth a slow stroll.

People's State Forest and Stone Museum (all ages)
One mile north of Pleasant Valley on East River Road to the forest's public entrance and the Stone Museum. Park office: (860) 379-2469; park open year-round 8:00 a.m. to dusk; day-use fee on weekends and holidays, $$. Stone Museum: (860) 379-6118; www.stonemuseum.org; seasonal hours; **free,** donations accepted.

Something **Fishy**

For nearly fifty years, the village of Riverton has hosted the annual **Riverton Fishing Derby,** held traditionally on opening day of fishing in Connecticut (the third Saturday in April). The West Branch of the Farmington River is stocked with rainbow, brown, and brook trout, and each year 500 or more anglers try to catch the biggest of them all.

Free to all participants and spectators as well, the derby starts with a Fisherman's Breakfast at the Riverton Firehouse at 6:00 a.m. and ends at 10:00 a.m. regardless of the weather. No registration or fee is required, but anyone over the age of sixteen must have a Connecticut fishing license. If you arrive without a license, you can buy one ($$$$) at the old-time (but renovated) Riverton General Store.

Children under the age of twelve have their own area slightly upriver from the rest of the crowd. Anyone old enough to handle a pole can join the Kid Derby and share in the wholesome fun. Prizes are awarded in adult and youth divisions of this classic event. For information, call (860) 379-4826.

Christmas in Riverton

This villagewide festival is quintessential New England for both Christian revelers and anyone, I suppose, who might like to share in the merriment during the winter holiday season. Everything is decorated and candlelit, and you can take a horse-drawn wagon ride, make a craft at the firehouse, blow your own ornament at Peter Greenwood's amazingly welcoming glassblowing studio, see a puppet show or a performance of Dickens's *A Christmas Carol* by the Riverton Theater at the Congregational Church, have a bowl of chili at the Chili Fest, you name it—it's Currier & Ives–style fun, typically on the first weekend in December, unless that overlaps with the last weekend in November. Some of the activities listed here have a fee, but much of the fun is **free.** See the Riverton Web site (www.rivertonct.com) so you can plan ahead.

Nearly filling the aforementioned rectangle scribed loosely by Routes 318, 181, and 20 and cut further by the East and West River Roads that flank the sides of the Farmington River's West Branch, this beautiful park is a great stop for families. It provides access to and views of the 14-mile section of the river that the National Park Service has designated an American Wild and Scenic River. The gorgeous Matthies grove overlooks the rushing water as it twists through the 200-year-old pines—be sure to have lunch here if you've packed a picnic. Anglers hip deep in the water during trout season are a pleasant addition to the majestic view.

Open every Sunday from Memorial Day to Columbus Day and every Saturday and Sunday in July and August, the park's Stone Museum has exhibits on native flora and fauna, natural history, and Native American and colonial history and industry. A seasonal series of slide programs is presented here on Saturday evenings at 8:00 in July and August, and hikes are led on varied Saturday mornings throughout the summer and early fall. Call for a schedule.

A blue-and-yellow-blazed trail called the Beaver Swamp Loop follows an old wagon path through the forest, across a bridged brook, and up to a kame terrace that was the site of native encampments from 2,000 B.C. to A.D. 600. Remnants of eighteen ancient Indian village sites have put this terrace on the National Register of Historic Places. As you descend the trail, still following the blazes, you can see a colonial house foundation and a meat-smoking chamber as well as other beautiful natural sites. The Beaver Swamp Trail is easy to moderate, takes about two and a half hours to hike, and is 3.5 miles long. A detailed description and map can be obtained through the park office. Descriptions of other trails leaving from the museum area are available on the Web site.

Cross-country skiing is allowed here in winter.

American Legion State Forest (all ages)

West River Road, Pleasant Valley; (860) 379-0922. No day-use charge; campsites, $.

On the western bank opposite People's State Forest, this quiet camping area has thirty wooded sites along the West Branch of the Farmington River. Clean pine woods, great shower facilities, flat tent sites, and good fishing spots make this a nice family campground. If no ranger is at the park office when you arrive, you just leave your registration in the box with your nightly fee. Open mid-April through December 1, the area has trails to some beautiful sights along the river (watch the steep hillsides as you go along some of the paths).

Where to Eat

Old Riverton Inn. See below. Breakfast for guests only. Lunch and dinner Wednesday through Sunday open to the public; reservations highly recommended. $$

Riverton General Store. Route 20; (860) 379-0811. Open Monday through Friday, 6:00 a.m. to 6:00 p.m., Saturday until 5:00 p.m., and Sunday from 6:30 a.m. to 3:00 p.m., for great sit-down breakfast and lunch, and perfect take-out picnic fare. Deli sandwiches and salads, pickles and ice cream, homemade soups and chili, coffee bar, and more. All this is offered in a charming setting with intriguing artifacts from its 120-year history. $

Sweet Pea's. 6 Riverton Road; (860) 379-7020. Old-fashioned charm spills from every pore of this 1880 house, and the food is even more delightful than the ambience. It's a little fancy, but not so much that children are not warmly welcomed—in fact, they have their own menu. Lunch and dinner, Tuesday through Sunday; brunch on Sunday. $$–$$$

Where to Stay

Old Riverton Inn. Route 20; (860) 379-8678 or (800) EST-1796. Doing business for 200 years, this inn, listed on the National Register, has 12 rooms with private baths; some rooms have canopy beds and fireplaces. Open year-round, it enjoys a front-row seat on the rushing river and has an award-winning dining room. Full breakfast. $$$

On the River B&B. 420 West River Road; (860) 738-9660. 1 spacious room with views of the water, gardens, and hills beyond, at the confluence of the Farmington and Still Rivers. King-size bed; rollaway cots or air mattresses for the kids. Wood-burning fireplace; air-conditioning; private bath, porch, and entrance. Country breakfast. Lovely innkeeper. Bring a canoe, fishing poles; relax, have fun. Nonsmoking 1920s feel-good house. $$$$

New Hartford

This tiny community has put itself on the map as one of the state's most popular sports and recreation destinations. From tubing in summer to skiing in winter, it's a town few families miss in a search for fun in the great outdoors.

Farmington River Tubing—Satan's Kingdom State Recreation Area (ages 10 and up)

Route 44; (860) 693-6465; www.farmingtonrivertubing.com. Open every day in July and August and on weekends and weekday afternoons only from Memorial Day through June from 10:00 a.m. to approximately 6:00 p.m. Call for hours on Labor Day weekend, for limited hours through mid-September, and to check on river conditions. $$$

This adventure is certainly on our top-ten list of best family summer activities in Connecticut—that is, if you're ten years or older, 4 feet 5 inches tall, and can swim alone without a doubt no matter your age. On some days, the river is chock-full of other tubing enthusiasts; on others you may be alone except for the dragonflies.

When you arrive at Satan's Kingdom, park in the lot right next to the river and the **North American Canoe Tours Inc.** outpost. Wear cutoffs and a T-shirt or change into your swimsuit in one of the changing huts provided at the lot. Put on some sunscreen and old sneakers, preferably your own. If you arrive barefoot, NACT makes you put on one of the spare pairs of soggy previously owned sneaks. Put on a life vest (mandatory equipment for everyone), pay your money, then walk down to the river with your tube and put your warm body into the cold water, bottom first, as you sit down in the hole of your tube with your feet up over the side. Sound like fun yet? It is, really—I promise. Now all you have to do is float and soak up the Vitamin D rays for 2.5 miles in about as many hours. The segment lies within the nationally designated Wild and Scenic River portion of the Farmington River.

The best parts for some are the mild rapids—three sets, with NACT lifeguards on duty in kayaks at the largest set only—others like the placid stretches where mergansers nest and the living is easy. This outfitter won't allow you to bring food on the river, so don't arrive hungry. When your ride is over (at a clearly marked take-out point), haul out with your tube. A shuttle bus takes you back to the starting point.

Ski Sundown (ages 3 and up)

126 Ratlum Road, 2 miles northeast of New Hartford on Route 219 off Route 44; (860) 379-9851; www.skisundown.com. Open from 9:00 a.m. to 10:00 p.m. Sunday through Thursday and until 11:00 p.m. on Friday and Saturday during the ski season, usually from early December to late March. For current lift rates and special packages, call or check the Web site.

For winter fun just a half hour from Hartford and an hour from Danbury and New Haven, Ski Sundown is a convenient alternative to out-of-state skiing. Special trails,

Gently Down the **Mainstream**

For guided canoe, kayak, and bicycle trips in the rolling beauty of north-western Connecticut, call **Main Stream Canoes & Kayaks** (170 Main Street, which is Route 44; 860-693-6791; www.mainstreamcanoe.com) in New Hartford. These folks will set you up for full-day or half-day guided river trips on the Wild and Scenic Farmington River. Flat-water, quick-water, and rapids tours ($$$$) on the upper and lower segments of the river are among the choices for canoes and kayaks. Moonlight trips are among the most entrancing options (ask about age limitations). They also rent bicycles for half and full days.

FlexTix, and a First-Time package for novice and beginner skiers and snowboarders make Sundown perfect for families new to the sport. Other programs are geared especially to children of moderate and advanced skills. Even accomplished skiers can enjoy the challenges of the three most difficult trails out of the total fifteen. Four chairlifts keep lines moving quickly and efficiently to the top of the sixty-five-acre property.

Proud of their well-groomed runs and friendly professional staff, the operators also like to crow about their rental shop, which provides top-drawer skis, boots, bindings, and snowboards, and Ski Shop, which offers similar goods and clothing for sale. A casual cafeteria helps hungry skiers get back to the slopes with renewed energy. An expanded lodge and lounge provides a place to rest and relax with fellow skiers.

All-day, after-school, twilight, and evening sessions include reasonable rates for adults, juniors, preschoolers, and seniors. Bring Grandpa and the baby, too, and enjoy the winter in the Berkshire foothills.

Where to Eat

Chatterly's. Two Bridge Street; (860) 379-2428. After skiing or tubing, replace carbohydrates in this landmark eatery in the old New Hartford Hotel in the center of the village. Light fare for kids—soup, salads, sandwiches, burgers—or full dinners for adults—steaks, roast pork, seafood. Lunch and dinner daily. $–$$

Portobello's Ristorante and Pizzeria. 107 Main Street; (860) 693-2598. Great Italian fare of traditional sorts, plus pizza and seafood. You can count on family-welcoming service here. Lunch and dinner daily from 11:00 a.m. to 10:00 p.m. $$–$$$

Where to Stay

Alcove Motel. 87 Main Street, which is Route 44; (860) 693-8577. 15 basic, affordable, clean rooms. Nightly rentals; no long-term residents. $

Chapin Park Bed & Breakfast. 45 Church Street; (860) 379-1075; www .chapinparkbandb.com. In the Pine Meadow historic district of New Hartford, right on its green, is a beautiful blue Victorian B&B awaiting children of all ages. Lovely innkeeper, happy to meet your needs and direct you to area attractions and entertainments. Full country breakfast; cheerfully quilted beds in spacious guest rooms, each with private bath. $$$–$$$$

Litchfield

From the Pleasant Valley and New Hartford areas, families may want to head south on Route 8 through Winsted and Torrington and then take Route 118 west about 5 miles to Litchfield. Settled in 1719, Litchfield remains one of the prettiest towns in the state, attracting visitors in droves to its meticulously preserved colonial architecture, its boutiques, and its restaurants. Antiques shops, elegant inns, and vineyards lure travelers looking for pastoral pleasures of a sophisticated nature. Judging these elements alone, it seems an area more suited to adults than to families, but we discovered a few places everyone should visit.

White Memorial Foundation and Conservation Center Museum
(all ages)

80 Whitehall Road, 2 miles west of Litchfield Center off Route 202; (860) 567-0857; www.whitememorialcc.org. Grounds open daily, year-round, from dawn to dusk. Free admission. Museum open daily 9:00 a.m. to 5:00 p.m. Monday through Saturday and Sunday noon to 5:00 p.m. Winter hours slightly reduced. Museum admission, $.

The state's largest nature preserve, with 4,000 acres and 35 miles of trails, White Memorial is a wonderful place to hike, ride horses, cross-country ski, fish, and picnic. Two campgrounds offer lakeside or woodland sites, and a public boat launch provides access to Bantam Lake. A specially landscaped bird observatory area includes thirty viewing stations created for bird-watchers and photographers. The interpretive Trail of the Senses invites youngsters to touch, smell, and listen as they traverse the quarter-mile pathway.

Guided walks and special programs are frequent. At the annual Family Nature Day in late September, bird banding, tree identification, old-time outdoor games, and a pond life study are offered.

The excellent hands-on Conservation Center Museum, housed in the former Whitehall mansion, artistically arranges dioramas and interactive exhibits on birds, bees, soil, seeds, woodland animals, and much more in a bright, open atmosphere. Upstairs, an outstanding natural science library with a special children's section is open even to day-tripping visitors.

Bantam Lake and Sandy Beach (all ages)

East Shore Road, Morris; (860) 567-7550; www.litchfield.bz/id433.htm. Open to the public on weekends only from Memorial Day through the end of June, daily from late June through Labor Day from 9:00 a.m. to 7:00 p.m. Daily fee, $ per car or boat; non-resident season passes ($$$$) are also available and can be purchased at the beach or at the Litchfield or Morris Town Halls.

If you want to take a dip in pretty Bantam Lake, leave Litchfield center on Route 202 West, take a left on White's Woods Road, and another right on East Shore Road. Just before the bend in the road, you'll find the entrance to Sandy Beach. Actually in the town of Morris, the secluded beach provides 800 feet of clean sand on the shore of Connecticut's largest natural lake.

Lifeguards, bathrooms and bathhouses, and a snack bar are among the amenities. A canoe launch, a volleyball "court," and a picnic area with tables and firepits make this a great place to spend the day. Return in winter to see the ice boaters clip across the frozen lake or to try your luck at ice fishing.

Lee's Riding Stable (ages 4 and up)

57 East Litchfield Road (Route 118); (860) 567-0785; www.windfieldmorganfarm.com. One-hour guided trail rides, $$$$ (7 years and older only); pony rides (all ages), $$ for twice around and $$$$ for a half hour or an hour. Open 365 days per year 9:00 a.m. to 5:00 p.m.

If you love horses, horseback riding, and truly decent people, go directly to Lee's. Only positive things happen for kids at this peaceful horse farm. Visitors are welcome any time; reservations for trail rides are preferred but not absolutely necessary. Trail ride groups are normally limited to six to eight riders, so you don't get that mule-train feeling, and the attitude of the staff is friendly and enthusiastic. No one has a hint of reluctance to take you over the same trails they've seen time and time again—a pleasant change from the bored demeanor of staff at other stables. The trails take you through some 5 miles of exceptionally pretty country in and adjacent to Topsmead State Forest.

A miniature petting zoo with goats, chickens, geese, sheep, rabbits, a cow, a donkey, and an adorable Shetland pony is a hands-on operation. Buy a bag of feed or bring your stale crackers, and the penned animals will adore you.

If the staff is not too busy, they'll give you a tour of the stables and pastures. Riding lessons are also offered. An indoor ring is used in bad weather; it is also the home of the Litchfield Little Britches program, offering therapeutic riding for the handicapped (call for information). Birthday parties, longer outings, and custom group rides can all be arranged. The registered Morgan horses are gorgeous, and Lee Lyons, the special angel who runs the whole show, has a down-to-earth approach that makes everyone feel comfortable and want to come back.

Mount Tom State Park (all ages)

Route 202, southwest of Litchfield Center, in Bantam; (860) 868-2592. Open daily April 1 to October 15, dawn to dusk. Parking fee on in-season weekends, $$.

A small lake offers fishing, swimming, scuba diving, and non-motor boating in summer; ice fishing and ice-skating are possible in winter. A beach and picnic area with a snack bar concession, lifeguard, picnic tables, grills, restrooms, and changing houses (but no showers) make this a good family-fun destination.

Those who want more vigorous recreation can take the short hike to the top of the 1,325-foot mountain. The yellow-blazed trail is little more than a mile, but it's a pretty steady climb; older kids may do it in fifteen to twenty minutes, younger ones may need a half hour. The extra 30-foot climb up the wooden interior staircase of the black granite tower at the top is well worth it. The view over the treetops is spectacular—you'll be glad you did it.

Litchfield History Museum and Tapping Reeve House and Law School (ages 8 and up) 🏛

7 South Street and 82 South Street; (860) 567-4501; www.litchfieldhistoricalsociety .org. Open mid-April through November, Tuesday through Saturday 11:00 a.m. to 5:00 p.m. and Sunday from 1:00 to 5:00 p.m. Adults $ for both museums; children under 14 free.

If history lessons intrigue your children, have a brief look at the collections in the seven galleries of the historical museum for insight into the town's culture and community. Afterward, stop at the Tapping Reeve House and Law School if you want to inspire future attorneys to emulate the 130 members of Congress who graduated from this first law school in the nation, open to the public as a historical exhibit.

Where to Eat

Aspen Garden. 51 West Street near the Green in Litchfield center; (860) 567-9477. Omelets, salads, pizzas, Greek specialties, pasta, seafood, reasonably priced. Terrace dining in nice weather. Lunch and dinner daily from 11:00 a.m. $$–$$$

Saltwater Grille. Route 202; (860) 567-4900. On Litchfield Commons where Chuck's Steakhouse used to be, this family-friendly fish house offers lunch and dinner from noon every day (except no lunch on Monday). Steaks, flatfish and shellfish of all sorts, salads, sandwiches, chowder, and much more. Patio outdoors in warm weather; paper and crayons on the tables inside; children's menu ($). $$–$$$

Ming's. Route 202; (860) 567-0809. Dependably good Chinese cuisine in a relaxed setting. Lunch and dinner Tuesday through Sunday. $–$$

Bantam Bread Company. 853 Bantam Road; (860) 567-2737. If you think you can make a meal from delightful French cheeses and the world's tastiest organic breads, tarts, pies, and quiches, bring a picnic basket to this bakery and prepare for ecstasy. Strawberry rhubarb pie counts as a fruit in my book, and pumpkin custard is a vegetable. Open 8:30 a.m. to 5:30 p.m. Tuesday through Saturday and until 5:00 p.m. on Sunday. $

Where to Stay

The Litchfield Inn. Route 202; (860) 567-4503. Set back from the road, this inn offers 32 rooms with private baths, continental breakfast, and lovely common areas. Bistro East restaurant (860-567-9040) offers lunch and dinner daily. $$$$

Washington/Washington Depot/ New Preston/Bridgewater

Often called unspoiled and compared to the alpine lake regions of Austria and Switzerland, the town of Washington and its village of New Preston, with its most famous attraction, Lake Waramaug, are among Connecticut's most popular day-tripping destinations. If you can't get to Europe to check out whether the comparison works, take my word for it and come here to enjoy the four-season beauty of this delightful area just about 10 miles southwest of Litchfield. If you're exploring awhile in this region, you'll more than likely come upon such towns and hamlets as Warren, Washington Depot, Roxbury, and Bridgewater, as well as northern sections of Brookfield, which is officially in Fairfield County, and Southbury, which officially lies in New Haven County. For the purposes of school districts and day trips and such, these towns are closely linked despite their labels. Be sure you have a good map on the car seat when you head out.

Speaking of labels, you may be hard-pressed to find a sign for the below-mentioned CT Route 458 around Lake Waramaug, which is sliced roughly in half by the boundary between the town of Warren and the town of Washington. Route 458 is one of the state's "secret" routes, often unmarked with a numbered sign but no less real. A designated CT Scenic Roadway, it curls all around the 680-acre lake, which is Connecticut's second-largest natural inland body of water. From Route 7 if you are traveling from parts north or south, or Route 202 if you're coming southwestward from Litchfield, find Route 45, which is also called Cornwall Road or, when it reaches the lake area, is called both Lake Road and East Shore Road. Follow Route 45 to North Shore Road, which loops around the lake to Lake Waramaug Road (past the state park, which actually lies in the town of Kent), which then links to West Shore Road to take you back to Route 45. The drive is about 8 miles. The village center of New Preston lies south of the lake, at the junction of Routes 45 and 202, and is chockablock with antiques shops; the kids will probably want to move right along to other attractions.

When Lake Waramaug loosens its grip on your soul, take Route 45 south to Route 202 (that's where you'll find New Preston's commercial center) and head northeast for a bit on 202, then take Route 47 south from Route 202 to Washington and Washington Depot. Don't blink or you'll miss the towns hidden in the twists and turns of these lovely hills. The fourth town in the colonies to be named for George, the pretty little village of Washington is a true New England gem, and the depot, another hub of regional community life, is in its own way equally charming. As beautiful as these villages are, however, the special treasures here are the natural environment and the legacy of the native Algonkian people, whose civilization preceded that of the colonists by several thousand years.

Lake Waramaug State Park (all ages)

Lake Waramaug Road (Route 478), in Kent, 5 miles north of New Preston center; park maintenance office: (860) 868-2592; campground office: (860) 868-0220. Open year-round from 8:00 a.m. to dusk; camping from May 15 to September 30. Camping fee, $; day-use fee, $$ on weekends and holidays only from Memorial Day through Labor Day.

Although this state park lies officially in the town of Kent, few travelers would arrive here by way of Kent's village center. The lake itself is bordered on the west by Kent, on the north by Warren, and on the south and east by Washington, which includes New Preston, the village most closely associated with the lake. It is from New Preston's roadways that most folks find their way to this beautiful spot. To start with the basics, Waramaug, also the name of a chief of the Wyantenock tribe, means "good fishing place." If you're so inclined, this sounds like the plainest fishing tip I've ever heard. In addition to this most popular sport, the park offers opportunities for picnicking, swimming, scuba diving, and sailing (you bring your own gear), and it provides paddleboats (which you rent). Trails for hiking and seventy-seven very nice sites for camping are also available. Nightly camper nature programs are scheduled in summer, and ice-skating, cross-country skiing, and ice fishing are possible in winter.

Gunn Historical Museum (ages 6 and up)

5 Wykeham Road; (860) 868-7756; www.gunnlibrary.org. Museum open Thursday through Saturday 10:00 a.m. to 4:00 p.m. and Sunday noon to 4:00 p.m. Closed major holidays. Family programs, workshops, and exhibits throughout the week year-round in the Junior Library (860-868-2310). Free.

If you fall in love with the village, a visit to the museum at the Gunn Memorial Library on the town green will flesh out the area's colonial history and lifeways. Within the lovely 1908 fieldstone building is a collection of quilts, needlework, kitchenware, spinning wheels, furniture, and other household decorative and utilitarian items. A children's room includes dolls, dollhouses, toys, children's clothes, and other objects of interest to youngsters. Here, too, you can see original signatures of George Washington and Thomas Jefferson. Be sure to look up—a magnificent ceiling mural decorates the lobby of the original library building.

Institute for American Indian Studies (ages 4 and up)

38 Curtis Road off Route 199; (860) 868-0518; www.birdstone.org. Open Monday through Saturday from 10:00 a.m. to 5:00 p.m. and Sunday from noon to 5:00 p.m.; closed on Monday and Tuesday from January through March. $

Magnificently displayed in a discreet building smack dab in the woodlands near Steep Rock Nature Preserve, the exhibits here are interpretations of the institute's research on the history and culture of Indian America. The permanent exhibit, titled *As We Tell Our Stories: Living Tradition and the Algonkian Peoples of New England,* includes the taped stories of Algonkian people and an extensive collection of Native American tools, baskets, implements, and art. Also inside the museum are a re-creation of an Algonkian longhouse as it might have looked prior to the arrival of the Europeans and a simulation of a northeastern reservation house from the early 1900s; both of these are filled with artifacts used in everyday life. A Children's Discovery Room features an interactive exhibit called *If You Lived in the Woodlands*. Learn about the woodland creatures and plants; learn how the Algonkian peoples used these gifts; feel different kinds of fur, try on deerskin clothing, and more. An excellent gift shop and an art gallery for changing exhibitions are also inside.

Outside, an authentically constructed seventeenth-century settlement with three wigwams, a longhouse, a rock shelter, native-plant trails, and a garden planted each season with corn, beans, and squash provides a peek into the proud 10,000-year history of these people. A simulated archaeological site offers intriguing insights into their moving story.

Craft workshops, dances, films, storytelling, and more are on the annual events calendar. Children's summer camps are also on the schedule.

Steep Rock Reservation (all ages)

(860) 868-9131; www.steeprockassoc.org. Open dawn to dusk year-round. Small parking area off River Road. No facilities. Free.

After a morning at the Indian studies institute, you might want to stay in the great outdoors to reflect on all you've learned about the fragile, life-sustaining ecology of the Eastern Woodlands. Linked to the institute property by a common border, this 700-acre natural preserve is one section of a two-parcel land trust owned and maintained by the Steep Rock Association. Dedicated to preserving and protecting, for the good of future generations, the beauty and integrity of this important ecosystem and all of its flora and fauna, the association has opened its trails to hikers. With pathways that hug the Shepaug River and climb to Steep Rock, the sanctuary offers incredible vistas that should keep families mindful of their integral role in conservation of our remaining wild places. Come here to the cool woods to hear the whispering wind in summer, enjoy the glorious blaze of the foliage in autumn, linger as the snows fall silently in winter, and walk softly beside the wildflowers as the new leaves open in the springtime. The association fears that overuse of these lovely footpaths may force them to close to the public, so please remember to walk respectfully only on cleared trails, pack out every scrap of what you carry in, and take nothing but memories with you as you leave.

Shepaug Bald Eagle Observation Area (all ages)

Off I-84 exit 13 or 14; River Road, Southbury, in the Shepaug Recreation Area. Observation area open from 9:00 a.m. to 1:00 p.m. on Wednesday, Saturday, and Sunday (except New Year's Day) from the last week in December through mid-March. Free, but reservations required. For reservations, which can be made from early December, call (800) 368-8954, Tuesday through Friday, from 9:00 a.m. to 3:00 p.m.

During the coldest months, nature lovers should bundle up well and go see the annual reunion of bald eagles that gather near the Shepaug Dam, especially from January through mid-March. Through a program managed by Northeast Utilities, guided by the Connecticut Department of Environmental Protection, and staffed by volunteers from the Connecticut Audubon Society, visitors can come to the NU Shepaug Bald Eagle Observation Area near the Shepaug hydroelectric station on the Housatonic River in Southbury. The dam area is attractive to wintering birds because the station's operation prevents the water from freezing, making fishing below the dam easy for the birds. One of the largest concentrations of wintering eagles in Connecticut may be seen at this site.

A blind equipped with spotting scopes is set up to provide excellent viewpoints, and exhibit panels on the eagles' habits and conservation issues help to educate visitors. NU staff and CAS volunteers are on hand to assist visitors, and they are always happy to answer questions. You might also want to bring binoculars and a camera (and mittens!). In addition to the eagles, you may see red-tailed and sharp-shinned hawks, goshawks, great blue herons, and a great variety of waterfowl.

Where to Eat

Doc's Trattoria and Pizzeria. Lake Waramaug South Shore Road (Route 45), New Preston; (860) 868-9415; www .docstrattoria.com. Housed in a charming cottage overlooking the lake, Doc's offers the best pizza in Litchfield County, plus other delicious Italian favorites in a casually sophisticated setting. Lunch is served daily from noon to 3:00 p.m., dinner served daily starting at 5:00 p.m. Innovative salads, pastas, chicken, and seafood keep the place popular with parents; kids love the imaginative pizzas and half-orders that help them leave room for dessert. Reservations are a good idea. $$–$$$

G.W. Tavern. 20 Bee Brook Road (Route 47), Washington Depot; (860) 868-6633. Traditional favorites like meatloaf, chicken pot pie, steaks, pastas, soups, salads, and a cheerful staff and adaptable chef who welcome children. Special children's menu, and lots of side dishes make choosing easy. Lunch and dinner daily; brunch Saturday and Sunday. $–$$

The Pantry. 5 Titus Road, Washington Depot; (860) 868-0258. Gourmet fare in a simple setting often used by adults with fancy tastes and deep pockets. Good for families needing picnic fare. Muffins, croissants, and other delicious bakery treats; salads; and sandwiches. Open 10:00 a.m. to 6:00 p.m. Tuesday through Saturday. Table service from 11:00 a.m. to 5:00 p.m. $

Bridgewater Village Store. 27 Main Street South (Route 133), Bridgewater; (860) 354-2863. Right on the green of the last dry town in the state, this charming store is the place to come for down-home and gourmet deli sandwiches and salads, homemade baked goods, coffee, teas, a local newspaper, and much more in a vintage store that has preserved all the right old-fashioned touches even as it has updated with modern conveniences and comforts. Built in 1899, it has worn wood floors, tin ceilings, and even a delectably tempting candy counter where you can buy locally made Bridgewater Chocolates by the piece. Come here for breakfast, lunch, and picnic foods; eat inside or spread your blanket on the green. Open year-round, Monday through Friday from 6:00 a.m. to 6:00 p.m., Saturday from 7:00 a.m. to 5:00 p.m., and Sunday from 7:00 a.m. to 4:00 p.m. $

Where to Stay

The Heritage Inn. 34 Bridge Street, New Milford; (860) 350-3097; www.theheritage innct.com. This 20-room bed-and-breakfast is owned by the folks who own the Newbury Inn a distance to the south, near Lake Candlewood. Visitors to Lake Candlewood, Squantz Pond, and the "greater" Washington area described above will find a warm welcome for children in this smoke-free inn in historic New Milford center. All rooms have private baths. Kids under 16 stay **free.** A deluxe continental breakfast is complimentary. $$$–$$$$

Bethlehem

About 6 miles east of Washington as the crow flies (14 miles by Route 109 east to Route 61 south), Bethlehem is Litchfield County at its best—gorgeous hills, pretty village, quiet byways of unsurpassed serenity. Its evocative name conjures images of peace and sentiment that its residents play upon in a few special ways. In the months before Christmas, folks deluge the Bethlehem post office with holiday cards they would like to bear the Bethlehem postmark. A Christmas festival in early December celebrates the spirit of the season, and an annual country fair in late summer celebrates the bounty of Bethlehem's fields and orchards. And, as in most towns in this state, there's a historical society museum and an ancient homestead that spans two and a half centuries of history in its furniture, art, and gardens.

Together these features portray a part of the magic of Bethlehem. The village is so tiny that you can easily find the shops, the post office, the fairs, and the historic homes. The town Web site (www.ci.bethlehem.ct.us) can lead you to the facts about these attractions. The information below will help you out if you wish to call for details before you visit. Following those are the details on a very quiet but special place just a bit off the gently worn paths in Bethlehem.

- **Bethlehem Post Office.** 34 East Street; (203) 266-7910.

- **Bethlehem Fair.** (203) 266-5350. Often the second full weekend in September. $$, accompanied children are **free.**

- **Old Bethlehem Historical Society Museum.** Corner of Routes 132 and 61; (203) 266-5188. Open Sunday 1:00 to 4:00 p.m. from June through August. $

- **Bellamy-Ferriday House and Garden.** 9 Main Street North (Route 61); (203) 266-7596. Open May through October on Wednesday, Friday, and weekends from 11:00 a.m. to 4:00 p.m. Exquisite house and glorious gardens with property linked to the nature trails of a nearby land trust. $

The Abbey of Regina Laudis and the Monastic Art Shop
(ages 6 and up) 🎵

273 Flanders Road between Route 6 and Route 61; (203) 266-7637; www.abbeyof reginalaudis.com. Abbey church open year-round for daily mass (8:00 a.m.) and vespers (5:00 p.m., except Sunday 4:30 p.m.). Art shop and gallery open daily except Wednesday from 10:00 a.m. to noon and 1:30 to 4:00 p.m. When its restoration is complete, the crèche will be open daily 10:00 a.m. to 5:00 p.m. from the day after Easter through January 6. Call ahead to confirm these hours.

A treasured presence just a jog off Route 61 is Bethlehem's beautiful abbey. No wonder that the inspiring Benedictine nuns chose this place to build their wonderful community—it is on a magnificent hillside overlooking the glory of creation. Traditionally, each summer in early August, the sisters opened the gates of the abbey and welcomed visitors to share in the festivities of their Abbey Fair. Sadly for us, this splendid outpouring of spirit and celebration grew too large for the sisters to manage, as thousands of guests showed up for a taste of their remarkable experience. Today a simple theater production for the whole family replaces the old tradition with a new one.

Though there is no guarantee that a production will be performed every August, the show has gone on every year since the fair ended. Staged in the abbey's open-air covered theater, the productions are often the first weekend in August, with three performances on Friday and Saturday. There is a suggested donation for the show— adults, $$; children under 12, $.

At other times of the year, you can come to hear daily mass and evening vespers at the church on Robert Leathers Road. The voices of the sisters at vespers are especially moving. You can also browse in the abbey's Monastic Art Shop, which has an art gallery as well as books, crafts, and comestibles made by the sisters.

The best family attraction here is the abbey's magnificent Neapolitan crèche, which illustrates the Nativity in a starlit scene of more than a hundred eighteenth-century figures beautifully dressed in silks and brocades and placed against the backdrop of an Italian hillside. Displayed in one of the abbey's barns, it is a fascinating and intricate work of art that families of every faith can appreciate. Closed temporarily for a restoration by conservators from the Metropolitan Museum of Art, the crèche will be well worth the wait for its reopening. Call ahead to check on its progress.

Where to Eat

Painted Pony. Route 61; (203) 266-5771; www.paintedponyrestaurant.com. Best known for juicy prime rib up to a whopping forty ounces, this place is also great for salads, pastas, chicken, and seafood. Special menu for children. Open daily from 11:00 a.m. to 11:00 p.m. on weekends and to 10:00 p.m. on weekdays. $$

Theo's Pizza. 15 Main Street; (203) 266-5558. Great pizza, salads, lasagna, stuffed shells, manicotti—you get the picture. Theo says, "If you want it, we're going to try to make it!" Open daily 10:00 a.m. to 10:00 p.m. Greek specialties, simple desserts; casual, friendly atmosphere. $

Thomaston

East of Bethlehem (take Route 61 south, then Route 6 east through Watertown and onward to Route 8) is the town of Thomaston, named for clockmaker Seth Thomas. Thomas's clocks were made right in Thomaston with brass gears manufactured in the mills of Waterbury. Today those two communities are linked in other ways. One of these links is a railway: the original Naugatuck Railroad that opened in 1849 to connect Bridgeport with all the towns north to Winsted. Located in the beautiful and still rugged Naugatuck Valley, Thomaston welcomes families to its historic downtown (where one can see the famed Seth Thomas clocktower and its magnificently restored opera house), its Victorian railroad station, and the vintage train that offers travelers splendid views of the scenic Naugatuck River, its wildlife, and the communities along its banks.

Railroad Museum of New England/Naugatuck Railroad Scenic Excursion (all ages)

242 East Main Street; (860) 283-7245; www.rmne.org. Operates May through October, Saturday and Sunday at noon and 2:00 p.m.; Tuesday, 10:00 a.m. Pumpkin and Halloween excursions in October; Santa Express on first three weekends in December. $$–$$$; children 2 and under, free.

This moving museum is actually a scenic railroad excursion that resulted from the signing of a thirty-year lease of the 19.5-mile Waterbury to Torrington Line, which gives the Naugatuck Railroad Company operating rights over the 150-year-old track. The new "Naugy" now operates between the 1881 Thomaston Passenger Station in downtown Thomaston and the Waterville Station in Waterbury. Sunday afternoon trips in July and August run from Thomaston to Torrington.

Grab the kids and jump aboard for the great sights and sounds of this grandly exciting adventure. What is it about train rides that is so appealing? Maybe it's the bells and whistles or the clackety-clack, maybe the huge sighs and shudders of the enormous locomotives, maybe just the heart-tingling joy of heading off to new horizons on a beast so mighty it can scale mountains. Ride this baby with your eyes and ears wide open to all the fabulous wonders around you—from inside one of the factory complexes near the historic Brass Mills of Waterbury to the Mattatuck State Forest's cool green canopy in summer or blazing patchwork of scarlet and bronze in autumn. Travel past small towns with charming old houses and tiny depots, and onward across—yes, right across the face of—the spectacular Thomaston Dam.

The train consists of restored historic New England passenger and freight cars pulled by historic New Haven and Maine Central locomotives. The usual hour-and-a-quarter excursions are 20-mile round-trip rides. No reservations are required.

I could give you a whole history lesson on the economic importance of this line in the olden golden days of industry in the Naugatuck Valley, but you'll hear some of that on the train. For now, just pull on your pin-striped overalls, buy your ticket, and have a ball.

Thomaston Opera House (ages 4 and up)

158 Main Street; (860) 283-6250; www.thomastonoperahouse.org. Open year-round. Season tickets for varied series are available, as are individual tickets ($–$$$) for all productions. Call the box office Monday through Saturday from 1:00 to 6:00 p.m. for tickets or buy tickets online.

Built in 1884, the beautifully restored Thomaston Opera House is a perfect venue for families. Shows are affordable, especially compared to Broadway and even Bushnell prices, and more family-friendly shows were staged here in 2007–08 than in any other theater in the state. In this most recent season, families and other young audiences could see a stage production of Roald Dahl's novel *The BFG* (Big Friendly Giant); Dickens's *A Christmas Carol; The Wizard of Oz;* a musical version of E. B. White's *Stuart Little; Little Red Riding Hood; I Have a Dream,* a staged story of the life and times of Martin Luther King Jr.; Cole Porter's family-friendly romance *Anything Goes;* a Holiday Pops concert; and at least two classical music recitals. The opera house is, well, gorgeous, with frescoed ceilings, an incredible pipe organ (ask about the organ concerts), and amazing acoustics. If it was good enough for Enrico Caruso and Marian Anderson, it's good enough for Connecticut families. Get tickets today; don't hesitate.

General Information

Northwest CT Convention & Visitors Bureau. P.O. Box 968, U.S. 202, Litchfield, CT 06759; (860) 567-4506; www.litchfieldhills.com. Call or write for the tours booklet, which provides itineraries for walking, hiking, driving, and boating tours of the area. Also ask for a free getaway planner called *Unwind*.

Litchfield Web site: www.litchfieldct.com.

Connecticut Angler's Guide. Published by the State Department of Environmental Protection Bureau of Natural Resources Fisheries Division, this booklet describes everything you'd need to know about fishing in the state of Connecticut. Call (860) 424-FISH to request a copy.

Hartford County

Capital Ideas in the Heart of Connecticut

Sliced into unequal parts by the Connecticut River, the north-central region of Connecticut is a region of diversity including farming communities, towns with a long history of industry, and a city of pre-Revolutionary importance as a seat of government. This diversity makes for perfect touring conditions, as it offers something for all tastes, interests, and ages.

Hartford itself offers a full slate of attractions typical of an urban cultural center. The arts, sciences, history, and industries of the city, its suburbs, and the nation are well represented on its long list of museums and exhibits. Traveling families should try to plan at least a day in the state's capital city, keeping in mind that even if you were to visit only the most important museums and family-fun sites, you could easily spend three days here.

TopPicks for fun in Hartford County

1. Lake Compounce Theme Park and Entertainment Complex

2. Huck Finn Adventures

3. Imagine Nation Museum

4. Talcott Mountain State Park and Heublein Tower

5. Old New-Gate Prison and Copper Mine

6. Old State House

7. Mark Twain House

8. Connecticut Science Center

9. New Britain Museum of American Art

10. Dinosaur State Park

HARTFORD COUNTY

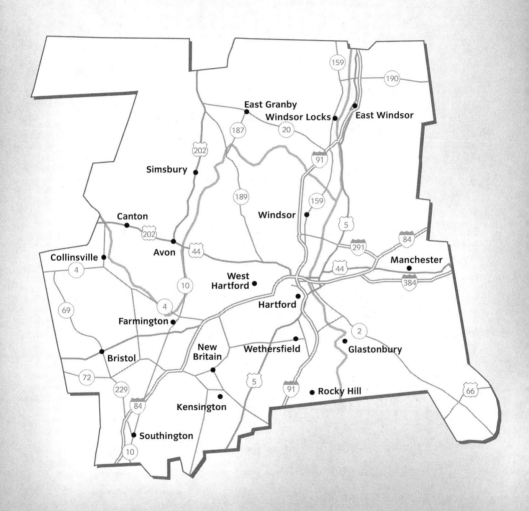

East Granby
Windsor Locks
East Windsor
Simsbury
Canton
Collinsville
Avon
Windsor
West Hartford
Hartford
Manchester
Farmington
New Britain
Wethersfield
Glastonbury
Bristol
Kensington
Rocky Hill
Southington

In the towns surrounding Hartford, you will find attractions that reflect each community's unique history and importance. Defined by such tourist district names as Tobacco Valley or Olde Towne, every area of this county provides opportunities for family fun.

Southington

The town of Southington lies halfway between New York and Boston just east of I-84, a location that even in prehighway days helped it become an important industrial community, producing cement, tinware, and carriage hardware in the nineteenth century and aircraft parts, electronic equipment, and medical instruments in the twentieth. With all the work they do, folks in these parts need a time and place for play. Southington offers both.

Ski Mount Southington (ages 4 and up)
Off I-84 exit 30; follow signs to 396 Mt. Vernon Road; business office: (860) 628-0954 or (800) 982-6828; snow phone: (860) 628-SNOW; www.mountsouthington.com. Open from early December through April for skiing.

If hiking in summer or skiing in winter appeals to your family, Mount Southington is a good place to start. Fourteen downhill trails with five surface lifts and two chair-lifts provide a convenient and state-of-the-art alternative to out-of-state facilities for young families who don't want to travel too far to ski.

Night skiing, snowboarding, and ski parties are all part of the business here. Be sure to check the Web site for the great variety of specials, passes, flex tickets, and other chances to make skiing and boarding affordable. More than 100 professional instructors give group and private lessons, including the SKIwee program for four- to twelve-year-olds and learn-to-race programs on four electronically timed courses for ages eight to adult. Snowmaking machines keep the slopes active from early December through much of early spring. A Terrain Park with tabletops, spines, and rails has made this an especially popular site for boarders. A snack bar/cafeteria and the Mountain Room restaurant give you a chance to refuel, and a ski shop and rental shop help you get the equipment you need. Come to the annual Ski Swap in late October for great deals on equipment.

Where to Eat

Agave Grill. 461 Queen Street; (860) 329-0387. Mostly Mexican cuisine that also wraps its arms around the Caribbean; fresh guacamole prepared tableside, great traditional and inventive entrees, salads, and more. Agave Amigos children's menu ($).

Kids eat for half price Monday and Tuesday. Open from 11:30 a.m. for lunch and dinner daily. Lunch, $–$$; dinner, $$.

Anthony Jack's Wood-Fired Grill. 30 Center Street; (860) 426-0500. Family-owned and family-friendly American-cuisine

Nuts about **Apples**

Every October, Southington's population swells by many thousands as the annual **Apple Harvest Festival** attracts an estimated 300,000 revelers. For nearly forty years, this street festival has celebrated the Southington apple crop in every way possible—a parade, a carnival, a road race, a variety talent show, apple foods and ethnic foods, music, arts and crafts, and dancing. Admission is free. Follow the crowds to the town green on Route 10. Depending on the way the weekends fall on the calendar, the festival is usually held the last weekend of September and the first weekend in October, including the Fridays of both weeks. Check the Web site for this year's schedule.

The festivities extend to the orchards themselves. Two in Southington have apples to pick or buy, plus cider, candies, other produce, and gifts. Call Roger's Orchards (860-229-4240; www.rogersorchards.com) or Karabin Farms (860-621-6363; www.karabinfarms.com). For information on the festival, check the official Web site: www.appleharvestfestival.com.

restaurant right downtown. Booths and brick walls, Angus steaks and fresh seafood cooked over oak and apple fires. Children's menu ($); daily specials; open for lunch and dinner Wednesday through Sunday. Closed Tuesday. $$–$$$

Where to Stay

Holiday Inn Express. 120 Laning Street; (860) 276-0736 or (800) 221-2222. 122 units, outdoor pool, continental breakfast. $$$

Residence Inn by Marriott. 778 West Street; (860) 621-4440. 94 suites with full kitchens. Pets welcome. Exercise room, outdoor pool. Buffet breakfast. $$$–$$$$

Bristol

Though firmly in Hartford County, the small industrial city of Bristol is classified by the State Tourism Commission as part of Connecticut's Northwest. The city's history as a center of venerable Yankee industries, however, gives it a distinctive character much more in line with Hartford than with rural Litchfield. To arrive here from Southington, take Route 10 north to Route 229, and you'll reach Bristol about 8 miles from that junction.

American Clock & Watch Museum (ages 4 and up)

100 Maple Street; (860) 583–6070; www.clockmuseum.org. Open daily from April 1 through November 30 from 10:00 a.m. to 5:00 p.m. except Easter and Thanksgiving Day. $, children under 8 free.

In honor of those industrious craftsmen, you might start a day in Bristol here. More than 1,400 clocks and watches are beautifully displayed in a nineteenth-century colonial home with two modern wings filled with the largest of the ticking, striking, and chiming clocks.

A forest of grandfather clocks shares one wing with a marvelous representation of an eighteenth-century wooden-works clock workshop that displays ledger books, manuals, and clocks in various stages of finishing. Back in the main house, a charming clock shop is re-created with hundreds of clocks that would have been sold in the 1890s, including the original fixtures from an actual 1890s shop in Plymouth, Connecticut.

The collection is magnificent and very appealing to children. A guided tour takes about one hour. We found clocks shaped like Old King Cole, a bumblebee, a frying pan, a pumpkin, a violin, a town crier . . . the list could go on and on. The museum also contains the largest collection of Hickory Dickory Dock clocks held anywhere. Children may enjoy finding familiar figures such as Mickey Mouse, Bugs Bunny, Barbie, and other licensed characters among the antique cabinet clocks, pocket watches, wristwatches, and much more.

The New England Carousel Museum (ages 4 and up)

95 Riverside Avenue (Route 72); (860) 585-5411; www.thecarouselmuseum.org. Open April through November, Monday through Saturday 10:00 a.m. to 5:00 p.m. and Sunday, noon to 5:00 p.m.; and December through March, Thursday through Saturday 10:00 a.m. to 5:00 p.m. and Sunday noon to 5:00 p.m. Closed New Year's Day, Easter Sunday, Memorial Day, Independence Day, Labor Day, Thanksgiving, and Christmas. $–$$; children under 4 are free.

One of the nation's largest displays of antique carousel pieces has its home in Bristol. The golden age of the carousel, from 1880 through the 1930s, is portrayed in the restored hosiery mill—the "Stockingnet Factory"—that houses both the museum and the restoration workshop of carousel expert Bill Finkenstein. The main hall contains a changing parade of Coney Island, Philadelphia, and Country Fair–style figures so colorful and stately that one cannot help but be drawn into their magic. Many horses have been rescued from demolition and restored here, or kept on long-term loan from private collectors, a situation that infuses the museum with new life each time an exhibit is brought in.

The simplicity of the hall underscores the grandeur of the horses, chariots, band organs, and rounding boards. You can't help but smile and you might even feel like dancing when you hear the beautiful band organ music that fills the hall.

Guides tailor their tours to the age and interests of the visitors. Children are invited to feel a horsehair tail and to guess at details of carousel construction. A re-creation of a carver's workshop reveals the secrets of the craft; the particular details of master carvers such as Illions, Stein and Goldstein, Denzel, and Looff are pointed out.

Call for information on the museum's birthday parties, which include crafts, games, and tours. Also explore the rest of the building, which also houses the **Bristol Center for Arts and Culture,** the gallery of local artist Glo Sessions, and a Museum of Fire History that includes a collection of firefighting equipment and memorabilia. Other galleries of fine art and folk art are also here.

Imagine Nation Museum (ages 1 to 10)

1 Pleasant Street; (860) 314-1400; www.imaginenation.org. Open Wednesday to Friday 9:30 a.m. to 5:00 p.m.; Saturday 11:00 a.m. to 5:00 p.m., Sunday noon to 5:00 p.m., and until 8:00 p.m. on the first Friday of the month. $, infants under 1 free. Admission may be higher during special events.

Operated by the Family Center of Bristol and affiliated with the Boys & Girls Club of Bristol, the Imagine Nation Museum is a nonprofit hands-on learning facility targeted to the youngest of visitors. Its focus is on interactive exhibits that encourage exploration and experimentation in the sciences of sound, air, and motion.

The Sandsational Pendulum, for instance, allows children to experiment with pendulum motion and art at the same time, as fascinating designs are created while sand runs out of a swinging pendulum. At the Gravity Well, children discover the principles of gravity and inertia as they roll balls of different weights down the

Connecticut Carousels

The carousel museum may make you ache for a ride, but you can't do it there. Luckily, you're in a great state for carousels. Although by the end of the nineteenth century more than 3,000 carousels operated in the United States, fewer than 100 still exist. Connecticut is home to three antiques, plus a few more recent and brand-new ones, such as the one in the Danbury Fair Mall, the one at Lake Compounce (see next page), and the one at Lake Quassapaug (see Middlebury section of New Haven County chapter). Of the three antique carousels, two are currently operating, and we test-rode them for you in New Haven and Hartford (see Lighthouse Point Park and Bushnell Park, respectively). The third, the restored Pleasure Beach carousel, is partly displayed in Bridgeport at Beardsley Park, next to the operating reproduction that twirls in the specially constructed Carousel House on the zoo grounds (see Beardsley Zoological Gardens). At Sound View Beach in Old Lyme is a 1925 kiddie-sized carousel that is pure summertime fun for the wee ones.

mouth of a well. At the Tuning Fork Table, visitors experiment with sound vibra-
tion, learning the principles of frequency and resonance. An oversize glockenspiel
provides a way to explore musical notes, with colorful charts that invite young
musicians to play songs. Children of all ages will love the Stretch-It Pegboard, which
employs rubber bands to form original shapes and patterns. Whisper Dishes invite
visitors to learn how sound waves can be channeled, and an exhibit called Air Time
uses a complex of ping-pong balls, hand-held blowers, and launch tubes to show
how directed air produces power. Sponsored by ESPN, one of the museum's most
popular attractions is the Play Your Way exhibit, which uses advanced green-screen
technology to allow kids to role-play as their favorite athletes along with a digital-
image backdrop. Parents can watch the action from the bleachers and view the final
product on monitors.

In the Kids Zone, caution lights, street signs, and chain-link fencing create
a construction-zone theme where children can don construction hats, safety
goggles, and work aprons and construct any variety of structures from plumb-
ing pipes, plastic and wood blocks, Erector sets, and gears. For fine artists,
the creative arts center has a huge supply of recyclable materials available for
self-directed activities as well as some conducted by museum staff. Candle- and
jewelry-making, bookmaking, weaving, rug hooking, and basketry classes are also
offered in this area.

As if that weren't enough, the museum also has a collection of international dolls;
a cyber-lab of PC workstations; a greenhouse where young visitors can learn about
ecology, botany, and conservation; a water-play area with bubble wands and giant
bubble machines; a jungle-theme playscape with tunnels, a slide, and climbing wall
sections; a birthday party room; and a dark room with black lights and glow-in-the-
dark toys where visitors can explore the science of luminescence and phosphores-
cence. There's even a real 1940s soda fountain that serves up kids' lunches and ice
cream treats. You have to come play here—it's great!

Lake Compounce Theme Park and Entertainment Complex
(all ages)

**822 Lake Avenue (Route 229 North), 2 miles from I-84 exit 31; (860) 583-3300; www
.lakecompounce.com. Open most days from Memorial Day to late August, then weekends and holidays only until late September. Call for specific hours and days of operation. Ride-all-day rates: $$$$; children 3 and under free. Season passes good for
unlimited visits, $$$$. Evening rates and group rates also. Parking, $.**

Lake Compounce upholds its record as the oldest continually operating amusement park in the United States. After a $50 million face-lift, its more than thirty
rides and other amusements have charmed the crowds back to its 325 acres of
merriment.

Besides the old-fashioned fun in the sun encouraged by its twenty-eight-acre
lake and its sandy beach, the park still operates its 1911 carousel with Wurlitzer

organ, a 1927 white wooden Wildcat roller coaster, and its century-old open-air sky trolley. Along with those are new temptations for thrill-seekers: Boulder Dash (the East Coast's longest and fastest roller coaster); Zoomerang coaster with corkscrew turns; Splash Harbor wave pool and Tunnel Twister water slides; Thunder Rapids raft ride; Mammoth Falls flume ride; Rainbow Riders balloon ride; and the Zoomers Gas 'n' Go mini-Corvette ride. The Vacation Village Lakeside Theatre features changing acts from circuses to magic shows; a 100-foot Ferris wheel competes with the 750-foot ascent of the Southington Mountain Sky Ride; the Shoreline Trolley car shuttles passengers to a 2,400-seat picnic pavilion. Young visitors will enjoy the Kiddieland Circus World, with ten rides for children under 48 inches. A miniature golf course and paddleboats (both an extra charge) add to the entertainments.

Bring along a bathing suit or a change of clothes and a towel so you can enjoy a ride on the water slide or a dip in the lake. Lockers and changing rooms are provided. Several food concessions and a large full-service restaurant provide lots of choices for snacks, meals, and beverages. Groups of twenty-five or more can request special rates, so visitors might consider the reduced price a good excuse for a neighborhood outing, a family reunion, or a birthday bash.

Where to Eat

Super Natural Market and Deli. 430 North Main Street in Northside Square; (860) 582-1663. Excellent hot and cold buffet and deli with small eating area; perfect for takeout or picnics, or pull up a stool and eat here. Terrific soups. Open Monday through Friday 8:00 a.m. to 6:00 and Saturday 9:00 a.m. to 5:00 p.m. $

Carmine's Italian Grill. 650 Farmington Avenue; (860) 314-1501. All the best traditional Italian specialties, some of which are offered in wonderful family-sized portions, along with salads and fresh bread, plentiful for sharing with the whole table. Children's menu ($). Open every day for lunch and dinner. $$–$$$

Where to Stay

Clarion Hotel. 42 Century Drive; (860) 589-7766. 120 units, including 2 suites. Health club, sauna, indoor pool. Full breakfast available ($) at Jillian's Restaurant on premises. Special packages. $$–$$$

Canton/Collinsville

Fishing and antiquing are probably the most popular tourist activities in the Canton/Collinsville area near Route 179 north of Burlington and west of Avon, but they are not likely to sustain the long-term attention of everyone in the family. Luckily, some other options make the area a crowd-pleaser anyway.

Huck Finn Adventures (all ages)

(860) 693-0385; www.huckfinnadventures.com. Open in spring, summer, and fall. Call for reservations and directions. Mini solo kayaks, catamaran canoes, a wooden raft, and an inflatable raft are also available. $$$$

First of all, this operation is run by an easygoing fellow with a great appreciation for the beauty and adventure to be enjoyed in the outdoors. An all-around nice guy, John Kulick offers leisurely trips specially designed for families with young children or beginner canoeists. You choose from 3-, 5-, or 9-mile trips in waist-high flat water along a quiet section of the sandy-bottomed Farmington River between Avon and Simsbury.

Everything you need for the self-guided outing is provided, except the picnic or snacks you bring along. The outfitter sets you up with stable 17-foot canoes, paddles, life vests, and so on. The canoes have seats in the middle for the kids, so two adults and two young children are usually comfortable in one canoe. Instruction on paddling, put-in, and take-out is offered at the outset for novices, but this is gentle enough for little risk to true beginners.

You'll paddle past King Philip's Cave high up on the Talcott Mountain Ridge. On the ride back to your put-in spot, the driver of your shuttle van will tell you the story of King Philip, or Metacomet, chief of the Wampanoags. A bloody three-year war began in 1675, when Metacomet began to massacre the settlers he feared would destroy his people. When Simsbury, among other towns, was burned by the Wampanoags in 1676, their notorious leader supposedly watched from the cave. You might want to stop in the small park near the old iron bridge along the way for a picnic at the Pinchot Sycamore, the largest tree in Connecticut. Actually located in Simsbury in the Weatogue section on Route 185, the tree's circumference is 25 feet, 8 inches. It is 93 feet tall and its branches spread 138 feet. A picnic area with tables is there for your use.

Two adults paddling at a leisurely pace can do these trips in two to three hours (paddling time), but you're welcome to spend the day picnicking and exploring, or drifting like Huckleberry himself. Twilight and moonlight trips can also be arranged. Whitewater instruction usually takes place in May and June as water conditions allow.

Collinsville Canoe and Kayak (all ages with some limits)

41 Bridge Street (Route 179); (860) 693-6977; www.cckstore.com. Seasonal hours, depending on weather and water conditions; call to inquire. $$$–$$$$

This outfitter offers guided and self-guided canoe and kayak trips on flat water, whitewater, and the Sound. Self-guided trips on flat water are commonly taken from the put-in points near the Collinsville Canoe store on Route 179. Guided tours are offered on the Farmington River as well as Bantam Lake in Bantam, Lake McDonough in Barkhamsted, and White Memorial in Litchfield, plus Selden Neck, Great Island, Fishers Island Sound, the Mystic Seaport, the Thimble Islands, the Norwalk Islands, and other areas. Reservations are necessary for all guided tours and are highly recommended, especially for weekends, even for the self-guided Farmington River flatwater trips.

The age minimum for kayaks and canoes is up to parental discretion, but the child must be able to fit snugly into a life vest. They also offer instruction in beginning canoeing and kayaking for whitewater, flat water, and the sea.

Canton Historical Museum (ages 6 and up)

11 Front Street; (860) 693-2793; www.cantonmuseum.org. Open April through November, Wednesday through Sunday from 1:00 to 4:00 p.m.; open until 8:00 p.m. Thursday. December through March, Saturday and Sunday from 1:00 to 4:00 p.m. $, children under 6 free.

If you're intrigued by the history of the area after a day on the river, visit this marvelous museum. A complete, original post office, a general-store re-creation, a blacksmith area, a barbershop area, a Victorian bride's parlor with wedding dresses, a late-nineteenth-century kitchen setting, and tons of farming equipment, medical equipment, household implements like looms and spinning wheels, and much more await your perusal on the one-hour guided tour. A special children's area includes dolls, toys, and other items of interest, and a true highlight is an operational model train diorama of the whole Collinsville village and countryside as it appeared about 1900.

Roaring Brook Nature Center (all ages)

70 Gracey Road; (860) 693-0263; www.roaringbrook.org. Open year-round Tuesday through Saturday 10:00 a.m. to 5:00 p.m. (also Monday from July through August) and Sunday 1:00 to 5:00 p.m. Hiking trails open daily, dawn to dusk. $

Canton's sanctuary is perfect for families. An excellent longhouse typical of the Wampanoag people is still among the recently re-created *Changing Land and Wildlife* indoor exhibits, which reveal how changes in land use during the past 500 years have affected the flora and fauna of the Eastern Woodlands. Among these updated and interactive areas are colorful and fascinating walk-in dioramas, including a beaver wetland re-creation and an ancient forest and Native American area. Here too are a wild animal attraction area, a live-animal area with native creatures, and a small gift shop. Six miles of trails through exceptionally pretty country are on the sanctuary. A wildflower trail is especially lovely in spring and summer. Ask at the nature center for wildlife and flora guides and checklists before you venture into the beautiful Werner's Woods property. Indoor programs as well as guided walks are offered throughout the season for families. A full slate of concerts ($–$$$), some especially designed for young children, is one of the best and most unique features of this nature center. See the Web site for the schedule.

Where to Eat

La Salle Market and Deli. 104 Main Street, Collinsville; (860) 693-8010. Open daily year-round from 6:00 a.m. to 7:00 p.m. Monday through Friday, from 7:00 a.m. to 8:00 p.m. on Saturday, and Sunday 7:00 a.m. to 5:00 p.m., this village market has five eat-in tables or take-out service if you need picnic food for a canoe or road trip. Bagels, muffins, breakfast sandwiches, deli sandwiches and salads, hot dogs, burgers, meatballs, and much more. Pizza is served in the evening, and open-mike entertainment is offered Thursday through Sunday. A friendly throwback to the good old days, it's great for families. $

Crown & Hammer Restaurant and Pub. 3 Depot Street; (860) 693-9199. In the former freight station, this busy local favorite is open Wednesday through Sunday for lunch and dinner; pub stays open late. Great setting with intriguing historic photos; great burgers, wraps, crab cakes, and fried green tomatoes, of course. $$–$$$

Bagels Plus Canton. 220 Albany Turnpike (Route 44), Canton; (860) 693-3799. In the Canton Village Shopping Center, this bagel shop/cafe offers breakfast and lunch options every day and can help you pack a pretty good picnic. Bagels and bagel sandwiches of every description; great deli sandwiches and soups. Eat here at a few tables, or pack it out. Open from 6:00 a.m. to 2:00 p.m. on weekdays; 7:00 a.m. to 1:00 p.m. on Saturday, and 7:00 a.m. to noon on Sunday. $

Where to Stay

Hillside Motel. 671 Albany Turnpike (Route 44); (860) 693-4951. 16 units in this neat, clean, owner-occupied motel. No-frills basic place to rest your head comfortably and safely. Complimentary coffee in the morning. $

Avon

Named for the river in Stratford, England, Avon originated in 1645 as a section of Farmington. First known as Nod, for North District, it grew substantially in the following century when the new stagecoach route from Boston to Albany came through town. Along with the Albany Turnpike came prosperity for the farmers and traders of the region, who capitalized on the needs of the travelers passing through town. Inn and tavern keepers, blacksmiths and harness makers, merchants, and even bandits all benefited from the construction of the road we now call Route 44.

Avon has retained all signs of the affluence it achieved in its past. Now a bedroom community populated largely by commuting Hartford executives and professionals, it is plump with restaurants and shops catering to a comfortable clientele. For tourists, of course, this means wonderful food and great places for shopping. Unfortunately, the kids might lose interest after a while. No worry—Avon is home to a few places the kids might really enjoy, albeit with one caveat: It's best to be here in summer or fall.

Avon Cider Mill (all ages)

57 Waterville Road (Route 10); (860) 677-0343. The mill's market is open daily, mid-September to October 31 from 9:00 a.m. to 6:00 p.m.; November 1 to December 25, they close at 5:00 p.m.

When the trees show signs of turning, come here. From apples trucked in from upstate New York, the Lattizori brothers make 35,000 to 40,000 gallons of cider every year, starting in mid-September. You can actually watch them make the cider in the press their grandfather bought in 1919, but you'd have to get up pretty early in the morning. Cider-making begins at 2:00 a.m. and is usually done by 7:00 a.m. Set the alarm if you want to see the press in action. If you like to sleep a little longer, just plan on tasting the wonderfully sweet cider—the ultimate chaser for the melt-in-your-mouth cider doughnuts sold here as well.

The market also offers local produce and crafts, pumpkins, and fall accoutrements like Indian corn, gourds, mums, and more. Later in the season, they truck in the Christmas trees. After Christmas, the Lattizoris rest a bit; they close shop until spring, when they bring out plants for your gardens. In midsummer, local produce, such as sweet corn, tempts the tourists right off the road.

Pickin' Patch (all ages)

276 Nod Road, off Route 44; (860) 677-9552. Open daily in season from 8:00 a.m. to 6:00 p.m. Open 8:00 a.m. to 5:00 p.m. in November and December.

In the same vein, only more so, you might like to stop by the Pickin' Patch, just a mile and a half up Nod Road, which begins at the Avon Old Farms Inn at the corner of Routes 10 and 44. Owned by Janet and Don Carville, the farm has been in the Carville family since 1666 when their ancestors came from Hartford after accompanying Thomas Hooker to Connecticut.

This farm is a fountain of riches, namely nearly everything growing under the sun from asparagus to zucchini. As the name suggests, this is a pick-your-own place from roughly mid-April onward to December until the Christmas trees are gone and they turn the lights out on Christmas Eve. The tenth-oldest family farm in Connecticut, the farm grows the largest variety of berries, vegetables, and flowers in the state. Strawberries, blackberries, blueberries, squash, spinach, collards, peas, cucumbers, tomatoes, peppers, and much more are sold at half the cost of retail if you pick them yourself.

The joint really starts hopping when pumpkin season and the **free** hayrides begin. On Saturday and Sunday in October from 10:00 a.m. to 5:00 p.m., you can ride the tractor-driven hay wagons out to the fields to pick your own pumpkin.

Farmington Valley Arts Center (ages 6 and up)

25 Arts Center Lane, just under a half-mile west of the junction of Routes 44 and 10 North, in Avon Park North office/industrial complex. Turn from Route 44 into Ensign Drive, then left onto Arts Center Lane. The second and third buildings slightly askew

at your left are the Arts Center buildings, numbers 25 and 27; (860) 678-1867; www
.fvac.net. Studios open year-round (see below) by chance or by appointment; store
open year-round Wednesday through Saturday from 11:00 a.m. through 5:00 p.m.
and on Sunday from noon to 4:00 p.m. Open Monday through Saturday 10:00 a.m. to
5:00 p.m., Thursday until 8:00 p.m., and Sunday noon to 5:00 p.m. in November and
December.

Historically important as former factory buildings, these century-old brownstone
structures now house the studios of about twenty-five resident working artists
who compose the center. Painting, ceramics, weaving, and sculpture are just a
few of the media explored here by professional artists and their students. Classes
are offered for children and adults at every level—beginners as well as advanced.
Artists work on individual schedules, but someone is almost always here to
watch, and you are welcome to stroll from studio to studio throughout the year,
especially on Saturday and Sunday from February through October or as many
as seven days a week in November and December. Open Arts Day in early June
is a festival event with demonstrations, classes, musicians, dancers, a theater
performance, and other experiences related to the arts. Check the calendar for
Art Nights, which are **free** or very affordable—and great. Adults as well as children ages six to seventeen are welcome. Creativity Workouts, also excellent, are
designed for adults, but call to inquire for an exception if the topic is of interest
to a child you know; instructors here are known to soften the rules for passionate
learners of all ages.

From the first Saturday in November until Christmas Eve, the annual holiday
exhibit, called the Art of Giving/The Giving of Art, features strolling musicians, lumi-
naria, and festivities on opening night, plus sales of contemporary American crafts
thereafter in the Fisher Gallery and in the Visitors' Gallery, which is the FVAC store.
This shop offers a varied collection of pottery, jewelry, toys, prints, clothing, and
other exceptional crafts made by U.S. crafters only. Ask for a course catalog in the
FVAC office on your way to the gallery or check the Web site. The teen and children's
summer classes at the Learning Center Annex are wonderful.

First Company Governor's Horse Guards (all ages)

Military Reservation, 232 West Avon Road (Route 167); (860) 673-3525; www.gov
horseguards.org. Public viewing of drills on horseback every Thursday evening, usually shortly after 7:30 throughout the year. Open horse show in June. Call for schedule or check the Web site. Visitors welcome at other times daily to view horses. The
driveway to the compound is actually on Arch Road, just off Route 167.

If you are in Avon at a time that coordinates with the activities of the Governor's
Horse Guards, stop for a look. The nation's first cavalry unit organized in 1658 as the
mounted guards of Connecticut Colony, the original thirty or so riders and horses
served both as ceremonial escorts and in active duty in the War of 1812, World War
I, and World War II. The company's current responsibilities are mostly decorative.
Their choreographed maneuvers are amazingly intricate "dances" performed at such

events as presidential and gubernatorial inaugurations. You are welcome to watch them practice their astounding routines at the compound on Route 167 between Routes 4 and 44. Each Thursday evening, the caretaker and the mounted troopers go through the drills, both inside the barn and outside. You can also ask for a tour of the compound on other days if you are visiting nearby; an advance call is a good idea.

Where to Eat

Avon Old Farms Inn. 1 Nod Road, at the junction of Routes 44 and 10; (860) 677-2818; www.avonoldfarmsinn.com. A splurge for many families, this classic is one of the ten oldest restaurants in the country and one of the best in the state. New American cuisine freshly prepared and presented in a beautiful setting. Open year-round daily. $$$$

To spend a bit less, try the Tavern Room, which offers a wonderful lunch buffet. $$

Bakers Dozen Bagel Company. 315 West Main Street; (860) 676-2245. This spic-and-span family-owned bakery has made thirty-five varieties of bagels on-site for the past twenty-five years. Bagel sandwiches, stuffed bagel pockets, soups in winter, and more. Eat in or out for breakfast, lunch, and beyond. Open daily from 6:30 a.m.; closings vary (earliest is 2:00 p.m. on Sunday). $

Max a Mia Ristorante and Cantinetta. 70 East Main Street (Route 44); (860) 677-MAXX. Northern Italian contemporary cuisine is what they call it; we call it delicious. Fresh focaccia, excellent salads and pastas galore, thin-crust pizza made in wood-fired oven. Open for lunch, dinner, and Sunday brunch. $$–$$$

Where to Stay

Avon Old Farms Hotel. 279 Avon Mountain Road, at the junction of Routes 44 and 10; (860) 677-1651; www.avonoldfarms hotel.com. Across the street from the Avon Old Farms Inn, which is a restaurant, is this cream-of-the-crop, 160-unit hotel with standard and luxury rooms and 3 suites. Luxury amenities, from the soap to the chocolates, from towels to apples. Continental breakfast. Outdoor pool, sauna, health club. Seasons Restaurant and Pub. $$$$

Simsbury

Six miles north of Avon, Simsbury is an appealing suburb of 22,000 people, many of whom work in Hartford, just twenty minutes south. Established in 1670 by English colonists, Simsbury was built on land long populated by the Wampanoag Indians, who had no understanding of the English concept of land claims when they began to share local tribal lands with the newcomers. Their misapprehension of the situation led to turbulence that culminated in the burning of Simsbury by the Wampanoags on March 26, 1676. Sad to say, the Wampanoag people underestimated the tenacity of the settlers and were nearly eradicated in the bloody King Philip's war that ensued. Reconstruction of colonial Simsbury commenced in 1677 when it was clear that no further resistance was possible. The settlers of Simsbury soon had a community that flourished, as did industries of copper mining, smelting, steel production, copper coinage, silver plating, and safety fuse manufacturing. Now largely residential, Simsbury offers to the public one of the best historical settlements in the state.

The Phelps Tavern Museum and Phelps Homestead
(ages 6 and up)

800 Hopmeadow Street (Route 10); (860) 658-2500; www.simsburyhistory.org. Open year-round, Tuesday through Saturday from noon to 4:00 p.m. Last full tour at 3:15 p.m. Closed holidays. $–$$

Once called Massacoh Plantation, this property has eight structures—some reproduction, some original, and some transported here for the purpose of creating a museum. A tour of the property usually begins at the replica 1683 meetinghouse wherein the Simsbury founding fathers decided matters of church and state and from which supposed witch Goody Griffin is said to have departed by flying through its keyhole.

The 1771 Elisha Phelps House, occupied by the Phelps family for nearly 200 years, is restored to the period of 1830–40 when it served as a hotel/tavern for travelers on the New Haven–Northampton Canal. The site also includes a Victorian carriage house with an authentic tin peddler's cart, a 1740 one-room schoolhouse, a barn, an icehouse, a 1795 cottage also owned by the Phelps family, and a re-creation of the safety fuse manufactory with fixtures, records, and furnishings of the original factory.

Tours by (sometimes) costumed guides of the Simsbury Historical Society are thorough and excellent, though a full tour for children under eight may be longer than they can bear. Feel free to ask for a short version if you are the only folks in the group. You can stroll the grounds unguided, but you cannot tour the buildings alone. The museum typically offers a holiday festivity of one sort or another in late November or early December. Living-history reenactments with costumed actors have been among past events; staged readings of holiday tales or visits from Saint Nicholas might occur. Check the Web site for these and other special events of interest to families.

Talcott Mountain State Park (all ages)
Route 185; (860) 242-1158. Park open year-round dawn to dusk. Heublein Tower open mid-April to late August Thursday through Sunday 10:00 a.m. to 5:00 p.m. and, for foliage season, from early September through October, open daily at same hours. Free.

If the excellent history lessons at the Phelps Tavern Museum overwhelm some in your party, refresh yourselves with a brisk hike. A popular family area because of the amazing Heublein Tower at the 1,000-foot summit of the Talcott Mountain Ridge, it has moderate trails, benches, picnic sites, and, on clear days, views of four states from the tower. Some, including Mark Twain, who used to walk this ridge, say it's the finest view in all of Connecticut. The park overlooks many of the fertile Farmington Valley farms and pretty towns like Avon. From Route 10 between Simsbury and Avon, you can't miss seeing the white 165-foot-tall tower built in 1914 by businessman Gilbert Heublein.

Once you're in the park, you hike the 1.5-mile King Philip's Trail to the tower and then climb up. The observation deck, at the top of several flights of stairs, provides a 50-mile view on clear days. A local history exhibit is also at the tower base, with interesting facts about the park and tower.

International Skating Center of Connecticut (ages 3 and up)

1375 Hopmeadow Street (Route 10); (860) 651-5400; www.isccskate.com. Public ice skating Monday through Friday from 11:45 a.m. to 12:45 p.m., Saturday from 4:30 to 5:50 p.m. and Sunday from 6:15 to 7:35 p.m. Added sessions on some holidays or during school breaks. Visitors welcome daily 6:00 a.m. to midnight. $–$$

You want to skate, and you'd love to see the example of Ekaterina Gordeeva, Oksana Baiul, Viktor Petrenko, Scott Davis, and other skating champions. Come here to the world-class twin facility that is their home rink. An Olympic-size and an NHL-size rink are both linked to the Sk8ters Cafe, a restaurant and coffee shop that allow diners a view of both rinks. Two thousand seats allow spectators to watch figure skating and hockey events and practices. Small classes for beginners to pros are offered here, and the instruction programs and scholarships bring young skaters from all over the world. Learn-to-Skate programs include special kids' classes for ages three and up. Skate rentals, purchases, and sharpening and repair services are all available to the public. Private birthday parties can be arranged.

Flamig Farm (ages 2 to 10)

West Mountain Road; (860) 658-5070; www.flamigfarm.com. Open daily 9:00 a.m. to 5:00 p.m. or dusk, April 22 (Earth Day) to late November. Pony rides weekends only 11:00 a.m. to 3:00 p.m., $ for children up to 75 pounds. Other rides offered, weather permitting. Zoo admission $ for folks over 1 and under 80.

A petting zoo of farm animals is the big ticket at this farm most of the season. See Belgian draft horses and miniature horses, llamas, pigs, goats, sheep, chickens, rabbits, turkeys, geese, ducks, and even a pair of Texas longhorns named Strawberry and Oreo. You can buy a cupful or a handful of grain if you'd like to give the animals a snack, and you can pet them all, of course. You might also like to visit the barns and bring your own meal to the picnic area.

Pony rides are given on weekends only; occasionally a draft horse is saddled as well for larger riders. In pumpkin season, public hayrides to the pumpkin fields are given on weekends only on the half-hour from 11:00 a.m. to 4:00 p.m. Private horse-drawn rides and tractor hayrides can be arranged in advance; sleigh rides can also be arranged when the weather cooperates. Pony-ride birthday parties at their place or yours are also frequent; a covered pavilion is available here for that use. Check the Web site for rates for all of these kinds of rides and parties and for news of the farm's seasonal events. In the fall, haunted hayrides are typically sold out, as are their Breakfasts with Santa. A Summer Farm Adventure Camp is fabulous. You can also buy fresh eggs here year-round and cut flowers in season at the farm store.

Where to Eat

Pettibone Tavern. 4 Hartford Road; (860) 658-1118. For good American fare in a historic setting, come here for dinner daily, 4:00 to 9:00 p.m., and for lunch on week-days. Steaks, seafood, and simple choices for children, such as grilled cheese and spaghetti. $$–$$$$

Amelia's American Bistro. 2 Wilcox Street, at Fiddler's Green; (860) 408-1234. Open for lunch and dinner Tuesday through Saturday and on Sunday for brunch only, this pretty bistro offers a casually elegant approach to family fare. Children's menu ($). $$–$$$

Maple Tree Cafe. 781 Hopmeadow Street; (860) 651-1297. Sandwiches, burg-ers, salads, pastas and seafood with an emphasis on Italian favorites, soups, and typical American appetizers. Children's menu. Patio tables in fair weather. Live music on Friday and Saturday evenings. $

Sakimura. 10 Wilcox Street; (860) 651-7929. For a delicious and cultural food adventure, try lunch or dinner at this excellent Japanese establishment. A sushi/sashimi bar, more than two dozen appetizer dishes, teriyaki, tempura, and American favorites made Japanese style are among the many choices. Open daily. $–$$$

Where to Stay

The Simsbury Inn. 397 Hopmeadow Street; (860) 651-5700. 100 "luxury rooms with a country inn ambience" is how the inn's owners describe it. They're right. Indoor pool, 3 restaurants, health club, sauna, tennis, jogging paths, and continen-tal breakfast make this a special place for families. $$$$

East Granby

This little town 4 miles east of Granby (north of Simsbury by means of Route 10/202) is downright bucolic, and it's a pleasure merely to explore the gentle twists and hills of its rural roadways. Just a handful of miles from the Massachusetts border, its village center is a quiet place of refuge from the busy hub that grows in an ever-widening circle around Hartford.

Old New-Gate Prison and Copper Mine (ages 4 and up)

Newgate Road off Route 20; (860) 653-3563. Open from mid-May through October, Wednesday through Sunday from 10:00 a.m. to 4:30 p.m. $, children under 6 free.

Amid the beautiful hills of East Granby is a National Historic Landmark. The first North American copper mine chartered by the British monarchy in 1707, New-Gate is also Connecticut's first prison, named after London's notorious New-Gate Prison. When copper mining ceased in the facility in 1773, the subterranean tunnels and chambers were designated as a perfect place to confine the burglars, horse thieves, and counterfeiters who had broken the laws of the English colonies. Soon, however, English sympathizers were imprisoned here as the American Patriots revolted against the monarchy and took New-Gate as their own. During the Revolution, George Washington sent captured Tories here along with American deserters. Just to make sure no one was having any fun underground, prisoners were forced to mine the tunnels and to make nails and shoes.

Now the old brick rooms and ruins of the prison and much of the mine are open to the public. A self-guided tour of the 65-foot-deep mine takes about thirty minutes. I recommend highly that you call ahead and ask for a guided tour, which the staff is happy to provide. All the guides are wonderfully educated as to the facts and fictions of this remarkable site.

The view from the prison grounds is one of the finest views in the state. The fall foliage here is glorious. You can picnic on the lawn or on tables. A great wildlife nature trail designed to demonstrate wildlife habitat–management practices homeowners can use on their own property is accessible from the parking lot. Pick up a trail guide inside the prison.

Windsor

Six miles north of the state capital lies Windsor, which calls itself Connecticut's oldest town, settled in 1633 by Englishmen from Plymouth Colony in Massachusetts. These adventurers camped at the confluence of the Connecticut and Farmington Rivers in a place the native inhabitants called Matianuck. Briefly named Dorchester by the newcomers, the town was renamed Windsor in 1637 and has enjoyed a prosperous history ever since, based on the varied enterprises of brick making, cigar tobacco farming, and the milling of woolens and paper. Now largely suburban in nature, this town of just over 30 square miles on the western bank of the Connecticut River has a variety of attractions that will add to a family's appreciation of the state's north-central Heritage Valley.

In addition to the main attractions listed in the following paragraphs, the town of Windsor offers a pleasant array of places and events where families might enjoy a day or a weekend. Summer concerts on Thursday evenings on the historic town green, a winter carnival, a clown day, and a just-for-fun dog show are the kinds of

History in the **Heritage Valley**

Windsor is proud of its history as the cradle of European settlement and development in the Connecticut River Valley, and it celebrates that through several museums and events that may be of interest to families. Most of these are located in or near the town's historic district, which centers roughly on the Broad Street town green and the Palisado Green, on or near Routes 75 and 159. The marvelous Windsor Historical Society (96 Palisado Avenue near the corner of North Meadow Road; 860-688-3813; www.windsorhistoricalsociety.org) has three galleries with changing art and artifact exhibitions and a hands-on history learning center that covers three centuries of life in Windsor. Here, for instance, you can try on colonial-style clothing, pretend to attend the one-room schoolhouse, or learn about hearth cooking. The society also operates the adjacent 1758 Strong House and nearby 1765 Chaffee House. The museum is open and tours of these homes are given year-round, Tuesday through Saturday, from 10:00 a.m. to 4:00 p.m. ($). The 1780 Oliver Ellsworth Homestead (778 Palisado Avenue; 860-688-8717; www.ctdar.org/oeh) re-creates the life of its namesake Revolutionary patriot and statesman through domestic furniture, implements, and ephemera. It is open for tours from noon to 4:30 p.m. May through October on Tuesday, Wednesday, and Saturday; $, children under 12 are free.

activities that characterize this family-oriented town. Other annual events include the one-of-a-kind Shad Derby Festival the third Saturday in May, a Yankee Doodle Fourth of July Celebration, and an early autumn Revolutionary War Encampment (see www .revolutionarywindsor.com). Walking and cycling on the Windsor Center River Trail, ice-skating on the town green, and canoeing on the Farmington River are among the town's many outdoor activities; indoors are museums that explore 300 years of history (see sidebar). Consider booking a room at a local hostelry and have an old-fashioned good time.

Northwest Park and Nature Center (all ages)
Luddy/Taylor Connecticut Valley Tobacco Museum (ages 8 and up)
Lang Road; park and nature center: (860) 285-1886; www.northwestpark.com; tobacco museum: (860) 285-1888; www.tobaccohistsoc.org. Park open daily year-round, dawn to dusk. Nature center open daily year-round, Monday through Saturday from 10:00 a.m. to 5:00 p.m. and Sunday noon to 4:00 p.m. Tobacco museum open March to mid-December, Tuesday through Thursday and Saturday from noon to 4:00 p.m.,

with somewhat longer hours in summer. Admission to the park, nature center, and museum is free.

Lovely Northwest Park has nearly 475 acres and 10 miles of trails, along with picnic areas and pavilions, community and demonstration gardens, a playground, and much more of appeal to visitors of all ages. Explore the Wetland Forest Trail, the Bog Loop, the Softwood Forest, or the Woody Succession Trail. Check out the Hemlock Trail or the Pond Trail. All of these are open any time of year. Stop at the live-animal exhibits in the Animal Barn and Nature Center. See the demonstration maple-sugaring house or linger quietly in the bird and butterfly gardens. Hiking, biking, and picnicking are among the self-guided activities you might pursue here, or take a guided walk or participate in a family nature program or kids' camp. An annual Country Fair offers games, races, hayrides, and entertainment especially for children ages two to ten. Call or check the Web site for this year's date.

Snowshoeing and cross-country skiing are possible here during snowy winters; a rental center offers equipment ($$). Throughout the academic year, come in the evening or on occasional afternoons on selected Saturdays for the Northwest Park Coffee House Concert series. All performances are alcohol- and smoke-free and are suitable for families ($$$). Check the Northwest Park Web site for the current schedule.

At the Luddy/Taylor Connecticut Valley Tobacco Museum, located in Northwest Park, you can explore a restored tobacco curing barn to gain a sense of the venerable history of tobacco farming in this valley. The world's finest cigar wrappers are still grown in this area, although the total acreage is reduced to 2,000 acres from a peak of 30,000 acres in 1921. Learn how the shade-leaf tobacco was grown and cured; see the authentic equipment stored in the barn; and peruse the historical displays in the museum building near the barn to gain an appreciation for the ways the tobacco industry contributed to the region's economy and even its ethnic culture.

Where to Eat

Albert's Riverside Restaurant and Pub. 1530 Palisado Avenue; (860) 285-0878. In the warm months only (typically May through October), you can eat in or out at this dependably good American and Italian restaurant right on the Connecticut River. Ribs, roasts, steaks, salads, soups, sandwiches, pasta specials, and more. Open for lunch and dinner daily in season. $$–$$$

Bart's Deli and Restaurant. 85 Palisado Avenue; (860) 688-9035. Within the historic district not far from the center of town is this cozy and down-to-earth place right on the banks of the Farmington. Great breakfasts and, for lunch and early dinner, hearty sandwiches of all kinds, rings and dogs, burgers, and traditional American hot meals. 7:00 a.m. to 7:00 p.m. daily year-round, except until 5:00 p.m. on Saturday. Picnic tables by the river if you'd like to eat outdoors. $–$$

Dom's Broad Street Eatery. 330 Broad Street; (860) 298-9758. Try Dom's for cuisine similar to Bart's—hearty traditional American breakfasts, and generous sandwiches, soups, salads, and such for lunch. Open year-round from 7:00 a.m. to 2:00 p.m. on weekdays, from 6:00 a.m. on weekends, and breakfast only on Sunday. $

Where to Stay

Residence Inn by Marriott. 100 Dunphy Lane; (860) 688-7474; www.residence inn.com. 96 suites with fully equipped kitchens. Complimentary continental buffet breakfast; outdoor pool, whirlpool, sports court. Pets welcome. $$$$

Windsor Locks

Best known for its current role as the home of Bradley International Airport, Windsor Locks is on the Connecticut River about a dozen miles from downtown Hartford and has a large concentration of hotels, motels, and restaurants serving travelers. It also has one of the nation's best aviation museums.

New England Air Museum (all ages)
Route 75; (860) 623-3305. Open daily year-round, except New Year's Day, Christmas, and Thanksgiving, from 10:00 a.m. to 5:00 p.m. $, children under 6 free.

Right within sight of the runways at Bradley International Airport is the largest aviation history museum in the Northeast and one of only four such collections in the United States. From a 1909 wood-and-canvas Bleriot XI monoplane to modern jets, the museum includes eighty aircraft of military and civilian origins. Most are restored and housed inside two hangars, transformed to museum-gallery quality.

Excellent exhibits tell the story of flight from the drawings of Leonardo da Vinci to the space flights of NASA astronauts. The evolution of humankind's mastery of gravity is chronicled at every turn, nowhere more evidently than in the aircraft themselves. The museum owns the oldest aeronautical artifact in the United States—a beautiful wicker balloon basket built by Silas Brooks of Plymouth, Connecticut, in 1870. From that vintage onward, the museum houses biplanes, Piper Cubs, Seabat helicopters, B-25 bombers, Grumman Hellcats and Wildcats, F-4 Phantom jets, hang-gliders, and many other fully and partially restored aircraft.

Lindbergh memorabilia, an outstanding Igor Sikorsky exhibit, and an air-mail display are among the special areas. Films on flight, the space program, and other topics are played continuously in the museum's theater. On Open Cockpit Sundays (offered a few times annually) you can climb inside several restored aircraft. Most of the signage of the exhibits is directed to adults. Parents of young children will have to read or paraphrase most of the excellent information the museum provides. Despite this problem, the museum is well suited to children, and the museum shop is full of merchandise perfect for kids.

By the way, the road to the museum runs right alongside the airport runway. Pull over and sit there awhile for great views of the comings and goings of local, national, and international aircraft.

Where to Eat

Skyline Restaurant. 106 Ella T. Grasso Turnpike (Route 75); (860) 623-9296. For good Italian food in a family-friendly place close to views of the air traffic, come here from 11:30 a.m. to 10:00 p.m. for lunch or dinner. On its extensive children's menu are such great choices as chicken parmigiana and ravioli along with the typical tenders, dogs, and the like. You can't see the planes take off or land, but they are there in the sky. Ask for a window seat in the front atrium. Open daily year-round, except major holidays. $–$$

Where to Stay

Doubletree Hotel. 16 Ella T. Grasso Turnpike (Route 75); (860) 627-5171. 200 rooms, 2 suites, indoor pool, sauna, fitness center, whirlpool, restaurant. $$$

Fairfield Inn by Marriott. 2 Loten Drive; (860) 627-9333 or (800) 228-2800. 135 rooms, outdoor pool, continental breakfast. $$$

Ramada Inn at Bradley. 5 Ella T. Grasso Turnpike (Route 75); (860) 623-9494 or (800) 2-RAMADA. 148 rooms, indoor/outdoor pool, restaurant, buffet breakfast, weekend packages. $$$–$$$$

East Windsor

Follow Route 20 East from East Granby and pick up Route 140 East to get to East Windsor. Once the northernmost point that could be reached by steamboats before encountering rapids on the Connecticut River, it became a busy freshwater port with a crowded warehouse area still known as Warehouse Point. Now an interesting mix of suburban and rural areas, East Windsor holds a few treasures for families who look past the fast-food joints and businesses that line the main thoroughfares close to the airport and Interstate 91.

Connecticut Trolley Museum (all ages)

58 North Road (Route 140); (860) 627-6540; www.ceraonline.org. Memorial Day through Labor Day, open 10:00 a.m. to 5:00 p.m. Monday and Wednesday through Saturday, and from noon to 5:00 p.m. on Sunday; Labor Day through late November and from April to Memorial Day, from 10:00 a.m. to 5:00 p.m. Saturday and from noon to 5:00 p.m. Sunday; and from late November through December, 10:00 a.m. to 4:00 p.m. Saturday and noon to 4:00 p.m. Sunday. Closed Thanksgiving Day, Christmas Eve, Christmas Day, and January 1 through March 31. Also open weekday evenings during the Winterfest Light Display, from the first weekend after Thanksgiving through December 23 and then for a few days after December 26. See the Web site for this

year's Winterfest schedule. $–$$. Includes admission to the adjacent fire museum. Festival admission slightly higher.

Enjoy the nostalgia of riding on real trolleys as they make 3.5-mile round-trip excursions through the East Windsor woodlands. The museum owns nearly eighty trolleys collected from all over the world, and you can learn lots about these vintage cars in the beautiful visitor center, which also includes a library, theater, gift shop, and restrooms. Half of the trolleys are housed in five storage barns; the remainder sit on the side of the tracks, waiting for restoration. Of the dozen or more that have been restored, two to eight may be out on the tracks on any given day. The cars run every fifteen minutes; your admission ticket buys you unlimited rides and a tour of the visitor center, which houses several restored cars, a steam locomotive (for Thomas the Tank Engine fans), and a large model trolley collection.

Come in October and December for special festivities. From mid-October to just before Halloween, come for the Pumpkin Patch ride on the weekends. Planned especially for children ages three to ten, it features games, treats, prizes, and rides to a nearby pumpkin field, where each rider chooses a pumpkin to take home. In December, the Winterfest features decorated cars and a canopy of colorful lights along the track through the woods. This evenings-only (5:00 to 9:00 p.m.) festival often begins shortly after Thanksgiving and goes on through December 30.

The museum also has a Trolley Stop Snack Shop with an outdoor seating area; birthday parties and group outings can be arranged here.

Connecticut Fire Museum (all ages)

58 North Road; (860) 623-4732; www.ctfiremuseum.org. Open in May and June on Saturday from 10:00 a.m. to 4:00 p.m. and Sunday noon to 4:00 p.m.; in July and August on Wednesday through Saturday and on Sunday at those same hours; and in September and October on weekends only, noon to 4:00 p.m. $–$$. Includes admission to the adjacent trolley museum.

This museum next door to the Connecticut Trolley Museum houses an amazing collection of vintage fire-fighting vehicles and equipment. An original 1904 switchboard alarm system, which still operates, is preserved exactly as it would have been used in decades past. The main hall contains twenty-one trucks, from a turn-of-the-twentieth-century horse-drawn sleigh to a 1955 Zabek pumper. Other memorabilia, tools, and model fire trucks are also displayed. This museum is crowded, but if you love fire engines, this is the place to come.

Where to Eat

Maine Fish and Seafood Restaurant. Bridge Street (Route 140); (860) 623-2281. Seafood, sandwiches, burgers, and more. Open Monday through Saturday at 10:30 a.m. and Sunday at noon, for lunch and dinner, pretty much daily, year-round. $–$$

Where to Stay

Best Western Colonial Inn. 161 Bridge Street; (860) 623-9411. 120 rooms, outdoor pool, patio, and gardens, whirlpool, steam bath, restaurant, continental breakfast. $$

Holiday Inn Express–Bradley Airport. 260 Main Street; (860) 627-6585. 115 rooms, continental breakfast, exercise room. $$$–$$$$

Manchester

First the summer camping ground of the Podunk Indians and later called "Silktown" because of its fabrics and paper mills, Manchester is now a mostly residential area just 9 miles to the east of Hartford. It seems that shopping mall developers like the open farmlands around Manchester, a fact that has forever altered the rural landscape outside of the historic town center. Visiting families may want to shop till they drop—or just drop in to one of Connecticut's children's museums and a few other attractions instead.

Lutz Children's Museum (ages 2 to 10)

247 South Main Street; (860) 643-0949; www.lutzmuseum.org. Open Tuesday through Friday 9:00 a.m. to 5:00 p.m., and Saturday and Sunday noon to 5:00 p.m. $

Devoted to making interesting concepts in art, history, science, and nature accessible to children, the Lutz offers hands-on experiences for children from toddlerhood to ten. Special activities, experiments, and workshops lead to discoveries that are reinforced by the opportunity to participate. Live domestic, native, and exotic animals engage the youngest visitors most dramatically. Other do-touch exhibits on natural history and science capture the attention of older siblings. A large playground on the grounds provides an outlet for energy. Another outdoor portion of the museum is the **Oak Grove Nature Center** on Oak Grove Street. Its nature trails are open daily from dawn to dusk at no charge.

The Fire Museum (all ages)

Connecticut Firemen's Historical Society, 230 Pine Street; (860) 649-9436. Open mid-April through mid-November on Saturday only, from noon to 4:00 p.m. or by special arrangement. $, children under 5 free.

If the trucks at the Connecticut Fire Museum in East Windsor weren't enough to please you, come here to see more. Located in a turn-of-the-twentieth-century firehouse, the collection includes hand-pulled, horse-drawn, steam-powered, and motorized trucks, along with other fire-fighting equipment such as buckets, hats, helmets, tools, and lanterns. The model and toy fire engines are very appealing. Exhibits were recently revamped over the two spacious floors of this vintage building.

Wickham Park (all ages)

1329 West Middle Turnpike; (860) 528-0856. Open April through October daily from 9:30 a.m. to dusk. Parking fee, $.

This former estate has a breathtaking spread of more than ten acres of formal ornamental gardens. Panoramic views of the woodlands, ponds, and brooks of the 215 acres of the park provide incentive to play and picnic here. Walking trails, a playground, an aviary, a log cabin, a snack bar, and sports facilities encourage day-tripping families to stop for a break from the museums.

Where to Eat

Romano's Macaroni Grill. 170 Slater Street; (860) 648-8819. Primarily Italian food plus steaks, chops, and chicken, for lunch and dinner from 11:00 a.m. daily. Kids' menu. Not exactly picturesque, but convenient, especially if you went to the mall. $–$$

Where to Stay

Clarion Suites Inn. 191 Spencer Street; (860) 643-5811 or (800) 992-4004. 104 suites with kitchen, dining area, living room, fireplace. Outdoor pool, sports court, exercise room. Pets welcome. Full breakfast. $$$$

Hartford

The hub of the county is, of course, the state's capital city of Hartford. Connecticut's oldest city, it holds a wealth of historical, cultural, and educational attractions. Founded in 1636 by Thomas Hooker and his Puritan followers, Hartford evolved from a peaceful agrarian community to a bustling industrial metropolis by 1900. The first city in the United States to be fully electrified, Hartford was by that time reputedly the wealthiest city in the nation. Well-established as the center of the insurance industry, it was also a center for the production of firearms, machine tools, typewriters, and bicycles.

Hartford's neighborhoods grow more diverse with each wave of immigrants, and the people within the city limits invested their talents in building a city of "firsts." Bushnell Park was the first public park in the United States to be conceived, built, and paid for by its citizens through popular vote. Elizabeth Park Rose Garden was the first municipal rose garden in the country. The Wadsworth Atheneum was the nation's first public art museum. These and other important fixtures of the city provide ample incentive to explore Hartford time and time again. This guide contains only the best sites for families. Try to get your hands on a Greater Hartford tourism pamphlet for thumbnail descriptions of all of Hartford's excellent museums, parks, and historic sites. To get around town, consider the **free** Hartford Star Shuttle, which operates about every twelve minutes, Monday through Friday from 7:00 a.m.

to 11:00 p.m. and on Saturday from 3:00 to 11:00 p.m. (see http://Hartford.com/shuttle_map.php).

Connecticut Science Center (all ages)

50 Columbus Boulevard and Phoenix Plaza at Adriaen's Landing; (860) 727-0457; www.ctsciencecenter.org. Check the Web site or call for details of hours and admission prices.

The flashiest—and undoubtedly the most well-funded—and pretty much inarguably the *best* new attraction in Connecticut, if not all of New England, is the amazingly interactive Connecticut Science Center, at Adriaen's Landing in Hartford. Slated to open in late spring 2008, the new center offers lifelong science learning opportunities, but its primary mission is to inspire children to appreciate and embrace the world of science. As they put it in their own publicity materials, which, other than the skeleton of the building, was all that was available before this volume's press time, this nonprofit center "will spark creative imagination and an appreciation for science by immersing visitors in fun and educational hands-on, interactive experiences."

Now that's an understatement from a place that promises to be phenomenal.

More than 200 exhibits are in development for this dynamic—and enormous—learning and discovery place taking shape in our capital city. You'll see that the minute you enter Science Alley, the 130-foot-high central artery that leads into the center from both Columbus Boulevard and the new Phoenix Plaza, part of the dramatic revitalization of Hartford's Connecticut River waterfront district. Bridges crossing Science Alley connect to such exhibit galleries as Forces in Motion, a series of stream channels, vortex pools, water jets, and fountains that present interactive experiments with forces and properties found in nature. This gallery of physical science offers large-scale elements that magnify motion-related phenomena and accommodate multiple users who can compare efforts, strategies, and results. A low-friction air table with toy sailboats, for instance, engages visitors in experiments that reveal that sailboats are pulled rather than pushed from behind by the wind. A high-speed camera records the changing shapes of a dropped object on impact. Other exhibits invite visitors to explore robotics and to hear, see, and feel the energy of sound and light.

The Sight and Sound Experience makes sound and music visible, using varied media to display the patterns and behaviors of music. In the Groove Room, for instance, you can orchestrate a symphony of sound and light using your own hand gestures in thin air. The Sports Lab invites you to use math and science to analyze your performance at games and activities. You can bounce, balance, or just about bonk off the walls in this space and still find a parallel science concept to help you define and refine your endeavors. Here and in the Picture of Health gallery, you'll discover the center's strong message about the mechanics and health benefits of physical activity and cardiovascular fitness, not to mention mental fitness. Through face captures and voiceprints, among other intriguing interactive elements, you'll learn about DNA, genetic traits, stress, motivation, and choice-making. The Planet Earth and Exploring Space galleries include solar system exhibits about exploration for signs of life in our galaxy; the Galaxy and Beyond exhibits focus on remote exploration of the Milky Way and cosmic questions about the universe. You can even "fly over" Mars in a joystick-equipped flight chair, surrounded by real images of the red planet from recent missions.

The Invention Dimension gallery features made-here products such as the Wiffle Ball but also explores the process of invention. Visitors can solve puzzles and apply imagination and logic to solve physical and abstract riddles. In the earth sciences galleries, you'll explore the River of Life (using the Connecticut River as a window to lessons on ecology and more), and you'll explore weather as a window to the environment and considerations of climate change and the effects that life on earth has on the earth itself. The story of energy is told in the Smart Energy Gallery, where a realistic driving simulator puts visitors in an urgent "race against resources." The 3-D Science Theater is a 200-seat venue for state-of-the-art science and nature films.

Much more is evolving here as the months go on, and some of the above may even change before opening day. The outcome of that development process is bound to be impressive if the dramatic building at the riverbank is any reflection of the creative team of scientists at work on this premier education center. Come here as fast as you can, as soon as the opening of this space is announced. Visitor information (as it becomes available), images, and descriptions of the galleries are posted on the Web site. Check it out—it's amazing!

Old State House (ages 4 and up)

800 Main Street; (860) 522-6766; www.ctosh.org. Open year-round (except major holidays), Tuesday through Friday 11:00 a.m. to 5:00 p.m., and Saturday from 10:00 a.m. to 5:00 p.m. Special programs (free with admission) for children and families on Saturdays in the Holcombe Education Center; other programming $–$$; children under 6 are free.

Many tourists begin a trip to Hartford here. Having undergone a complete restoration, the state house is the perfect place in which families can orient themselves to the city and gain some perspective on its laudable history. Designed by Charles Bulfinch and constructed in 1796, on the site of the founding of the colony in 1636 by Thomas Hooker, the building is the oldest state house in the nation, established in service of the American people and their new Constitution.

The site on which George Washington greeted French General Rochambeau in 1780 when he arrived to assist the Patriot cause, the halls of the Old State House have also echoed with the footsteps of Lafayette, Andrew Jackson, and many other principal players of American history. Both the *Amistad* and the Prudence Crandall trials took place here. If you are thinking that this must be, therefore, a dusty, stodgy relic that expects quiet awe from whispering students on class trips, you've made a terrible mistake.

Canoe Cruises under the City

One of the most amazing of all day trips a family might make in Connecticut is the incredible underground canoe trip offered by **Huck Finn Adventures** (see the Canton/Collinsville section). Limited to eight to twelve people ages nine or older, these guided tours under the city of Hartford go belowground after a shuttle ride that leaves from Charter Oak Landing. For about two hours (with a trip total of about three and a half hours), you explore the buried Park River, which flows through a fascinating system of flood control tunnels. In water of about bathtub depth, you'll glide in the dim underworld, doing some sound and light experiments and even drifting in the total darkness for three to seven minutes when you all turn off your headlamps. John Kulick provides a narration explaining the mechanics of the system and pointing out sites of interest. What an experience! Call (860) 693-0385 for more details. $$$$

The beautifully restored Old State House is anything but stodgy. With public restrooms, total handicapped (and stroller) accessibility, public telephones, and an Acoustiguide audio tour option, the building is bright, sparkling, airy—and yes, entertaining—despite its hallowed-halls reputation. It actually invites children to touch, to run, to cheer, to ask questions. In addition to a fabulous museum store (which specializes in Connecticut-made crafts), you'll find gallery exhibits of art and history. Don't miss the colorful and interactive multimedia *History Is All around Us* exhibit, which tells the story of the city across six centuries. You can also see portions of the collection of Steward's Museum, a re-creation of the state's first museum, founded by Joseph Steward, collector of everything extraordinary, impossible, and downright fraudulent. A smorgasbord of delights Barnumesque in nature, the museum has among its many "natural and other curiosities" a unicorn's horn, an elephant's molar, a whole Bengal tiger, and an ostrich egg, just to name a few.

Wadsworth Atheneum (ages 4 and up)

600 Main Street; (860) 278-2670; www.wadsworthatheneum.org. Open year-round except on Monday, Tuesday, and major holidays (check the Web site for the exact schedule of holiday closings. Regular hours are 11:00 a.m. to 5:00 p.m. Wednesday through Friday; 10:00 a.m. to 5:00 p.m. Saturday and Sunday; and 11:00 a.m. to 8:00 p.m. the first Thursday of each month. $–$$, children 12 and under free. Discounted admission ($) on First Thursdays from 5:00 to 8:00 p.m.

Just two blocks from the Old State House is the Wadsworth Atheneum, currently a midsize museum housing more than 45,000 works from ancient to modern times. The nation's oldest continuously operating public art museum, the atheneum has a well-deserved reputation as one of the finest museums of its kind in the United States, and it is likely to become even better when it unveils its upcoming multimillion-dollar, 50,000-square-foot expansion across Prospect Street, into the 1920 neoclassical building that once was home to the *Hartford Times*. Even now, visitors can enjoy spacious exhibition galleries showcasing an excellent collection of nineteenth-century French and American Impressionist masters, major works from the Hudson River School, Old Master paintings, American and European decorative arts, a costume and textile gallery, several rooms from important architectural periods, the *Amistad* collection of African-American art, and a gallery of contemporary art.

The museum offers a wonderful service to children—ask the folks at the main desk for "art cards," which make the museum appealing to and manageable for kids. Each of the fifteen or more colorful cards has a game, a search, or an idea for exploring the galleries with young children.

The museum's cafeteria has a children's menu, the exceptional gift shop is a place in which you could do all your holiday shopping, and the calendar of events includes films, workshops, concerts, and tours for families with young children. Special family activities and gallery tours directed to children are offered on First Thursdays, the first Thursday of each month. An annual festival of holiday trees is staged each December.

Bushnell Park and Carousel (all ages)

Elm and Jewell Streets; Bushnell Park Foundation (860) 232-6710; www.bushnellpark .org. Park open daily year-round, dawn to dusk; free. Walking tours typically offered from noon to 1:30 p.m.; call for schedule. Carousel (860-585-5411 for the New England Carousel Museum, which oversees the carousel) open from May through August, Tuesday through Sunday from 11:00 a.m. to 5:00 p.m., and September and October, 11:00 a.m. to 5:00 p.m. Thursday through Sunday; it is closed in severe weather. $1 per ride.

Just west of Hartford's Ancient Burying Ground Cemetery on Main Street, pass under the Soldiers and Sailors Memorial Arch on Jewell Street at the entrance to the park.

Spend some time exploring America's oldest public park, established in 1854. Landscaped as an arboretum, its plantings, monuments, fountains, and bridges are pointed out in the wonderful free pamphlet *Bushnell Park Tree Walks,* available in the Old State House, the capitol building, or from the DEP office at 165 Capitol Avenue. An art gallery showing works by local artists is in the park's pumphouse, which is an actual working pump station for the city's flood control authority. Throughout the park are statues of famous Connecticut citizens, such as Israel Putnam, and monuments honoring veterans of foreign wars. The memorial arch, for instance, is dedicated to the 4,000 Hartford citizens who served in the Civil War. This huge sandstone arch depicts scenes from the war on its terra-cotta frieze. Very interesting guided walking tours of the park can also be arranged (call the Bushnell Park Foundation or visit the Web site), but younger children especially will gladly skip the tour and head straight for the park's most popular feature: After you pass through the soldiers' arch, immediately look to your left and you'll find the Bushnell Park Carousel in a low brown pavilion with stained-glass windows encircling its upper walls.

Managed for the City of Hartford by the New England Carousel Museum in Bristol, this gorgeous 1914 carousel was hand carved by master craftsmen Stein and Goldstein; its band organ is a 1924 Wurlitzer. Charming murals, lit by 800 lights, portray the seasons of the year. Forty-eight exceptionally well-restored prancing horses on gleaming brass poles provide the best carousel ride we've had in the state. Thirty-six of the steeds are jumpers, which go up and down; the rest are stationary. Two ornate chariots complete the set. Compared to others we rode, this carousel is fast. Hold onto toddlers, parents, and don't be fooled by the slower warm-up of the first pass. You pay for each ride, so bring a pocketful of bills. I think you'll ride this one more than once. If you're in the city on December 31, come for the carousel's First Night celebration, a great way to hail the New Year. You might also enjoy the Haunted Carousel festivities in late October, of course, for Halloween.

State Capitol Building (ages 6 and up)

210 Capitol Avenue; (860) 240-0222; www.cga.state.ct.us/capitoltours. Free one-hour tours of the capitol and the Legislative Office Building year-round on weekdays on the quarter hours between 9:15 a.m. and 1:15 p.m. and on Saturday from April through October between 10:15 a.m. and 2:15 p.m. In July and August, a 2:15 p.m. tour is added on weekdays. Closed on state holidays.

When you escape the enchanting music of the Wurlitzer, you might notice the gleaming gold dome of the state capitol building high on the hill to the right (or west) of the carousel. You can't miss it, actually. It's the icing on a rather overstated piece of cake, so to speak. Opened in 1879, the Connecticut State Capitol Building features architecture that has been the subject of much commentary. Words like "monstrosity" have been used to describe this remarkable structure, but few families will be offended by its departures from architectural purism. To a child, this behemoth is just grand.

You can take a guided tour or stroll here yourselves. Pick up a self-guided tour brochure in Room 101 (to your left and toward the back of the lobby if you've entered from the front vestibule). The tour includes visits to the public galleries of the assembly rooms, explanations of the functions of major offices, and information on how a bill becomes law.

If you are touring on your own, your first stop might be the main rotunda from which you can look up at the magnificent dome. The first floor also includes several pieces of sculpture—some huge, some graceful, like the young Nathan Hale. A large collection of Civil War memorabilia in the west wing is impressive; it includes uniforms, many former U.S. flags, and the equipment of important personages.

Hartford **Extras**

If you are on a whirlwind tour of Hartford, visit the above-described attractions first. If your schedule allows other pleasures, choose from among the following sites.

- **Connecticut Historical Society.** 1 Elizabeth Street; (860) 236-5621; www.chs.org. A beautiful facility with hundreds of products, furnishings, artifacts, and portraits related to Connecticut history. Open noon to 5:00 p.m. Tuesday through Friday and Sunday. Excellent multimedia exhibit on the *Amistad* incident; charmingly low-tech but really fun interactive exhibit called *Choice, Chance, and Change,* on immigration; and excellent hands-on and dress-up opportunites in *Tours and Detours through Early Connecticut,* which focuses on the colonial and Revolutionary periods. Great library, great bookstore, family events throughout year. $–$$
- **Charter Oak Landing.** Riverfront Plaza; follow signs from Brainard Road exit off I-91; (860) 722-6505. Thankfully rescued from decay as part of the work of an organization called Riverfront Recapture (860-293-0131; www.riverfront.org), the plaza has a playground, gazebo, benches, walkways, a boat launch, and tons of activities from the arts to sports. It is now linked to Great River Park across the river. Riverside Park is also right nearby. Check the Web site or call either phone number to get the schedule of events, or just grab a picnic and have a good time here. Free; events might charge a fee.
- **Travelers Tower.** 1 Tower Square; (860) 277-4208. If it's a clear day, this is a great place to have a look at the lay of the land. Elevator ride, then 100 stairs. Open year-round, but free tours mid-May to late October. Check out the Web site, http://hartford.omaxfield .com/travelers.html.
- **Bushnell Memorial Hall.** 166 Capitol Avenue; (860) 246-6807. Designed in the 1930s by the architects of New York City's Radio City Music Hall, this National Historic Landmark has a year-round slate of top-billed performing arts, including a family matinee series. Home of Connecticut Opera, Hartford Ballet, Hartford Symphony. Promenade Gallery features works of area artists. Visitors are welcome to see the theater; free forty-five-minute backstage tours are available year-round by appointment. Call (860) 987-6000. $$–$$$$

Museum of Connecticut History (ages 8 and up)

231 Capitol Avenue; (860) 566-3056; www.museumofcthistory.org. Open year-round, Monday through Friday from 9:00 a.m. to 4:00 p.m., Saturday from 9:00 a.m. to 3:00 p.m. Closed on Sunday and state holidays. Free.

This beautiful collection is housed in the same magnificent building as the Connecticut Supreme Court and the Connecticut State Library, opposite the capitol building. Check out the library's incredible main reading room while you are here. The museum exhibits include aspects of Connecticut history from all periods, with examples of Connecticut products such as Colt firearms, clocks, hats, furniture, and more, with a focus on government, industrial, and military history. See the table on which Lincoln signed the Emancipation Proclamation. See the 1622 Royal Charter of the Colony of Connecticut and learn the Charter Oak story. Have a look at Freedom Trail quilts, which portray the important story of the state's African-American experience, and see the portraits of Connecticut's governors. Changing exhibitions, special tours, and events of interest to families are on the calendar. This museum is well worth a second day in the city if your kids are old enough to appreciate it.

Elizabeth Park and Rose Gardens (all ages)

Prospect and Asylum Avenues; (860) 722-6514 or (860) 231-9443; www.elizabethpark .org. Open daily year-round, dawn to dusk. Greenhouses open Monday through Friday, except holidays, from 8:00 a.m. to 3:00 p.m. Free.

The first municipal rose garden in the country, this beautiful park has 15,000 rose bushes of 800 varieties. With lanes, arbors, and gazebos that bring *The Secret Garden* to mind, the formal garden is most glorious in late spring and throughout summer. Truly a haven within the bustle of the city, Elizabeth Park's rock gardens, ornamental grasses, perennial and herb beds, and a trail through its forest of specimen trees make it a lovely spot to play.

Special events such as concerts, poetry readings, or storytellings are sometimes on the calendar here. Check the Web site calendar for events that might interest your family. In mid-June come to the park's gala celebration of peak rose season. Called Rose Weekend, the event features music, food, art, tours, and activities for the whole family.

The park extends across Prospect Avenue to acres of athletic fields and a children's play area with swings, tennis courts, and a picnic grove. The Elizabeth Park Overlook provides a panoramic view of the city as well as a gorgeous spot to watch the sun rise. Frisbee players, kite flyers, joggers, in-line skaters, bicyclers, and brides and grooms regularly inhabit this space in spring, summer, and fall. In winter you can sled on the huge hill near the overlook or skate (conditions permitting) on the pond. The Pond House Cafe (860-231-8823) is open from Tuesday through Saturday for lunch from 11:00 a.m. to 2:30 p.m. and for dinner from 5:00 to 9:00 p.m. or for Sunday brunch from 10:00 a.m. to 2:30 p.m.

Mark Twain House and Museum Center (ages 6 and up)
351 Farmington Avenue, at Woodland Street; (860) 247-0998; www.marktwainhouse .org. Open year-round Monday through Saturday from 9:30 a.m. to 5:30 p.m. and on Sunday from noon to 5:30 p.m. January through March, closed on Tuesday. Closed January 1, Easter Sunday, July 4, Thanksgiving, and December 24 and 25. $$$, children under 5 free. Last tour 4:30 p.m. daily.

Next on a must-do tour of Hartford is the home of novelist Samuel Langhorne Clemens, who gained fame as Mark Twain. It is located on a property known as Nook Farm, once the site of a lively community of artists, writers, and other literate folk. Quite bucolic in the last decades of the nineteenth century, Nook Farm is now nearly eclipsed by the sprawl of Hartford and its suburb of West Hartford. Nevertheless, the homes and grounds give visitors a sense of the area's former air of gentility and simplicity.

Of course, simplicity is nowhere to be found in the Twain house. The Gilded Age with all its splendid cacophony of detail is apparent in every inch of this remarkable home. Guided tours here are among the most excellent tours we have taken in the state. You will hear marvelous tales of the family's life and a generous sampling of the owner's sardonic wit and wisdom. While living here from 1874 to 1891 with his wife, Olivia, and their three daughters, Clemens wrote *Tom Sawyer, Huckleberry Finn, The Prince and the Pauper, A Connecticut Yankee in King Arthur's Court,* and *Life on the Mississippi.*

The nineteen rooms of the house are restored to reflect its appearance in 1881, when the house was redecorated by a guild of artisans including Louis Comfort Tiffany. The tour includes the family living quarters and Twain's private study (where he did much of his writing). Nearly half the decorations and furnishings in the house were owned by the family, including many photographs, a feature that gives the suggestion that Twain himself might appear in a doorway at any moment.

Before or after a tour, don't miss the magnificent three-story Museum Center with exhibit spaces, a lecture hall, classrooms, a museum store, and a seventy-five-seat cafe with an outdoor terrace.

Harriet Beecher Stowe Center (ages 6 and up)
77 Forest Street at Farmington Avenue; (860) 522-9258; www.harrietbeecherstowe center.org. Open year-round Tuesday through Saturday from 9:30 a.m. to 4:30 p.m. and Sunday noon to 4:30 p.m. Open on Monday also from Memorial Day through Columbus Day and in December. Closed major holidays. $$, children under 5 free.

Just across the lawn from the Twain House is the 1871 cottage built for Stowe and her family. The house is austere compared to its gaudy neighbor, but it is in itself a serenely beautiful Victorian dwelling that has been restored in every detail. The last residence of Stowe, whose *Uncle Tom's Cabin* can be said to have changed the course of U.S. history, this house is furnished mostly with items belonging to the Stowe family. The kitchen is patterned closely after the model kitchen described by Stowe and her sister Catherine in their book *The American Woman's Home.* In this home, too, one fairly expects its owner to step into the room and continue the grand tour.

Docents here present the center's renewed emphasis on family-friendly tours; in fact, there is a special children's tour option. The house is filled with many decorative artworks done by Stowe herself. An accomplished painter, she often painted the flowers she loved to grow in her gardens. Outside, the gardens have been replanted with the many exotic and native perennials that Stowe grew here before her death in 1896.

Tours of the Stowe house include a trip to her niece's house on the corner of the Nook Farm property at Farmington Avenue and Forest Street. The Katherine Seymour Day House contains Stowe's personal belongings and excellent historical exhibits that explain the effect of *Uncle Tom's Cabin* on the abolitionist movement and the Civil War. It also includes exhibits on nineteenth-century architecture, decorative arts, history, and literature. An extensive research library on these subjects as well as social reform, the women's suffrage movement, and women's studies in general is also open by appointment. Children are welcome to use the library, but a letter of recommendation from a teacher or librarian is necessary to gain access.

Tour tickets are purchased in the Carriage House Visitors Center, which has an introductory exhibit on the Beecher family as well as an excellent gift shop. The Stowe Center hosts a few annual events designed especially for children. A celebration of Stowe's birthday is among these, typically in mid-June. Check the center's Web site for this year's dates and for other events.

Where to Eat

Black-Eyed Sally's. 350 Asylum Street; (860) 278-RIBS. Award-winning Cajun, creole, and barbecue, gumbo, grits, collard greens—all the real, down-home Southern cooking you can eat. Come for po' boy sandwiches, pulled pork or chicken, or chicken-fried steak. Absolutely delicious. The joint hops after 9:00 p.m. with the best open-mike blues jam anywhere around; come early with the kids. Closed on Sunday; dinner only on Saturday; lunch and dinner Monday through Friday. $–$$$

Agave Grill. 100 Allyn Street; (860) 882-1557. Zesty, fresh, spicy, fun Mexican-Caribbean food in a zippy place right in the heart of downtown, not far from Bushnell Park. Excellent "guac" made right at your table. Entirely family-friendly. Open daily for lunch and dinner. $$–$$$

Firebox Restaurant. 539 Broad Street; (860) 246-1222. Not far from the capitol building, the establishment in a vintage brick factory complex serves up locally produced foods with a true flair for flavor and freshness. Children's options are not on the menu, but the folks here are eager to please families. Lunch Monday through Friday; dinner Monday through Saturday. $$–$$$

In the city's South End is Franklin Avenue, also known as Hartford's Little Italy. Stroll the sidewalks between Elliot and Eaton Streets and search for your own favorite eatery among the espresso cafes, bakeries, grocers, and full-service restaurants. Our favorite is **Carbone's** (588 Franklin Avenue; 860-296-9646). Pricey but delicious. Children very welcome among adult diners. $$$

Where to Stay

Crowne Plaza Hartford–Downtown. 50 Morgan Street; (860) 549-2400. 350

units, restaurant, exercise room, outdoor pool. $$$

The Goodwin. 1 Hayes Street, at Goodwin Square, opposite the Civic Center; (860) 246-7500 or (800) 777-7803. 124 units, including 11 suites, restaurant, health facilities. $$$$

Hilton Hartford Hotel. 315 Trumbull Street at the Civic Center; (860) 728-5151 or (800) 325-3535. 390 units including 6 suites, restaurant, health club, sauna, indoor pool. $$$$

Residence Inn by Marriott Hartford Downtown. 942 Main Street, near Market Street; (860) 524-5550 or (800) 331-3131. 120 rooms, studios, and suites. In-room kitchens, complimentary hot breakfast buffet. Restaurant. $$$$

West Hartford

West Hartford sashays outward from the left of Hartford just as smoothly as Fred Astaire and with just as much debonair grace. In its upscale downtown less than 5 miles from downtown Hartford you'll find terrific shops and restaurants and a couple of attractions great for a family day trip. Peruse the boutiques, visit the Noah Webster House, spend some time at the Children's Museum, and have dinner at one of nearly thirty restaurants.

Noah Webster House/Museum of West Hartford History
(ages 6 and up)   🏛
227 South Main Street; (860) 521-5362; www.noahwebsterhouse.org. Open for tours Thursday through Monday from 1:00 to 4:00 p.m. Last tour 3:00 p.m. Call for extended summer hours and holiday closings. $–$$, children under 6 free.

The birthplace and childhood home of the author of the first American dictionary, Noah Webster House is one of the best colonial restorations in the state, not least of all because it was the home of one of America's finest citizens. An excellent short film introduces visitors to Webster's story and the history of the house, and guided tours by costumed docents fill in the gaps of the tale.

The house has an active calendar of family and children's events—genealogy workshops, open-hearth cooking, colonial dancing and games, and more. Children going into grades four, five, and six can participate in the Colonial Child Summer Camp, a week of activities typical of an eighteenth-century childhood.

Even if you come only for the day, you'll see Webster's desk and clocks and 200 original editions of his books, including his *Blue-Backed Speller* and the dictionary he spent nearly twenty-seven years writing.

The Children's Museum (ages 2 through 10)

950 Trout Brook Drive; (860) 231-2824; www.thechildrensmuseumct.org. Open year-round, Tuesday through Saturday 10:00 a.m. to 5:00 p.m. and Sunday from noon to 5:00 p.m. Closed on Easter, Thanksgiving, and Christmas. Also open on Monday holidays, school vacations, and in July and August. $$–$$$, children under 2 **free.** Planetarium and laser shows are an additional charge, which varies according to program.

One of the oldest children's museums in the state, this facility has a brand-new name and renewed focus on igniting preschool and toddler curiosity through science and nature. The newest exhibit areas have at their heart the guiding philosophy that scientific principles are best learned through experience. All exhibits are interactive, allowing children and adults to discover a range of scientific facts or truths and to conduct experiments that reinforce those findings.

Major changing exhibitions, which run approximately two months, occur in an exhibition hall beside the permanent exhibit areas. In the Idea Zone, learn about gears and motion, race a car on the LEGO racetrack, or walk through a kaleidoscope. In Critter Crossing, explore the toddler play space with nature-themed, hands-on discovery centers. In the Kids' Corner, you can explore concepts of sound, light, touch—and bubbles. Outside are a wildlife sanctuary area that provides a home for a diverse collection of birds, reptiles, and mammals from around the world and an outdoor full-scale walk-in model of Connecticut's state animal, the sperm whale. The Gengras Planetarium, featuring a new SciDome digital projection system, explores the sun, stars, and galaxy along with laser light shows accompanied by environmental or mythical narratives. These shows are suitable for the whole family, including children of all ages.

Where to Eat

A. C. Petersen Farms Restaurant. 240 Park Road; (860) 233-8483. Open for breakfast, lunch, and dinner from 7:00 a.m. to 11:00 p.m., this landmark was renovated but is still old-fashioned at heart. Great traditional American meals and terrific ice cream, perfect for families. $–$$

Back Porch Bistro. 971 Farmington Avenue (rear); (860) 231-1922. Friendly service, cheerful decor, tasty American fare. Outside dining in season. Open from 11:30 a.m. Monday through Friday for lunch, and from 5:00 p.m. Monday through Saturday for dinner. $$

Elbow Room. 986 Farmington Avenue; (860) 236-6195. This cheery place has great nooks and the best macaroni and cheese on the planet. Eat up on the roof in warm weather. So fun. Open daily for dinner; lunch Monday through Saturday; Sunday brunch. $$

Where to Stay

West Hartford Inn. 900 Farmington Avenue; (860) 236-3221. 50 units, exercise room, restaurant, continental breakfast. $$$

Farmington

From West Hartford take Route 4 south to the pristinely restored seventeenth-, eighteenth-, and nineteenth-century homes that line the main street of affluent and elegant Farmington. From these homes to the prestigious Miss Porter's School to the upscale shops and restaurants, Farmington presents the polished side of Hartford County. Having played a principal role in the *Amistad* story, Farmington also was an important station on the Underground Railroad, contributing to its importance in the history of the state and the nation.

Farmington Historical Society Tours of the *Amistad* Sites
(ages 8 and up)

Main Street; (860) 678-1645; www.farmingtonhistoricalsociety-ct.org. Tours offered in May and September. $

This organization has created a guided tour of the nine Farmington sites associated with the Africans of the *Amistad.* Visit the places where the Africans lived and studied while in Farmington; see the gravesite of one who lost his life. Tour the hall where abolitionists met and the homes and churches of citizens who spoke out against slavery and in support of the *Amistad* group. Most of the sites are in private hands today, so a tour provides the best and easiest access.

Hill-Stead Museum (ages 8 and up)

35 Mountain Road; (860) 677-9064 or (860) 677-4787. Open May through October, Tuesday through Sunday 10:00 a.m. to 5:00 p.m. and November through April, Tuesday through Sunday 11:00 a.m. to 4:00 p.m. One-hour guided tour; last tour an hour before closing. $–$$, children under 6 free.

This colonial revival home is not the place to come with small, squirmy folk who'd rather be chasing the butterflies on the gorgeous front lawn of this 150-acre country estate. It is, however, a fine place to come if you and the children would like to see the magnificent artworks that hang in the mansion designed by Stanford White and owner Theodate Pope Riddle, herself an architect. The house is beyond reproach in its taste and gentility as well as its elegant design, and its outstanding art collection is unparalleled by other house museums. Cassatt, Degas, Manet, Monet, and other French and American Impressionists are on the walls of this beautiful home. The decorative arts are of the caliber that make docents turn ashen at the sight of toddlers.

The *Amistad* Story

From Havana, Cuba, on June 28, 1839, the Spanish ship *Amistad* set sail with fifty-three Africans who had been taken from their homeland to be sold as slaves. On their way to another part of Cuba for what they knew would be a lifetime of enslavement and hard labor, the captives, led by Joseph Cinque, seized control of the ship and forced its owners to set a course for Africa. Under cover of night, however, the navigators charted a northward course, hoping to reach an American slave state before their plot was discovered. Instead, the boat sailed into Long Island Sound, where it was apprehended by the U.S. Navy and taken into custody in New Haven. A two-year trial in which the Africans were defended by John Quincy Adams centered on the question of whether the captives were to be considered slave or free. Eventually declared free, the *Amistad* Africans were sent to Farmington to live while funds were raised to return them to the area in Africa now called Sierra Leone. Thirty-seven survivors from the original group set sail for home as free people again in November 1841, reaching their home shores in January 1842. Nine sites linked to the case and to the lives of the Africans during the waiting period remain in Farmington. The First Church of Christ Congregational in Farmington has maintained its connection to the enslaved Africans of the *Amistad* through ongoing support of the people of Sierra Leone, especially during its recent brutal civil wars. In December 2007 the re-created vessel *Amistad* (see *Amistad* entry in the New Haven section) sailed to Sierra Leone to celebrate the rebuilding of the Hope Primary Day School in Freetown, funded in large part by donations from the church.

School tours are common here, however, and the docents are warmly welcoming and comfortable with youngsters.

Be sure to stroll the wonderfully restored sunken garden and walk the wooded paths through the naturalized bulbs and wildflowers.

Stanley-Whitman House (ages 6 and up)

37 High Street; (860) 677-9222; www.stanleywhitman.org. Open year-round, May through October, Wednesday through Sunday from noon to 4:00 p.m. and on Saturday and Sunday at the same times from November through April only. $

An impeccable restoration of this 1720 house brings the period alive again in this amazingly well-curated site. Tours include a peek behind the scenes through windowlike panels that offer a look at early-eighteenth-century construction methods.

Among the programs directed toward children are family history hikes, toddler programs, ghost walks, a colonial fair, cooking demonstrations, and a holiday candlelight tour. Check the Web site for details. Among the other inside points of interest are a gift shop and an exhibit of archaeological artifacts and discoveries. Outside is a kitchen herb garden.

Day-Lewis Museum (ages 6 and up)
158 Main Street (rear); (860) 677-2754. Open only on Wednesday from 2:00 to 4:00 p.m., March through November, except in August. Call ahead to be sure of hours. $

This small museum, owned by Yale University, is in a colonial post-and-beam house on a piece of property discovered to be the site of human habitation, as well as a trading place, as early as 10,000 years ago. The Native American artifacts unearthed at the site during an archaeological dig are on display here. Arranged by date in four display cases, these objects span several centuries, from the precontact era to the European contact period. Recently renovated extensively, this property also includes Yale's renowned noncirculating research library of English eighteenth-century literature.

Winding Trails Recreation Association and Cross-Country Ski Center (ages 4 and up)
50 Winding Trails Drive, off Route 4; (860) 678-9582; www.windingtrails.org/ski/index. html. Open daily 9:00 a.m. to dusk, weather permitting. Weekend and holiday trail fees are posted each season for adults and children 5 to 12. Children under 5 are always free. Weekdays are less expensive than weekends. Ski rentals also have adult's and children's prices. Ice-skating and sledding at the daily ski rates. Check the Web site for the current rates.

Since 1972, this pretty 350-acre property has been the site of a 20-kilometer trail system for cross-country skiers. Skaters will love the eight-acre natural ice rink on picturesque Walton Pond. Through woodland and past brooks and other spring-fed ponds, the trails are groomed daily and are clearly mapped and posted with signs noting degrees of difficulty. Snowshoeing and back-country trails are also on the property.

Rental skis are available here, as are wooden toddler sleds so the whole family can enjoy a healthy day in the crisp air. You can also try out demo equipment and purchase your own in the retail shop. Waxes, gloves, and hats are among the other goods you can buy there.

The Winding Trails Lodge offers a place for you to warm your toes by the fireplace and wrap your cold fingers around a warm mug of cocoa. If you prefer, remain outside at the tables near the snow-draped pines. Instruction is offered to beginners on weekends at 9:30 and 11:00 a.m., 1:00 and 2:30 p.m., and 10:00 a.m. and 1:00 p.m. on weekdays.

In other seasons, Winding Trails also offers a summer day camp and varied family programs and events; family memberships to the full range of year-round recreation options can also be purchased.

Where to Eat

The Silo Restaurant. 330 Main Street; (860) 677-0149. Children are welcome and will be offered kid-pleasing choices at this family-owned casually fine dining establishment with a basically Italian flair and no pretensions. It tends to cater to a loyal grandma-and-grandpa kind of crowd. Barn-sided dining rooms with a silo in the middle. Open for lunch Monday through Friday; dinner Monday through Saturday. $$–$$$

Scotty's Aurora Cafe. 222 Main Street; (860) 677-6411. In Post Office Square, this friendly little eatery offers breakfast and lunch Monday through Saturday from 7:00 a.m., and on Sunday, breakfast only from 8:00 a.m. to 1:00 p.m. House-made soups, chilis, burgers, and more. $

Where to Stay

Centennial Inn Suites. 5 Spring Lane; (860) 677-4647 or (800) 852-2052. Elegant country inn with 112 suites with kitchen, living room, fireplace, and one or two bedrooms. Outdoor pool, whirlpool, continental breakfast. Pets welcome. $$$$

The Farmington Inn. 827 Farmington Avenue; (860) 677-2821 or (800) 648-9804. 72 units, with 13 suites, restaurant, passes to health club, continental breakfast. $$$$

Hartford Marriott Hotel–Farmington. 15 Farm Springs Road; (860) 678-1000. 381 units, restaurant, health club, indoor and outdoor pools, tennis, game room, jogging trail. $$$$

New Britain/Kensington

Ten miles southeast of Hartford is the small city of New Britain, once nicknamed "Hardware City" with an ethnic population that included every major European nation and most of the minor ones. The steady pace at the Stanley tool works has slowed in recent years, and the immigrant groups have mixed and changed, but the city is much the same—a modest metropolis with a low-key reputation that keeps it well out of the limelight. It has some special treasures, though, inside its city limits and in nearby Kensington. Less than 5 miles southeast of downtown New Britain on Route 372, the small town of Kensington is home to Hungerford Park and the Youth Museum's nature center.

New Britain Youth Museum (ages 2 to 12)

30 High Street; (860) 225-3020; www.newbritainyouthmuseum.org. Open year-round, Tuesday from 10:00 a.m. to 5:00 p.m., with a storytime/activity program at 10:00 a.m.; Wednesday through Friday from noon to 5:00 p.m.; Saturday from 10:00 a.m. to 4:00 p.m., with a themed craft/activity program at 2:00 p.m. Free.

The New Britain Youth Museum is not new—in fact, it recently passed the half-century mark—it's not big, either, or slick, sleek, or sophisticated. Some days it's downright sleepy, and on some days just a few activities take place in its exhibit rooms and play areas. Still, it is a two-thumbs-up terrific place for kids. At this little wonder you

Walnut Hill Park

The New Britain Museum of American Art overlooks **Walnut Hill Park,** designed by Frederick Law Olmsted, who also designed New York City's Central Park. Its sweeping lawns and towering oak trees make it a perfect place to play or picnic. A children's playground, playing fields, and bicycle paths make the park a family destination. A **free** summer music festival at the Miller Bandshell is held in July and August on Monday and Wednesday at 7:30 p.m. An annual American Arts and Crafts Fair in mid-September includes admission to the nearby museum ($$).

may see some of the best exhibitions you've seen anywhere. You also may participate in some of the best and least expensive children's workshops offered anywhere.

Curated by its ever-creative director, Deborah Pfeiffenberger, the museum has an extensive permanent collection of dolls and toys, and a continuing focus on historical and cultural artifacts of childhood. It also has a terrific puppet theater area, a dinosaur room, and a wonderful outdoor play area. For information on the museum's natural history exhibits at Hungerford Park in Kensington, see the separate entry on the next page.

New Britain Museum of American Art (all ages)

56 Lexington Street; (860) 229-0257; www.nbmaa.org. Open year-round, Tuesday, Wednesday, and Friday 11:00 a.m. to 5:00 p.m.; Thursday 11:00 a.m. to 8:00 p.m.; Saturday 10:00 a.m. to 5:00 p.m.; Sunday noon to 5:00 p.m. Closed Monday and holidays. Cafe on the Park is open Tuesday through Saturday 11:30 a.m. to 3:30 p.m. and Sunday noon to 3:30 p.m. $$, children under 12 free. Saturday from 10:00 a.m. to noon is free for everyone.

If you have never taken the children to an art museum, begin here, "where art meets life." Perfect for young families because of its manageable size—even with its recent addition of a stunning 43,000-square-foot wing—this attraction is in every way a gem. Originally housed in the contiguous early-twentieth-century mansion built by William Hart, founder of the Stanley Works tool company, the museum has a full slate of educational programs and three themed audio tours especially designed for children. In the vintage portion of the museum are two features of special importance for families: The Art Lab, created for children ages three to twelve, offers twenty or more hands-on art activities in a variety of media, each of which youngsters can accomplish independently. Computer stations offer art games, a costume rack interprets clothing portrayed in the permanent collection, and puzzles, collage and sculpture opportunities, and music and poetry explorations accompany these. Outfitted with easels, computer stations, and drying racks, the Art Studio offers weekly drop-in children's art classes, special workshops, and exceptionally well-planned birthday parties that feature hands-on arts activities. Check the NBMAA calendar online for information on the Art Start program for preschoolers (Tuesday and Saturday mornings; $; drop-ins welcome) and the Art Explorers program for children ages six to eight (Saturdays; $$; drop-ins welcome); both are excellent introductions to making art. School-vacation programs provide more activities throughout the year; these programs are **free** for the participants when their chaperone pays admission. Whenever you visit, be sure to ask for the *Art Elements* children's booklet—it's a terrific introduction to the collection and a handy aid to enjoying a visit. The museum's 5,000 holdings from the early eighteenth century to the present include some of the greatest treasures of American art. Gilbert Stuart, Asher Durand, Thomas Cole, Frederic Church, Winslow Homer, Maxfield Parrish, John Singer Sargent, Mary Cassatt, Childe Hassam, Georgia O'Keeffe, N. C. Wyeth, Andrew Wyeth, Norman Rockwell, and Thomas Hart Benton are just some of the artists represented here. If that were not enough, the museum offers **free** monthly concerts suitable for families, a gift shop, and a cafe, which overlooks the lovely Walnut Hill Park.

Copernican Space Science Observatory and Planetarium
(ages 4 and up)

1615 Stanley Street, Central Connecticut State University; (860) 832-3399 or (860) 832-2950; www.ccsu.edu/astronomy/. Planetarium shows year-round on the first and third Saturdays of the month at 8:00 p.m. Closed on state holidays. Free.

Located at the top of Copernicus Hall at CCSU, this observatory boasts one of the largest public telescopes in the United States. Special programs on a variety of fascinating themes related to the stars and space science are offered throughout the year for both children and adults. Weather permitting, planetarium shows are followed by a session in the observatory. Exhibits on flight and the American space program are adjacent to the observatory and planetarium.

New Britain Youth Museum at Hungerford Park (ages 2 to 10)
😀 👫 🎮 🍁

191 Farmington Avenue (Route 372); (860) 827-9064; www.newbritainyouthmuseum .org. Trails open dawn to dusk, free of charge. Open year-round, Tuesday through Saturday 10:00 a.m. to 4:30 p.m. Closed on Sunday and Monday. Live-animal programs on Saturday at 11:00 a.m., 1:30 p.m., and 3:30 p.m. year-round; open to those who have paid admission. Exhibit hall admission, $, children under 2 free.

Located on twenty-seven acres of wooded park, swamp, pond, and wetland habitats, the New Britain Youth Museum at Hungerford Park represents the natural history collection of the museum. Indoor exhibits are housed in a restored 1920s show-horse stable. Long-term exhibits are stimulating and detailed, changing sometimes for just a season or lasting a year or two. We have observed outstanding exhibits here, curated by the remarkable Ann Peabody. Check the Web site for the latest installations.

A weather station, aquariums, terrariums, an iguana rain forest habitat complete with waterfall, and a small variety of animals are also indoors. Outside the main exhibit hall are extensive and wonderful gardens, designed as sensory experiences for visitors, who are welcome to taste, feel, look, smell, and touch the plants.

A pig, goat, steer, sheep, and turkeys, ducks, and geese are among the animals in the Hungerford Barnyard; among the animals you might see inside in the Exotic Animal Room are lizards, turtles, snakes, and a leopard tortoise. A trail system and a pond with observation stations are also part of the complex. Picnic tables and trash containers are provided. Frequent programs are open to members and visitors. Some are intended for children only; others are whole-family events. Check the Web site.

Where to Eat

Fatherland. 450 South Main Street; (860) 224-3345. Delicious, authentic Polish food in a low-key setting friendly to families. Excellent house-made soups, several kinds of pierogies, traditional stuffed cabbage, and perfect potato pancakes, including sweet potato ones. Half-size servings for kids. Open for lunch and dinner, Monday through Thursday noon to 8:00 p.m., Fri-day and Saturday until 9:00 p.m., and Sunday to 7:30 p.m. $

Where to Stay

La Quinta Inn and Suites. 65 Columbus Boulevard; (860) 348-1463. Newly rebuilt, stem to stern. 135 rooms, with 4 suites; complimentary full breakfast; restaurant. $$

Rocky Hill/Glastonbury

If your children are attracted to dinosaur research, they'll love Rocky Hill, about 8 miles south of Hartford off I-91. The hills and valleys just west of the Connecticut River are relatively new, you see. The area commonly called "Rockie Hill" in its colonial days was far different 185 million years ago. Then it was a bona fide Jurassic Park—a wide mudflat on the edge of a broad, shallow lake that filled a basin carved by glaciers a few million years before that. The lake was densely populated with vegetation, fish, and small reptiles of a roughly crocodilian description. The dinosaurs roaming nearby liked the menu, so they stayed until their luck ran out in the next ecological disaster.

Now only their tracks remain, a fact discovered during excavations in the 1960s for a modern ecological disaster called an office building. Bulldozer operator Ed McCarthy recognized something unusual about the ground he was clearing, and soon the place was crawling with paleontologists. Now families are the most frequent pilgrims to this ancient site.

Dinosaur State Park (all ages)

400 West Street; (860) 529-8423 or (860) 529-5816; www.dinosaurstatepark.org. Exhibit center open Tuesday through Sunday 9:00 a.m. to 4:30 p.m. year-round, except holidays. $, children under 6 free. Casting area open daily (except holidays) May 1 to October 31 from 9:00 a.m. to 3:30 p.m. at no charge. Park open daily year-round (except holidays) from 9:00 a.m. to 4:30 p.m. at no charge.

Many of the 2,000 Jurassic-period tracks uncovered have been recovered to preserve them, but about 500 are exposed to public view in this amazing park. A giant geodesic dome protects the mostly three-toed impressions from the elements. A walkway around the tracks provides a good view, and a full-scale reproduction of the sort of dinosaur most likely to have made the tracks stands in a running pose on the platform above the pit. The exhibit center also has exhibits on geology, history, and dinosaurs, and two murals show how the region may have looked in the Triassic and Jurassic periods. An auditorium shows related films on weekends and during school vacations.

In the warm months, visitors are invited to make plaster casts of some of the tracks in the outdoor casting area. Signs provide the instructions, but you must provide the supplies necessary to complete the project. Bring a quarter-cup of vegetable oil, ten pounds of plaster of paris, a five-gallon plastic container, and clean-up rags and paper towels. If you decide to do this, you have to be finished by 3:30.

Outside the dome there is no evidence (except in the casting area) of prehistoric animal life, but the park offers sixty acres of nature preserve with more than 2 miles of hiking trails and a picnic area. The Dinosaur Park Arboretum is home to more than 250 species of conifers, plus gingkoes, redwoods, magnolias, and other plants that originated in prehistoric times.

Connecticut Audubon Holland Brook Center at Glastonbury
(all ages)

1361 Main Street; (860) 633-8402; www.ctaudubon.org/centers/glastonbury. Open Tuesday through Friday 1:00 to 5:00 p.m., Saturday 10:00 a.m. to 5:00 p.m., and Sunday 1:00 to 4:00 p.m. Closed major holidays. Free, except for $1 for Discovery Room in nature center.

Explore native flora and fauna in person along the trails of forty-eight-acre Earle Park, then inside at the exhibits of the nature center. Other exhibits examine the ecosystem of the Connecticut River. A hands-on Discovery Room has natural objects to touch, smell, and see as you discover interesting facts about the birds, the bees, the trees, and so much more. A nature shop and bookstore provide great materials for continuing your learning at home and in the field. Year-round programs for families include guided walks, animal observation, and much more.

Ferry 'Cross **the River**

Another way to examine the ecosystem of the Connecticut River is aboard the *Hollister III*, the latest boat in the 350-year-old ferry service that crosses from Rocky Hill to Glastonbury. The original ferry service dates from 1655, when local families used long poles to push along a small raft. Later, a horse on a treadmill in the center of the craft supplied the power for the river crossings, and, in 1876, steam power made the job faster and easier, at least on the horse. Now a diesel towboat leads an open flatboat. Four minutes from one side to the other, the ferry ride is accessible from the Rocky Hill Landing on Route 160 off the Silas Deane Highway or the Glastonbury Landing on Route 160 off Route 17. It runs from May 1 through October 31, weekdays from 7:00 a.m. to 6:45 p.m. and weekends from 10:30 a.m. to 5:00 p.m. You can pay $1 per person to walk on (or $3 per vehicle); pay a bit more for ice cream at the Pilot House at the riverside in Rocky Hill.

Where to Eat

Max Amore. 140 Glastonbury Boulevard in the Somerset Square Shopping Area; (860) 659-2819. You can't miss here—the pizza is wonderful, the toppings are creative, and the pasta dishes are on par with the pizza for innovation. Seafood, poultry, and vegetarian choices are here, too, as are special dishes for children under 10. Lunch and dinner daily, plus a Sunday brunch menu. $$

Min Ghung Asian Bistro. 39 New London Turnpike, #311; (860) 659-2568. Open daily for lunch and dinner, this is a do-not-miss kind of place, perfect for palate-pleasing plate-sharing for the whole family. Excellent, snappy, fun, delicious. Sushi, Korean specialties, and more. $–$$$

Rose's Berry Farm. 295 Matson Hill Road, South Glastonbury; (860) 633-7467. On Sundays in season, have breakfast on Rose's deck overlooking the picking fields of strawberries, blueberries, raspberries, pumpkins, mums, and Christmas trees. When you are full, pick fruit for a home-cooked breakfast tomorrow. Buy fresh-baked muffins and pies, cider, and picnic goodies. $

Where to Stay

Hartford Marriott Rocky Hill. 100 Capital Boulevard; (860) 257-6000 or (800) 228-9290. 250 rooms and suites, restaurant, fitness center, whirlpool, indoor pool. $$

Udderly Woolly Acres B&B. 581 Thompson Street, Glastonbury; (860) 633-4503. Open year-round, this small, certified-organic working farm offers families a two-room suite that includes a sitting room and a spacious bedroom with two twin beds, one child-size trundle bed, and a rollaway bed upon request. A private bath, private entrance, small refrigerator, and hearty breakfast make this a cozy place for families to rest their heads. $$$

Wethersfield

Preserved a mere 5 miles south of the modern hub of Hartford, the historical center of Wethersfield is in itself a miniature museum. Its pretty Main and Broad Streets are chock-full of seventeenth- and eighteenth-century homes that reflect Wethersfield's past. The first permanent settlement in the colony and the most northerly trading post on the Connecticut River, the town has the largest authentic historic district in the state. It is easy to enjoy the fantasy that you have stepped back in time in Wethersfield.

The Wethersfield Historical Society (ages 6 and up)

150 Main Street; (860) 529-7656. Old Academy and Cultural Center open year-round Monday through Saturday from 10:00 a.m. to 4:00 p.m. and on Sunday from 1:00 to 4:00 p.m. The Francis and Hurlbut-Dunham Houses are open mid-May through mid-October, Saturday from 10:00 a.m. to 4:00 p.m. and Sunday from 1:00 to 4:00 p.m. Cove Warehouse open mid-May to mid-October, at those same times. $, children under 16 free.

The Wethersfield Historical Society owns and maintains five historic buildings, four of which are open to the public. The 1790 Hurlbut-Dunham House at 212 Main Street is an elegant late-Georgian brick beauty updated in the mid-1800s in the Italianate style. The Cove Warehouse, at the end of Main Street at Cove Park on the river, is the only warehouse to have survived the flood of 1692 that created the cove; it has exhibits on local maritime industry and history. A research archive and a library of local and state history, genealogy, and architecture are in the 1804 Old Academy. A museum shop, exhibits on Wethersfield's history, and a gallery of changing exhibitions are housed in the Keeney Memorial Cultural Center (860-529-7161) at 200 Main.

Webb-Deane-Stevens Museum (ages 6 and up)

211 Main Street; (860) 529-0612; www.webb-deane-stevens.org. Tours from May 1 to October 31 on Wednesday through Monday from 10:00 a.m. to 4:00 p.m. (last full tour at 3:00 p.m.; 30-minute highlights tour at 3:30 p.m.) and Sundays 1:00 to 4:00 p.m.; in April and November, Saturday 10:00 a.m. to 4:00 p.m. and Sunday 1:00 to 4:00 p.m. December holiday tours daily throughout the month, on weekdays from 10:00 a.m. to 4:00 p.m., on Saturday from 10:00 a.m. to 8:00 p.m., and on Sunday from 1:00 to 4:00 p.m. Closed January 1 to March 31. Tickets are sold for the three-house tour ($$); the Buttolph-Williams House alone ($), and half-price highlights tours ($). Family rates are offered; children under 5 free.

This wonderful museum is composed of three eighteenth-century homes, each restored and furnished to provide a glimpse into distinct periods of American life. Each house, respectively, offers a look at the family lifestyle of a merchant, a diplomat, and a tradesman spanning the years from 1690 to 1840. A lovely children's bedroom is arranged to reflect the lifestyles of the five children who grew up in the house in the 1830s. A doll and toy collection displayed in cases is charming. The terrific full tours take one hour; you can also include a twenty-minute tour of the Buttolph-Williams House. The gardens behind the three houses are extraordinary, featuring flowers and herbs of the eighteenth century. Check the Web site for the extensive children's programming and special events.

Buttolph-Williams House (ages 6 and up)

249 Broad Street; (860) 529-0460 or (860) 529-0612. Open from May 1 to October 31 from 10:00 a.m. to 4:00 p.m., Wednesday through Monday. $ ($$ if you include the Webb-Deane-Stevens Museum).

This beauty reflects the medieval architecture of an early-eighteenth-century "mansion" house. Furnished to provide a sense of an affluent family within a Puritan community, the 1710–20 house is the site of many fine family events, workshops, and celebrations.

Eleanor Buck Wolf Nature Center (all ages)

156 Prospect Street; (860) 529-3075. Open Tuesday through Saturday, 10:00 a.m. to 5:00 p.m., plus First Thursday programs from 4:30 to 6:30 p.m. Free. Registration is required for special programs offered throughout the year.

This environmental education center at the entrance to Mill Woods Park offers science and outdoor explorations especially for children in grades kindergarten through six. Live animals, including native mammals, reptiles, and birds, are here, along with hands-on science displays, a wildlife and botanical library, and a gift shop. Trails link the center to the 110-acre Wintergreen Woods Park, which is also a nice place for day-tripping families to rest, relax, and explore.

Where to Eat

Vito's. 673 Silas Deane Highway; (860) 563-3333. This Wethersfield classic provides creative Italian cuisine, including pizza, terrific pasta, wonderful pesto, and a marsala sauce second to none. Lunch and dinner from 11:00 a.m. to 10:00 p.m. on weekdays, until 10:30 p.m. on Friday and Saturday, and from noon to 9:00 p.m. on Sunday. $–$$

Where to Stay

Motel 6. 1341 Silas Deane Highway; (860) 563-5900. 145 units, clean and basic for families. $

Best Western Camelot. 1330 Silas Deane Highway; (860) 563-2311. Remodeled, 110 units, whirlpool, exercise room, sauna, extensive continental breakfast. Nonsmoking rooms. $$$

General Information

Central Regional Tourism District. River Valley/Connecticut. 31 Pratt Street, 4th floor, Hartford 06103; (860) 244-8181; (800) 793-4480; www.visitctriver.com or www .enjoycentralct.com. Info for the leisure traveler and tour groups.

Greater Hartford Convention and Visitors Bureau. 31 Pratt Street, 4th floor, Hartford 06103; (860) 728-6789; www.enjoyhartford.com.

Farmington Valley Visitors Association. 33 East Main Street, Avon 06001; (860) 676-8878; (800) 4-WELCOME; www.farmingtonvalleyvisit.com. Info on special events and attractions in Avon, Simsbury, Canton, Farmington, and West Hartford.

New Haven County
Urban Culture and Country Adventure

Shaped sort of like a five-point star, this county reaches widely from its historic center in New Haven. The small cities of Meriden and Waterbury in the north are balanced by suburban towns and rural villages to the east and west. Sliced into three parts by the Quinnipiac and Naugatuck Rivers, the county is usually perceived more along those divisions than as a whole.

New Haven is most definitely the cultural center of the county, a situation made difficult by the unfortunate struggle to overcome the public perception that the city might be a dangerous place. In fact, New Haven has much to offer and little to fear. Areas of interest to tourists are well cared for, well lit, and well protected. Both in and outside of its cities, New Haven County is a great place for families.

TopPicks for fun in New Haven County

1. Connecticut Audubon Coastal Center and Silver Sands State Park

2. Yale Peabody Museum of Natural History

3. Eli Whitney Museum

4. Freedom Schooner *Amistad* at Long Wharf

5. Thimble Islands cruises

6. Lake Quonnipaug and Dudley Farm

7. Hammonasset State Park and Meigs Point Nature Center

8. Lake Quassapaug and Quassy Amusement Park

9. Barker Character, Comic, and Cartoon Museum

NEW HAVEN COUNTY

Madison
Guilford
Stony Creek
Branford
East Haven
New Haven
Milford
Hamden
Cheshire
Waterbury
Middlebury
Derby

79
80
1
95
1
95
91
15
5
691
15
91
80
15
5
91
10
15
10
63
34
1
69
63
84
8
63
8
15
63
84
6

Clogged Arteries in Greater New Haven

The largest roads through and into New Haven are Interstate 95 (running east–west but labeled north–south) and Interstate 91 (running north–south and actually labeled north–south). Both are usually jammed with cars during rush hours, though I-91 tends to run a little more smoothly than I-95. From roughly 7:00 to 9:00 a.m. and again from 3:30 to 6:30 p.m., drivers are likely to encounter slow-moving traffic on both roads. My advice is that families stay put at those hours and avoid the madness. Eat breakfast or an early dinner, or linger at home, in the parks, or at the museums for an extra hour. You are unlikely to get anywhere quickly by trying to exit the highway to find alternate routes. Type A personalities who convince themselves that traffic is an evil opponent they must circumvent at all odds can try Route 1 (an option only for the insane), Route 80 (a viable option but also likely to be crowded single-file with commuters if the interstate is really backed up), or Route 34. Route 10 will take you north or south between I-95 and Route 15 (called the Wilbur Cross Parkway in this county and the Merritt Parkway in Fairfield County); this is an option for skirting the I-95/I-91 interchange.

Major Routes throughout New Haven County

The Wilbur Cross Parkway (Route 15) sweeps diagonally on a northeast–southwest course through the county, from Milford in the south to Meriden in the north. Traffic can become heavy on this road at rush hour or on summer weekends, but it rarely is so heavily congested that the flow nearly stops. Route 8 runs north–south through the western part of the county, from Derby to Waterbury, then on up to Litchfield County. Often crowded at rush hour in its Fairfield County portion, it is rarely crowded in New Haven County once the northbound traffic passes Ansonia. Interstate 84 passes in an arc right across the northernmost part of the county from Southbury through the northern part of Cheshire. In Cheshire the road splits; I-84 continues to New Britain and Hartford, and I-691 connects to Meriden and I-91.

If you prefer slower or quieter suburban and rural routes, you can travel north–south on Route 69 all the way from the Wilbur Cross Parkway in northern New Haven through Waterbury and on to Hartford County, Route 63 from the Wilbur Cross through Naugatuck and on to Litchfield County, or Route 10 from I-95 or the Wilbur Cross through Cheshire and on to Hartford County. To travel east–west, pretty Route 68 will link Route 8 to Route 15 and on to Durham in Middlesex County. Route 80 meets I-91 in New Haven and travels east–west across North Haven, North Branford, and the northern parts of Guilford and Madison and onward to Middlesex County.

Milford

This community on the western border of the county is Connecticut's sixth-oldest town, settled in 1639 by families from New Haven and Wethersfield. It now has enough citizens to qualify it as a small city, but its pretty green, duck ponds, beaches, and residential neighborhoods have helped it retain the charm of a New England shore town. Although busier than most, especially along the Boston Post Road, where few signs of charm are at all apparent, it still draws families to its downtown arts-and-crafts shows, its summer concerts at the gazebo on the green, its coastal attractions, and its famed Oyster Festival.

Connecticut Audubon Coastal Center (all ages)

One Milford Point Road, off Seaview Avenue; (203) 878-7440; www.ctaudubon.org/ visit/milford.htm. Open year-round. Outdoor areas open dawn to dusk at no charge. Center open Tuesday through Saturday from 10:00 a.m. to 4:00 p.m. and Sunday noon to 4:00 p.m. Suggested donation, $.

This pristine habitat is composed mostly of salt marshes that border the Sound and the mouth of the Housatonic River. It provides families the opportunity to see one of the last surviving unaltered coastal properties in Connecticut. Just a few of the sanctuary's 800 acres of marshland and shore are passable to foot traffic, but these reveal the treasures of the rich ecosystem that flourishes here. A pathway provides access to the area's beach, a serene place for exploring and enjoying the native flora and fauna. Observation platforms help you gain a better view of the shore birds and other wildlife. This is not a park, so no picnic areas or trash receptacles are provided. Simply stroll peacefully through the habitat and learn about this fragile environment through the signage, the guided walks, and the displays and workshops in the coastal environment education center.

Among exhibits on the coastal environment, the center includes a 300-gallon saltwater tank with specimens native to the area. One such denizen is a diamondback terrapin, an endangered creature that inhabits the tidal estuaries. Though this one cannot be returned to the seashore, she serves as a reminder of the beautiful life forms we all have a responsibility to protect. Birthday parties that include beach walks and other nature fun can be arranged here. Inquire about the lecture series, summer camp programs, craft workshops, and family activities.

Historic Wharf Lane Complex (ages 6 and up)

34 High Street; (203) 874-2664 or 874-5789; www.geocities.com/SiliconValley/Park/ 3831/. Open Memorial Day through Columbus Day on Saturday and Sunday from 1:00 to 4:00 p.m. Free.

Revisit the past through a visit to the three historic houses maintained by the Milford Historical Society. Featuring the 1700 Eells-Stow House, the 1780 Clark Stockade

Milford Beaches

In addition to the passive recreation possible on the beach at the coastal center, Milford offers families a chance to enjoy its public beaches for fun of a more active nature. The State of Connecticut also owns a stretch of shoreline in Milford, and visitors are welcome at its as-yet-undeveloped beach. For further information, call the Milford Parks and Recreation Department at (203) 783-3280 or check the town Web site at http://milfordct.virtualtownhall.net.

Gulf Beach. Gulf Street. Visitor per-vehicle parking fee ($) from Memorial Day through Labor Day. Concession, restrooms, lifeguards, bird-watching/fishing pier.

Walnut Beach. Corner of East Broadway and Viscount Drive. Small pavilion, restrooms, picnic tables, lifeguards. Nice, wide-open views of the famed Charles Island, convenient location adjacent to Silver Sands State Park and close to Milford Point CAS Coastal Center. Open daily July 1 through mid-August. Weekends-only earlier and later in the season. Per-vehicle parking fee ($) or free street parking.

Silver Sands State Park. Off Mayflower Avenue between Robert Treat Drive and Nettleton Avenue; call the Department of Environmental Protection at (860) 485-0226 or check www.dep.state.ct.us/stateparks/parks/silversands.htm. Approximately 300 acres of shoreline and marshland. Lifeguards, portable toilets, and a boardwalk across the top of the beach and into the salt marsh are the current amenities. A bit removed from the beach is a picnic area with tables and barbecue grills. Restrooms, a first-aid station, and a pavilion are on the agenda for phase two of the park's development project. Bring drinking water, picnic foods and beverages, and trash bags. **Free.**

House, and the circa 1785 Bryan-Downes House, the complex has been curated to portray three centuries of life in New England through the furnishings, artifacts, and tours given in the trio of homes. One of the homes contains the Claude C. Coffin collection of Native American artifacts, touted as one of the finest archaeological records ever gathered in Connecticut. Period flower and herb gardens add a touch of authenticity to the site.

Milford **Oyster Festival**

Slap on the sunscreen and load your wallet with a wad of cash for the irresistible fun at this annual celebration of the gustatory delights of the homely but delicious oyster and other pure pleasures of summer on the shore. The third Saturday of August (and the previous Friday evening) is the usual date of the Milford Oyster Festival, which brings tens of thousands of visitors and nationally and regionally known performers to the harbor, the green, and Fowler Field on New Haven Avenue. An arts-and-crafts show, a classic car show, children's activities, a canoe race, a moonlight music dance party, and a food court featuring oysters, of course, as well as other family-friendly treats are all part of this popular festival. The action typically starts on Friday at 5:00 p.m. and begins again at 10:00 a.m. on Saturday. Admission is free; the food, the crafts, and the boat rides will cost you at least a little something. Call (203) 878-5363 or check www.milfordoysterfestival.org for more information.

Where to Eat

Cafe Atlantique. 33 River Street; (203) 882-1602. This little corner bistro advertises itself as a fine wine and espresso bar, and it is also something much simpler: a great place for families for breakfast, lunch, snacks, and a light dinner. Open Monday through Thursday from 7:00 a.m. to 10:00 p.m., Friday from 7:00 a.m. to midnight, Saturday from 8:00 a.m. to midnight, and Sunday from 9:00 a.m. to 8:00 p.m. Live music on weekends. Great sandwiches, soups, salads, baked goods. $–$$

Paul's Famous Hamburgers. 829 Boston Post Road; (203) 874-7586. This classic drive-in offers the finest in burgers, dogs, grilled chicken, fish sandwiches, fries, rings, real milkshakes, and other American fast-fare. Eat at tables inside and out, or take it on the road. Open Monday through Saturday, 10:00 a.m. to 8:00 p.m. $

The Olive Tree. 2009 Bridgeport Avenue; (203) 878-4517. Very, very good falafel made from scratch in this small Middle Eastern–Mediterranean deli with a few eat-in tables (thank goodness). Excellent wraps and pitas, salads, baba ghanoush, and baklava. How can you go wrong? Olives and other groceries to take out. Open Monday through Saturday from 9:30 a.m. if you are here to shop; 11:30 a.m. if you're here for lunch; and until 6:30 to 7:30 p.m., depending on the day and season, for whatever else you need. $

Where to Stay

Comfort Inn. 278 Old Gate Lane, off exit 40, I-95; (203) 877-9411 or (800) 221-2222. 120 units, including 4 suites, sauna, indoor and outdoor hot tubs, continental breakfast. $$

Fairfield Inn by Marriott. 111 Schoolhouse Road; (203) 877-8588. 104 rooms, outdoor pool, fitness center, continental breakfast. $$

Hampton Inn-Milford. 129 Plains Road; (203) 874-4400 or (800) HAMPTON. 148 rooms, fitness center, continental breakfast. $$

Howard Johnson Hotel. 1052 Boston Post Road, off exit 39A, I-95; (203) 878-4611 or (800) I-GO-HOJO. 165 units with 3 suites, restaurant, coffee shop, in-room refrigerators, health and exercise facilities, sauna, whirlpool, playground, indoor and outdoor pools, miniature golf. $$

New Haven

Once the site of a Native American village called Quinnipiac, which means "long water land," New Haven was renamed by English settlers who established a colony here in 1640. Since its earliest days an important center of industry, education, and culture, New Haven remains one of the most vital cities in the state. A treasure chest of attractions and historic sites appealing to every generation of visitors, the city takes pride in its firsts—fact and folklore support evidence of America's first football, Frisbees, burgers, dogs, pizza, and even lollipops being birthed right here in New Haven.

This chapter contains the best family attractions in the city, but by no means does it attempt to consider all the possibilities your family may enjoy. Check the *New Haven Register,* the *New Haven Advocate,* the *Connecticut Post,* or the Connecticut section of the *New York Times* for listings of events scheduled at New Haven's universities, museums, galleries, parks, and theaters. New Haven is a not-to-be-missed city.

West Rock Ridge State Park
Wintergreen Avenue; (203) 789-7498; http://cityofnewhaven.com/parks/parks/westrock park.htm or www.nochildleftinside.org/parks/westrockridge.php. Open year-round daily for walk-in visitors from 8:00 a.m. to sunset. The south overlook drive to the summit is open to vehicles Thursday through Sunday from Memorial Day through the last weekend in October. No restrooms. In-season entrance fee for cars, $.

If the layout of the city mystifies you, you might want to start a tour of New Haven high above the urban clamor. Overlooking the entire city (and the Sound and other parts of Connecticut on a clear day), West Rock is one of two ridges of basalt forced skyward through volcanic action 200 million years ago. The state park runs along the top of the western ridge and has a variety of recreational areas including hiking trails, a fishing and boating (car-top vessels only, such as canoes and kayaks) pond called Lake Wintergreen, and a picnic area.

A scenic drive traverses parts of the park. Its southern portion is open to motor vehicles only on a seasonal basis (see information in boldface, above). The northern section is closed to vehicles but open to hikers, cyclists, and skiers year-round. Pets are welcome on the trails, but they must be leashed. Folks in cars wishing to hike when the scenic drive is closed can park at the nature center on Wintergreen Avenue

Help for **Visitors**

Be certain to call the Greater New Haven Convention and Visitors Bureau (203-777-8550 or 800-332-7829) to ask for its terrific guides to the city and its 'burbs. You can also write to or visit the bureau at 59 Elm Street, New Haven 06510. The visitors guide is also on the Web site, www.visitnewhaven.com.

or at Lake Wintergreen. The park entrance is about 200 feet south of the nature center entrance, also on Wintergreen Avenue.

The park's blue-blazed main trail, called **Regicides Trail,** is accessible at the top of the ridge via the scenic drive or you can walk in off-season from the nature center (see following paragraphs). This 6.3-mile trail begins near the summit at Judges Cave and follows the crest of the West Rock Ridge range northward, ending at its junction with the Quinnipiac Trail in Hamden. The trail offers some beautiful views of the harbor and, of course, leads through scenic woodlands, as you might expect. The most infamous site on the trail is **Judges Cave,** where in 1661 John Dixwell, Edward Whalley, and William Goffe hid from bounty hunters hoping to claim the £100 reward for their capture as traitors against the Crown, having signed the warrant for the execution of Charles I many years earlier.

West Rock Nature Center (all ages)

1020 Wintergreen Avenue, not far from exit 59 off Route 15; (203) 946-8016; www.city ofnewhaven.com/parks/parksinformation/westrockpark.asp. Open year-round Monday through Friday 10:00 a.m. to 4:00 p.m. Closed holidays. Free.

Listed on the state's register of historic places, this forty-three-acre parcel of upland woods and fields is believed to be the first urban nature center in the nation. Owned and operated by the city, this separate area just north of the entrance to West Rock Ridge State Park on Wintergreen Avenue hosts a great variety of ranger-led, nature-related interpretive programs and guided walks. At the visitor center is a backyard-birding area, displays on pond life and aquatics, and exhibits on local wildlife and nocturnal denizens of the woodlands. The Nature House includes live reptiles, amphibians, and insects. Short nature trails take you past the ravine, a small waterfall, and so on. The center also has a picnic shelter and restrooms. Come in the wintertime with your sleds and toboggans.

East Rock Park (all ages)

Enter from East Rock Road in New Haven or Davis Road in Hamden; playground, environmental education center, and ranger station in College Woods at corner of Cold Spring and Orange Street; (203) 946-6086; www.cityofnewhaven.com/parks/parksinfor mation/eastrockpark.asp. Park open daily year-round from sunrise to sunset. Summit

Road open daily from April 1 to October 31, 8:00 a.m. to sunset, and at the same time on Friday and weekends only from November 1 through March. Two other roads are closed to vehicles but open to cyclists, in-line skaters, and walkers. Hiking trails are closed to mountain bikes. Free.

The twin of West Rock, East Rock is on the other side of the city, recognizable by its matching sandstone and traprock cliffs. Its 425-acre park is city-owned and is most well known for its spectacular views of the city and harbor from its monument-topped summit. Long-range binoculars and benches at the scenic overlook add to your enjoyment of the view as you rest here awhile and get your bearings on the city below you. A large, grassy picnic area with barbecue grills is frequented by visitors who pause here to explore the area around the towering Soldiers and Sailors monument, which honors New Haven veterans, and the Compass Rose, which identifies New Haven points of interest within sight.

The Trowbridge Environmental Center contains displays about local wildlife and plant life. Guided nature walks, workshops, and talks appropriate for families and

Yale University Visitor Information
and Walking Tours

Whether you're in a consumer-minded mood or not, Yale is a wonderful university to tour. See the Gothic splendor of the Sterling Memorial Library (where you can peruse newspapers in dozens of languages). Slip into the dimly lit galleries of the Beinecke Rare Book and Manuscript Library (where you can see a Gutenberg Bible, among other treasures). Walk through Phelps Gate, listen to the bells in Harkness Tower, stop at the statue of Yale grad Nathan Hale outside the 1750 Connecticut Hall (the oldest building in New Haven and the last remaining structure from Yale's Old Brick Row), where Noah Webster, Nathan Hale, and William Howard Taft perfected their studies.

You can join a free one-hour guided walking tour on Saturday and Sunday at 1:30 p.m. and on Monday through Friday at 10:30 a.m. and 2:00 p.m. (no tours on Thanksgiving Day or December 22 through January 1). It leaves from the Yale Visitor Information Center (203-432-2300) at 149 Elm Street, across from the north side of the New Haven green. No reservations or tickets are necessary. You can also pick up a self-guided tour pamphlet from the visitor center and explore the campus on your own. A second tour option covers important downtown sites near the New Haven green. Those tours are given by the New Haven Preservation Trust; you can call (203) 562-5919.

children are on the schedule at this center. Visitors can also walk the 10 miles of hiking trails, including the 1,000-foot, 285-step cliffside ascent called the Giant Steps Trail. A bird sanctuary, a self-guided nature trail, playing fields, picnic pavilions, playgrounds, an ice-skating rink, a basketball court, and opportunities for sledding, fishing, and kite flying are also located within park boundaries. Stop at the Trowbridge Center for a map.

Connecticut Children's Museum (ages 3 to 10)

At corner of Orange and Wall Streets; (203) 562-5437; www.ctchildrensmuseum.org. Open most Fridays and Saturdays, noon to 5:00 p.m. Call ahead or check the Web site for calendar of closings. $; children under 3 are free.

This educational play center/museum is housed in the Children's Building, not far from the city green district and the arts district of Audubon Street. Although public visiting hours are limited, this center is well worth a visit and is especially cheerful on wet, too-hot, or too-cold weekends when little spirits get dampened by the weather. No one can manage to be cranky in this stimulating play space.

Exhibit areas are carefully shaped to engage the eight intelligences as described by Howard Gardner and others. In the musical intelligence room, for instance, you will find children "Making Music" everywhere. A piano, a saxophone, and a guitar invite them to see and touch. A work station has wind chime components, an ocean drum makes rhythm visible, and a steel drum and pipe drum reveal that instruments can be made from found objects. In the bodily/kinesthetic room, mirrors reflect faces and children explore emotions in English, Spanish, and American Sign Language. Sculptures portray the characters from *Frog and Toad Are Friends, Blueberries for Sal,* and *Caps for Sale,* and children can "become" a frog, bear, or monkey with props and costumes on a stage with spotlights.

In the mathematical room, kids can adjust their green visors and gather at a kidney bean–shaped table, adding, subtracting, and counting the room's collections. A maze wall has movable slats so children can create pathways for rolling balls; a gear wall allows kids to arrange the gears and turn a crank to rotate them; tangrams, mosaics, and fraction games are available for quiet problem-solving. In the space place, architectural blocks, a chalkboard house, gravity tubes, and a garbage sculpting center provide exercise for spatial intelligence. Another room has beekeeper gear, an observation hive with thousands of live bees, and a sitting space of hexagonal honeycombs where visitors can just nest awhile. Magnifying glasses help young naturalists examine an ant farm and other earthly wonders. There's even a "great, green room" complete with a bunny in a bed and a little red house as well as the famous "comb and a brush and a bowl full of mush." The words of Margaret Wise Brown's beloved classic *Goodnight Moon* are on large magnets in different languages and braille for children to assemble on the great, green magnetic wall.

On Saturdays at 2:00 p.m., artists and educators engage children with dramatic readings of favorite books. The aim is to engage young readers in a hands-on book experience through creative interpretation of the story. You can't go wrong here with children ages three to seven; you might even have trouble getting many ten-year-olds to go home.

Yale University Art Gallery (ages 4 and up)

1111 Chapel Street at York Street; (203) 432-0600; http://artgallery.yale.edu. Open Tuesday through Saturday from 10:00 a.m. to 5:00 p.m. and Sunday from 1:00 to 6:00 p.m. Closed Monday and major holidays. Free; donation suggested.

Founded in 1832, the oldest university art museum in the United States has recently undergone a $44 million–dollar restoration that has uncovered the original design of its renowned architect, Louis Kahn. Engaging for children, especially in the sense that the scene changes markedly from gallery to gallery, it provides families with an excellent overview of the history of art. Take the kids here to see selections of its 85,000-piece collection of objects from ancient to modern times. Among the ancient treasures are many from Egypt, elsewhere in the Middle East and Africa, the Pacific islands, and the Far East. The American paintings and decorative arts are exquisite; O'Keeffe, Kandinsky, and Pollack are among the twentieth-century notables; earlier works from artists of the Hudson River School and the American Impressionist colonies also abound. The European collection includes van Gogh, Manet, Monet, and Picasso, among other greats. The sculpture garden—now beautifully revealed—provides an intriguing outdoor respite.

The museum hosts wonderful changing exhibitions of work that may never again be collected in one place in this area, plus other tours, programs, and concerts designed to appeal to families.

Yale Center for British Art (ages 4 and up)

1080 Chapel Street at High Street; (203) 432-2800; http://ycba.yale.edu/index.asp. Open year-round Tuesday through Saturday 10:00 a.m. to 5:00 p.m., Sunday noon to 5:00 p.m. Closed Monday and major holidays. Free.

Home to the largest collection of British art outside Great Britain, the center exhibits paintings, drawings, prints, rare books, decorative arts, and sculpture from the Elizabethan period to the present. Works by Stubbs, Hogarth, Turner, Constable, Blake, Lear, and Reynolds are among the treasures here. Aligned with a research institute, a reference library and photographic archive, and a paper conservation laboratory, the museum has a serene and serious aura, but families are most welcome here. You should aim to enjoy at least some of the collection, even if only for a brief visit with young children.

Many of the museum's **free** lectures and symposia are best suited to adults and students, but children are welcome to all gallery tours, concerts, and films. Programs especially for children occasionally appear on its calendar of events. The monthly Sun-

Carillon Concerts at **Harkness Tower**

If you are in New Haven in summertime on Friday night at 7:00, grab a blanket and a picnic dinner and head to Harkness Tower, near the Old Campus between Chapel and Elm Streets. Settle yourselves in the courtyard of Saybrook College, on Elm Street near the corner of High Street, and relax awhile and listen to the incredible music of the carillon. Students of the art as well as international artists play here several times each summer for about an hour. Don't pack anything crunchy in your picnic and make sure you close your eyes for the full and unforgettable effect of the glorious classical pieces on each concert's program. For a schedule of these free performances, call the Yale Events Hotline (203-432-9100), the Yale Guild of Carillonneurs (203-432-2309), or check the Web site www.yale.edu/carillon. In case of rain, the concerts are held at Phelps Hall at 344 College Street. Please leave pets at home.

day afternoon concerts are especially wonderful and are offered at no charge, as are the tours and films. The museum gift shop is exceptional and very child-oriented—a great place to shop for the holidays or special occasions.

The Yale Collection of Musical Instruments (ages 8 and up)

15 Hillhouse Avenue, between Trumbull and Grove Streets; (203) 432-0822. Open from September through June, Tuesday through Thursday from 1:00 to 4:00 p.m. Suggested donation, $. Call for the concert schedule ($$–$$$).

The public hours scheduled here make it mighty hard to arrange a visit with a school-age child, but if you have a little someone who really loves music, this awe-inspiring collection is well worth a half day out of school. More than 850 European and American instruments from the sixteenth to twentieth centuries are on display, and an annual concert series is offered from September through March.

Yale Peabody Museum of Natural History (all ages)

170 Whitney Avenue; (203) 432-5050; www.peabody.yale.edu. Open year-round daily, Monday through Saturday 10:00 a.m. to 5:00 p.m. and Sunday noon to 5:00 p.m. $–$$, children under 3 free; admission is free to all on Thursday from 2:00 to 5:00 p.m.

Last in the Yale neighborhood is one of the most popular family destinations in the state. Everybody has probably already been here, but for those people who have not, just think dinosaurs, dinosaurs, dinosaurs, plus fossils, birds, insects, seashells, rocks, shrunken heads, minerals, meteorites, mummies, mastodons, mammals, and much, much more. A two-story life-size statue of the dinosaur *Torosaurus latus* sits in a garden outside the museum amidst plants of the Cretaceous period. Also here is the enormous mural in the Great Hall depicting beautiful (although outdated) images of how the dinosaur age might have looked. Excellent wildlife and cultural dioramas from many habitats and periods include studies of Neolithic, Pacific, Meso-american, ancient Egyptian, and Connecticut Native American peoples. A Discovery Room designed especially for young visitors meets the need to touch, feel, and smell interesting natural objects. Changing exhibitions and tons of special events, classes, workshops, and hands-on activities are offered throughout the year.

The New Haven Museum (ages 6 and up)
114 Whitney Avenue; (203) 562-4183; www.newhavenmuseum.org. Open year-round from Tuesday to Friday 10:00 a.m. to 5:00 p.m. and Saturday from noon to 5:00 p.m. Closed major holidays. $; children under 6 free.

This beautiful building designed expressly as the museum of the Colony of New Haven is alone worth a visit—a colonial revival masterpiece built in 1930 in the late Georgian style, it has a most lovely skylit rotunda, marble staircases, an alluring salmon-colored ballroom, and magnificent moldings at every doorway. Kids may not appreciate the architecture, but they may enjoy the exhibits focusing on the inventions and indus-tries begun in New Haven County. See Eli Whitney's cotton gin, Charles Goodyear's rubber inkwell, an organ made by the New Haven Organ Company, and an original Mysto Magic Erector Set. Enjoy a marvelous three-story dollhouse with a veritable bevy of silent inhabitants and a thousand other details of decoration. Be sure to linger at the exhibit on Sengbe Pieh and the *Amistad*. Along with these are maps, ships' models, and other wonderfully curated, often interactive changing exhibitions.

Historic New Haven **Walking Tours**

The staff at the New Haven Colony Historical Society (114 Whitney Ave-nue; 203-562-4183) have designed a walking tour of Historic New Haven's buildings, parks, monuments, and other historic and cultural sites. Begin the self-guided tour near the eighteen-acre green that was planned in 1638 for the common use of New Haven residents. See its three historic churches, its famed Bennett Memorial Drinking Fountain, and the World War I Memorial Flagpole. Check out the finest sites of Yale University, then browse through the Grove Street Cemetery, looking for the graves of Noah Webster, Eli Whitney, Roger Sherman, Lyman Beecher, Timo-thy Dwight, Charles Goodyear, Roger Sherman, Walter Camp, and other famed Americans. Walk past the mansions of Hillhouse Avenue on your way to the Peabody Museum, then stop at the Historical Society, the New Haven City Hall, and the *Amistad* Memorial.

Amistad Memorial and the Freedom Schooner *Amistad* at Long Wharf Pier (ages 4 and up) 🏛

The memorial is located in the plaza at 165 Church Street at the New Haven City Hall. Accessible year-round and around the clock **free** of charge. The Freedom Schooner *Amistad* is berthed, when she is not sailing as an educational ambassador to other ports, at Long Wharf Pier off Long Wharf Drive. For a schedule of *Amistad* homeport tours and voyages, call *Amistad* America at (203) 495-1839 or visit the Web site (www .amistadamerica.org), an excellent source of facts about the *Amistad* incident and the construction of this historic replica. Tours, $–$$; sails, $$$$.

Lessons of courage, honor, and justice are to be learned at the base of the marvelous bronze sculpture outside New Haven's City Hall and aboard the re-creation of the *Amistad* itself at Long Wharf Pier. Created by Kentucky artist Ed Hamilton, the *Amistad* Memorial reminds visitors of the bravery of Joseph Cinque and the commitment of his American supporters to take a moral stand against the outrage of slavery and the illegal capture of free Africans from their homelands.

The story of the *Amistad* Africans started in the seas off Havana, Cuba, in 1839, when fifty-three Mendi captives seized control of the merchant ship *La Amistad*, which was taking them closer and closer to the unspeakable ordeal of a lifetime of slavery. Days under sail on an eastward course toward Africa were compromised by the slavers' alteration of the course toward the northern United States by night. Eventually apprehended by the U.S. Navy as the ship met the waters of Long Island Sound, the slavers accused their captives of piracy, and the Africans were taken into custody and held in the New Haven jailhouse, then on a site opposite the present city hall. Here the captives awaited trial, as abolitionists and attorneys and former president John Quincy Adams joined the battle to restore the Africans' freedom.

Connecticut **Freedom Trail**

In recognition of the importance of numerous Connecticut sites associated with the abolition of slavery and the movement toward freedom and equality for African Americans, the Connecticut General Assembly authorized the development of the Connecticut Freedom Trail. From monuments such as the *Amistad* Memorial to Underground Railroad sites to notable birthplaces, gravesites, and museum exhibits, the Freedom Trail traces the historic importance and contributions of Connecticut's African Americans and their supporters. An excellent pamphlet providing a map and details about the thirty-six sites throughout the state is available at tourism information centers, tourism district offices, and the Connecticut Historical Commission (59 South Prospect Street, Hartford 06106; 860-566-3005). You can also visit the Web site www.ctfreedomtrail.com.

The heroic acts of the group's leader, Sengbe Pieh, also known as Joseph Cinque, are celebrated on the 14-foot, three-sided bronze sculpture that stands near the site of the jailhouse where the kidnapped Mendi Africans were imprisoned. Although the morally laudable and eventually triumphant teamwork of the principal players in this incident did not lead directly or immediately to the release of other captive Africans, it did contribute greatly to the abolitionist movement and inspired the courage of countless other Africans who sought, fought for, and won their own freedom. This monument reminds all visitors of the importance of pursuing justice, freedom, and equality for all people against all odds. A tour of the re-creation of the schooner itself (usually in port from April through October) is a moving, eye-opening experience that makes the reality of the Mendi ordeal all the clearer. When the schooner is in port, it also does three-hour public sails on Friday and Saturday from 5:00 to 8:00 p.m.; reservations are necessary.

Lighthouse Point Park and Carousel (all ages)
2 Lighthouse Road, off Woodward Avenue, from I-95 exit 50 northbound, or exit 51, Frontage Road, southbound; follow the signs down Townsend Avenue to Lighthouse Road and the park; park manager: (203) 946-8005; ranger station: (203) 946-8790; http://cityofnewhaven.com/parks/parksinformation/lighthousepoint.asp. Park open daily year-round, sunrise to sunset, free of charge except from Memorial Day to Labor Day, when each out-of-town carload pays a day-use fee ($$). Carousel operates daily from Memorial Day to Labor Day, from 10:00 a.m. to 5:00 p.m. Private rentals available.

New Haven is not often characterized as a city on the sea, but it is a major working port in New England, and some of the best the city has to offer is by the shore or on the Sound. Although it is not known for its fine beaches, the city does have a great seaside park and swimming area.

Now popular mostly with city residents and bird-watchers, Lighthouse Point Park was once the enormously popular last stop on the New Haven trolley line. In those olden days the park had bathhouses, boat rides, and baseball games, with such legends as Babe Ruth and Ty Cobb playing here on Sunday afternoons in the Roaring Twenties. Nearly destroyed in the hurricane of 1938, the park later was home to a small amusement park.

Today only one of its famed rides remains. Housed in a New Haven landmark building listed on the National Register of Historic Places is the Lighthouse Point Carousel, an astonishingly well-restored treasure and a joy to ride. Assembled around 1911 from new and used parts, this sparkling beauty carved mostly by masters Looff and Carmel has seventy-two figures mounted in twenty ranks on a 60-foot platform. Jumping horses that slide on gleaming brass poles stand four abreast, alternating with the steadfast steeds, which stand shoulder to shoulder in rows of three. With these are a beautifully saddled camel and twin dragon chariots, the latter carved by Charles Illions. For 50 cents per ride, you can hop on any one of these gorgeously

Theater and Music in New Haven

The arts flourish in New Haven, but it takes some investigation to find the best performances for families. Check the Web sites of these groups and theaters, or call to inquire about single concerts and plays as well as series suitable for children.

New Haven Symphony Orchestra. 33 Whitney Avenue; box office: (203) 776-1444 or (800) 292-NHSO; www.newhavensymphony.com. The fourth-oldest orchestra in the United States, this symphony offers an October to June concert season in beautiful Woolsey Hall at the corner of College and Grove, plus a free summer series on the green. In addition to these, they offer the festive and family-friendly annual Holiday Pops! concert, a joyous collaboration of orchestra and choruses singing traditional carols, gospel, and even reggae tunes.

Shubert Performing Arts Center. 247 College Street; (203) 562-5666; www.shubert.com. This recently refurbished theater offers Broadway shows, ballet, opera, modern dance, comedy, and more in a full season from September through May. Many shows are suitable for or aimed especially at families, and some are offered at special prices as low as $10 per ticket.

Long Wharf Theatre. 222 Sargent Drive; box office: (203) 787-4282; www .longwharf.org. Renowned for its excellence and intimacy, this award-winning theater has two stages; inquire about affordable Kids on the Wharf plays and other productions suitable for the whole family. Summer camps for teens and middle-schoolers; workshops for kids 6–9.

New Haven Folk. www.ctfolk.com. These traditional and contemporary folk artists sponsor acoustic concerts and workshops featuring national and regional touring artists and local performers. They also produce the wonderful Connecticut Folk Festival and Green Expo each September. Check the Web site for dates of this and their concert series.

Music on the Green. Presented by New Haven Office of Cultural Affairs; concert hotline: (203) 946-7821; www.infonewhaven.com. Free summer concerts in July and August on selected Saturday evenings. Bring a blanket and picnic or eat at the food booths set up at the edge of the green. Dance in the twilight with music all around you.

International Festival of Arts and Ideas. (203) 498-1212 or (888) ART-IDEA; www.artidea.org. Musicians, dancers, puppeteers, storytellers, theater performers, and children's entertainers come from nearly every continent to raise our awareness and our spirits in an outpouring of artistic energy that spans five days in late June each year. Of the scores of indoor and outdoor performances staged on or near the green and on the Yale Campus, most are free; a handful require paid tickets. See classical and modern dance; hear opera, folk, salsa, reggae, jazz, and classical artists; participate in art activities, dances, or mask and puppet pageants.

painted Coney Island–style mounts, with names like Wild Wind, Sweet Sue, City Lights, Sea Dreamer, and Sundance. The beveled mirrors at the center of the ride reflect the glimmer of hundreds of twinkling light bulbs; the refurbished antique murals on the rounding board at the top of the carousel depict scenes from the history of New Haven; the air-driven Stinson Band Organ makes heavenly music. Group reservations are accepted—what a great place to party.

The eighty-two-acre park also has the pre–Civil War Five Mile Point Lighthouse and a great little nature center at the East Shore Ranger Station. When Ranger Terry is here, you may learn something about natural history, marine ecology, and maritime history at a program. Lighthouse tours are among the programs on the calendar.

The park's beach is clean and safe; a first-aid station, a snack bar, spotless changing rooms and showers, a small wooden playground, several swing sets, and a picnic grove are here. A splash park with ten fountain displays provides cool fun for visitors of all ages. A public boat launch, a fishing pier, volleyball nets, a nature trail, and several excellent bird-watching areas in the bird sanctuary are also here. Hawk-watching during the annual migration, from late August through November, brings birders from all over the state.

In mid-November, look for announcements of the **UI Fantasy of Lights** (info line: 203-777-2000) holiday display that is staged each year at the park (from 5:00 p.m. daily November 15 through December 31). Cruise the park's roadways past sixty colorful oversized symbols of Christmas joy. Fees ($$ per car or minivan) benefit the Easter Seals rehabilitation programs. Each vehicle is loaned a cassette tape (or tape plus tape player) that features a musical program timed for the ride through this animated holiday spectacle.

Fort Nathan Hale and Black Rock Fort (ages 6 and up)

Woodward Avenue; (203) 787-8790; www.fort-nathan-hale.org. Open daily Memorial Day to Labor Day from 10:00 a.m. to 4:00 p.m. Free.

After you leave Lighthouse Point, you might want to make a historical pit stop as you travel north again on Townsend Avenue. Take a left on Fort Hale Park Road to visit two of New Haven's oldest historic sites. Black Rock Fort was built in 1776 by order of the Connecticut Colony to protect the Port of New Haven from the British. Unfortunately, by the time the British arrived in 1779, only nineteen defenders remained at the fort; they were swiftly captured by the enemy, which then marched on to New Haven.

Fort Nathan Hale was built near the same site in the early 1800s as the British and Americans prepared again to fight. This time, during the War of 1812, the defenders successfully repelled the British invaders. Rebuilt in 1863 with new ramparts, bunkers, a drawbridge, and eighteen guns, the fort was prepared for Civil War action, but it never came.

Now you can make a self-guided tour of both sites. The drawbridge, its moat, the ramparts, bunkers, and other fortifications either still exist or have been restored. It's a neat site with terrific views of the harbor, but it's very low-key. In addition to the remains of the forts, there is a handsome statue of the young Nathan Hale, a colorful flag display, and some signage and self-guided tour brochures at the information booth at the entrance to the site.

Schooner Sound Learning Cruises (ages 4 and up)

60 South Water Street; (203) 865-1737; www.schoonersoundlearning.org. Late May through September. Private charters of varying duration and price, plus public sails. Among the latter, the best for families are Educational Sea Adventures, Pirate Sails, and Sunset Cruises; other specialty cruises are offered as well, so check the Web site calendar and call to inquire about suitability for children. Cruises leave from the Long Wharf. $$$$

If you want to see New Haven from the Sound and get a history and ecology lesson and a great boat ride to boot, call this tour operator during the warm months. Weather permitting, they'll take you out on chartered half-day, full-day, and sunset sails aboard the *Quinnipiack,* a 91-foot gaff-rigged wooden schooner. On the public sails, the lively crew offers entertaining and educational stories about the history of New Haven, the ecology of the Sound, and the cultures that affected the present ecosystem. Sea Adventures offers hands-on activities about marine science; Pirate Sails include costumed reenactors (very fun and very popular). On both chartered and public cruises, passengers are welcome to bring picnics and beverages; some of the specialty public cruises include food and/or beverages as part of the cruise package. Inquire also about the birthday parties that can be arranged here and the excellent weeklong summer day camps for children ages four through grade twelve.

Other New Haven **Parks**

New Haven has a variety of small parks that serve the needs of the families of its many neighborhoods. Among these parks are a few that are notable for special reasons. Call the city Department of Parks, Recreation, and Trees (203-946-8025) for details about each park's hours of operation and special events.

Edgerton Park. On Whitney Avenue and Cliff Street near the Hamden line; enter observatory area at 75 Cliff Street; (203) 777-1886; http://edger tonpark.org. Listed on the National Register of Historic Places; twenty-two-acre property originally owned by Eli Whitney and later the site of the Edgerton mansion. Crosby Conservatory of tropical plants with a simulated rain-forest path. Greenbrier Greenhouse with culinary herbs and seasonal plants for sale year-round, plus a children's corner with modestly priced plants. Outdoor flower gardens and magnificent trees, walking, biking, and cross-country skiing paths, picnicking areas, community garden center; seasonal fairs and concerts.

Edgewood Park. 720 Edgewood Avenue between Whalley Avenue and Chapel Street; (203) 946-8028; http://cityofnewhaven.com/parks/ parksinformation/edgewoodpark.asp. 120 acres with nature walkways, playground, ranger station with wildlife displays, duck pond, tennis and basketball courts, playing fields, Holocaust memorial, and Spanish-American War monument.

Wooster Square Green. On Chapel Street between Academy and Wooster Place; www.nhpt.org/Historic_District_Pages/woostersquare .html. Near New Haven's Little Italy is a historic district of some of New Haven's prettiest architecture designed in the early 1800s around a central square named for New Haven's Revolutionary War hero David Wooster. Have a look at the monument to Christopher Columbus, sit on benches under flowering cherry trees, and breathe deeply—the aromas of olive oil, garlic, and spicy tomato sauces will remind you that you are steps from the city's finest Italian restaurants and the world's best pizza and pastries.

Where to Eat

Chow. 962 Chapel Street; (203) 772-3002. Chinese-fusion-Asian; lots of dim sum–style small plates perfect for sharing. A great fun place for families. Funky modern design that's urban/industrial in flavor and casual in spirit. Open for dinner Wednesday through Saturday from 5:00 p.m. $–$$

Claire's Corner Copia Cafe. Corner of College and Chapel Streets; (203) 562-3888. Close to the green, the university, and the museums, Claire's offers the best soups in the city, plus other flavorful vegetarian main dishes, sandwiches, quesadillas, and baked goods. Takeout or tables with a semi-self-service, casual flair. Open for breakfast, lunch, and dinner year-round daily from 8:00 a.m. to 10:00 p.m. $

Kudeta. 27 Temple Street; (203) 562-8844. Striking, dramatic decor; tiny jewels of appetizers and zesty trans-Asian dishes. Traditional Chinese and Thai flavorings and pairings in abundance; excellent sushi; tons of choices. Terrific family-size tables with spinner in the middle to make sharing fun and easy. Open for lunch and dinner daily from 11:30 a.m. $$–$$$

Louis' Lunch. 263 Crown Street; (203) 562-5507. Louie Lassen opened this landmark luncheon stand in 1895 and claimed responsibility for the first hamburger cooked in America in 1900. Now this famed eatery has its place on the National Register. Fresh-daily burgers and cheeseburgers, served on toast in adult- and child-size portions. Tuna salad served year-round on Friday. Open Tuesday and Wednesday 11:00 a.m. to 4:00 p.m. and Thursday through Saturday from 11:00 a.m. to 2:00 or 3:00 a.m. Closed Sunday and sometimes Monday and for the entire month of August.

New Haven's Little Italy–Wooster Street. Whether it's pizza, pasta, or pastries you crave, a walk down Wooster Street will be sure to satisfy you. If you don't mind waiting in line for pizza, both Pepe's Pizzeria Napoletana (157 Wooster Street; 203-865-5762; $–$$) and Sally's Pizzeria (237 Wooster Street; 203-624-5271; $) offer up coal-fired brick-oven thin-crust pizza to die for. Pepe's is closed on Tuesday and Sally's on Monday. For pasta, try Tony & Lucille's (150 Wooster Street; 203-787-1621; $$) or Consiglio's (165 Wooster Street; 203-865-4489; $$–$$$). The latter looks fancy, but the service is warm and welcoming, and they love children. If you have room for a small treat—or at least to take one home—go to Libby's Italian Pastry Shop (139 Wooster Street; 203-772-0380; $) for the best cannolis and rice and ricotta pie for miles around and Italian ice so good it's exported to many other Connecticut establishments.

Where to Stay

Fairfield Inn by Marriott. 400 Sargent Drive; (203) 562-1111 or (800) 243-0059. 152 units, including 55 suites, outdoor pool, health club, sauna, continental breakfast. $$$

Courtyard by Marriott at Yale. 30 Whalley Avenue; (203) 777-6221. 160 units, restaurant, exercise facility, outdoor pool. $$$

Econo Lodge Conference Center. 100 Pond Lily Avenue; (203) 387-6651. 123 units, health club, sauna, Jacuzzi, indoor pool, continental breakfast. $$

Residence Inn by Marriott. 3 Long Wharf Drive; (203) 777-5337. 112 suites with kitchens, outdoor pool, Jacuzzi, continental breakfast. $$$$

East Haven

This shoreline community is a bustling outgrowth of New Haven's sprawl, seen mostly by travelers passing along I-95 through the shopping areas on Frontage Road. If it weren't for the seemingly endless construction on or near the Lake Saltonstall Bridge, few travelers would slow down along this route to see what the town has to offer. Those who exit the highway in East Haven will find one of Connecticut's most popular family attractions.

Shore Line Trolley Museum (all ages)

17 River Street; (203) 467-6927; www.bera.org. Open Memorial Day to Labor Day from 10:00 a.m. to 5:00 p.m. Also in April on Sunday only, and in May on Saturday and Sunday at the same hours. Weekend tours in September and October, plus Columbus Day and in November on Sundays only, prior to Thanksgiving. Call for a special events schedule for December. Trolleys run at least every thirty minutes; first one leaves at 10:30 a.m.; last one leaves at 4:30 p.m. $–$$; children under 2 free.

The efforts of the Branford Electric Railway Association have kept alive and well one of Connecticut's oldest tourist attractions—the oldest continually operating trolley line in the United States.

Nearly 100 classic trolley cars are stored on the grounds and in the car barns of the property. Admission buys you unlimited 3-mile round-trip rides on the beautifully restored cars, plus a guided or self-guided tour of the museum's display areas, which include the history of the technology and the local lines, plus some interactive and audio-video exhibits. The trolley rides themselves are great fun, especially for young children, and special days are offered throughout the year, broadening the appeal for older children. Among these are Pumpkin Patch days in October, Santa on the Trolley days in late November and December, and Illuminated Nights rides on Friday, Saturday, and Sunday (6:00 to 9:00 p.m.) from late November through December 23. Call to ask for a special events schedule or check the Web site.

You can picnic on the grounds, but there is no food concession or snack bar. You can also arrange birthday parties and special charters at a group discount if booked in advance.

Branford/Stony Creek

One of the prettiest and most relaxing family excursions in the state centers in and around Branford's Stony Creek, as quintessential a quaint New England fishing village as can be found in these parts. Only Stonington, in New London County, transports one more thoroughly to the nautical past.

Less than 10 miles from New Haven, Stony Creek has a long and lively history, complete with tales of pirate treasure and other romances of the sea and

Shoreline Greenway and
CT Coastal Access

Families who love the outdoors are sure to appreciate the **Shoreline Greenway Trail,** a multi-use recreational footpath that is being built, one section at a time, from Lighthouse Point in New Haven to Hammonasset State Park in Madison. Hugging as closely as possible to the coastal environment, it will eventually snake 25 miles through the four shoreline towns of East Haven, Branford, Guilford, and Madison. When the work is finished, the trail will connect parks, railroad stations, village centers, and other existing trails. Designed for nonmotorized recreation, the Greenway will be suitable for walkers, hikers, bicyclists, runners, and cross-country skiers. Approximately 10 feet wide and made of hard-packed crushed stone, the improved sections of the trail are accessible to outdoor enthusiasts of all ages, from senior citizens to babes in strollers, and, in some sections, may be accessible to in-line skaters and folks in wheelchairs.

The trail's first improved section, just about 2,500 linear feet, opened in 2005 in Branford, parallel to Birch Road, from the west side of Young Park to the east end of the Branford Day Care Center's Nature Classroom. To reach it from the Branford Green, travel east on Main Street and turn right on Montowese Street, which is Route 146. Turn left onto Pine Orchard Road and then left onto Birch Road. The Branford Day Care Center is at 16 Birch Road.

Another section, as yet unimproved, is the old Trolley Trail, also in Branford, which winds about 1 mile through the tidal salt marshes and woodlands between Pine Orchard and Stony Creek, offering up-close-and-personal experiences of the estuary habitat and its wildlife, as well as views of Branford Harbor and the Thimble Islands. Currently listed in the Connecticut Coastal Access Guide, this portion is perfect for hikers. A few years back, the Long Island Sound (LIS) Fund, which collects money, in part, from the sale of LIS license plates, provided a grant to the Town of Branford to construct a 480-foot-long footbridge in the footprint of the historic trolley track. The bridge connects to a nature walk from which visitors can see a seasonal variety of shorebirds, mammals, and invertebrates nesting, feeding, and wading in the creek and marsh areas. To reach this trail portion, take I-95 to Leetes Island Road at Exit 56. Follow that road south to Thimble Islands Road, then take a right on West Point Road to the parking lot.

A third section, still a rough trail about 1 mile long, has been cleared in Madison. Look for announcements of its opening in 2008–09. For further information about the development of the Shoreline Greenway, check the Web site at http://shorelinegreenwaytrail.org. For the **CT Coastal Access Guide,** check the Web site www.lisrc.uconn.edu/coastalaccess.

heart. Once home to farmers, fishers, and quarriers, the village is now famed for its quiet Yankee charm and its sprinkling of pink granite islands just offshore—the Thimbles.

In fact, the village's principal industry, if one can call it that, is the Thimble Islands sightseeing tour business. Three enterprising captains have updated the centuries-old trade of ferrying livestock, groceries, visitors, and even the occasional piano from the town dock to the islands. Now, from mid-May through Columbus Day, landlubbers can board ship to enjoy the sea breeze and scenery while listening to the colorful tales of the islands' past and present.

To reach the Stony Creek Dock, take I-95 to exit 56, and go south on Leetes Island Road for two miles. At the stop sign, go straight on Thimble Island Road, and follow the signs to the dock. For more information about this village and its history and attractions, check the Web site www.thimbleislands.com.

Volsunga IV (all ages)

Stony Creek Dock; (203) 488-9978 at the dock; (203) 481-3345 for reservations and information. Cruises every hour on the hour, weather permitting, from 11:00 a.m. to 4:00 p.m. daily except some Mondays July 1 to day before Labor Day. From mid-May through June and from Labor Day through Columbus Day, the tour times differ somewhat, with fewer cruises daily and no operation on Monday of several weeks at either end of the season. Call ahead or check the Web site www.thimbleislands.com for current schedule. $–$$. Groups of more than 12 should make reservations. Two-hour evening charters ($375 for thirty people) are also available.

From Captain Kidd to General Tom Thumb, the stories told by Stony Creek native Captain Bob Milne aboard the *Volsunga IV* are exceeded in quality only by his sure navigation of the reefs surrounding the 23 inhabited islands of the total 365. Milne's 40-foot vessel is rated for forty-nine passengers.

All seats are great seats for parents and kids alike on its single deck, and Captain Bob's easygoing manner makes for terrific storytelling, easily heard over the *Volsunga IV*'s sound system (the engine is soundproofed). Along with views of the islands' ninety-five homes, which range from a palatial Spanish mansion to Victorian cottages to a veritable aerie on stilts, you will enjoy the sights of human and winged islanders—kids wearing life jackets in their yards, teens diving from rocks, and seabirds to spare.

Sea Mist II (all ages)

Stony Creek Dock; (203) 488-8905; www.seamistcruises.com. In May and September (including Memorial Day and Labor Day) forty-five-minute cruises depart Friday through Sunday at 10:15 a.m. and 12:15, 2:15, and 4:15 p.m. In July and August cruises depart Wednesday through Monday on every quarter hour from 10:15 a.m. to 4:15 p.m. In October cruises depart on Saturday and Sunday at 12:15 and 2:15 p.m. $–$$. Two-hour charters available ($450 for up to 34 people). Reservations suggested for large groups. Public seal watches at noon on weekends only in March and April; two hours; $$$.

Captain Mike Infantino Jr. offers a similar ride on his similar boat, a 45-foot vessel that carries forty-six passengers. The navigation is just as sure, the stories are an entertaining mix of myth and fact, and the views of the sea, the birds, the islands, and the islanders are basically identical. All passengers are seated comfortably and can easily hear both the stories and the sounds of the sea. Chartered seal and bird watches can also be planned for groups of ten or more. Call for details. Bird watches are arranged year-round; seal watches are typically December through mid-April.

Islander (all ages)

Stony Creek Dock; (203) 397-3921. Fifty-minute cruises every hour leaving at twenty minutes before the hour, from 10:40 a.m. to 4:40 p.m. daily from mid-June through Labor Day. Reservations suggested for groups of more than 12. $–$$

The smallest of the three cruise options, Captain Dave Kusterer's 26-foot port launch carries about twenty-five passengers on a fifty-minute tour. The size of his boat allows exploration of a few spots the larger boats can't reach and allows Captain Dave to be right there in the middle of the more intimately sized deck. Like Captain Bob's, his stories reflect his personal knowledge of the lifestyles and histories of the islanders.

Stony Creek Village (all ages)

On your ride down to the water, you may notice Stony Creek's other attractions. Be sure to have a look at the small array of shops between the railroad bridge and the dock and rest or play awhile in the village park, which has a popular children's playground. The Stony Creek Market (203-488-0145) is great for breakfast, lunch, dinner (some nights), soft drinks, and picnic fare, and Creekers at Stony Creek Marine and Cuisine (203-481-2836) offers drinks, deli, and snacks, and does summertime-only lunch and dinner under a tent at the waterside. When your appetite is satisfied, stroll the rest of the village. When you return to your car, you can reach the Branford town green by following Route 146 to its end and continuing straight into the center of town. There are many stores and restaurants in that area plus the beautiful landmark Blackstone Library and the historic Harrison House museum.

Where to Eat

La Cuisine Market and Cafe. 750 East Main Street; (203) 488-7100. This bright and immaculate eat-here or take-out establishment offers terrific picnic choices, dinners to go, and delightful baked goods along with its cheerful table service of soups, stews, chili, and great hot and cold sandwiches for lunch. Open Tuesday through Sunday (market 7:00 a.m. to 7:00 p.m. and cafe 8:00 a.m. to 3:00 p.m. Tuesday through Friday; market and cafe open 8:00 a.m. to 4:00 p.m. on weekends; breakfast served on weekends until 3:00 p.m. $

Lenny's Indian Head Inn. 205 South Montowese Street; (203) 488-1500. Come here for a menu of New England seafood, epitomized in Lenny's Famous Shore Dinner of clam chowder, cherrystones, sweet corn on the cob, lobster, steamers, and watermelon. Steaks, burgers, fries and rings, and a children's menu served in the casual ambience of worn wood floors and wooden booths makes this a happy, noisy, thumbs-up place for families. Open daily year-round for lunch and dinner. Indoor seating year-round; patio in warm season. $–$$

Stony Creek Market. 178 Thimble Island Road; (203) 488-0145. For simple breakfasts and baked goods, arrive from 8:00 to 11:00 a.m. For lunch, come between 11:00 a.m. and 3:00 p.m. and take their over-stuffed sandwiches out on the front deck for a great view of the harbor. For dinner, from 5:00 to 9:00 p.m. Tuesday through Sunday, the market doubles as Stony Creek Pizza, serving pizza, salads, and occasional pasta specials. $

Where to Stay

Days Inn and Conference Center. 375 East Main Street; (203) 488-8314 or (800) 329-7466. 78 units with 3 suites and 2 mini-suites, outdoor pool and Jacuzzi. Continental breakfast. $$

Best Western Stony Creek Inn & Suites. 3 Business Park Drive; (203) 488-4991. 85 units, with some suites and efficiencies; spa/pool; exercise room; complimentary continental breakfast. $$–$$$

Guilford

One of the most exceptional colonial greens in New England is in the center of Guilford, one of the prettiest towns along the New Haven County shoreline. Lying south of the Boston Post Road, as you drive toward the Sound, its twelve acres are crisscrossed by walkways and dotted with benches that make this a popular site to relax and to play. Shops, restaurants, churches, galleries, and beautiful colonial, federal, and Victorian homes surround this classically lovely spot. Bring the kids here for bicycling or in-line skating, to listen to a summer concert, or to browse at one of the frequent fairs or festivals held on the site. Afterward, leave the green to explore other parts of Guilford. Walk or cross-country ski on the wooded trails through an old quarry site or an ancient farm. Stroll, snooze, or sift for forgotten treasures on

Guilford **Craft Expo**

Surely the most magical of all the events held on the green, this fabulous three-day festival, now in its fiftieth year, celebrates American handcrafts created by 170 juried artists from all corners of the nation. Displayed under huge, cheerfully lit tents, the pieces demonstrate an astonishing array of talent in every medium. Basketry, weaving, jewelry, toys, clothing, candles, leather goods, sculpture, pottery, paper crafts, glass, musical instruments, furniture—you name it, it's here.

A special Guilford Art Center tent features hands-on activities and demonstrations by crafters who practice their arts at the center. Entertainments such as storytellers, face painters, and other live performers help make the event a happy experience for all visitors. A food concession sells unremarkable fast-food fare. We always pack a picnic to enjoy under the trees.

The tents are lit from noon to 9:00 p.m. on Thursday and Friday and from 10:00 a.m. to 7:00 p.m. on Saturday in the middle week of July. A perfectly lovely and inspiring way to spend a summer afternoon, the expo is also a great opportunity for exposing children to the creative arts. Who knows? You may have a budding artist in your clan. Call (203) 453-5947 for more information. $$, children under twelve free.

the beach. Visit one of the four historical homes representing lifeways of the seventeenth, eighteenth, and nineteenth centuries. Just 15 miles east of New Haven, Guilford feels like a country town.

Guilford Art Center (ages 4 and up)

411 Church Street (Route 77), north of Route 1 and approximately 200 yards north of the I-95 overpass; (203) 453-5947. Studios open year-round for classes and visitors; call for schedule and course catalog. Gallery and shop open year-round Monday through Saturday from 10:00 a.m. to 5:00 p.m. and Sunday from noon to 4:00 p.m. Extended hours for annual Holiday Exhibition and Sale in December. Closed Thanksgiving, Christmas, and New Year's Day. Free.

Composed of a shop, a gallery, and a school, the Art Center was founded in 1962 by the local artists who organized the first of its remarkable annual expositions (see sidebar). Still a home away from home for many of those artists, the center has pottery, weaving, painting, and metalsmithing studios, plus multiuse classrooms for instruction in basketry, etching, printmaking, and woodcarving. Visiting artists also travel here to offer workshops for adults and children. A bounty of talented role models offers instruction, guidance, and encouragement as young artists tease from their own minds and fingers the wondrous creations born in these studios. The Mill Gallery hosts small expositions throughout the year, and the shop sells the works of as many as 300 artisans. Craft birthday parties and other special events are also offered here.

Henry Whitfield State Museum (ages 6 and up)

248 Old Whitfield Street, south of the green at the corner of Stone House Lane; (203) 453-2457 or (860) 566-3005; www.whitfieldmuseum.com. Open for mostly self-guided tours on Wednesday through Sunday from April 1 to December 14 from 10:00 a.m. to 4:30 p.m. and for groups year-round by appointment. $, children under 6 free.

This historic home is the oldest stone house in New England and the oldest house in Connecticut. Built in 1639 by Reverend Henry Whitfield, the post-medieval house has stone walls 3 feet thick and is the last remaining of four such houses strategically placed in Guilford as strongholds for the citizens during threat of war. No record confirms that the house was ever in fact used for this purpose.

Now restored more as a museum than a period house, the structure contains an outstanding collection of furniture, housekeeping implements, textiles, weapons, and other important Connecticut pieces. The entire house, including the attic, is open to the public, as are the gardens and lawns. Among the large collections displayed in the attic, you can see the 1726 Ebenezer Parmelee steeple clock, the first wooden-works tower clock made in the colonies. In the separate, adjacent visitor center is a tourist information center, a reference library, an exhibit gallery with excellent changing displays, and a charming gift shop, which reopens for a week in late December for holiday shopping.

Special events are planned throughout the public season, and, as now is true for most of the state's historic museums, educational and entertaining programming for families is the order of the day. Check the Web site for a list of these inventive and interactive events. Among the best are the Puritans at Play day of old-fashioned games, annually in June on the state's Open House Day; the Holidaze exhibit with costumed interpreters and period foods in late November; and the Firelight Festival in December with luminaria, chestnut-roasting over an open outdoor fire, and other seasonal activities and refreshments.

Hyland House (ages 6 and up)

84 Boston Street, which leads east from the south side of the green; (203) 453-9477; www.hylandhouse.com. Open from early June to early September daily except Monday from 10:00 a.m. to 4:30 p.m. and on weekends from Labor Day to Columbus Day. Suggested donation: $, children under 12 free.

This red overhung saltbox frame house was originally the home of the Hyland family. One of the Hyland daughters married Ebenezer Parmelee of clockmaking fame; it was through their efforts that the house was expanded from its original two-rooms-over-two size. Though the house was built in 1660, the museum's focus is on the fifty to seventy-five years before the Revolution. Everything the family might have used during that period is here for your education.

Here visitors step into the eighteenth century, especially in the house's wonderful kitchen in the lean-to addition at the back of the house. How we wish the friendly docents would leave us alone to play here.

The architectural details and the collections in this house are among the finest in the state. Gorgeous paneling, wide-board floors, walk-in fireplaces, and artifacts of every sort are abundant. Outside, the flower and herb garden is lovely in summer and fall.

The house docents are in tune with the interests of children of every age level, making the house come alive with scores of facts and stories. The house is the site of the Historic Foodways Festival on the last full weekend in September. Hearthside cooking and other activities are among the special events designed for families.

Thomas Griswold House (ages 6 and up)

171 Boston Street; (203) 453-3176 or (203) 453-4666; www.thomasgriswoldhouse.com. Open June through September on Tuesday through Sunday from 11:00 a.m. to 4:00 p.m. October, weekends only at same hours. $, children under 12 free.

Greatly restored by the Guilford Keeping Society, this 1774 saltbox home has a large number of important architectural details, including an original Guilford cupboard and a 10-foot-wide fireplace. This house also includes period rooms set with furnishings and implements in positions of use. Samplers, coverlets, costumes, dolls and toys, and a whimsical napkin-ring collection are among the treasures here.

Special events such as twilight tours, an antiques show, or reenactments are sometimes offered. Check the Web site's calendar of events. On these special days the museum's blacksmith shop and barn are usually open.

Westwoods Trails (all ages)

Trail entrance on Sam Hill Road near its junction with Route 146; (203) 453-8068; www .westwoodstrails.org. Open year-round from dawn to dusk. Copies of the trail map available at Guilford's town hall, library, and police station, and at the Guilford Parks and Recreation Department on Church Street. The Guilford Land Conservation Trust (P.O. Box 200, Guilford 06437) can also provide copies. Free.

For those of you who are fatigued with art and history, a walk in the woods may be the answer to your prayers. Head, therefore, to Guilford's Westwoods Trails, located less than a mile from the green in an open area of more than 1,000 acres. Forty miles of very pretty trails lace through forest and marshland.

Take Route 146 west from the green to Sam Hill Road and park in the small lot right near that corner. Follow the white-blazed trail from that point and connect with the other trails that lead to waterfalls, rock cliffs, colonial caves, an Indian cave, rock carvings, and vistas of the Sound and lake. The "G" Trail connects the Westwoods Trails to the Stony Creek Quarry Preserve; here you can see the remains of old quarrying operations.

Jacobs Beach (all ages)

Seaside Avenue off Whitfield Street; Guilford Parks and Recreation: (203) 453-8068. Park and playground area open year-round from 8:30 a.m. to 9:00 p.m. Swimming allowed only when lifeguards are present, from Memorial Day to Labor Day, on Monday through Saturday from 9:00 a.m. to 5:00 p.m. and Sunday from 11:00 a.m. to 5:00 p.m. Out-of-town visitors pay a day-use parking fee ($$ per vehicle) from Memorial Day through Labor Day.

Hikers and bikers may want a refreshing swim or at least a cool wind through their hair after some trail exercise. Head down to the Sound for a rest on the sand at Jacobs Beach. Comb the beach for treasures swept in on the tide, play on the playground, listen to the rustling marsh reeds. You can swim if the lifeguards are on duty, but you can use the beach and volleyball court even if the guards are off duty. Restrooms and a pavilion with picnic tables and nearby grills are also here. The beach is relatively small, but it's a pretty spot, and out-of-towners are more than welcome. Season passes cost families $50.

Lake Quonnipaug (all ages)

Route 77 in North Guilford, about 3 miles north of Route 80. Open Memorial Day through Labor Day; gated during remainder of year. Monday through Saturday 9:30 a.m. to 7:30 p.m., Sunday 11:00 a.m. to 7:30 p.m. Purchase per-vehicle day tickets at the lake ($$). Best buy for families is a season pass ($50), which allows unlimited visits per season and can be purchased only at the Guilford Parks and Recreation Department (203-453-8068) at 32 Church Street downtown.

If freshwater swimming is pleasing to you, head north to Lake Quonnipaug for salt-free water play, boating, fishing, and picnicking. This pretty lake is in a rural area dotted with barns, pastures, stone walls, and fences—the perfect setting for a New England day trip.

A good-size beach and grassy area are open to the public. Bathrooms with two outdoor showers are also provided. Small car-top boats such as inflatables, canoes, kayaks, sailboards, or tubes may be launched from the grassy area, but no snorkeling or scuba diving is allowed. A state-owned public boat launch ramp is at the north end of the lake, outside of the Guilford property.

Dudley Farm (all ages)

2351 Durham Road (Route 77), north of Route 80; (203) 457-0770; www.dudleyfarm .com. Open May through October, Monday through Saturday 10:00 a.m. to 1:00 p.m. Farmers' market June through October on each Saturday from 9:00 to noon; markets on only the first Saturday of each winter month. Grounds, trails, and market are free; house tour, $; children under 16 free.

Settled in the arms of nature, the eight standing buildings and nearly two dozen remnant structures at this peaceful ten-acre farm site are the legacy of the Dudley family, who tilled the soil and tended animals through two centuries in Guilford. Now the Dudley Foundation has as its mission the preservation of the farm and its structures

and the restoration of its meadows, fields, and flower gardens. Through this ongoing process, the foundation hopes to inspire present generations to recognize their
own connection to the soil. A visit here may rekindle in both children and adults an
appreciation for the natural environment and an attitude of stewardship toward the
earth. The farm offers an ever-increasing array of guided and self-guided tours, activities, workshops, and demonstrations. A 2-mile loop trail through ninety-five acres of
woodland traces the path of eighteenth-century wagon roads.

Tours of the farm and adjoining mill site feature a seventeen-room 1840s farmhouse, with many of those rooms restored to their beginning-of-the-twentieth-century
state, an enormous U-shaped barn that evolved through two centuries of farm life,
the large Munger Barn (reconstructed here for special events and activities), a sugarhouse, a small barn restored for use as a schoolhouse for visiting classes, an herb garden and restored flower gardens, a vegetable field, beehives, and animal enclosures
sheltering goats, oxen, sheep, chickens, and geese.

Families may prefer to visit on Saturday, when the farm is often at its busiest. In
the morning it offers a market of its own produce as well as that of other local farmers and crafters. Browse among fruits, vegetables, flowers, honey, and other goodies, then see what the farm staff is demonstrating in the house, the barns, or on the
grounds. Depending on the weather and season, you may see, or even participate
in, sheep-shearing, beekeeping, maple-sugaring or syrup-making, twig furniture construction, quilting, rag rug weaving, tool repair and maintenance, or barn chores. On
the first Saturday of each month, musicians play acoustic instruments under the trees.

Special events throughout the warm season include an Arbor Day celebration,
May Day festivities, and a Farm Day. In winter, two weeks or so are spent on the old-
fashioned adventure of tapping the running sap of the farm's majestic maples. The
foundation produces a newsletter to let folks know what's happening at the farm as
its restoration continues. Call to ask for a copy; check the Web site for the schedule
of markets and events.

Anne Conover **Nature Trail**

The National Audubon Society offers a 1-mile trail through the Guilford
Salt Meadows Sanctuary near the East River. Open dawn to dusk year-
round, the sanctuary and the trailhead are accessible from Meadowlands
Road off Clapboard Hill Road, not far from exit 59 (Goose Lane), on the
north side of I-95. Secondary-growth forest and meadow-, river-, and
tidal marshland are habitats for herring and eels, eastern box turtles, salt
marsh sparrows and osprey, and many other birds and beasts of the Eastern Woodlands. The trail is easy, short, and quite beautiful. A kiosk at the
parking area provides trail guides. Admission is free. For more information, check the Web site www.audubon.org/local/sanctuary/guilford.

Where to Eat

Anthony's of Guilford. 2392 Boston Post Road; (203) 453-4121. Reasonably priced and well-prepared mostly Italian specialties in a comfortable setting welcoming to families. Open year-round for lunch and dinner. $–$$

Som Siam. 63R Whitfield Street; (203) 458-0228. In the rear of Whitfield Alley, directly across from the town green, this little place graciously serves delicious Thai favorites in a pretty, thimble-size setting warmly welcoming to families. Open for lunch Tuesday through Sunday and dinner daily. $–$$

Little Stone House Cafe. 514 Whitfield Street at the Guilford Dock; (203) 458-2554. Practically in the water, this great little family-friendly cafe offers gourmet-quality soups, sandwiches, paninis, wraps, baked goods, and meals to go. Be sure to try the lobster gazpacho and the best BLT wrap on the planet. Eat in or outside on the patio. Open 10:00 a.m. to 6:00 p.m., year-round, Tuesday through Sunday. $–$$

The Place. 901 Boston Post Road; (203) 453-9276. Seasonal dining in the rough at one of Connecticut's most unique eateries. Outside under tents, sit on rough-hewn seats at picnic tables and eat charcoal-grilled steak, pit-roasted corn on the cob, and fresh seafood. Open from late April through October on Monday though Thursday from 5:00 to 10:00 p.m., Saturday from 1:00 to 11:00 p.m., and Sunday from noon to 10:00 p.m. $$

23 Water Street. (203) 453-1153. This wee place sells Durham's famous super-premium 80 Licks ice cream, plus soups and pastries in the cooler seasons. Rock on! Opens at noon Monday through Saturday; closing varies with the day and season. $

Where to Stay

Comfort Inn. 300 Boston Post Road; (203) 453-5600. 45 rooms in brand-new facility. Complimentary continental breakfast; access to nearby health club. $$–$$$

Tower Inn and Suites Motel. 320 Boston Post Road; (203) 453-9069. 15 efficiency suites. Nonsmoking suites available. $$$

Guilford Suites Hotel. 2300 Boston Post Road; (203) 453-0123 or (800) 626-8604. 32 suites with bedroom, sitting room, bath, and kitchenette. Continental breakfast. $$$

Madison

Perhaps the loveliest town on the New Haven County shoreline, Madison was one of Connecticut's earliest settlements. Once called East Guilford and connected geographically and politically to the town of Guilford, it was incorporated as a separate town in 1826. In previous centuries a fishing and shipbuilding center and later a seaside resort area, Madison is now primarily a comfortable residential suburb whose population increases sizably in the summertime. Despite its limited ethnic diversity, many Madison families love their town because of its community-centered ambience—and its beautiful beaches. In fact, Connecticut's longest stretch of public beach is located here, and all visitors are welcome.

Hammonasset State Park (all ages)

Off the Boston Post Road, exit 62 off I-95; (203) 245-2785. Open daily year-round, 8:00 a.m. to sunset; most planned activities held in summer. Per-vehicle admission charge ($$–$$$) from Memorial Day to Labor Day and weekends only from mid-April to Memorial Day and from Labor Day through mid-October. Weekdays free to all during those weeks. In season, reduced fee after 4:00 p.m.; free after 6:30 p.m. Season pass ($$$$) allows unlimited visits. No charge off-season. Alcohol-free. Campsites, $ nightly.

Enormously popular, this park offers a 2-mile beach with pavilions and picnic shelters, a 550-site campground, playing fields, a spiffy year-round nature center with an amphitheater and walking trails, a bike path, and sun, sand, rocks, and salty spray in abundance.

Come here, then, to camp, swim, fish off the jetty, scuba dive, picnic, play ball, hike, sailboard, or boat on Long Island Sound. Stop at the **Meigs Point Nature Center,** a modest facility with several fresh- and saltwater aquariums, a marine touch tank, a few well-executed dioramas, and a variety of live amphibians and reptiles. Outside, the Willard's Island walking trail winds out through the salt meadow and onto the island, once farmed in colonial times and now home to the mammals and birds of the marshlands. See the nesting sites of the ospreys that soar overhead in spring, summer, and fall.

The nature center rangers provide walks, slide presentations, and craft workshops for children all summer long. The Junior Naturalist program for children nine to twelve and the Outdoor Explorer program for six- to eight-year-olds include free activities such as fishing, crabbing, tidal pool exploration, and bird and bat house building. Held midweek in July and August, the program is open to drop-in visitors.

The windswept seaside campground is extremely popular in the summertime. The sites are almost all open, so if you like the hills and woods, you are in the wrong

Downtown **Madison**

Families may enjoy a stroll through Madison's shops, which provide a marvelous alternative to cookie-cutter mall stores and impersonal outlets. Many of the boutiques, galleries, antiques stores, coffee shops, cafes, delis, and restaurants of Madison are in vintage homes and historic commercial buildings centered mostly on Wall Street, the Boston Post Road, and Samson Rock Road in the village center.

Be sure to stop for hot cocoa and great baked goods at the Madison Gourmet Beanery, children's books at R. J. Julia Booksellers (once voted the best independent bookstore in the nation), and toys and trinkets at Belles and Beaus. Parents may want to enjoy a cup of tea at the incomparable tearoom at Harp and Hearth. Savvy kids will ask for a treat at the Mad Bean ice cream shop behind the Beanery.

park. Bring a metal tub or fire ring (or rent one here); there are no grills or firepits, and campfires are permitted only in metal containers. Campfire programs, bingo, movies, an occasional dance, and a children's playground are part of what you'll enjoy here. Bring bikes and in-line skates—the campground has excellent lanes for both sports.

Allis-Bushnell House (ages 6 and up)

853 Boston Post Road; (203) 245-4567; www.madisoncthistorical.org. Open mid-June through August, Wednesday through Saturday from 1:00 to 4:00 p.m., and year-round by appointment. Free; donations gratefully accepted. The Lee Academy, formerly a one-room schoolhouse and now a satellite property of the museum, is located at 14 Meeting House Lane, on the Madison green.

Owned by the Madison Historical Society, the 1785 Allis-Bushnell House is notable for its unusual corner fireplaces and cupboards, its stenciled floors, the exceptional collection of tools and fishing and farming equipment in its annex, and its eighteenth-century herbs in the lovely rear garden. The birthplace and childhood home of Cornelius Bushnell, a founder of the Union Pacific Railway and chief financier of the Civil War ironclad ship, the USS *Monitor,* it also has a collection of fascinating memorabilia regarding that famed vessel and Madison's maritime history.

Special guided tours by a costumed interpreter of Cornelius's mother, Chloe Bushnell, are offered on select Saturdays in summer; during other special exhibitions, self-guided tours are also offered. Children may particularly enjoy the museum's small collection of toys, dolls, period costumes, and interesting medical implements. During the summer months, some parts of the collection are moved to the historic Lee Academy, on the Madison green, for special exhibitions on varied themes. These exhibitions are typically open on Saturdays from 11:00 a.m. to 3:00 p.m.; call or check the Web site for more information.

Deacon John Grave House (ages 6 and up)

581 Boston Post Road; (203) 245-4798. Open mid-June through Labor Day on Saturday only from 1:00 to 4:00 p.m. or by appointment throughout the year. $, children under 6 free.

Just a block east of Madison's town green, surrounded by stately period homes and its classically New England white Congregational church, is one of Connecticut's oldest homes, on a pretty parcel known in the past as Tuxis Farm. Occupied for more than 300 years by descendants of its original owner, Deacon John Grave, the house is a fine example of seventeenth- and eighteenth-century architecture, easily seen through the fine restoration work that has taken place here.

Adapted for use in the past as an ordinary, a school, a wartime infirmary and weapons depot, and even a courtroom, the house also was home to ten children at one time—and that was before its eighteenth-century additions were added! Come here to imagine the life of a farming family in pre-Revolutionary days, see the secret staircase that led to a hidden room used for storing arms during the French and Indian War, hear the ghost stories associated with the house, and sample open-hearth cooking done on special events days.

Where to Eat

Lenny and Joe's Fish Tale. 1301 Boston Post Road; (203) 245-7289. Serving the shoreline since 1979, this classic seafood shack-plus upholds a long tradition of fresh fish, chowder, traditional American sandwiches, award-winning lobster rolls, shrimp, scallops, and more. Eat inside, daily year-round, or outside, March through November. From mid-May to mid-September, they serve terrific ice cream and operate a great tyke-size carousel in its own separate outdoor pavilion. All profits ($) are donated to charities. $–$$

Friends and Company. 11 Boston Post Road; (203) 245-0654. The perfect blend of casual and refined, this riverside establishment is a longtime local favorite. Healthfully prepared and often locally grown, the meals on its seasonal menu are offered year-round, daily at dinner from 4:30 p.m. and for Sunday brunch from 11:00 a.m. to 2:00 p.m. Children's menu; appetizer portions. $$–$$$

Red Tomato Pizzeria. 37 Boston Post Road; (203) 245-6948. From 3:00 p.m. Tuesday through Sunday, order out or eat in at this cheery eatery that makes excellent thin-crust New Haven–style pizza baked right on the bricks. Fresh vegetable and meat toppings—even the clams are freshly shucked. Closed Monday. $–$$

Zhang's. 44 Boston Post Road; (203) 245-3300. Open daily for lunch and dinner, this sit-down or take-out restaurant with a Far Eastern flair offers Chinese and Japanese fare at moderate prices. $–$$

Where to Stay

Beech Tree Cottages. 1187 Boston Post Road; (203) 245-2676. In summertime, this three-acre enclave just steps from Hammonasset Beach offers bedroom-and-bath guest houses, plus more ample cottages with bath and kitchen facilities, large enough for a small family. Clean, simply furnished, and well-equipped; queen beds in every cottage. Friendly hosts; lovely grounds with rope swing, volleyball net, barbecues, walkways. Guest houses, $$$ nightly; cottages, $$$$ nightly; weekly rates available.

The Madison Beach Hotel. 94 West Wharf Road; (203) 245-1404. Directly on the beach, this restored 1800s hotel offers 35 units with 6 suites; complimentary continental breakfast. The Wharf (203-245-0005) restaurant has indoor dining and balcony seating in its Crow's nest bar. Open March 1 to January 1. $$$

Hamden

The most conspicuous feature of Hamden (north of New Haven) is in fact one of the most conspicuous features of all of Connecticut. Best viewed from a distance for the fullest impact, the rounded hills of Sleeping Giant State Park look exactly like a figure in repose, its head toward the west, its chest and body stretching eastward. (A great view is possible from I-91.) Hamden is also famous for its notable early citizen, inventor Eli Whitney.

Sleeping Giant State Park (all ages)

200 Mount Carmel Avenue off Route 10; ranger station: (203) 789-7498. For other information and a schedule of free guided walks, call (203) 272-7841 or check www .sgpa.org. Open year-round daily from 8:00 a.m. to sunset. Parking fee ($$) charged in season (usually April 15 to November 1) on weekends and holidays only.

Up close, the park is a great outdoor recreation area. Just off Route 10 a few miles north of Hamden's business center, its 1,500 acres of rolling woodland are traversed by hikers and cross-country skiers on 32 miles of trails. You can fish for trout in Mill River or you can hike the Tower Trail, an easy walk on a wide gravel path to the top of the ridge. At the top is a four-story stone building completed in 1939 as a WPA project. Go inside and walk up its ramps (not wheelchair-accessible) for scenic views of the area. The park also offers a pine-canopied picnic grove with tables, an open-air picnic shelter, drinking water, restrooms, and grills.

A booklet available at the park entrance booth explains the forty-point self-guided nature trail, which takes somewhat over an hour to traverse. You may also join one of the many free guided trail walks offered here mostly on Sundays in the spring and fall. Six to eight of these are scheduled during each of these seasons at 1:30 p.m. The hikes are fine for all members of the family.

Eli Whitney Museum (ages 4 and up)

915 Whitney Avenue (Route 10); (203) 777-1833; www.eliwhitney.org. Open year-round; Memorial Day to Labor Day, 11:00 a.m. to 4:00 p.m. daily. During remainder of year, open noon to 5:00 p.m. Wednesday through Friday, 11:00 a.m. to 4:00 p.m. Saturday, and noon to 5:00 p.m. Sunday. Closed Thanksgiving, Christmas, and New Year's Day. Fee for workshop projects.

Back down Route 10 toward the center of town is the Eli Whitney Museum. Not at all another historic home, this child-focused learning museum and projects workshop happens to center on the remaining and restored buildings of Whitneyville, a factory complex founded by Eli Whitney in the nineteenth century, but is entirely a hands-on place for inquiring young minds. On the site is a covered bridge, a wonderful outdoor Water Learning Lab (open May through October, weather permitting), and exhibits and project stations inside the restored armory and gun factory.

The exhibits in the armory focus on the scientific principles Whitney used in his inventions, including interchangeable gun parts and the cotton gin. A fascinating one-third-scale model of the factory village once centered in this neighborhood is also here.

The museum hosts many special events and activities of interest to children. Some of these, especially the daylong and weeklong projects, require advance registration. Walk-in visitors, however, can also participate in projects such as building a toy boat, a birdhouse, or a pinball or maze game. A marvelous toy train exhibition has been an annual event during the weeks around the winter holidays; call to inquire if it will happen again this year. Summers and school vacation times are when you are most likely to find wonderful, special hands-on fun provided for children. An extensive summer camp program offers excellent workshops and classes by registration only. An 1816 barn offers a summer theater series, country dances, and numerous folk concerts.

Brooksvale Park (all ages)

Brooksvale Avenue, off Route 10; Hamden Parks and Recreation: (203) 287-2579. Open daily year-round from dawn to dusk. Free.

Take a left turn off Route 10 going north to reach Brooksvale Park, a 190-acre recreation area that families flock to for hiking, picnicking, softball, basketball, and good old relaxing in the outdoors. A small petting zoo with domestic animals such as peacocks, a horse, oxen, rabbits, geese, and ducks is there for the delight of young visitors. Weather permitting, you can also enjoy ice-skating, cross-country skiing, and sledding here, and a maple-sugaring shack operates in late winter.

This popular park is a great place to stop if you are using the Farmington Canal Linear Park, which spans nearly 6 miles between Hamden and Cheshire. Brooksvale Park is directly adjacent to the linear walkway and happens to be nearly midway between the southernmost and northernmost end points, so it is a wonderful place for families to lace on their skates or have a rest before or after beginning a trek along the canal.

Farmington Canal Linear Park (all ages)

Park at Todd Street across from Sleeping Giant Golf Course or at Brooksvale Park on Brooksvale Avenue. Open year-round from dawn to dusk. Free.

New Haven County's **Best Ice Cream**

Just north of Sleeping Giant State Park, back out on Route 10, is **Wentworth Old-Fashioned Ice Cream,** which is worth a drive from practically anywhere. Fifty flavors, twenty-four toppings, freshly made cones, egg creams, root beer floats, fresh-squeezed lemonade, coffees, and baked goods are served up by friendly faces in this cheerfully painted parlor. They are open daily year-round, from 10:00 a.m. to 10:00 p.m. Sunday through Thursday and until 11:00 p.m. on Friday and Saturday in the summer; in the spring, fall, and winter, they close earlier, depending on the weather and business on the particular day. Call (203) 281-7429. $

Season Pass for **State Parks**

Frequent visitors to Connecticut's state parks may want to purchase a season pass that can be used in every state park for the entire Memorial Day through Labor Day season. The pass exempts users from any additional parking fees for individual parks. Unlimited visits to the parks are allowed, and no parks are excluded, except that in Gillette Castle State Park and Dinosaur State Park, the pass covers only the entrance fee to the outdoor areas. Visits to the castle itself and the Exhibit Dome of Dinosaur Park incur an additional fee. For information on obtaining passes, contact the State Parks Division at (860) 424-3200 or check the Web site at www.ct.gov/dep.

This recreational pathway lies along the abandoned railway that previously ran along the old Farmington Canal from Northampton, Massachusetts, to New Haven. Measuring a total of 83 miles, the canal required a 10-foot towpath, a depth of 4 feet, a width of 36 feet, and twenty-five locks to control the flow of water. All this was constructed using only manpower, horsepower, and simple tools like scoops and dregs. Twenty years later, the canal system was outmoded—replaced by the swifter and less expensive railroad in 1848.

See the Cheshire section (later in this chapter) for other details on this wonderful reuse of land through some of the county's prettiest woodlands. The two sections now provide 11 miles of paved and soft-shoulder pathway suitable for walkers, bikers, bladers, joggers, and cross-country skiers. Picnicking is possible along the route on benches made from stone taken from Sleeping Giant State Park. You can also linger at Brooksvale Park in Hamden or Lock 12 Historical Park in Cheshire. This is a great place for a simple family outing on a nice day.

Where to Eat

Aunt Chilada's Mexican Eatery. 3931 Whitney Avenue; (203) 230-4640. Overlooking the Sleeping Giant Golf Course near one of the entrances to the Linear Park, this establishment invites kids to eat free (one child per parent) on Sunday from 4:00 to 8:00 p.m. Clowns and prizes on that night draw in crowds of families. On Tuesday it's $2 taco night—a good deal for children. You can also choose salads, enchiladas, fajitas, and much more. Open daily for lunch and dinner year-round. $–$$

Where to Stay

Days Inn. 3400 Whitney Avenue; (203) 288-2505. 34 units, Jacuzzi. $$$

Howard Johnson Inn. 2260 Whitney Avenue; (203) 288-3831. 90 units, restaurant, outdoor pool. $$$

Cheshire

Centered near the junction of Routes 10 and 70 toward the north of the county, Cheshire was founded in 1690 by families who made their living as farmers, a fact that still influences this eclectic suburb. Close to New Haven, Meriden, Hartford, and Waterbury, Cheshire is a bedroom community for those cities, but it is also a region of nurseries, orchards, dairy and tree farms, and even a vineyard.

Bishop Farm (all ages)

500 South Meriden Road (Route 70); (203) 272-8243. Open from June through December. Hours are 9:00 a.m. to 5:00 p.m. on weekends and 10:00 a.m. to 5:00 p.m. during the week. In the fall, they may open earlier and close later. Free.

Right on Route 70 is one of the oldest and best of Cheshire's farms. The Bishop Farm represents the work of five generations. In business since 1805, Bishop grows and sells six varieties of apples, ten of peaches, four of pears, and five of plums, plus blueberries and raspberries. Some of these crops are pick-your-own; call for information and remember that the level of activity varies with the weather and the season. During most autumns, more than 70,000 pounds of pumpkins leave their fields. Fall is also a perfect time for walking the trails through the orchards and relaxing near the pond while you enjoy an apple cider doughnut. Also in the fall, they make cider and apple juice at their mill—watch them do so on pressing days and then buy some to take home.

In the snack bar, you can purchase apple crisp, baked goods, gourmet coffees, and soft drinks, or cruise for take-home treats in the gift shop. A Christmas Shop is open in season, and Christmas trees are for sale from Thanksgiving through December 24. They close up shop here on January 1 and typically reopen in late March.

Barker Character, Comic, and Cartoon Museum (all ages)

1188 Highland Avenue (Route 10); (203) 699-3822 or (800) 995-2357; www.barker museum.com. To renovate and take inventory of the collection, the museum will be open only on Saturdays until June 2008 from 11:00 a.m. to 5:00 p.m. Closed on all major holidays. Check the Web site for expanded hours after June 2008. Group tours (up to 12 visitors) are by appointment only; these are appropriate for ages 8 and older. Handicapped accessible on the first floor only. Free.

Want to just smile and smile and smile some more, Mom and Dad? Cheshire is home to another pair of ambitious entrepreneurs who bring a world of pure pleasure to children and parents. Herb and Gloria Barker, who own **Barker's Animation Art Gallery** here, share their private collection of vintage Disney characters, cartoons, comics, advertising characters, TV westerns, and all the toys and gewgaws that have been manufactured in association with them. The oldest such item dates to 1873.

Located on two landscaped acres, the complex includes the Barkers' huge animation art gallery, but it is in the museum and on its grounds that visiting baby boomers will begin to grin. Remember Lone Ranger cereal box rings, Dennis the Menace sling shots, Popeye Pez dispensers, and Little Orphan Annie Decoder badges? You name it, it's here.

Toys, trinkets, lunchboxes, and other memorabilia of the art and industry of cartooning are everywhere. This is the place to learn the complete stories of Betty Boop, Raggedy Ann and Andy, Sylvester, and hundreds of other characters. Inside its own building, a cartoon theater plays cartoon movies from the 1930s to 1950s on a big screen (summertime only). You'll learn some of the fascinating details of the art and history of many classic films and characters. Make a visit to this happy place and be inspired to take up collecting—or animation—yourself.

Farmington Canal Linear Park (all ages)

Parking areas at Cornwall Avenue, Mount Sanford Road, and Lock 12 at North Brooksvale Road; Cheshire Parks and Recreation Department: (203) 272-2743. Open daily year-round from dawn to dusk. Free.

Cheshire has joined hundreds of other communities across the United States in reclaiming for both recreational and historic preservation purposes the valuable land of abandoned railroad lines and canal routes. Thus far, the town maintains a 2.84-mile section that ends at the Hamden town line. The Hamden section picks up where this one leaves off (see earlier in this chapter) and conceptual plans indicate that the trail will eventually reach New Haven Harbor.

This ribbon of land was once on the property of the Farmington Canal, built in 1828 and extending from New Haven Harbor to Northampton, Massachusetts. The longest canal in New England, it was eventually replaced by a railroad along the same corridor. A 12-foot-wide pathway has replaced the railway, and the picturesque canal flows beside it (when the rains and snowmelt permit). Visitors to the linear park can stop at the park-within-the-park at Lock 12 of the canal. Engineered by Henry Farnum under the direction of James Hillhouse and Eli Whitney, the canal was an astonishing feat for that period. The Lock 12 site includes the lockkeeper's house, a helicoidal bridge, and a picnic area. On rare occasions, a park guide is available to explain the history of the site and the technology of the locks. (For further information, call Cheshire Parks and Recreation at 203-272-2743. This portion of the park is open March through December daily from 10:00 a.m. to 5:00 p.m.) The wooded pathway is used by joggers, walkers, in-line skaters, and cyclists in the summertime, and whenever there is snow, a swath is left unplowed for cross-country skiers. Mostly paved with asphalt, the path has a stone dust shoulder perfect for joggers. No skateboarding is permitted.

Where to Eat

Shangri-Lee Fine Chinese Cuisine. 965 South Main Street; (203) 250-8888. This sit-down restaurant offers tasty Chinese traditional dishes, with a dim sum buffet on the weekends. A favorite of loyal locals. $$

Vespucci's. 150 Main Street; (203) 271-9143. Just past the library, this restaurant offers mostly old-world Italian cuisine and pizza, with a children's menu that also adds American kid-favorites. Pretty murals. Open for lunch and dinner, from 11:30 a.m. to 10:00 pm. $$

Blackie's. 2200 Waterbury Road; (203) 669-1819. In business since 1928, this famed roadside stand transports you right back to, well, let's say the summer of '64. Hummel dogs are boiled in cottonseed oil and then grilled; you can top yours with their renowned hot green-pepper relish. Burgers, chips, and shakes as well. Open year-round Saturday through Thursday from 11:00 a.m. to 8:00 p.m. Closed Friday. $

Bagelicious Bagels. 945 South Main Street; (203) 250-9339. This casual eatery is open daily year-round for breakfast and lunch from 7:00 a.m. Very good fresh bagels, a nice sandwich menu, salads, and freshly made soups, plus coffee, etc. $

Where to Stay

Cheshire Welcome Inn. 1106 South Main Street (Route 10); (203) 272-3244. 25 units with 8 efficiencies and 2 apartments in clean, nicely landscaped setting. $$

Waterbury

Known for nearly two centuries as one of the nation's most industrial cities, Waterbury is also one of Connecticut's best embodiments of the term "melting pot." For three centuries its citizenry has been among the most diverse of all Connecticut populations, as wave after wave of immigrants has come here in search of the American dream.

Though their toil in the factories and mills of Waterbury was often far from idyllic, many of these workers would say their dream did come true. This success is evident in the thriving, busy neighborhoods, the beautiful early-twentieth-century architecture, and the rich variety of cultural entities like the Waterbury Symphony, the nearby Thomaston Opera House, and the exceptional and innovative Mattatuck Museum.

Mattatuck Museum (ages 4 and up)

144 West Main Street; (203) 753-0381; www.mattatuckmuseum.org. Open Tuesday through Saturday 10:00 a.m. to 5:00 p.m., Sunday noon to 5:00 p.m. Closed on major holidays. $, children under 16 free.

Excellent for families wishing to expand their appreciation for the unique contributions the little state of Connecticut has made to American culture, the Mattatuck Museum shows off its valuable collection in a recently built facility on the Waterbury green. Elaborately designed to enhance the "museum experience" for children, this

Cultural Arts in Waterbury

Waterbury and nearby Thomaston also offer other excellent opportunities for family fun. All of the following groups have reputations for presenting arts performances of the highest caliber for audiences of all ages. Single tickets for productions at all these venues range from $–$$$ for children to $$$–$$$$ for adults. Subscription rates available at most.

- **The Brass City Ballet;** (203) 573-9419. This celebrated company offers performances throughout the year.
- **The Waterbury Symphony Orchestra;** (203) 574-4283. Full season of symphony concerts, special pops concerts, and a Discovery series especially for families. Children's tickets for the last are $5.
- **The Seven Angels Theatre;** (203) 757-4676; www.sevenangels theatre.org. Awarded several Connecticut Critic Circle Awards for direction, acting, and design, this Equity venue stages a year-round professional series of Broadway-quality musicals, plays, children's theater, and cabaret concerts.

engaging museum is the only one in Connecticut that has selected the works in its art galleries entirely from American masters who have been associated with Connecticut. This exclusivity is not at all a drawback. It allows visitors to celebrate both Connecticut artists and Connecticut themes through the work of John Trumbull, Frederic Church, Maurice Prendergast, Alexander Calder, and others.

Fine arts of the nineteenth and twentieth centuries, decorative arts, and furniture are part of the permanent collection, but the period settings are among the best exhibits in the state for children. In the Brass Roots history exhibit, you can examine a re-created seventeenth-century house frame, you can wander through a nineteenth-century boardinghouse re-creation that has the voices of immigrants telling their stories, and you can explore a nineteenth-century brass mill while listening to the voices of workers describing their workdays in the factory. You'll learn what a colonial house looked like, you'll discover the pastimes of wealthy Victorians, and you'll even find out what role a saloon may have played in the lives of the workers who populated this busy industrial city at the end of the nineteenth century.

You will also learn of the amazing number of products that originated in the industries of Waterbury and other towns of western Connecticut. Clocks, watches, buttons, cameras, tableware, rubber products, and furniture made the Naugatuck Valley one of the most productive areas of the nation during and after the Industrial Revolution.

One of the best permanent exhibits is the fascinating story of the African-American captive named Fortune, who lived in Waterbury during the 1700s with other free and enslaved Africans. Learn their remarkable stories in this installation. The Mattatuck has a museum store and a cafe overlooking a courtyard garden. This complex also includes a 300-seat performance center, a research library, and a studio art classroom. Special events such as music festivals, dance performances, children's workshops, and lectures are listed on the online calendar. Be sure to cruise the Web site for one of the Mattatuck's best features: its online "exhibits," which provide excellent educational materials related to the museum's themes and collections.

Where to Eat

Diorio Restaurant. 231 Bank Street; (203) 754-5111. Excellent Italian fare is served at this elegant Waterbury landmark. High-backed booths and an etched-glass mirror across the back of the bar add to the old-time charm, and the great food earned high marks from the *Hartford Courant*. Lunch and dinner Monday through Friday, dinner only on Saturday. $$$

Domenic's and Vinnie's Apizza. 505 Wolcott Street; (203) 753-1989. Apparently it is understood that north of New Haven's Wooster Street there's been no finer place for pizza than Domenic's. Who am I to argue? More than thirty years' practice

makes perfect pies—now perfect-plus since their merging with Vinnie's. Open Wednesday through Sunday from 3:30 to 8:30 p.m. (9:30 p.m. on Friday and Saturday). $

Where to Stay

Courtyard by Marriott. 63 Grand Street; (203) 596-1000. 200 units, including 11 suites, 2 restaurants, fitness center, sauna, Jacuzzi, indoor pool. $$$

Holiday Inn Express. 88 Union Street; (203) 575-1500, (203) 573-1000, or (800) HOLIDAY. 111 units, fitness center, outdoor pool, continental breakfast. $$$–$$$$

Middlebury

Way out in the middle of the hills that begin the rise toward Litchfield County and the Berkshires is the pretty community of Middlebury, about 6 miles southwest of Waterbury. And right in the middle of Middlebury is one of the state's most popular family amusement parks.

Quassy Amusement Park (all ages)

Route 64; (800) FOR-PARK or (203) 758-2913; www.quassy.com. Open nearly daily Memorial Day through Labor Day and on April, May, September, and October weekends. Be sure to check the Web site for hours of operation and current pricing before you go. Parking fee ($$ per vehicle). Regular admission rate, $$$ for an all-rides/all-day pass. Saturday night after-5:00 carload specials. After 5:00 on any night, a rides pass is $$. Season passes available.

Located on the shores of Lake Quassapaug, Quassy Amusement Park is a sort of old-fashioned affair similar to the Savin Rock park old-timers may remember in West Haven.

Not quite as sophisticated as other New England amusement centers, such as Connecticut's Lake Compounce or Massachusetts's Six Flags New England, Quassy is newly refurbished and a whole lot of fun for families, especially those with young children.

Twenty-four rides, an eighteen-hole miniature golf course, a narrow-gauge miniature railway, paddleboats, a petting zoo, a lakeside entertainment theater, and a swimming and picnic area at the lake make this a perfectly happy place for a family outing. You can ride the carousel (a beautiful fiberglass repro of the original), two roller coasters, bumper cars, and all kinds of carnival-style rides with names like the Whip, the Monster, and the Himalayas. At the Saturation Station near Lake Quassy's beach, you can find thirty ways to get wet. The Big Flush water coaster is one of the park's newest rides. Take a wild rubber-raft ride down its 400-foot twisting tube of rushing whitewater. You might also try the Frog Hopper, a vertical thrill designed for kids two to thirteen. Or climb the catwalk up the Titanic and slide 45 feet down the deck to a soft landing.

Along with these features are the usual arcades, games of chance and skill, and a special area for children under five. The park's food concessions sell typical American fare, such as hot dogs and barbecued chicken. Special events like concerts, ethnic festivals, and fireworks add to the seasonal fun.

Where to Eat

Vinnie's Pizza. 504 Middlebury Road (Route 64); (203) 758-8846. Strictly pizza is the rule here, with the only exceptions being soda, beer, and wine to help the tasty pie make its way to your happy tummy. Clean, comfortable, and great for families leaving Quassy. Open Wednesday through Sunday from 3:30 p.m., closing at 8:00 p.m. on Wednesday, 8:30 p.m. on Thursday and Sunday; 9:00 p.m. on Friday, and 9:00 p.m. on Saturday. After pizza, stop next door for ice cream at Johnny's Dairy Bar. $

Derby

One of the oldest towns of the Naugatuck Valley, Derby has been characterized largely by the development of manufacturing since the Industrial Revolution. Luckily, a small portion of its lush woodlands, once the hunting grounds of the Paugussett Indians, has been preserved for future generations. To reach Derby from New Haven, take Route 34 10 miles west.

Osbornedale State Park/Kellogg Environmental Center/ Osborne Homestead Museum (all ages) 🕸 🐾 🎿 🏛

Park at Chatfield Street; Kellogg Center and Homestead Museum at 500 Hawthorne Avenue; park office: (203) 735-4311; Homestead Museum: (203) 922-7832; Kellogg Center: (203) 734-2513. State park open year-round 8:00 a.m. to dusk daily. Homestead Museum open late April through December 15 on Thursday and Friday from 10:00 a.m. to 3:00 p.m., Saturday from 10:00 a.m. to 4:00 p.m., and Sunday noon to 4:00 p.m. Environmental Center open year-round Tuesday through Saturday from 9:00 a.m. to 4:30 p.m. **Free.**

This pretty property lies in the hills just north of the confluence of the Housatonic and Naugatuck Rivers. Once the site of a silver mine and a spring water operation, the 400-acre park was for many years a famed breeding farm for prize-winning Osbornedale Holstein cows owned by Frances and Waldo Kellogg.

Activities at the park include hiking and fishing in the summer and skating and cross-country skiing in the winter. However, most activities here center on the Kellogg Environmental Center and the Osborne Homestead Museum, located on the property immediately adjacent to the park. The nationally registered 1850 colonial revival homestead is the former residence of Frances Eliza Osborne Kellogg, who willed Osbornedale Park to the state of Connecticut. The house and its formal rose and rock gardens are open for tours (April through December) that focus on the history of its first occupants and the fine art and antiques collection that they amassed here. Please consider offering a small donation if you take one of their hourlong tours. At other times of the year, the grounds of the mansion can be explored daily from 8:30 a.m. to 3:30 p.m.

The Kellogg Environmental Center is a natural science and environmental education facility. Wonderful both in its physical design and in its mission to educate the public, the center includes a solar exhibit area, a water study area, a nature store, a solar greenhouse, and classrooms and labs. Talks, walks, slide presentations, and activity workshops are offered here on a drop-in and registration basis.

General Information

Central Regional Tourism District: Connecticut's Heritage River Valley. 31 Pratt Street, 4th Floor, Hartford 06103; (860) 244-8181 or (800) 793-4480; www.enjoycentralct .com or www.visitct.com.

Greater New Haven Convention and Visitors Bureau. 59 Elm Street, New Haven 06510; (203) 777-8550 or (800) 332-STAY; www.newhavencvb.org.

Waterbury Region and Visitors Bureau. 21 Church Street, Waterbury 06702; (203) 597-9527 or (888) 588-7880; www.waterburyregion.com.

Northwest CT Convention and Visitors Bureau. P.O. Box 968, U.S. 202, Litchfield, CT 06759; (860) 567-4506; www.litchfieldhills.com.

Middlesex County
Riverside Villages and Shoreline Towns

I f you were to stand on the bare, windblown summit of Great Hill in the Meshomasic Forest, you would be easily convinced that Middlesex is the most beautiful county in Connecticut. On a clear day, the water of Long Island Sound glimmers far to the south. Four hundred feet below you, Great Hill Pond laps at the forest. And out of the north curls the broad ribbon of the Connecticut River on its way to the sea. The small country charms of the northern counties are eclipsed by this spectacular vista that reveals the best-kept secret of the region. From sea to river to vernal ponds, Middlesex County is a land shaped by water.

Also shaped by the sea and the river have been the lives of the inhabitants of these shores. Many of the attractions families visit in these parts are closely linked to the culture and industries that developed in response to the geography. Come to Middlesex for saltwater taffy, seafood of every sort, steamboat rides, covered bridges, and riverside rendezvous. Enjoy the bounty of its forests and farms—the water has nourished these well, and the riches they yield are jewels in Connecticut's crown.

TopPicks for fun in Middlesex County

1. Connecticut River Museum and *RiverQuest* Expeditions

2. Essex Steam Train and Riverboat Ride

3. Gillette Castle State Park

4. Devil's Hopyard State Park

5. Brownstone Exploration and Discovery Park

6. Kidcity Children's Museum

7. Durham Fair

8. Air Line Trail

MIDDLESEX COUNTY

- East Hampton
- Middletown
- Middlefield
- Durham
- Haddam
- East Haddam
- Chester
- Deep River
- Killingworth
- Ivoryton
- Essex
- Clinton
- Westbrook
- Old Saybrook

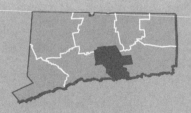

Essex

North of Old Saybrook on Route 9 or 154, Essex must fall on nearly everyone's list of favorite Connecticut towns. Honored in the past by the accolade "best small town in America," Essex is most certainly a New England gem, especially at the height of summer and in the stillness of winter. Elegant, gracious, and welcoming to families, Essex is another of Connecticut's windows to the past. Three-masted schooners, whale-oil lamps, scrimshaw, taverns with steaming bowls of chowder, sailors and captains and patient wives waiting at the widow's walks—these are the stuff of Essex's past.

Today, Essex offers a reminder of all that. Its concentration of eighteenth- and nineteenth-century homes on narrow village lanes, its wharf and marinas, its shops and restaurants—all are evocative of earlier centuries when Essex was one of the busiest ports on the Connecticut River.

Connecticut River Museum (ages 4 and up)

67 Main Street at Steamboat Dock; (860) 767-8269; www.ctrivermuseum.org. Open year-round, Tuesday through Sunday from 10:00 a.m. to 5:00 p.m. The museum closes at 4:00 p.m. in winter. Closed on Monday and major holidays. $–$$, children under 6 free.

This small, top-notch museum presents the history of the Connecticut River from its geology to its inhabitants, from its industries to the cultures that developed in the area because of the river. New gallery arrangements and exhibits literally explore the river from A to Z in this restored 1878 dockhouse. Among the artifacts and displays are scale models of the river's most famous warships, steamboats, and pleasure crafts as well as shipbuilding tools, marine art, and archaeological treasures unearthed in the area. One gallery focuses on the first submarine, the *American Turtle,* represented by a working replica.

Every year between Thanksgiving and New Year's Day, an exhibit of interest to children is in the changing exhibition gallery. Past exhibits have included dollhouses and snow globes, but the most popular of these are the magnificent model trains crafted by Connecticut artist Steven Cryan. Don't miss this year's show; Steven is often on hand to talk to kids about his work.

On summer weekends, hands-on activities are often planned especially for families. In the past, such topics as navigation by the stars, native and colonial knife-making and flint-knapping, rope-making, and knot-tying have been explored. These work-shops may have an extra admission charge.

RiverQuest **Expeditions**

If any young sailor in your party is in the mood for a little "expotition," check out the daytime excursions on *RiverQuest*, leaving from the Connecticut River Museum's Steamboat Dock. These adventures in Essex Harbor and the lower Connecticut River last approximately ninety minutes. In summer, five cruises are offered daily; in the cooler months of spring and early November, the cruise schedule is more limited; check the Web site or call ahead to be sure of sailing times. In February and March, come aboard for naturalist-guided eagle cruises, offered on Tuesday at 10:00 a.m. and on weekends at 9:00 and 11:00 a.m. and 1:00 p.m. Return later in the spring for cruises focusing on the nesting and migrations of ospreys and swallows; in autumn, celebrate the foliage; The schedule also includes two-hour sunset cruises, but these are limited to passengers over the age of twelve.

The twin-hulled, 54-foot *RiverQuest* has a fully enclosed cabin that is heated in the winter months; it holds fifty passengers. The narrated cruises reveal the many reasons the Connecticut is a designated National Heritage River, also declared "one of the last great places" by the Nature Conservancy. Learn about its abundant wildlife and the natural and cultural history of the river itself. Reservations are not required but are strongly encouraged. Tickets are one price ($$$$) for all passengers; children under two are **free.** Private charters can be arranged for groups of passengers. In 2008, a larger vessel, the *Adventure*, will be used primarily for special charters. For more information, call Connecticut River Expeditions at (860) 662-0577 or (860) 767-8269 or check the Web site www .ctriverexpeditions.org.

Essex Steam Train and Riverboat Ride (all ages)

Valley Railroad, 1 Railroad Avenue, off Route 154, about a quarter mile from Route 9 exit 3; (860) 767-0103 or (800) 377-3987; www.essexsteamtrain.com. Open early May through December, plus special events and combination rides throughout the year (riverboat combos only in warm season). Call for information or check the Web site. $$–$$$$, parlor car extra, children under 3 **free.**

Essex is also home to one of Connecticut's most popular family tourist activities, offered by the Valley Railroad Company. On a typical daily run, these vintage steam locomotives and railcars take passengers on a 12-mile, one-hour, round-trip ride from Essex to Deep River. At Deep River Landing, you can opt to board the triple-decker riverboat for a one-hour cruise upriver, past Gillette Castle to the East

Haddam Bridge and then back downriver. The total trip takes about two and a half hours if you take the boat ride. Each segment of the ride includes an entertaining narration about the railroad and the steamship lines. The sights and sounds of the river and countryside—and the trains—are wonderful. Bells, whistles, and the clackety-clack of the railroad track are accompanied by the shouts of blue-capped conductors calling, "All aboard!"

At the trainyard, before or after your ride, you can visit the station (which offers exhibits and children's activities), the car barns, and the gift shop. A stationary grill car called the Trackside Cafe offers hot dogs, deli sandwiches, salads, soft drinks, and such ($). If you want a special dining experience, book tickets for the Essex Clipper Dinner Train. Dine aboard a 1920s dining car, with a two-hour excursion through the river valley as you feast (May through October). Other special events for kids include an Easter Eggspress in March or April, a Trick or Treat Special in October, and a Santa Special and North Pole Express in December. Thomas the Tank Engine is also a regular visitor here; check the Web site for the schedule.

Where to Eat

Crow's Nest Gourmet Deli. 35 Pratt Street in the Brewers Dauntless Shipyard; (860) 767-3288. This dine-in, take-out, or out-on-the-deck eatery is the only restaurant overlooking the water in Essex. Breakfast and lunch daily from 7:00 a.m. to 4:00 p.m. from mid-June to Labor Day; closing at 3:00 p.m. in spring and fall; closed on Tuesday from Columbus Day to Memorial Day. Come for omelets, pancakes, create-your-own sandwiches, lobster, chicken, ribs, and chowders, plus fresh-made cookies, muffins, scones, and cheesecakes. $–$$

Griswold Inn. 36 Main Street; (860) 767-1776. Stop here for a meat pie in winter near one of the fireplaces or in sum-

The Parade of **Lighted Ships**

Early in December (or, rarely, in late November) the Connecticut River Museum sponsors a charming festivity that draws many visitors eager to experience the magic of Essex in winter. Called **Trees in the Rigging,** this free festival features a lantern-lit community caroling march, led by the Cappella Cantorum and the Ancient Mariners' Fife and Drum Corps, and a parade of lighted ships on the river. Beginning at the Essex Town Hall at 4:00 p.m. on Sunday of the selected weekend, carolers make their way down West Avenue and Main Street to the waterfront park at historic Steamboat Dock to see the colorfully lit garlands and nautical flags on scores of participating boats. Santa himself arrives on the dock by tugboat, and children can greet him and warm themselves with hot mulled cider at the museum.

Ivoryton

Officially a section of the town of Essex, this little village just a few miles east of Route 153 gained its name from its production of ivory products, in particular piano keys, in the nineteenth century. First settled in the mid-seventeenth century, Ivoryton maintains an interest in preserving the traditions of the early colonials that comes as no surprise in its museum celebrating one of the colonies' oldest traditions. The **Museum of Fife and Drum** (62 North Main Street; 860-399-6519 or 860-767-2237; donation; children under 13 free) is dedicated to the history and development of parade music, with a special emphasis on the traditional fife and drum corps that are called ancients. See the uniforms, parade and performance gear, musical instruments, music, and photographs of corps from all over the nation and Europe. Learn about the history of fifing and drumming from the Middle Ages through modern times. Usually open June 30 through Labor Day weekend, on weekends from 1:00 to 5:00 p.m.(except for the third weekend of July and the fourth weekend in August), the museum offers evening performances featuring two corps per night on selected Tuesdays at 7:30 p.m. in July and August.

Ivoryton also boasts a regional reputation in the arts because of its venerable theater at the village center. The **Ivoryton Playhouse** (103 Main Street; 860-767-8348; www.ivorytonplayhouse.org), which since 1930 has been home to some of Connecticut's best repertory and summer-stock theater companies. In addition to its year-round professional slate of comedies, dramas, and musicals, for adult and general audiences, it also hosts a terrific summer series of seven productions perfect for children two to ten. Among these are fairy tales, magic shows, and puppet theatres. Staged from late June through much of August, the performances are at 11:00 a.m.(and sometimes also at 1:00 p.m.); all seats are $10. **Note:** The River Rep (www.riverrep.com), at publication time of this guide, was awaiting completion of its new home in Old Saybrook. Check the Web site for any news of their location for the 2008 season.

mer for fresh seafood in the room with the moving mural of the steamboat on the Connecticut River. A special "young sailor's" menu and helpful suggestions for plate-sharing options make the place nice for young diners. Sunday Hunt Breakfast is served from 10:00 a.m. to 2:00 p.m.; kids 7 to 12 are charged half-price; kids 6 and under are free. $$–$$$

Oliver's Tavern. 124 Westbrook Road (Route 153), not far south of Valley Railroad, but not in the center village of Essex; (860) 767-2633. Good American fare (steaks, seafood, specialty sandwiches, chowder) in a warm, friendly setting. Lunch and dinner daily from 11:00 a.m., with the exception of Thanksgiving and the evening of December 24. $–$$

Where to Stay

Griswold Inn (same address and phone; www.griswoldinn.com) is also a very fine hostelry, offering 30 rooms and suites and even a charming guest cottage. Beautiful maritime and river artworks, fireplaces, private baths, and continental breakfast served in the library for all guests make this a cozy place for families. $$$–$$$$

Deep River/Chester

These two small towns are two of the most charming country villages in the state, although neither is exactly the family entertainment center of its county. Still, there are some excellent opportunities in both places for families.

Chester is quiet, quaint, and tiny. Located on Route 148 and surrounded by the Cockaponset State Forest, Chester was founded in 1692 as Pattaquonk Quarter, the fourth parish of Saybrook. An independent town by 1836, it seems content to remain in that century. Its winding lanes lined with historic buildings are unblemished by purveyors of fast food, slushy red soft drinks, or other atrocities of modern civilization. In Chester you will find lovely shops, great restaurants, and serenity.

Chester's **Norma Terris Theater** (www.goodspeed.org) offers the premieres of new musicals on its stage, and its famed **Connecticut River Artisan's Cooperative** (5 West Main Street; 860-526-5575) showcases the creative output of more than twenty visual artists who offer their work for sale here. Chester's downtown is, of course, primarily a retail center, but it is, in my opinion, one of the most charming and idiosyncratic in the state. So if you would like your children to see a thriving New England village that doesn't include glaring evidence of the corporatization of retail America, come here and enjoy the adventurous and serendipitous nature of independent emporiums. You might venture here also for annual events such as the Chester Fair (late August), the Lobster Festival (September), the Winter Carnival (mid-February), or the Holiday Stroll (mid-December).

When I first heard the name Deep River as a child on a family day trip to Gillette Castle, I thought Tom Sawyer must live in this town. Somewhere he sits dangling his feet in the water, chewing on a piece of straw and watching the steamboats pass by.

Forty years later, Deep River is not much different than it was the first time I saw it. Centered on the main thoroughfare of Route 154, it is a quiet town that still has the look and feel of a town of the 1950s. Famed in the more-distant past as a steamboat port accepting cargo and passengers to its docks, Deep River was once at the heart of the ivory trade that gave neighboring Ivoryton its name and supported the piano factories that you can still see in Deep River along Route 154. In the late 1800s,

Deep River Muster of **Ancient Fife and Drum Corps**

Held every third Saturday in July, this must-see family-style event may be the only one of its kind—or at least the largest. A gathering of up to seventy separate corps from all over the nation and overseas, this famed muster includes a colorful parade up the main street (Route 154) of Deep River. Chairs and blankets line the parade route long before you hear the first salute. Authentic uniforms, unforgettable music, and even bagpipers, pirates, Uncle Sam, and Dan'l Boone are part of the show.

After the parade, which can easily last two hours, walk to Devitt Field (at the bottom of the parade route), where the corps meet for food, drink, and special performances. Buy fifes, drums, music, tricorner hats, and other related items in the tents lining the perimeter of the field. Find out how to join a corps yourself. The parade and admission to the field are **free,** but parking will cost you ($) in one of the many "lots" set up on the front lawns of the townsfolk. For information, call (860) 767-2237.

three-quarters of the ivory taken from Zanzibar was shipped to Deep River. Today piano keys are long forgotten as the principal product of the area, and the tourists arrive mostly just to savor its quaint aspects.

Canfield-Meadow Woods Nature Preserve (all ages)

Access from the east side of 377 South Main Street, Deep River, just south of the Sunoco station. Open daily year-round, dawn to dusk. **Free.**

Three hundred acres of woodlands, wetlands, ridges, and valleys are the habitats and terrains in this preserve. Open for passive recreation such as hiking and wildlife watching, the preserve has an easy 3.5-mile trail; maps are usually at the trailhead.

Where to Eat

The Wheatmarket. 4 Water Street, Chester; (860) 526-9347. These friendly folks serve delicious, out-of-the-ordinary sandwiches, soups, cheeses, and breads. Vegetarians will find food they can eat here, thank goodness, and families who arrive early can have dinner here or buy to take out. Open Monday through Friday from 9:00 a.m. to 6:00 p.m. and until 4:00 p.m. on Saturday. $

Simon's Marketplace. 17 Main Street, Chester; (860) 526-8984. Very popular sandwiches (on great French bread), savory and sweet crepes, and exceptional scones are the mainstay at this eat-in market/general store.Open daily year-round from 8:00 a.m. $

The Whistle Stop Cafe. 108 Main Street, Deep River; (860) 526-4122. You can't get any more small-town charming than this. Owner Hedy Watrous, continuing the business her grandfather started in 1928, offers children's specials at every meal. Breakfast is served all day, beginning at 7:30 a.m. Lunch begins at 11:00 a.m. and ends at 2:00 p.m., when the cafe closes.

Eat inside or outside. Open Thursday through Monday. $–$$

Main Street Sweet Shoppe. 162 Main Street, Deep River; (860) 526-9012. Get in line for bliss: excellent chocolates, super-rich ice cream, hot cocoa, espresso, in a delightful pink-and-chocolate setting. Open Wednesday through Sunday from noon to 6:00 p.m., at least in the late fall and winter; longer hours in the summer and warmer months. $

East Haddam/Haddam

Though it is famed as the home of Connecticut's castle and its riverside opera house, the town of East Haddam is also a rural enclave that few visitors explore past the sight and sound of the river. In actual fact, the town spreads far eastward for several miles where Middlesex County pushes itself squarely into the western boundaries of New London County. Adventurous families who love the woodlands as much as the water should spend an extra day near East Haddam just to be sure they've seen all its wonders. Take Route 9 or Route 154 to Route 82 to reach its center.

In the town of Haddam, the Connecticut River beckons to visitors, this time from the west bank. In this town, too, the boundaries far exceed the visitor's concept of the few structures that hug close to the river. The town actually goes westward all the way to the Durham town line, but it is near the water that the action for families centers. Luckily a historic and remarkable bridge links both towns, and if you have the patience for the openings and closings of the swing bridge (which most kids do), you'll have fun making the crossings from place to place.

Gillette Castle State Park (ages 3 and up)
67 River Road; (860) 526-2336. The park is open daily year-round from 8:00 a.m. to sunset; no entrance fee is charged. From the Saturday of Memorial Day weekend through Columbus Day, the castle is open from 10:00 a.m. to 5:00 p.m. every day, but please note that the last castle tour tickets are sold at 4:30 p.m. $, children 5 and under free.

I have yet to find a Connecticut guidebook that can resist mentioning the medieval-looking wonder perched on a bluff called the Seventh Sister, high above the eastern bank of the Connecticut River. Recent restorations to this splendid fieldstone fortress have ensured that many more generations of visitors can enjoy this enchanting structure, toured by 100,000 visitors each year.

Completed in 1919 as the retirement home of the eccentric actor William Gillette (famed for his stage portrayal of Sherlock Holmes in the early part of the twentieth century), the house was built according to his exact specifications. The turrets, terraces, archways, and fountains found outside are awesome enough, but the interior will make you gape.

The twenty-four rooms contain gorgeous stonework, extraordinary hand-carved woodwork, and many of Gillette's original furnishings and possessions. A separate visitor center includes a gift shop, a picnic deck with tables, and restrooms. (A food concession operates in the summer season in yet another building.) The visitor center houses exhibits on Gillette's life and career, along with a portion of the castle's incredible collection of Holmes-related memorabilia. Here, too, is one of the restored electric engines from Gillette's train that used to loop the property; it is on display along with a passenger car from the original assortment of cars that Gillette used to take such guests as Albert Einstein and Calvin Coolidge on tours around his estate.

Only on the weekends (10:00 a.m. to 4:00 p.m.) between Thanksgiving and the week before Christmas, the castle has an annual Victorian Holiday Celebration that features special decorations, musical performances, and other entertainments. Have a cup of hot cider at the bonfire outside (no charge) or come inside for a tour ($). Call ahead to be sure this tradition has continued.

The castle grounds are part of the nearly 200-acre **Gillette Castle State Park,** with breathtaking views of the river and valley. You will see some of the same views painted by Connecticut artists in earlier times; look for the Viewpoints signage of the Connecticut Art Trail. Three miles of trails allow you to explore safely; many spots are perfect for picnicking, napping, or playing knights and ladies.

Goodspeed Opera House (ages 6 and up)

Goodspeed Landing on Route 82; box office: (860) 873-8668; tours: (860) 873-8664; www.goodspeed.org.

As you cross the river on Route 82, you'll note a large, white Second Empire building that houses the state's best-known opera house, built in 1876. Restored inside and out, the beautiful Goodspeed presents a three-show season of hit musical productions from April through December. Mostly revivals of Broadway favorites from the 1920s through the 1960s, the shows in this intimate theater are great family entertainment. Except for the youngest members of your family, who might have trouble staying settled through these full-length performances, bring the whole family if you can afford the moderately priced (compared to Broadway) tickets.

Real theater buffs may enjoy the thirty-minute tours of the opera house offered in season on Saturday and Monday; call for specific times and reservations ($). You get to see the dressing rooms and all the inner workings, plus you hear great stories of the Goodspeed's illustrious past.

Thankful Arnold House (ages 8 and up)

Hayden Hill Road, Haddam (860) 345-2400; www.haddamhistory.org. Open year-round from 9:00 a.m. to 3:00 p.m. Wednesday, 2:00 to 8:00 p.m. Thursday, and noon to 3:00 p.m. Friday; from Memorial Day through Columbus Day, from 1:00 to 4:00 p.m. Sunday. Museum store open Wednesday and Friday, noon to 3:00 p.m., Thursday 3:00 to 6:00 p.m., and from Memorial Day to Labor Day on Sunday from 1:00 to 4:00 p.m. Tours and access to the archives and library are also available by appointment. Tours, $.

If you are spending a weekend in the area, you might enjoy a tour of this historic house museum, built between 1794 and 1810. It is one of the thirteen historic sites on the Connecticut Women's Heritage Trail. Visitors can hear the story of the Widow Arnold, her daughter, and her granddaughter, all of whom were heads of the household for three successive generations. Local history programs, walking tours, and hands-on workshops are often on the calendar of events; children are given special attention on house tours. A lovely garden is out back, and from time to time a special event such as a fall family apple festival is hosted on the grounds.

Haddam Meadows State Park (all ages)

Route 154, about a mile south of Route 82 in Haddam; (860) 663-2030; www.ct.gov/dep. Open year-round from 8:00 a.m. to sunset. No parking fee or individual day-use fee. Pets must be leashed.

Used for agricultural fields in colonial days, the Haddam Meadows floodplain also served as a common pastureland for the livestock of Haddam's first European settlers. Now 175 acres of parkland have replaced those fields of hay and grain. Very peaceful and low-key in nearly every season, this park offers a sweeping view of the river from its broad lawns and picnic areas. Fishing is allowed, and you can launch a boat right into the river from the state boat-launch ramp, but picnics are among the

Nathan Hale **Schoolhouse**

So-called because the Connecticut patriot taught here, at the age of eighteen, for six months in 1773 and 1774, this one-room building is at the rear of St. Stephen's Church property on Route 149, just north of the opera house. Exhibits under development here tell the story of our state hero. A Yale graduate, he taught in New London the year after he taught here and later joined George Washington's revolutionary forces in New York City, where he was hung by the British for treason against the Crown. Maintained by the Connecticut Sons of the American Revolution, this small museum is open on weekends and holidays from noon to 4:00 p.m. in the summertime only. The exact address is 29 Main Street, East Haddam; for more information, call (860) 873-3399. $

Ferry to **the Castle**

If you're headed to Gillette Castle or you need to cross the river for any other reason, catch a ride on the **Chester–Hadlyme ferry** (860-443-3856), which docks at the end of Route 148. The ride takes about four minutes. The flatboat *Selden III* begins each day's labor on the Hadlyme side at 7:00 a.m. Monday through Friday and at 10:30 a.m. on weekends; the last ride of the day leaves Chester at 6:45 p.m. on weekdays and at 5:00 p.m. on weekends. Running daily (with the exception of Thanksgiving Day) from April 1 through November, the Chester–Hadlyme ferry service is one of the oldest in the country; it's been in continuous operation since 1769. $

prime activities. The fields are also used for varied sports and field games (bring a Frisbee, for sure), and on rare occasions a festival or other special event occurs, but life is typically quiet in these parts, and you can happily eat, read, nap, and watch the Little League kids take a swing at the ball. You might wade a bit at the boat launch, but swimming is prohibited, and the park offers no beach area or lifeguards.

Devil's Hopyard State Park (all ages)

Route 82 to Mount Parnassus Road to 366 Hopyard Road; (860) 873-8566. The park is open year-round from 8:00 a.m. to sunset. Free entrance to park; camping fee, $. Picnic shelter with tables and pedestal cooking grills. Pit toilets. Call ahead in the summer to be sure the campsites are open; the camping season is April 20 through September 30.

Beautiful in all seasons, the moderate trails through the heavily wooded terrain of this lovely park are wonderful for families. Views of the countryside are especially breathtaking in the fall, but the 60-foot cascades of Chapman Falls are most impressive in the spring. Look for the potholes in the rocks at the base of the falls. Legend says that these formations were made by the hot hooves of the devil as he hopped from ledge to ledge so as not to get wet.

Leave your own footprints on the paths that lead to the many scenic overlooks of the pretty Eightmile River, which threads itself through the woods and farms in the area. Stay overnight (if you dare) in one of the twenty-one wooded campsites with drinking water and outhouses. You can call for reservations or try your luck at the first come, first served game. You can also fish from the streams and picnic wherever you like. A large picnic area with tables is provided near the parking area, but in our opinion the best spots for picnicking are actually at the trailside overlooks. Choose the one that pleases you most. Leave well before dark if you believe the stories that this wood is haunted by the devil and the ancient hags of Haddam.

Where to Eat

The Cooking Company. 1610 Saybrook Road at Swing Bridge Market Place, Haddam, near junction of Routes 82 and 154; (860) 345-8008. Open from 10:00 a.m. daily except Sunday, this gourmet deli/bakery/coffeehouse has excellent hot or cold sandwiches, wraps, salads, soups, and desserts. Eat in or take out. $

Hadlyme Country Store. Near the corner of Routes 82 and 148 (called Ferry Road after the intersection) on the eastern bank in Hadlyme; (860) 526-3188. Open daily from 6:30 a.m. to 6:00 p.m. (4:00 p.m. on Sunday), this charming little store is run by cheerful folks who sell great picnic/hiking food and supplies—sandwiches, salads, fresh baked goods, soda, ice cream, even charcoal and marshmallows. $

Me and McGee. 40 Saybrook Road (Route 154), on the western riverbank, in Higganum; (860) 345-3777. The great food and good company at this friendly eatery keep the locals coming back and the tourists glad they came. Excellent breakfast omelets, fresh-daily homestyle soups, famed fish and chips, seasonal specials,

Clip-Clop through **the Countryside**

No outing in Connecticut may be more enchanting than a horse-drawn hay or sleigh ride, and **Allegra Farm,** deep in the woodlands of East Haddam, has a collection of sixty-plus vehicles that can help you make a day-in-the-country dream come true. Home to the largest authentic livery stable in the state, the farm is located on beautiful Lake Hayward on the border of Colchester. The forest paths, agricultural fields, and dirt lanes in this part of the planet make a perfect setting for a journey down a time-warped road. John Allegra or one of his staff will be more than happy to hitch a team to a wagon, a surry, a carriage, a caleche, a sleigh, or even—gulp—a hearse and take you for a ride. Allegra Farm is also home to the **Horse-Drawn Carriage and Sleigh Museum of New England,** which means you can visit here if you just want to see the vehicles (and the horses). You have to call ahead for an appointment, but you'd be welcome nearly any day of the year. You can even arrange for a lesson in carriage driving. Sleigh and carriage rides can be pricey for many budgets, but some vehicles here carry multiple revelers, so that can bring the price-per-person down to a reasonable splurge. Leaves will crunch or snow will fly, and you'll be bundled safely under a toasty lap rug, out in the arms of Nature. Could be worth every penny for an unforgettable birthday or holiday treat. The farm/museum is located at 69 Town Road in East Haddam. Call (860) 680-5149 or (860) 537-8861 for reservations. For more information, check the Web site at www.allegrafarm.com.

and Mom-made bakery treats and breads. Open 6:00 a.m. to 2:00 p.m. every day except Sunday. $–$$

The Blue Oar River Bank Grille. 16 Snyder Road, off Route 154 in the Midway Marina, Haddam; (203) 345-2994. For a casual meal outdoors on picnic tables or on the veranda inside, come to this sailor's secret, 1 mile north of the swinging bridge. The views of the river are beautiful, the chowder is great, and the sandwich specials or grilled dinners will please yachters and landlubbers alike. Open mid-May through mid-October, for lunch and dinner, Tuesday through Sunday, 11:30 a.m. to 9:00 p.m. Dinner specials start at 5:00 p.m. $–$$

La Vita Gustosa. 9 Main Street, East Haddam; (860) 873-8999. Across from the opera house, this cheery family-owned place offers reasonably priced, home-cooked Italian favorites, plus individual pizzas, panini "sangwiches," and a special "bambini" menu for the kids. Lunch and dinner year-round from 11:30 a.m., Tuesday through Sunday. $$

Gelston House. 8 Main Street, East Haddam; (860) 873-1411. For a river view that's pretty much incomparable in a fancier place to dine, come to this lovely historic setting for special occasions. Affordable patio menu ($–$$) in the warmer months; children's menu offers choices taken from the simpler and more affordable tavern menu. Open year-round Tuesday through Friday for lunch; Tuesday through Sunday for dinner; and on weekends from 11:00 a.m. to 3:00 p.m. for brunch. Pre-theater prix fixe dinner. Closed Monday. $$$–$$$$

Where to Stay

The Bishopsgate Inn. Just steps from Goodspeed Landing on Route 82; (860) 873-1411. Children are more than welcome in this polished, six-guest-room inn. A lovely suite with a sauna will meet all your family's needs. Fireplace rooms, private baths, cozy common areas, and generous breakfasts.Bring your own portable cribs for little ones. $$$–$$$$

Sunrise Resort. Route 151; (860) 873-8681. Only open May through October, this family resort/campground on the Salmon River has 200 guest units, 30 campsites, an outdoor pool, a restaurant, playground, tennis, volleyball, shuffleboard and bocce courts, paddleboats, rowboats, and canoes. Nightly and weekly rates. $$–$$$

Wolf's Den Family Campground. 256 Town Street (Route 82); (860) 873-9681. Tent and RV sites for 209 campers. Swimming, fishing, and hiking nearby. Tennis on the property. Game room, laundry facilities, toilets, showers. Nightly and weekly rates. $$

Portland/East Hampton

Nestled against the Connecticut River on one side and the Meshomasic State Forest on the other, the town of Portland has been famed in state history for its incredible brownstone quarries. In operation from the 1600s right up to the present day and now designated as National Historic Landmarks, these quarries are undergoing a tremendous evolution in the twenty-first century. In two of the quarries, all Connecticut families will benefit from the efforts of three enterprising brothers who have the support of the Portland community in their spectacular new recreation site.

Not far to the east, near the shores of Lake Pocotopaug, is the center of East Hampton, the town in which I took my first childhood family vacation, saw my first snapping turtle, and learned both how to canoe and how to capsize a canoe. Whoops! Outdoor fun like that is still yours for the asking in these parts. The town of East Hampton also includes the villages of Cobalt, Haddam Neck, and Middle Haddam, which make the historic East Hampton town center near the lake seem like a metropolis. East Hampton was once famed in Connecticut's history as "Belltown, USA." From 1808 onward through a great deal of the twentieth century, a whole lot of bells were manufactured here. Only one of at least thirty bell-making firms remains today (and its bells are made overseas). Just yards from the lakefront is another historic industry: The famed T. N Dickinson witch hazel products are created here at American Distilling and Manufacturing, which processes raw witch hazel and extracts, purifies, distills, and bottles the therapeutic skin-care and pharmaceutical properties of this native Connecticut plant. Sadly, no public tours are offered at either the distillery or the empty bell factories, but the quarries, lake, and trails of this quintessentially New England area should ring the bells of your whole clan.

Brownstone Exploration and Discovery Park (all ages)

161 Brownstone Avenue; (860) 342-0668; www.brownstonepark.com. Seasonal limitations on some activities; canoeing, kayaking, and diving are permitted year-round. Hours vary by season; check the Web site for the full schedule. General day passes and Adventure Sports Passes, $$$; season passes for individuals and families, $$$$. Children under 3 free. Portland residents pay half the daily rate; proof of residency required. All park visitors must register at the main gate, complete a liability waiver (which is kept on file for the season), and pay admission. Scuba divers not accompanied by an instructor must present a valid certification card from a recognized agency to dive. Solo diving is not permitted. Zip line users must weigh more than 70 pounds and less than 250 pounds. Cliff jumpers must be over 18. All water-based activities require use of personal flotation vests, which are provided. Scuba equipment rentals available with advance notice. Canoe and kayak rentals available.

Simply unbelievably wonderful, this extraordinary outdoor recreation park on the eastern bank of the Connecticut River may well become the state's most popular attraction as it evolves throughout its five-year development plan. In two of the nation's few brownstone quarries, three Connecticut brothers have devised more fun for more people in less time than even seems possible. In operation from 1660, the sandstone quarries—now designated National Historic Landmarks—continue to yield the softly colored building material known the world over as brownstone. Quarrying operations are active, however, at just one of the three "holes" in Portland. In the other two, a fabulous recreation facility has taken shape in just the past two years.

Remarkably well tucked into an industrial zone just north of the Portland Bridge, the park is among the most surprisingly beautiful sites in the state, both within the quarries themselves and in the many nearby acres of parkland above the river. The latter, owned by the Town of Portland, offer expansive vistas of the river and are open to hikers and bikers, dawn to dusk, year-round. Before long, the Hayes brothers plan to add a forty-site campground to this area. The quarries are, quite simply, stunning. They have been one of the nation's premier sources of brownstone, and during the mid- to late nineteenth century, 1,500 quarriers, 500 oxen, and at least one locomotive cut, dragged, and toted the stone to quarry schooners that carried it to New York City and elsewhere for use in residences, public buildings, and monuments. The floods and hurricanes of the 1930s put an end to all that. One day in that era, the Connecticut River overflowed its banks, and two of the quarries filled to the brim with water in fourteen minutes. Fed by natural springs that opened under the weight of all that water, the quarries—60 to 90 feet deep from the water line down and with sheared cliffs up to 100 feet above the water line—remain flooded to this day, with nearly pure, crystal-clear freshwater. Due to the efforts, imagination, and ingenuity of the Hayes brothers and their many supporters, you can now swim, slide from the Aqua Tower, scuba dive, kayak, or canoe in the quarry, with those magnificent cliffs rising all around you. You can rock climb and rappel. You can zip line, cliff jump, or tower climb. Arrange for lessons in just about any of the above, or just picnic, wander, and soak up the excitement. Have a birthday party, boost your self-esteem, or master a challenging obstacle course. You can even rent a private floating party barge complete with a canopy and picnic table and a canoe to get your guests out to it!

By 2009, you should be able to camp; in future years, you may visit museum exhibits and explore the learning center to discover the site's geological and natural history. The staff is highly trained and certified in safety, first aid, and CPR. Lifeguards are everywhere, and personal flotation devices are required and provided for water sports. Safety rules are clear and strictly enforced. Hidden under the water are carefully mapped scuba stations, complete with underwater training platforms at varying depths; divers can learn and practice scuba skills with the park's certified instructors. A gift shop provides souvenirs and water activity gear; a concession provides light meals, snacks, and beverages. You've got to see this to believe it. It's gorgeous; it's historic; it's fun.

Happiest Paddler (ages 4 and up)

70 North Main Street, East Hampton; (860) 267-1764. West Shore Marine is open year-round but closes for seasonal transitions. Boat rentals are primarily from April through October. Call ahead to be sure they are in operation. Reservations are recommended during the summer. $$–$$$$

At West Shore Marine, you will find the friendly folks at Happiest Paddler, who rent canoes, kayaks, and other vessels you might take out on the peaceful waters of pretty Lake Pocotopaug. Call ahead for the current scoop on their vessels, rates, and regulations. Ask too about the sunset cruises they offer in conjunction with the folks at Angelico's Lake House Restaurant, just up the road. In past seasons, they have offered one-hour cruises at 5:30 and 6:30 p.m. on Wednesdays and Sundays, weather permitting. Hors d'oeuvres are served aboard the boat, then you debark for dinner at the Lake House. Not a bad outing for the kids or for Mom and Dad. Be sure to call for both reservations (required) and for this year's rates.

Sears Park (all ages)

62 North Main Street, on Lake Pocotopaug; East Hampton Parks and Recreation Department: 20 East High Street; (860) 267-6020. Open year-round, dawn to dusk. May 15 to Labor Day, open only to residents; early September through May 14, free to nonresidents. Alcoholic beverages are prohibited.

This town-owned park offers a sandy swimming area, a boat launch, a pavilion, and other recreational facilities only to residents during the summer months (May 15 to Labor Day), but nonresidents are welcome to swim, picnic on its wide lawns, or play on its playscape during the rest of the year at no charge. It is one of the few public access areas to Lake Pocotopaug, which is one of the state's largest inland bodies of water.

Hurd State Park (all ages)

South of East Hampton center, on Route 151, in Cobalt section; (860) 526-2336; www .ct.gov/dep. Free day-use; overnight camping fee ($).

Hurd State Park is another of the excellent facilities the State of Connecticut maintains for public use. Like other state parks, it is typically beautiful, clean, safe, and fun. It's special, however, because of its location overlooking the Connecticut River and because of its pretty Hurd Brook Gorge. Its 884 acres offer a variety of recreational activities, including rock climbing, snowmobiling, cross-country skiing, freshwater fishing, and hiking. The Split Rock trail takes you to some magnificent views of the river.

Most important, Hurd offers campsites for youth groups and boaters. Many folks camp and canoe from here to Gillette Castle or to **Selden Neck State Park,** a 528-acre island downriver toward Lyme. Accessible only by boat, those parks also have primitive riverside campsites available from May through September. The state provides toilets and drinking water at Hurd; drinking water, outhouses, and fireplaces are at Selden Neck.

Air Line Trail (all ages)

East Hampton trailhead off Smith Street, at Cranberry Meadow parking area; East Hampton Parks and Recreation: (860) 267-6020; www.easthamptonct.org/pdf/park/ airline_trail.pdf or CT DEP site, www.ct.gov/dep. Open year-round, dawn to dusk, for nonmotorized (except for wheelchairs) recreation. Pets must be leashed. Free.

This multipurpose greenway trail wends its way in a 22-plus-mile corridor carved by the former Air Line Railroad, which by 1873 ran from New Haven to Willimantic and

Great Hill **Overlook**

You might recall from the intro to this chapter a mention of Great Hill in the Meshomasic State Forest. It is from the Cobalt section of East Hampton that you will reach it. From the intersection of Routes 151 and 66 in Cobalt, drive north 0.8 mile on Depot Hill Road (which is a continuation from Route 151). Turn right at the Y intersection onto Gadpouch Road, which becomes gravel. The trail starts on the left, 0.4 mile from that Y intersection. Park at the trailhead, which is the southern terminus of the southern section of the Shenipsit Trail system, marked by blue blazes. From the trailhead on Gadpouch Road, take the path through a section populated by tall tulip trees; cross a small brook before you ascend a steep section to a plateau and then another short, steep climb to the Great Hill Ridge. So far, you've hiked about 0.4 mile. Continue along to reach the white-blazed Lookout Trail on your left. Follow that for 100 yards to see the view of the river and the pond. The trail goes on from there, but if you retrace your steps to your car from this point, you will have had a hike of just under 1 mile. It's relatively steep in sections, but it's a short distance for a spectacular view. Be sure to wear proper footgear.

Before you attempt this or longer sections of the trail, you might want to call the Connecticut Forest and Park Association at (860) 346-2372. They can confirm the trail's condition or refer you to the volunteer trail manager. The CFPA, by the way, are the dedicated folks who produce the wonderful *Connecticut Walk Book*, which actually has two volumes—one for the eastern part of the state and one for the west. These excellent guides to the state's blue-blazed hiking trails are the most accurate guides to state trails that are open for nonmotorized recreation. Seven hundred miles of such trails lace through the uplands, shorelands, and fertile river valleys, through state parks and forests, for sure, but also across privately held lands. The GIS maps in each *Connecticut Walk Book* are backed up by the carefully updated Web site www.ctwoodlands.org, on which you can check for any trail closings, openings, or improvements. You can also order the books on the Web site. The oldest private nonprofit environmental organization in the state, the CFPA works tirelessly for all of Connecticut's citizens. They like nothing more than seeing families exploring the natural heritage of the eastern woodlands.

from those points onward to other rail lines that connected New York and Boston. The railroad, which fell into decline by the twentieth century, crossed the Connecticut River and cut across prime farmland and woodland tracts. In 1996 the Department of Environmental Protection proposed its rehabilitation as a recreational linear park, formed through the cooperative effort of the DEP, funds provided through the National Recreational Trails Act, and the four towns of East Hampton, Colchester, Lebanon, and Hebron, through which the trail runs. Hiking, bicycling, cross-country skiing, and horseback riding are the most common activities. It's a great place both to observe plant and animal life in the Eastern Woodlands and to gain a sense of its human history. Hemlock forest, marshlands, waterfalls, cranberry bogs, ponds, rivers, historic railroad sites, viaducts, and bridges—including the Comstock covered span—are part of its beauty. Bring your own picnic and beverages as well as a trash bag to pack out. Pick up a trail guide and map at the trailhead. In time, this greenway is likely to be linked to the East Coast Greenway, which will connect cities from the Canadian border to Florida.

Where to Eat

Angelico's Lake House Restaurant.
81 North Main Street; (860) 267-1276. Right across the road from the lake, this restaurant is one of the fancier places to eat in the area but not too formal for families. Quite casual, actually, it features live entertainment and sunset cruise/dinner packages in season. A kids' menu includes every kind of comfort from smoothies and mac and cheese to a "kid kut" prime rib. Lunch and dinner daily; Sunday brunch buffet (10:00 a.m. to 2:00 p.m.) is **free** for kids under age 5.

The Bridge of **Middlesex County**

Over on Route 16, almost at the New London County line between East Hampton and Colchester, is the **Comstock Covered Bridge,** believed to be the oldest of the three remaining authentic covered bridges in Connecticut. Constructed in William Howe's covered-timber truss style, patented in 1840 and used often for highway and railroad bridges, this bridge served travelers on the main road from Colchester to Middletown. It's open only to pedestrians now. Built in 1873 and placed on the National Register of Historic Places in 1976, the two-span bridge has an overall length of 110 feet, which includes a rare 30-foot pony truss span on its east side. Artists, photographers, and those who would like to fish in the Salmon River frequent the area, as do visitors who just want to enjoy a quiet, cool refuge on a sunny day. If you happen to be nearby, stop and have a walk across this pretty remnant of the past.

Portland Restaurant. 188 Main Street, Portland; (860) 342-2636. Straightforward in both name and presentation, this old-fashioned, hometown-style place is clean, no-fuss, and affordable, in a nineteenth-century brick building with high ceilings, black-and-white floor tiles, and dartboards. Italian fare, pizza, subs, daily specials, desserts. Lunch and dinner Monday through Saturday from 9:00 a.m., even though the only "breakfast" dish might be a BLT or an egg-and-cheese sandwich. $

Rossini's Italian Restaurant. 62 West High Street, East Hampton; (860) 267-1106. Every employee in this made-for-families restaurant is gracious and warmly welcoming. Delicious Italian favorites—pastas, pizzas, seafood, salads, soups, and more. Tuesday through Sunday from 10:00 a.m. $$

Where to Stay

Riverdale Motel. 1503 Portland-Cobalt Road (Route 66), Portland; (860) 342-3498; http://riverdale-motel.com. Family-owned since 1928, this complex includes a 47-room motel built in 1989. Simple, clean rooms with refrigerators; 4 units have equipped kitchenettes; smoking and nonsmoking units. Children 16 and under, **free**; complimentary morning coffee and pastry. $–$$

Markham Meadows Campground. 7 Markham Road, off Route 16, in East Hampton; (860) 267-9738. Seasonal, weekly, and nightly spaces in 100-acre family-owned campground. Fishing, swimming, boat rentals, entertainment; all necessary hookups for outdoor lodging. Bring your own tent or camper. Open April through mid-October. $

Middletown

This small city, once the largest and busiest port on the whole Connecticut River, is now best known as the home of Wesleyan University, one of the nation's finest centers of higher education. The city's interesting history and architecture and its position on the river have led entrepreneurs to capitalize on the tourist business that may help to revive the formerly sleepy atmosphere of the refurbished downtown area. Shops and restaurants of every description now line several blocks of Main Street, and the new hotel in the old armory makes it easy to explore for a weekend. These efforts as well as some traditional favorite events and sites make Middletown a good destination for families looking for fun in one of Connecticut's funkiest small cities.

Kidcity Children's Museum (ages 1 to 8)

119 Washington Street; (860) 347-0495; www.kidcitymuseum.com. Open Sunday through Tuesday from 11:00 a.m. to 5:00 p.m. and Wednesday through Saturday from 9:00 a.m. to 5:00 p.m. $, babies under age 1 **free.** Annual family memberships available.

The brainchild of Wesleyan alumna and Middletown mom Jennifer Alexander, Kidcity is devoted to integrated learning and play experiences for young children. Located just steps away from the city's main street, the museum offers 13,500 square feet of play space in its two linked buildings. Dedicated to the idea that parents and kids who play together will also learn together and reach out to others together, this innovative attraction continually reinvents itself. Designed to entertain and challenge the intellects and energies of children ages one to eight, this museum always has something new on board. From the Toddler Sea Caves on the basement level to the Space Age Roadtrip on the top level of the east building, this hive of interactivity offers fresh ideas for fun and learning. Your kids might choose to explore a sailing ship, a farm room, a diner, a market, a bagel shop, a push-button streetlight, a post office, or a wooden train layout. A laundry nook features an old-time hand-crank wringer, a clothesline, and clothespins, as well as the laundry to hang. On the clipper ship, which recalls the days of Middletown's heyday as a shipping port, kids can hoist the sail, steer the vessel, walk the plank, and otherwise romanticize the olden days of wooden sailing vessels.

When the kids tire of that fun, they can rumble around the Farm Yard and climb the Apple Tree House, specifically designed for toddlers. Other play spaces include a construction zone, a schoolroom with a giant chalkboard, and an old-fashioned farm kitchen with a vintage fridge. In the farmhouse market garden, visitors can plant carrots and play store. Visual and musical thinkers will appreciate the video production theater and the instruments from around the planet; bookworms will love the Reading Room, a recreation of Arrietty's library from Mary Norton's beloved classic, *The Borrowers*.

Visit often just to keep up with all the creative energy here. Birthday parties are frequent, as are special exhibits and events.Be sure to come a few times annually, just to absorb it all. You won't be disappointed.

Oddfellows Playhouse Youth Theater (ages 4 and up)
128 Washington Street (Route 66); (860) 347-6143; www.oddfellows.org. Year-round. Tickets in advance or at door; $–$$.

The state's oldest theater dedicated to works performed by and for children, Oddfellows was started in 1975 by Wesleyan students. Now privately run, the renovated theater with a colorful marquee on its refurbished redbrick building on one of Middletown's main drags is spurred by the efforts of many Wesleyan folks. With a mission to provide educational, multicultural entertainment for all students, including disadvantaged and minority children, the theater stages high-quality productions enhanced by the direction of professionals who come from all over the country to direct the young actors.

Among recent productions performed by the Teen Repertory company were *The Grapes of Wrath* and *Treasure Island,* and *Chavez Ravine,* produced with the guidance of the visiting Chicano/Latino troupe Culture Clash. The annual—and amazing—Children's Circus, held outdoors at 6:00 p.m. on the Friday of the first full week of August, features Middletown schoolchildren ages eight to fourteen, who learn circus skills in a five-week summer camp. All other plays are open to student actors from out of town, and all productions are open to the public. As many as two shows per month run throughout the school year; summer productions vary in number.

ArtFarm: Theater. Simple Living. **Activism.**

These three concepts compose the umbrella philosophy of one of Connecticut's most dynamic performance arts organizations. Currently offering theater workshops for children, youth, and adults from Middletown specifically and the lower Connecticut River Valley in general, **ArtFarm** is the brainchild of Marcella Trowbridge and Dic Wheeler, both formerly associated with Oddfellows Playhouse. In the past few years they've developed a theater company with a social mission as well as an artistic and educational vision. They aim to purchase a river valley farm or other open space as a future permanent home with performance spaces, theater workshops, retreat possibilities, and even some sustainable organic gardens. For now they offer a Shakespeare in the Grove production each summer on the campus of Middlesex Community College at 100 Training Hill Road in Middletown. Performances, typically offered at 7:00 p.m. for several days in mid-July, are preceded by an EcoFestival that begins each evening at 4:00. The festival features musicians, circus performers, and interactive Shakespearean theater activities along with such eco-activists as local organic farmers, crafters, artisan bakers, green vendors, and environmental organizations with exhibits related to conservation and sustainable agriculture. Shakespeare in the Grove and the ArtFarm EcoFestival are offered to the public at no charge, but along with your picnic basket and blanket, you might consider bringing along a donation. The suggested amount is $10 per person, but these free-will kind of folks will accept whatever you can afford. For more information, call (860) 346-4390 or visit the Web site www.art-farm.org.

The Wesleyan Potters (ages 6 and up)
350 South Main Street (Route 17); (860) 344-0039; www.wesleyanpotters.com. Open year-round. Gallery/shop: Wednesday through Friday from 10:00 a.m. to 6:00 p.m., Saturday from 10:00 a.m. to 4:00 p.m., and Sunday from noon to 4:00 p.m. Studios: Check Web site for class schedule. Free.

One of Connecticut's finest craft centers, this prestigious studio was inspired by the work of a Wesleyan professor who began a pottery class for Middletown residents in 1948. Now housed in 9,000 square feet of studio and gallery space, this cooperative includes 100 potters, weavers, basket makers, and jewelry artists. They also teach a year-round schedule of classes and workshops, all of which are available to the public. The frequency of these classes nearly ensures that a visit here by a family could include observation of teachers and new crafters at work. Your interest is welcomed; just check the Web site to see when particular classes are offered; when you arrive, stop in the office to ask someone to escort you to a spot from which you can observe without disrupting the class. Sometimes the studios can be as quiet as a tomb; other times there is plenty of activity and lots to see. Call ahead to arrange a guided tour of the pottery and weaving studios (860-347-5925). Come in late November through mid-December to enjoy the wares at the very special and celebratory annual exhibit and sale.

Where to Eat

It's Only Natural. 386 Main Street; (860) 346-9210. ION is perfect for families who crave the delicious and fresh taste and texture of vegan and vegetarian entrees, soups, and sandwiches. Open daily from 11:00 a.m.; they close at 9:00 p.m. Monday through Thursday, 10:00 p.m. Friday, 8:00 p.m. Saturday, and 3:00 p.m. Sunday. $

Javapalooza. 330 Main Street; (860) 346-5282. A fine stop for lunch or very light dinner fare (sandwiches and salads) this café offers teas, smoothies, coffees, and some sweets. Enjoy the passersby and economical fare. Open until 9:00 p.m. Sunday through Thursday and until 10:00 p.m. Friday and Saturday. $

Tuscany Grill. 120 College Street, also known as 600 Plaza Middlesex; (860) 346-7096. In an old theater building with high ceilings and brightly lit galleries, enjoy fresh sauces over perfectly done pastas; well-seasoned soups; thin-crust brick-oven pizza; innovative salads. Children warmly welcome. Lunch and dinner Monday through Saturday; dinner only on Sunday. $$

Typhoon. 360 Main Street; (860) 344-9667. This reasonably priced establishment is owned by an energetic, super-friendly woman who moves around the place with a quip for everyone. When you finish your Thai, Vietnamese, or Chinese specialties, you'll get an American-style treat: bite-size Snickers and Milky Way candies with your bill. Lunch, 11:00 a.m. to 3:00 p.m.; dinner, 5:00 to 9:30 p.m., Monday through Saturday. $–$$

Vecchittos. 323 DeKoven Drive; (860) 346-2637. *The* place to go in all of Connecticut on a hot summer night, this classic seasonal stand offers lemon, raspberry, chocolate, watermelon, banana, you-name-the-flavor of Italian ice, from noon till 9:30 p.m. from Memorial Day until the crowds go away sometime after Labor Day. $

Where to Stay

The Inn at Middletown. 70 Main Street; (860) 854-6300; www.innatmiddletown .com. Once the city's National Guard Armory, this restored landmark is now a lovely 100-room inn. 12 two-room junior suites equipped with microwave and refrigerator; cribs available at no charge. Heated indoor pool; fitness center; 100-seat Tavern at the Armory, specializing in traditional New England cuisine with seasonal favorites. Three meals daily (dinner, $$$–$$$$); children's menu. $$$–$$$$

Middlefield

I mean no disrespect at all when I say that Middlefield is very aptly named. Situated north of Durham close to the New Haven County line, it is an area of fields and farms, the pretty Coginchaug River, and parts of the Cockaponsett State Forest. Along with these features are two attractions particularly suited to families.

Lyman Orchards (all ages)
At the junction of Routes 147 and 157; (860) 349-1793; http://lymanorchards.com. Open daily; seasonal hours; call for schedule.

A huge family-owned operation since 1741, this bucolic extravaganza includes apple and peach orchards, strawberry and pumpkin fields, raspberry and blueberry patches, a sunflower maze and a corn maze, and the Apple Barrel Farm Store. A grand destination in every season, the farm is very popular with families wanting to pick their own produce and see the countryside.

Many festival-style events are planned throughout the year, mostly in celebration of various harvests. Food tastings, barbecues, hayrides, and other festivities are planned on those days. The Apple Barrel store is filled daily to the brim with fresh produce and baked goods, cheeses, maple products, fudge, freshly pressed apple cider, and take-out sandwiches, soups, and wraps. Come anytime to enjoy the ducks on the pond and the fresh air and sunshine.

Wadsworth Falls State Park (all ages)
Route 157; (860) 566-2304. Open daily year-round from 8:00 a.m. to sunset. Day-use charge on weekends only from Memorial Day to Labor Day. $

This state park has hiking trails and picnic areas, but its special attractions are a swimming area, which is available for ice-skating in the winter, and a beautiful waterfall with an overlook. One of the prettiest cascades in the state, Wadsworth Falls is a great place to spend a country afternoon. The swimming area and the falls are distinctly separate. Ask rangers or follow trails to the falls. You can also visit this 285-acre park to cross-country ski in winter and fish in the streams in summer.

Durham

Durham has some of the prettiest farmland in the county. Centered on Route 17 just south of Middletown, this quiet rural and residential town is admired for its farms and its charming historical Main Street of vintage homes and (mostly) independent businesses. It also has an intriguing new ice cream factory, but nothing can beat its incomparable country fair.

Durham Fair (all ages)

Durham Fairgrounds, Route 17, right in the village center; (860) 349-9495. Third weekend in September, beginning at 9:00 a.m. on Friday. $$$, children 10 and under free. Parking charge if you use someone's temporary lawn lot or free shuttle bus to free parking at the high school and other lots.

The fairgrounds are hardly noticeable most of the year as you drive past the green, but for three days annually, the joint is hoppin'. Like all country fairs, the Durham Fair celebrates the culture and traditions of Connecticut agriculture through literally hundreds of exhibits, demonstrations, and food and craft booths.

The largest agricultural fair currently held in Connecticut, it displays sheep, llamas, cattle, draft animals of *major* proportions, and every other barn and farm animal you can name. Look at the quilts, pies, fruits, and flowers. Ride the Ferris wheel and go through the Fun House. Eat candied apples; hot cashews; delicious chili, chicken, and chowder; and strawberry-topped Belgian waffles. Wander through the farm museum; buy something pretty at the crafts show. A terrific section for the youngest fairgoers includes kiddie rides and special programs for tots.

Over the aroma of fried everything rise the sounds of country music, announcements of contest winners, and screams from the midway. If your family has sleek, sophisticated city ways, put them aside for a day and come to the fair for a down-home good time. The ballet can wait, and your kids really ought to see the oxen and draft horses. They are a tribute to biodiversity, evolution, or Supreme Intelligence. Whatever your belief system, you have to be amazed at these creatures.

80 Licks Ice Cream Factory (all ages)

Parsons Road, just north of junction of Routes 17 and 147; (860) 349-1190. Call for public hours and current tour information. $

If you love both rock 'n' roll and ice cream, you're going to be very, very happy in Durham. Jill and Johnny, the two cheery and hardworking owners of this ice-cream factory have recently opened its doors to visitors, who won't be disappointed by the super-premium treats manufactured here. Most of the flavors—most of the *dozens* of flavors, that is—have deliciously inventive rock 'n' roll names (such as Oreo Speedwagon, Vanilla Nice, Judas Peach, and the Almond Brothers, of course), and rock 'n' roll memorabilia decorate the plant's walls. Come here for a fascinating tour of the operation; sample the ice creams, gelatos, sherbet, sorbet, and Italian ices. In the recent past, these folks have also operated the **80 Licks Ice Cream Cafe** (201 Marlborough Street; 860-342-8080) in Portland, a bit north of Durham and across the river from Middletown. At press time for this book, there was some question about if and when that establishment might reopen for the warm-weather season. Call in spring 2008 to see if it's reopened. In the meantime, if you need Another Brick in the Walnut, you know where to come.

Where to Eat

Lily's Cafe. 325 Main Street; (860) 349-5459; http://lilys-cafe.com. This friendly establishment is a best bet year-round for lunch Tuesday through Friday from 11:00 a.m. to 2:30 p.m.; brunch on weekends only from 9:00 a.m. to 2:00 p.m.; and fully prepared take-out dinners Tuesday through Friday from 2:30 to 7:00 p.m. For lunch, try creative sandwiches, house-made soups, salads, mac and cheese, omelets, and much more. The dinners-to-go in the refrigerator case make going home easy. $–$$

Killingworth

Nearly completely residential and rural in nature, this hilly town south of Durham (take Route 79) supports a few small farms and nurseries and is usually missed altogether by tourists. Nevertheless, it has a popular site perfect for a day in the eastern woods, complete with pretty trails, a miniature covered bridge, and an ol' swimmin' hole.

Chatfield Hollow State Park (all ages)

Route 80, about 1.5 miles west of the rotary at the junction of Route 81; (860) 663-2030; www.ct.gov/dep. Open year-round daily 8:00 a.m. to sunset. Day-use vehicle charge Memorial Day to Labor Day, $$.

The hills in these parts are deeply etched reminders of the glaciers that passed this way thousands of years past; those icy masses carved out nooks and crannies well worth exploring in this pretty park. Crisscrossed by several miles of well-marked hiking trails that present a merely moderate challenge even to small children, the park also has a pond for swimming and fishing in the summer months and ice-skating, if the weather permits, in the winter. The pond's water is the color of iced tea, but don't let that stop you from plunging in. The clear, clean water is just tinged with the natural colors of the minerals loosed from the soil in the pond's basin.

Changing facilities, rustic flush toilets, and a picnic shelter provide a few comforts, but there are no showers and no concession. A privately owned mobile lunch truck is here all day most weekends in summertime.

Where to Eat

Cooking Company Killingworth. 187 Killingworth Turnpike (Route 81); (860) 663-3111. Sister store to the similarly named eatery in Haddam, the Cooking Company offers soups, salads, sandwiches, and baked goods. Open Monday through Friday from 10:00 a.m. to 7:00 p.m. and Saturday from 10:00 a.m. to 6:00 p.m. Closed Sunday. $

Old Saybrook/Westbrook/ Clinton

These three towns compose Middlesex County's trio of Long Island Sound shoreline towns. Easy to group together because of their geography, they are also similar in other quintessentially Connecticut shoreline ways. Heavy with salt and briny mud smells of the sea and shore and marsh, the air here carries the sounds of screeching gulls, slapping rigging, lonesome train whistles, and bellowing foghorns.

These are the towns where you eat crab cakes and clam strips and play real mini-golf with windmills and lighthouses. Where you stroll along seawalls, have double-dip ice cream cones, and skip stones off the jetty. Where you walk barefoot, break out in freckles, and let the sun bleach your hair. These are the towns of summer.

Very, very few true "suck-'em-in" tourist attractions are here, but you can wander for hours along the shore roads that splinter south from the Boston Post Road. Also known as Route 1, footpath of the Pequot Indians and stomping grounds of the beach bums of Connecticut, this road is richer than a sea captain's treasure chest. Seafood shacks, antiques shops, ice cream parlors, and all those sort of half-rundown Cape Cod-y kinds of emporiums are designed to make you put on your browsing shoes.

Begin a tour in Old Saybrook, taking Route 154 south, bearing left on Main Street and continuing basically straight on College Street (both of which are actually still Route 154) toward the water.

Saybrook Point Park and Saybrook Monument Park

(all ages)

Follow College Street (Route 154) to its end at Saybrook Point; Old Saybrook Parks Department: (860) 395-3152. Both park sites open dawn to dusk daily year-round. **Free.**

Proceeding down Route 154 you will find Saybrook Point Park and a few satellite sites. Stop for a while in the big parking lot to your left as you approach the dead end in the roadway here, and walk to the seawall along the park's edge. It is here that nature provided the Connecticut River Valley her first big break. Down here near the mouth of the river, a sandbar prevents huge oceangoing vessels from entering the river. Thanks to the sandbar, which makes the Connecticut the largest river in America without a port, the river has stayed healthier than many others, and her towns have retained many of their old-time characteristics.

At this popular destination for day-trippers, miniature golfers, and anglers, you will find great fishing spots on the seawall, long-range binoculars to help you get a better view of the boats and lighthouse, and benches and picnic tables that encourage you to linger here. From the paved walkway you can see the breakwater that protects the harbor, and you can watch the boats and gulls and swans. You can play eighteen

Ahoy! Saybrook **Sails**

In business for more than sixty years, **Captain John's Sport Fishing Center** (860-443-7259; www.sunbeamfleet.com) offers chartered winter nature cruises that depart from Saybrook Point. In February and March, their licensed captain and a naturalist will take groups up the Connecticut River to see the bald eagles that fish these waters during the winter months. Typically offered on Sunday mornings, the charters ($$$$) are by advance arrangement only; large family groups and scout troops are welcome. If your group is smaller than the minimum required, the captain may agree to combine your group with another. The boat has a heated cabin, but dress warmly, including hats and mittens, in case you venture into the open portions of the vessel. Bring your own snacks, hot cocoa, binoculars, and cameras. More than 100 bald eagles now make their winter home on Connecticut's largest waterways, including this river, so although sightings are not guaranteed, they are not at all unusual. Many other birds inhabit this beautiful stretch of river as well, and the scenery along the banks makes for fine viewing, too.

holes at the **Saybrook Point Mini-Golf Course** (203-388-2407). Affordable and well maintained, it provides picnic tables, lights, and bug zappers for your comfort.

Pick up a bite to eat at the **Dock & Dine Restaurant** (860-388-4665); while you're there, stop in the restaurant's Connecticut River Room to see the wonderful artwork of Old Saybrook artists Lauren and Steven Cryan (860-388-5010); see the Essex section for news of Steven's famed holiday train layouts at the Connecticut River Museum. When you've seen the sights at Saybrook Point, explore the **Saybrook Monument Park** just half a block up the street, with its own small parking lot. Storyboards there describe its historic remains and artifacts from Saybrook Plantation's early days; a lovely short boardwalk provides an observation area of the tidal marshlands and its bird life. When you've soaked up the sights, get back in the car and follow Route 154 across the causeway and all the way around the peninsula (you'll turn sharply to the left immediately after you leave the Point parking lot). Enjoy the water views as you drive, then, when you arrive back at Route 1, turn left and drive toward Westbrook.

You'll have a real dilemma soon if you're hungry for lunch. You can stop in Old Saybrook for my personal-favorite lunch stop, you can head west a bit for the best pizza made anywhere between Providence and New Haven, or you can hold out until you reach the seafood king in Westbrook. See the end of this section for descriptions of all three restaurants. No matter which you choose, head for the beach when you're done.

West Beach (all ages)

Seaside Avenue; (860) 399-3095; www.westbrookct.us. Open 8:00 a.m. to 10:00 p.m. Restrooms, concession, showers in season. Seasonal beach pass required for residents; nonresidents pay a day-use parking fee ($$$$ per vehicle) from late June through Labor Day, from about 9:00 a.m. to 5:00 p.m.

After you eat, drive along the Boston Post Road and turn south onto Seaside Avenue in Westbrook. Highlighted by one of the prettiest views of the water and the offshore islands, this drive also takes you to what might very well be the best public beach in the tri-town area. Nonresidents are welcome to use the beach year-round; once school gets out (usually the third week in June), a daily per-vehicle parking fee goes into effect. Space in the parking lot is limited, so arrive early in the day if you are coming from some distance and would like to be sure there is room for you. Free parking on the nearby side streets is mostly prohibited. You can spend the day on the sand or stroll the long seawalk past the cottages that line the roadway across from the shoreline. This very clean beach is great for young children. Its swimming area has an extraordinarily sandy bottom that slopes very gradually toward deeper water.

When you leave the beach area, continue toward Clinton by driving west on Route 1. Except for its pretty beach and views of the water from its various beach roads and marinas, no attractions set it apart as a place for families. Still, coupled with some time at the beach, a variety of restaurants, an ever-growing number of antiques shops, and an ice cream emporium or two make it a perfect town for whiling away a summer afternoon. Come on Thursday evenings in summer to the gazebo at the historic Pierson School for the outdoor concert series. Programs generally begin about 6:30 p.m.

Clinton Town Beach (all ages)

At the foot of Waterside Lane off Route 1; (860) 669-6901. Open year-round. Concession and restrooms in season only. Day-use per-vehicle parking fee for nonresidents, $$$, payable at the gatehouse from 9:00 a.m. to 3:00 p.m. only, from Memorial Day weekend through Labor Day weekend. Residents, $$ in season.

Visiting families are welcome at this small crescent-shape beach. Cross the wooden bridge at the foot of the narrow, pretty road that leads past some lovely old houses and enter the beach area. A children's playground, restrooms, and a snack bar that provides simple summer beach fare are here. This is a nice, quiet beach perfect for families with young children. Sometimes they show open-air movies in the evening—great fun!

Clinton Town Marina and Cedar Island Marina (all ages)

Riverside Drive, Clinton.

Ending a tour of the beach towns at this little slice of the shoreline in Clinton might be the perfect close to your day, especially if you visit near sunset. It may be a bonus if you are also hungry for dinner. Take Grove Street south from Route 1 at the weathered blue and gold sign that lists the harbor sites. This quiet, residential avenue reaches the water about ½ mile down, ending at a point where the Bluefin Charters leave the harbor for sportfishing trips and the freshest lobster for miles around comes into harbor at the Lobster Landing, a refreshingly ramshackle establishment that offers a variety of shellfish and bivalves you can take home or, if the sunset entices you to linger awhile, eat right here on the Landing's very casual deck. You can also step on the brakes just a bit before you reach the doors of that quintessential shanty, and take the right turn onto Riverside Drive instead. There you'll find the Clinton Town Dock and Marina, with a public boat launch and a seasonal seafood shack, the Galley Grille. It serves up the best—maybe the only—bluefish nuggets in the state, along with hefty haddock sandwiches and other great seaside fare, from 7:30 a.m. to sometime after the sun goes down in summer.

At the waterside, a row of benches along a small stretch of walkway provides a front-row seat on the colorful spectacle the sun may be painting on the sky as it drops into the Sound to the west of Cedar Island. The view here may not be exactly glamorous, but if you can't see the beauty in the palette above you as the boats return to their moorings, then you've definitely left your rose-colored glasses at home. If you savor such scenes, you can even let the kids play in the sand awhile at teeny-tiny Esposito Beach, immediately to the west of the main parking lot. It's just a pier-side patch of sand, with no lifeguard (you wouldn't want to swim here anyway; this waterway is also leeward of the gasoline dock), but it can make for a good place for the kids to construct a quick castle while the folks crack open some steamers.

You can also head for the full-service restaurant contiguous to this area but tucked within the parking area of the private Cedar Island Marina. The Aqua Restaurant, decidedly public and seasonal, is the place to come if you'd like table service inside (ask for a window table) or out on their deck. The folks at Cedar Island don't mind at all if you sit on their benches or stroll their walkways, too. The private areas for their members and transient boaters are pretty clearly marked (by a gate you'd need to swipe a card to get through), so just use your common sense and enjoy

Keeping Things **Uniform**

If the beach holds no interest for you, you might care to stop in Westbrook at the **Company of Military Historians Museum** at Westbrook Place on North Main Street. The nation's largest collection of American military uniforms is here, as are completely restored and operable military vehicles from World War II and other late-twentieth-century conflicts. Open year-round from 8:00 a.m. to 3:30 p.m. Tuesday through Friday and by appointment. Call (860) 399-9460. Free.

The Pink **Sleigh**

Last in Middlesex County is a little bit of magic before you head home. Best seen in the twilight when the air is crisp and your breath rises steamily from your throat is a haven of peace and beauty for anyone who delights in the wonder of Christmas. Housed in an old barn, this store is truly charming—a place where every small child will suck in his or her breath in awe of all its glitter and gold. Dazzling displays of every color and material fill the rustic two-story barn, which is in itself beautiful. Stepping into this place on a crisp autumn afternoon just as twilight falls is like stepping into an elfin workshop hidden in the hills. Be sure to search for the hidden Mark Roberts fairies sprinkled around this magical place. Halloween and harvest decorations are here as well, at 512 Essex Road (Route 153) in Westbrook, ½ mile north of I-95 (860-399-6926). Open from early July until Christmas Eve, Tuesday through Saturday from 10:00 a.m. to 5:00 p.m., from 11:00 a.m. to 4:00 p.m. on Sunday, and on Mondays from November 1 to December 24. Extended hours in December on Thursday, Friday, and Saturday, when closing is typically at 8:00 p.m.

the stretch of walkway where you can see the locals exercising their dogs or pushing their baby strollers. No matter what portions of this little enclave you choose to enjoy, you've probably had a full day by now. Wait till the stars come out, brush the sand from your toes, and head on home to brush the salt air out of your hair. You'll come back, I'd guess.

Where to Eat

Cloud Nine Deli Cafe. 256 Boston Post Road, Old Saybrook; (860) 388-9999. For healthful breakfast, lunches, and take-out dinners in a simple, sunny setting, come here year-round, Monday through Friday from 8:00 a.m. to 3:00 p.m. and Saturday from 9:00 to 3:00 p.m. Closed Sunday. $

Alforno Brick Oven Pizzeria and Ristorante. 1654 Boston Post Road in Old Saybrook; (860) 399-4166. For the shoreline's best pizza, come here for thin, crisp crust, fresh toppings, and excellent sauce. Great salads and good pasta, too. If you can wait for a table, you won't be disappointed. $$

Paperback Cafe. 210 Main Street, Old Saybrook; (860) 388-9718. Diner-style menu; live music on Friday, Saturday, and Monday evenings, and Sunday afternoons. Outside seating in warm weather. Breakfast and lunch daily; dinner Tuesday through Saturday. $–$$

Bill's Seafood Restaurant. Route 1 in Westbrook; (860) 399-7224. If seafood wins the toss of the coin, cross the deck of the singing steel bridge, and slip into Bill's, on the right. The food is good, the prices are reasonable, and the setting couldn't be more picturesque. Watch the swallows swoop and chatter; look for the ospreys nesting above the tidal marsh; feed the ducks that hang out near the riverside deck. If you're going to eat chowder, steamers, and clam strips, you might as well do it here. The place hums most nights with live jazz, Dixieland, rock 'n' roll, and old-time banjo played by locally famed combos. $–$$

Edd's Place. 478 Boston Post Road, Westbrook; (860) 399-9498. For quick and delicious breakfast, lunch, and early, casual dinner or takeout, Edd's is terrific for soups, panini, spaghetti pie, lasagna, pies and muffins, and much more, at outdoor tables at the riverside or in a screened gazebo, open daily year-round. $

Aqua Restaurant. Riverside Drive in Clinton; (860) 664-3788. This shoreside classic at Cedar Island Marina offers great views, a friendly ambience for families, and great adult-friendly seafood. There's no better place to watch the sailboats return to the marina. Open nearly year-round for lunch and dinner. $–$$$

Where to Stay

Days Inn. 1430 Boston Post Road, Old Saybrook; (860) 388-3453 or (800)

329-7466. 50 units with refrigerator; complimentary beach passes and continental breakfast. $$–$$$

Sandpiper Inn. 1750 Boston Post Road, Old Saybrook; (860) 399-7973. 45 units, outdoor pool, beach passes. Nicely kept and popular with families. $$–$$$

Comfort Inn. 100 Essex Road, Old Saybrook; (860) 395-1414. 120 units; sauna, indoor pool, exercise room; continental breakfast. $$$

Water's Edge Inn and Resort. 1525 Boston Post Road, Westbrook; (860) 399-5901 or (800) 222-5901. Fifteen acres on the Sound, 100 luxury units with beautiful beach, terraced lawns and gardens, tennis, indoor and outdoor pools, health club, spa, water-views public restaurant, entertainment, and activities for the kids. Year-round. $$$$

Westbrook Inn B&B. 976 Boston Post Road, Westbrook; (860) 399-4777. This Victorian beauty has 9 rooms, 1 suite, and a two-bedroom cottage perfect for families. On the river with a dock and fishing; three minutes to beach, full breakfast on the wrap-around porch in fair weather. Gear available for boating, biking, and fishing. $$$$

General Information

Central Regional Tourism District. 31 Pratt Street, 4th Floor, Hartford 06103; (860) 244-8181 or (800) 793-4480; www.visitctriver.com.

Tourism Information Center. I-95 northbound in Westbrook. Staffed in summer months; maps, vacation guides, brochures.

Tolland County

Simple Dreams and Country Comforts

The hills of northeastern Connecticut have magic in them. As with Washington Irving's Catskills, something within these knolls has defied the physical laws governing the passage of time. The traveler is transported centuries backward just by being here. The magic of Tolland County lies not in what one does here. This is not a place well known for action. Rather, its magic lies partly in the sweet relief of having nothing to do here. It is, simply, a nice place just to wander.

Families looking for the quieter pleasures of life in New England will find much to please them here. The museums are smaller and have fewer buttons to press, but they are no less excellent than their showy counterparts in the city. The activities have fewer moving parts and use little or no fossil fuel, but they'll invigorate the body, feed the soul, and leave time for the mind to restore itself.

Begin a circular tour of this county by starting in Coventry; its center is on Route 31, most easily reached from Route 44 to the north or Route 6 to the south.

TopPicks for fun in Tolland County

1. Nathan Hale Homestead

2. Mansfield Drive-in and Marketplace

3. Connecticut Archaeology Center events

4. Ballard Institute and Museum of Puppetry

TOLLAND COUNTY

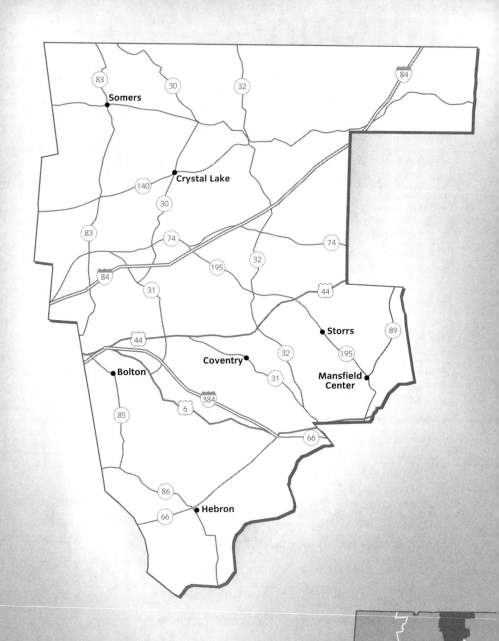

Coventry

Incorporated in 1712, Coventry describes itself as the gateway to the state's Quiet Corner, which is a fair appraisal of this truly charming country town. Centered on Route 31 neatly in the middle of the southern end of the county, its rolling, second-growth woodlands are laced by mile upon mile of twisting country road, beautiful in every season.

Like those of many towns in the area, Coventry's chief temptations are its scenic byways, farmstands, antiques shops, and inns. The slick stuff of the city is not to be found here. Still, Coventry provides a few attractions and a healthful trio of regular and annual events that will appeal to any family that enjoys history or nature. In the future, look for word of the expanded public hours of one of the state's newest history museums: The Museum of Connecticut Glass (www.glassmuseum.org) is under development in the John Turner House on North River Road, which is within Coventry's National Historical Glass Factory District. Plans are under way for the installation of a glass furnace that will demonstrate early techniques of glassmaking in Coventry and at other glassworks in the state.

Nathan Hale Homestead (ages 6 and up)
2299 South Street; (860) 742-6917 or (860) 247-8996; www.hartnet.org/als/nathanhale. Open Wednesday through Sunday from 1:00 to 4:00 p.m. from May 15 to October 15. Tours every half hour. $; children under 6 free.

The most famous spot in Coventry might be the home of Connecticut's state hero, Nathan Hale. On the fringe of the Nathan Hale State Forest off Route 31, the Nathan Hale Homestead is perhaps the most stately of Revolutionary-era historic homes in the country. Its situation on the property is a fitting memorial to the proud young man who lost his life in the service of his country in September 1776.

Nathan spent his boyhood on this lovely property, raised here in apparent harmony with his nine surviving siblings. While Nathan was serving in the Continental Army, the house currently standing on the property was rebuilt to add space to the original smaller house in which the ten brothers and sisters had been raised. Sometime after the death of the first Mrs. Hale (I presume from exhaustion), Nathan's

Coventry **Visitor Center**

Day-tripping families may stop at the Coventry Visitor Center (1195 Main Street; 860-742-1085) in the old brick post office in the heart of town. Open year-round on weekends only from 10:00 a.m. to 2:00 p.m., it offers maps, brochures from the tourism council, and assistance from volunteers who can add to your exploration of this pretty place.

The Story of a **Hero**

At just twenty-one years of age, the young Nathan, a graduate of the class of 1773 at Yale and a teacher by profession, set out on the most dangerous mission known to his generation. Acting under the principles of freedom that drove the Patriot cause, Nathan, now a captain in the rebel army, walked on foot in the disguise of a poor schoolmaster to infiltrate the British encampment at New York City and bring the plans of the enemy back to General Washington. Apprehended within sight of the smoke from the American campfires, Nathan was relieved of the secrets he had written on a parchment hidden in his boot and was hanged from the gallows without a trial for the crime of treason against the Crown.

Legend tells us that it was on this occasion, facing his death, that Nathan Hale uttered his most famous words: "I only regret that I have but one life to lose for my country." His body was left hanging for three days as a warning to other traitors and was buried in an unknown, unmarked grave in Artillery Field, now underneath the pavement near New York City's Sixty-sixth Street and Third Avenue. Back home in Coventry, years later, his father erected a headstone in his memory graven with these words: HE RESIGNED HIS LIFE A SACRIFICE TO HIS COUNTRY'S LIBERTY.

father, Deacon Richard Hale, married the second Mrs. Hale, a widow with seven children of her own. Clearly there was just cause for building a new homestead that represented not only breathing space but the prosperity that Nathan's father had achieved.

The homestead tour begins with an excellent short film shown in the small eighteenth-century barn, which also serves as the gift shop, to the left of the drive at the left of the house. The house includes many Hale furnishings and belongings. See Nathan's musket, his shoe buckles, the trunk he left with his friend Asher Wright when he left on his mission, and the Bible he received as a gift on his seventeenth birthday. The tours are among the best we have heard for children in the state—filled with detail but quick and not above the heads of young listeners. You may even see a costumed character cooking at the open hearth, making soap, or toiling in the period herb and vegetable garden. Hands-on activities are typically incorporated for children.

Several special days are planned annually. On Mother's Day the two Mrs. Hales appear to portray motherhood in the eighteenth century. Mothers are admitted at no charge. In early June Nathan's birthday is celebrated with cake and a performance by the Nathan Hale Ancient Fife and Drum Corps. On the first Sunday in June, an Antiques Festival draws one hundred or more exhibitors; in late July a Revolutionary War encampment takes over the grounds for a full weekend of camplife reenactments and a multicorps fife and drum muster. In late September a mourning day commemorates Nathan's death or some aspect of Hale family history. An October walking tour focuses on the homestead as well as the forest and other nearby historic sites. The Coventry Regional Farmers' Market is also on-site on Saturdays from May through October (see sidebar); if you are here on one of those Saturdays, you are in for an extra treat.

An exceptional Colonial Life weeklong day camp for children involves kids in colonial games, crafts, weaving, cooking, clothes making, plant study, and the opportunity to role-play a Hale historical character. Call early in the spring to register.

Patriot's Park (all ages)

Lake Street (Route 275 becomes Lake Street at the Route 31 junction); (860) 742-4068. Open 8:00 a.m. to dusk year-round; fees in summer only. Nonresident day-use in the summer, $ per vehicle on Monday through Friday and $$ on weekends. If you have more than 5 occupants in your car, pay a bit more ($) for each extra person over the age of 5. Concession in summer only; lifeguards from May 1 through September 30.

This seventeen-acre park with trails linked to the contiguous fifty-seven-acre Patriot's Forest trail system offers a public beach on 373-acre Lake Wambungaug, also known as Coventry Lake. A picnic pavilion and snack hut, a children's playscape, extensive open fields, an outdoor performance pavilion, and restrooms are all here for public use. In winter, weather permitting, enjoy the ice-skating pond with a warming hut; bring your own skates.

History **Lessons**

Families with history buffs among them might also like to check out Coventry's **Brick School House** on Merrow Road. Built from 1823 to 1825, it served as a one-room district school until 1953. Now restored, it is furnished with nineteenth-century artifacts. It's open on Sunday afternoons from mid-May to mid-October. The **Strong-Porter House** at 2382 South Street, just down the road from the Hale Homestead, includes local artifacts and memorabilia about the Hales, their relatives the Strongs, and the Porters. The property includes carriage sheds, a barn, and a carpenter's shop. It is open Saturday and Sunday afternoons from mid-May to mid-October. Both free. For more information, visit www.coventry cthistoricalsociety.org.

Rural and **Herbal Pleasures**

Part of the rural culture and agrarian legacy of the state's Quiet Corner is reflected in its agricultural fairs, farms, and farmers' markets. Coventry is home to some of the best opportunities for celebrating the gifts of the earth. **Topmost Herb Farm** (244 North School Road; 860-742-8239), owned and operated by Carole Miller, grows medicinal and culinary herbs and heirloom tomatoes according to organic standards. The display gardens and the greenhouse on her lovely twenty-acre property are open from May through September, Thursday through Saturday from 9:00 a.m. to 5:00 p.m. Always on the first Saturday in June (9:00 a.m. to 4:00 p.m.), Topmost hosts the Connecticut Herb Association's **HerbFest** ($$), with workshops, demonstrations, craft and herb vendors, food vendors, a bake sale, and children's activities. Topmost also hosts **Taste! Organic Connecticut** ($), a celebration of local organic agriculture on the first Sunday after Labor Day, from 10:00 a.m. to 4:00 p.m. Sponsored by the Northeast Organic Farming Association and the Willimantic Food Co-Op, this event offers fresh produce and plants, honey, maple syrup, crafts, and herbal products, along with workshops, music, and children's events. Both events are on the farm, which Miller's grandfather bought in 1915. For more information, visit www.ctnofa.org or call (203) 888-5146. The folks at **Edmondson's Farm** (2627 Boston Turnpike, which is Route 44; 860-742-6124) also welcome families to ride their hay wagons in September and October, when they are open daily from 9:00 a.m. to 6:00 p.m. Take a tractor-driven ride ($) guided by Mrs. Pumpkin through the woods and back to the farm stand. Buy a pumpkin, a bushel of crisp apples, or some mums. Veggies and herbs are all available seasonally, and Christmas trees and trimmings come out around Thanksgiving. Lastly, the award-winning and wonderful **Coventry Regional Farmers' Market** (www.coventryfarmersmarket.com) runs from June through October from 11:00 a.m. to 2:00 p.m. on the grounds of the Nathan Hale Homestead. If you like locally produced produce and regional crafts and other home-grown products, don't miss this exceptional market. Chock-full of every kind of deliciousness plus special demonstrations, themed events, and music, it is one of the very best farmers' markets in New England. All members of the family will find something to love here.

Where to Eat

Bidwell Tavern. 1260 Main Street (Route 31); (860) 742-6978. Famous for its chicken wings, this classic 1820s tavern is a local favorite that deserves its reputation for good steaks, burgers, ribs, and seafood. Lunch and dinner daily year-round except Thanksgiving and Christmas. $–$$

Hilltop Country Store and Deli. 2208 Boston Turnpike; (860) 742-9559. Eat in or take out excellent picnic food choices at this certified heart-healthy eatery. Breakfast and lunch Wednesday through Friday from 8:00 a.m. to 5:00 p.m.; weekends, 9:00 a.m. to 5:00 p.m. $

Where to Stay

Special Joys Bed and Breakfast. 41 North River Road; (860) 742-6359. This pink-towered B&B offers families (with children over the age of 6) a private balcony, private entrance, and dining room, plus 2 immaculate guest rooms with private baths. Glassed-in conservatory with fountain; extensive gardens; full country-style breakfast. Special Joys Doll and Toy Shop offers dolls, dollhouses, doll clothes and accessories (open year-round Thursday through Sunday, 11:00 a.m. to 4:00 p.m.). If you are not a guest at the bed and breakfast, be sure to call ahead to confirm the shop hours. $$–$$$

Hebron/Bolton

The trouble with Tolland County is that it's so rural that its towns are sort of rambling affairs without boundaries that are crystal-clear to the traveler. The boundaries exist, of course, but to find Point A in Town A, it might actually be easier to travel to Point A from Town B. And so on.

If you were to leave Coventry, for example, to find Gay City State Park (which is, from a north–south perspective, halfway between Hebron and Bolton), it would be absurd to travel to either Hebron or Bolton proper. You'd go to Andover first, and then on through the countryside to the park. You are much better off discovering and accepting this curious Yankee phenomenon right here in this slim volume because if you were to stop and ask an inhabitant of this strange land, they would likely smile wryly at your city-slicker type-A hang-ups and say something along the lines of, "W'aall, you found us, so you cain't be too far off." And then you're on your own again.

The fact of the matter is that Gay City State Park is in Hebron, but even the state campground guide explains its position as 3 miles south of Bolton on Route 85. I say it's 4 miles west of Andover at the junction of Routes 31 and 85. The bottom line is that it's actually easy to find and very worthwhile no matter how you get there.

Gay City State Park (all ages)
Entrance on Route 85 in Hebron; (860) 295-9523. Open year-round 8:00 a.m. to sunset. Parking fee on weekends and holidays, $$.

Adjoining the vast acreage of the Meshomasic State Forest, the park centers on the remains of an eighteenth-century mill village settled in 1796 by a religious sect led first by one Elijah Andrus and later by a man named John Gay. Quite successful and nearly self-sustaining, the community had, at its peak, a population of twenty-five families and a handful of thriving mills that produced lumber, woolens, and paper, among other goods. For nearly eighty years, the industrious citizens of Gay City managed to overcome their various hardships, but by 1879 the struggle to sustain themselves became overwhelming. In that year, the last of their mills burned to the ground, and the citizens abandoned the settlement. Soon the fields lay fallow, the silent ruins were home to wild dogs, and nature removed nearly every trace of human habitation. Now only some tumbling foundations, some cellar holes, a few gravestones, and the ruins of an old aqueduct remain.

When you enter the 1,569-acre park, leave your car at a parking area near the pond and pick up a trail map from the rangers or in the wooden box near the trail-head. Ten trails lace through the park, but the easiest ones for children are those with the greatest concentration of historic spots. The park offers swimming, fishing, hiking, and picnicking in warm weather. In winter, you can ice-skate and cross-country ski. The state provides picnic tables, drinking water, and flush toilets to make your visit comfortable. Leashed pets are permitted.

Fish Family Farm Creamery and Dairy (all ages)

20 Dimock Lane, Bolton; (860) 646-9745. Open Monday through Saturday, year-round, from 8:00 a.m. to 8:00 p.m. (6:00 p.m. in winter). Walking around is free, but they charge for the ice cream.

After a full day of hiking and swimming, there's no better place to replace some calories than at another of Connecticut's finest ice cream emporiums. Now you can go to Bolton (you see, you didn't miss anything at all arriving at Gay City through Andover), straight north on Route 85. This dairy is one of the very few operations in Connecticut that milks, pasteurizes, and bottles its own milk, and its enterprising owners also make fabulous ice cream.

Visitors are welcome to take a self-guided tour around the farm as long as the path taken is safe and doesn't endanger anyone, but do pay attention to any signage. You can explore the dairy barn and pet any of the adorable wee calves who might be here when you come. Twenty cows are milked here every day, and the best viewing place of the bottling plant is through a glass window in the farm store where you buy their ice cream. Be here around 3:30 p.m. each afternoon if you'd like to see the milking process; bottling is usually done between 6:00 a.m. and noon on Monday and sometimes Tuesday. Starting in 2008, you can arrange for a birthday party here, and these and other groups can make appointments for a one-hour guided barn tour as well. The store also sells the Fish family's own fresh eggs; best of all, though, is their ice cream—you won't get it any closer to the source anywhere in the state.

Where to Eat

Bolton Pizza and Family Restaurant. 270 West Street (Route 85); (860) 643-1014. Famed for its spinach pies and

calzones, this Italian eatery offers great food at great prices to families. Open year-round, Tuesday through Sunday. $–$$

Somers

Way up north in Tolland County just a stone's throw from the Massachusetts border is the small town of Somers, pronounced like the season. Once the home of the Scantic Indians and later settled by colonists who made use of the Scantic River to power grist and woolen mills, it remains a quiet community with rural charm.

If you have been lingering in the south of the county, make your way up Route 85 to the center of Vernon at Route 85's junction with Route 30. Take a right on Route 30, also called Hartford Turnpike, and go to the second light to the shopping center called 30 Plaza. Stop at **Rein's New York Style Deli** (435 Hartford Turnpike; 860-875-1344; open year-round daily except December 25) in the shopping center and buy some wonderful take-out sandwiches, kosher pickles, German potato salad, and whatever other picnic fixings you may need for a day in the country. Then go northward on Route 83 to Somers.

Shallowbrook Equestrian Center (ages 4 and up)
Route 186; (860) 749-0749; www.shallowbrook.com. Open year-round; call for seasonal hours, events, and information on lessons.

Those of you who love horses probably already know about this place; it's the largest family-owned complex of its kind in the United States, it has the largest indoor polo arena in the nation, and it enjoys a national reputation as one of the country's best riding schools. Indoor and outdoor riding rings, a hunt course, indoor and outdoor polo courses, forty hours a week of scheduled riding lessons for all levels and ages of riders, facilities for carriage shows, rodeos, and gymkhana competitions, and much more keep participants and spectators alike arriving for the year-round special events on this beautiful fifty-acre site. Whether you come to watch the pageantry or the sportsmanship or to develop your own skills, you will find much to occupy the family at Shallowbrook.

Soapstone Mountain (all ages)
Soapstone Mountain Road. Open year-round dawn to dusk unless closed due to weather conditions. Free.

If you want to save those sandwiches just a little bit longer, take Route 190 east from its junction with Route 83. Drive 1.2 miles to Gulf Road. Take a right on Gulf Road and drive 2 miles to the entrance of the Shenipsit State Forest. Pass the parking area and turn west onto Soapstone Mountain Road, which will twist upward to a beautiful vista just under a mile from Gulf Road. Stop at the overlook, then drive onward to a picnic area near the top of the mountain. Park here and enjoy your lunch. If the state forest trails are open when you visit, walk to the nearby weather-relay station and take the short trail to the wooden firetower beyond it.

Retrace your route to Gulf Road and take a right onto it so you're going south toward Crystal Lake, which is just a few miles away at the junction of Routes 140 and 30. If you have the equipment, stop at Crystal Lake's public boat launch and public fishing area and see if you can land some trout. Crystal Lake Brook, which runs parallel to Route 30, is a major trout stream, stocked in early spring and open from the third Saturday in April through March 1 of the following year. If the fish aren't biting, go east on Route 140 to Stafford Springs, and hook a right onto Route 32 toward Mansfield.

Mansfield

If you don't have a firm grip on the township concept, you'll have a great chance to process it fully in Mansfield. Composed of several village centers and a large university, it lies roughly between Routes 44 and 6 at the north and south and is crisscrossed by Routes 195, 275, 32, and 89.

I mention this because even if you have driven for miles you will know that you are still in Mansfield if you are between any two of these points, a fact that can become very important since the village names are Mansfield Depot, Mansfield Center, and Mansfield Four Corners. Plus Eagleville, Spring Hill, and Storrs (the home of the University of Connecticut and the name by which most out-of-towners refer to Mansfield). For the purposes of this book, we are going to group the university-related attractions under the town heading of Storrs, just a few pages onward.

A day in Mansfield can include all four of the following attractions if you plan well: the Mansfield Drive-in Theater, the Gurleyville Grist Mill, the Mansfield Hollow Dam and State Park, and the Mansfield Marketplace, which is held at the drive-in.

Mansfield Hollow Dam and State Park (all ages)
Just about a mile east of Mansfield Center near the junction of Routes 195 and 89; (860) 455-9057. Open year-round from sunrise to sunset. Free.

Created to protect the land around the 550-acre reservoir made by the damming of the Natchaug River by the Army Corps of Engineers, the park includes more than 2,300 acres of open space perfect for hiking, picnicking, cross-country skiing, and bird or wildlife watching.

Among the amenities are a field-sports area, a picnic grove (with some pretty tall pines, tables, firepits, restrooms, and seasonal water fountains), horseshoe pits, an interpretive nature trail, and miles of other hiking trails. Trash containers are not provided, so be prepared. The park is an alcohol-free facility, so leave the wine and beer out of your picnic fixings.

Unfortunately, because the lake is a public water supply, you can't swim here, but you can bring in your fossil fuel–burning powerboat at the public boat launch. As they say in New York, go figure. You can also fish here. I guess the fish don't mind the petrochemicals.

Follow the signs to the 1952 Mansfield Hollow Dam (you can walk to it along the top of the dike that runs through the first part of the park or you can drive to it on the roads). The dam is a fairly impressive structure, unless you've already seen Hoover, of course, and it overlooks the lake, the river, and Kirby mill, a stone structure dating from 1882.

Gurleyville Grist Mill (ages 5 and up)

Stone Mill Road; (860) 429-9023; www.mansfieldhistory.org/gurleyvi.htm. Open late May through mid-October on Sunday from 1:00 to 5:00 p.m. Free.

If historic structures intrigue you, head up Route 195, take a right onto Gurleyville Road, and follow the signs to the mill. A mill site since the 1720s, this small stone building is the state's only remaining gristmill. Dating from 1830, it contains its original nineteenth-century machinery and is open for **free** tours, as is the nearby miller's house, once the home of Governor Wilbur Cross and now a museum of Mansfield history.

This is a short stop, unless you want to walk awhile on the nearby Nipmuck Trail, which follows the pretty twists of the Fenton River, on which the mill is situated. To do that, park near the bridge that crosses the river and look for the blue blazes that lead northwest close to the west bank. The Nipmuck Trail is 39 miles long, but you can enjoy a short section right here near the mill. The riverside is a lovely place to stop for a picnic lunch. You can walk about a quarter-mile to where the trail crosses Gurleyville Road. From there you can retrace your steps to your car or continue up to Route 44 (about another mile) and then return to your car.

Mansfield Drive-In and Marketplace (all ages)

228 Stafford Road, which is at the junction of Routes 31 and 32; drive-in: (860) 423-4441; www.mansfielddrivein.com; marketplace: (860) 456-2578; www.mansfield marketplace.com. Drive-in open every Friday through Sunday evening from mid-April through May and in September, and every night in June, July, and August. $–$$. Wednesday night is Family Night; special per carload price. Opens at 7:10 p.m. Marketplace open 8:00 a.m. to 3:00 p.m. on Sunday from March 15 until Thanksgiving. Rain or shine. Free. Small parking fee.

For fun in a time warp, come for one of the first-run films playing on the big screen. If you were a child of the 1950s or '60s, you probably know how this works: The kids get into pajamas just before dark and pile into the Ford Country Squire, and the whole family cheerfully heads off to the drive-in to watch wholesome, family values–type movies under the stars.

If it's really warm, the kids spread a blanket on the roof of the car and pile on top, hoping to get a good view of anything interesting going on in the next car. There's lots of giggling involved and lots of popcorn, and when there's too much noise on the roof, Dad says something like "June, can you make those kids settle down?" and Mom says something like "Oh, Ward, they're just high-spirited," and everybody starts giggling again.

This drive-in is one of two remaining open in Connecticut and the only one east of the Connecticut River. The three screens offer "family" films, but call to be sure you share their opinion of appropriate films for your children. Often there are double features, with the earlier film being most oriented toward younger audiences. A full-service snack bar prepares dogs and burgers and such and hawks typical theater treats. Depending on your comfort level here, you can send the kids to play on the on-site playground. Restrooms complete the package.

Return here on Sundays from mid-March until Thanksgiving to check out the goods at the largest indoor/outdoor weekly flea market in eastern Connecticut. Don't be concerned that children won't have fun here. Of the 200 or so dealers who sell here regularly, a large percentage sell toys, crafts, candy, baseball cards, dolls, sporting goods, books, and other goods of appeal to families. Breakfast and lunch are offered for sale at the snack bar.

Storrs

Not surprisingly, the University of Connecticut provides several resources for family activities on its main campus at Storrs. If you enter the university near the information booth at the main entrance on Route 195, you can pick up campus maps and inquire about guided and self-guided tours of the campus. In addition to the attractions detailed below, you can visit the Kellogg Dairy Barn exhibits at the School of Agriculture daily from 10:00 a.m. to 4:00 p.m. and ask for the self-guided walking tour of the campus trees, which is actually pretty amazing. Planted with trees from all temperate parts of the world, the campus itself has achieved arboretum status, and its School of Horticulture maintains beautiful themed gardens, including one planted in the school colors. Be sure to visit the Little Stone House, which is constructed from stone taken from every town in the state of Connecticut and has an interior wall with a specimen stone from every state in the union. The Geology Park is made from stone taken from every working quarry in Connecticut and includes a set of Connecticut dinosaur footprints.

Connecticut Archaeology Center (all ages)
2019 Hillside Road, University of Connecticut, off Route 195; (860) 486-4460; www .cac.uconn.edu. Open Tuesday through Saturday 10:00 a.m. to 4:00 p.m. Closed

Sunday and Monday. Free; donations appreciated. Check the Web site for the calendar of special events, workshops, and activities. The center is in the building to the right of the UConn Co-op; it is labeled MNH on the campus map available at the Lodewick Visitor Center. Parking on weekdays is available in the garage behind the Co-op for a fee; on weekends free parking is permitted in the lots and on the streets as well.

The Connecticut State Museum of Natural History at UConn has hitched its team to the wagon of the Office of State Archaeology to create a new partnership and a new venue for the considerable collections and resources of these institutions. The Connecticut Archaeology Center now has a wonderful new permanent exhibit called *Human's Nature: Looking Closer at the Relationships Between People and the Environment.* One of the finest natural history collections in the state is kept here and is displayed, in part, in this exhibit exploring the effects of the land on its inhabitants and the impact of the people upon the land. Geology, ethnobotany, archaeology, and climatology are among the sciences explored here in several "story stations" and multimedia presentations.

A full slate of activities includes family programs, nature walks, science workshops, field trips, Sunday lectures by scientists and scholars, and guided tours. Children entering grades one through five, accompanied by an adult, may particularly

UConn Greenhouses and Animal Barns

At 75 North Eagleville Road, behind the Torrey Life Sciences Building, are the University of Connecticut Department of Ecology and Evolutionary Biology's greenhouses, which house the most diverse collection of plants between New York and Boston. Nearly 4,000 species thrive here, including cacti, succulents, bromeliads, and more than 500 species of orchids. The facility is open to the public for free from 8:00 a.m. until 4:00 p.m. Monday through Friday; it is closed on weekends and state holidays. Check the Web site for further information: http://florawww .eeb.ucon.edu/visiting.html. This may be the closest you come to a rain forest—it's lush, humid, and lovely.

UConn's animal barns are also open to the public for free self-guided tours. The barns are located on Horsebarn Hill Road and are open daily year-round from 10:00 a.m. to 4:00 p.m. (plus an hour or two later in summertime). You may see cattle, horses, and sheep; you may have even more fun if you pick up a copy of a brochure called *Follow the Animal Trail: A Children's Guide to the Animals at UConn Storrs.* The brochure is available at the UConn Visitor Center, at the Dairy Barn, and in the barns.

enjoy the **free** Saturdays at the Museum programs offered monthly (second or third Saturday) from 1:00 to 3:00 p.m.

William Benton Museum of Art (ages 8 and up)
University of Connecticut, 245 Glenbrook Road; (860) 486-4520; www.thebenton.org. Open year-round Tuesday through Friday 10:00 a.m. to 4:30 p.m. Saturday and Sunday 1:00 to 4:30 p.m. Closed during exhibit changings or some academic breaks. Free.

Housed in one of UConn's earliest buildings now on the National Register of Historic Places, this museum's galleries are devoted to changing exhibitions and displays from the university's 5,500 -piece permanent collection of American and European art.

The small size of the museum, even with the recent addition of new galleries and lecture areas, makes it a wonderful place in which to introduce young children to fine art, and the museum's changing exhibitions are of the highest caliber possible, often focusing on art from many cultures beyond the scope of its own collection. Although directed mostly at adult visitors and students of fine art, some exhibitions are of great appeal to children; summer exhibitions often have a special family focus. A convenient Cafe Muse provides a nice place to eat and relax; the museum gift shop is also excellent.

Ballard Institute and Museum of Puppetry (all ages)
Willimantic Cottage, Weaver Road, UConn Depot Campus, off Route 44; (860) 486-4605; www.bimp.uconn.edu. Open late April through mid-November Friday, Saturday, and Sunday from noon to 5:00 p.m. Free; donations appreciated.

One of the Benton Museum's special exhibitions was based on a collection so important and impressive, in fact, that a unique museum has been created to provide it a permanent home of its own. Named for professor emeritus Frank Ballard and dedicated to preserving and displaying the Ballard puppets as well as the puppets of other student, state, national, and international puppeteers, the museum also has as its purpose the aim to educate the public and promote the puppet arts.

Showcasing a collection of literally thousands of puppets from around the world, the institute and museum celebrate the wondrous art form of puppetry through changing exhibitions of marionettes, glove puppets, rod puppets, shadow puppets, and the props, paraphernalia, and publicity materials associated with puppet productions. Three of the museum's eventual five galleries are now open to visitors; a small gift shop is also here.

Honored by an award acknowledging its special contribution to the arts, the University of Connecticut is the only university in the nation with a degree program in puppetry arts. At the helm of that tradition for more than thirty years was Frank Ballard, directing the work of the latest generation of puppet creators. Ballard's own stories are inspirational tributes to the generous support he received from childhood onward as he carved out his life in the arts. He made his first puppet at the age of five. Inspire your own kids—bring them to this must-see museum and be sure to visit its "Try-It" room, where you too can be a puppeteer.

Contact the Department of Dramatic Arts at the university for information about student puppet productions. In September or October, the museum usually has an open-house special performance or hosts the Connecticut International Festival of Puppet Arts, with renowned performers from across the globe presenting puppet performances for families as well as adults. Call for ticket information.

Jorgensen Center for the Performing Arts (ages 4 and up)

2132 Hillside Road at UConn; (860) 486-4226; www.jorgensen.uconn.edu. October through May. Also Connecticut Repertory Theatre, (860) 486-3969. Check the Web site to select performances suited to your family's interests. Single tickets ($$$) and subscription series are available; you can also design your own series. Children, $$.

This 2,630-seat contemporary theater offers top-drawer entertainment in the form of musicals, comedies, Broadway classics, dance, opera, and drama. The full season of productions features professional touring companies as well as nationally and internationally known soloists and symphonies. Nearly all the productions are appropriate for the whole family.

The Jorgensen Children's Series offers several productions each academic season, featuring favorite tales such as *Sleeping Beauty* or the *Wizard of Oz.* Recommended for children ages five through eleven, these Sunday performances are at 1:00 and 3:00 p.m.

Where to Eat

You can eat on campus in the student union during the academic sessions in the coffee shop and cafe-style eateries or at the Blue Oak Cafe in the Nathan Hale Inn (open year-round for breakfast, lunch, and dinner). You can also try one of these local favorites:

Angellino's Restaurant. 135 Storrs Road (Route 195); (860) 450-7071. You just can't go wrong here. Pizza, great pasta, quick service, lots of families. $–$$

Kathy-John's. 643 Middle Turnpike, near the junction of Routes 195 and 44; (860) 429-0362. Sandwiches, burgers, soups, salads, breakfast dishes, ice cream and sundaes. Open daily year-round from 11:00 a.m. to 10:00 p.m. except major holidays; closes at 4:00 p.m. on the eves of major holidays. $

UConn Dairy Bar. 3636 Horsebarn Road Extension, UConn School of Agriculture, just north of Gurleyville Road on Route 195; (860) 486-2634. Sensational ice cream freshly made year-round by students. The portions are enormous, and the creative flavors change all the time. Monday through Friday from 10:30 a.m. to 5:00 p.m., Saturday and Sunday from noon to 5:00 p.m. Longer hours in summertime. Closed on major holidays. $

Where to Stay

Best Western/Regent Inn. 123 Storrs Road (Route 195) in Mansfield Center; (860) 423-8451. Near UConn, 88 rooms with two double beds, indoor pool, fitness center. Continental breakfast. $$–$$$

Nathan Hale Inn. 855 Bolton Road; (860) 427-7888. This inn and conference center offers 100 guest rooms and 18 suites right on the UConn campus. Restaurant, indoor pool, health club. $$$$

General Information

River Valley/Connecticut covers forty-six towns of the Central Regional Tourism District, including towns in Tolland County and other areas of the Connecticut River Valley. For free maps and brochures and information on attractions, dining, and accommodations, visit 31 Pratt Street, Fourth Floor, Hartford 06103; www.visitctriver.com; or call (800) 793-4480 or (860) 244-8181.

Mystic Country/Connecticut covers forty-two towns in the Eastern Regional Tourism District, including parts of Tolland County. Call (800) TO-ENJOY or (860) 444-2206, or visit 32 Huntington Street, New London 06320; www.mysticcountry.com; for brochures, maps, calendars of events, and information on attractions, dining, and accommodations.

Windham County
River Valleys
and Rural Byways

I don't know in what year some clever copy writer labeled Windham County the "Quiet Corner," but the name has stuck so thoroughly that you might think it is the region's official name. Though parts of Tolland County share the name, at least in the state tourism materials, it is here in Windham that the full impact of the term hits the traveler. It's quiet here.

Although a portion of the county is sliced by I-395, which leads travelers toward Worcester, Boston, and points beyond, the area is little altered by the traffic. In fact, the whole twenty-five-town region along the Quiet Corner's two major rivers has been designated the Quinebaug and Shetucket Rivers Valley National Heritage Corridor in recognition of its status as one of the last unspoiled and undeveloped areas in the Northeast. In keeping with that honor and spirit, the proprietors of the region's museums, shops, and inns have deliberately and successfully maintained the county's old-fashioned ambience, partly to please those very travelers who seek its peaceful thoroughfares.

Call it what you will—some folks call it the "Last Green Valley" amidst the sprawl that has spread from Boston all the way to D.C.—I just call it beautiful. Families looking for fun in Windham County are going to find mostly simple pleasures. Kick back, take your shoes off, sit a spell. Get ready to use your senses. This is the place

TopPicks for fun in Windham County

1. Diamond A Ranch

2. Quaddick State Park

3. Fort Hill Farms and Corn Maze

4. Mashomoquet Brook State Park

5. Creamery Brook Bison

6. Prudence Crandall Museum

WINDHAM COUNTY

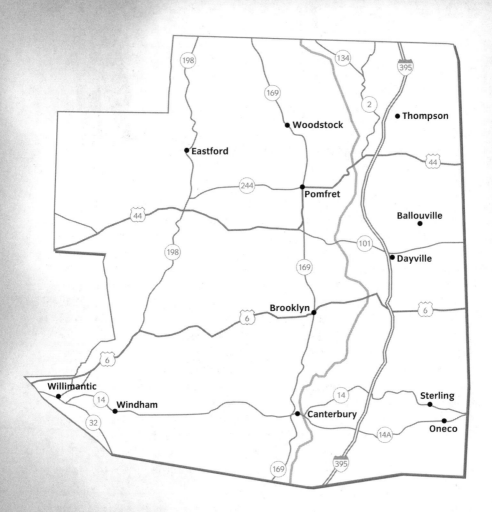

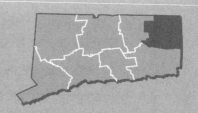

The Last **Green Valley**

The hills, valleys, rivers, and historic mill villages of the northeast corner of Connecticut constitute part of one of America's national heritage corridors, established by the National Park Service but managed by twenty-five towns and many private organizations that lie within this portion of Windham County. (Ten Massachusetts towns manage the Massachusetts portion.) Called the **Quinebaug and Shetucket Rivers Valley National Heritage Corridor,** the area extends northward from Norwich in New London County to ten towns in south-central Massachusetts. Notable for its tranquility, its pristine natural environments, and its historical importance as one of the birthplaces of the American Industrial Revolution, the region is much admired for its recreational opportunities and its preservation of natural and historic resources. Most of the important attractions within the corridor have been selected as destinations deserving treatment in this guide, but many others also could have been included had space permitted. For a complete understanding of this heritage corridor and its attractions, call the Quinebaug and Shetucket Rivers Valley National Heritage Corridor Inc. at (860) 963-7226 or check the Web sites www.thelastgreenvalley.org or www.visitthelastgreenvalley.info. From the Web site, you can download (or call to ask for) copies of these wonderful documents: the National Park Service brochure and map titled *The Last Green Valley, The Green and Growing Guide to the Agricultural Treasures of the Q&SRVNHC,* the *Walking Guide to the Q&SRVNHC,* the *Walking Weekend Guide,* and the three "Ventures" tour maps to the Green and Growing places, the Villages, and the Wild.

You can also call the Eastern Regional Tourism District at (860) 444-2206 or check the Web site www.mysticcountry.com.

to explore, to take a deep breath, to listen to the brooks, the breeze, and the birds. It's the place to contemplate how this land—all of this land, this whole now–United States—must have looked before 1636, when the European settlers came.

Dayville

Beginning right in the heart of the county, take a ride up I-395 to Dayville, a barely there village on the western side of the highway in the larger town of Killingly. This excursion will throw you right into the sort of down-home, laid-back, unhurried action typical of the county.

Diamond A Ranch (ages 3 and up)

975 Hartford Turnpike. From exit 93 off I-395, drive 1.1 miles east on Route 101 and look for the Diamond A; (860) 779-3000; www.daranch.net. Prices vary (all $$$$); call or check the Web site for current information. Rides range from one to three or more hours. Call a day or two in advance to make reservations; be prepared to give heights, weights, and level of ability for all riders.

Get on your jeans and some sturdy shoes and head up the trail to Dayville for a day or weekend of fun in the great outdoors. On the belief that children are very nice people, the folks here offer guided trail rides and riding lessons for all ages on their gently rolling property.

Owner Alicia Summar has created some great opportunities for families with children ages three and up to enjoy the pretty terrain of her ranch. Trail rides ranging from one-hour outings to weekend excursions are offered nearly year-round, as long as there is no ice on the ground. Reservations are pretty much required, especially during peak fall foliage season, but on occasion a call here on the same day you'd like to ride may net you a horse. On weekends from May through November, drop-ins might be able to be accommodated, but a call will ensure the best luck.

The trails at Diamond A traverse gentle hills and grassy meadows. They pass through an apple orchard and across numerous creeks. You can even ride through the canopy created by the trees at either side of the old Danielson-to-Providence trolley track that runs through the property. If you like horses and the New England woodlands and wildlife, come here.

For a family experience you won't easily top in terms of uniqueness, you might request a Wild West Trail Ride and Cookout, most often held in summer and fall. Specially designed for families with young children (but also adapted for teens), these trips are arranged by reservation only and usually consist of one- or two-family groups. Any day of the week, you leave the stables about an hour before dark and take a one-hour trail ride to a campsite in the middle of the woods. There a blazing campfire awaits you, complete with a steaming iron kettle of beans and a big old coffeepot for brewing river coffee. You eat beef jerky, beans, and biscuits or cornbread, and you sit around the campfire for an hour or two and tell tales and sing campfire songs until it's time to head back to the stables.

Other trips are available as well, including one-hour picnic-lunch trips and a five-hour trail ride to a pizza restaurant overlooking a lake. Warm yourselves with pizza by the stone fireplace in the restaurant and then head back to the stables. Pony-ride parties, beach rides, and moonlight rides are also offered, as are overnight camping excursions. Dinner and supplies are included in the price of these popular trips; you just bring a sleeping bag, pillow, and spending money for breakfast and snacks.

Where to Eat

Mozzarella's Italian Grill. 460 Hartford Pike, Route 101; (860) 774-3434. Perfect before or after a ride at the Diamond A. Delicious prime rib, steaks, grilled chicken, pastas, salads, soups, finger foods, and homestyle specials in a casually contemporary dining room of a quaint country house. In warm weather, dine on the patio near a water garden. Lunch and dinner from 11:00 a.m. until 11:00 p.m. on Friday and Saturday, until 9:00 p.m. on Sunday, and until 10:00 p.m. Monday through Thursday. Kids' meals, $1.99 on Wednesday, Saturday, and Sunday. $–$$

Zip's Diner. Junction of Routes 101 and 12; (860) 774-6335. Authentic stainless steel and spinning counter stools are here in this classic 1954 O'Mahoney diner. Nothing's changed here in fifty years, folks, and that's a good thing. Open daily from 6:00 a.m. to 9:00 p.m. $–$$

Where to Stay

Holiday Inn Express Hotel and Suites. 16 Tracy Road, off exit 94, I-395; (860) 779-3200. 78 rooms and suites, indoor pool, fitness room, restaurant, continental breakfast. $$$

Thompson

Some people think that Connecticut's most northeastern town of Thompson has the quintessential village of the Quiet Corner. Tiny and serene, it is lined with houses, churches, inns, and merchants that still seem almost eerily reminiscent of the eighteenth century. Were the town managers to outlaw automobile traffic, this village that grew alongside the stagecoach route to Boston and Providence would be surreal indeed. A stroll along the main avenue (Route 193) of town is pleasant for parents and patient children, but the real family values in Thompson lie off the main thoroughfare.

Quaddick State Park (all ages)
East Putnam Road off Route 44; (860) 928-9200. Open year-round from 8:00 a.m. to sunset. Free, except parking fee ($$) on weekends and holidays from Memorial Day through Labor Day. No lifeguards.

Unless you've had your fill of simple pleasures, you'll find Quaddick a great place to spend an afternoon. Located on East Putnam Road off Route 44, the land and the lake was once the summer camp and fishing ground of the Nipmuck Indians. Later it was the Thompson town farm, where elderly citizens spent their dotage in peaceful contemplation. It's a fair bit noisier now, being one of the most popular state parks in the county.

The 466-acre reservoir and sandy beach are the source of most of the activity. You can swim, fish, water-ski, Jet Ski, and sail or canoe here in the summertime. Those delights are made easier with such facilities as changing houses, restrooms, drinking fountains, a boat launch ramp, a picnic pavilion, and a food concession. You can also hike through 116 acres on well-marked woodland trails or play ball or horse-shoes on the sports fields. In winter you can ice-skate or ice-fish on the reservoir as long as the weather permits. Cross-country skiing is not possible on the trails, but you can hike or snowshoe if the spirit moves you to take the kids out for a brisk walk in the crisp air.

Fort Hill Farms (all ages)

Quintessential Gardens and Corn Maize Quest, 260 Quaddick Road; (860) 923-3439 or (866) 919-2204. Gardens open April through November; tours, May 10 through October 9. Maze open August 17 through November 11. Garden tours, $$ per person; corn-maze admission, $$ per person. Admission to the Lavender Labyrinths, $$$ per person. Horticulture classes, $$$$ per class. Check the Web site for information on classes and preregistration.

Ten thousand visitors have come to tiny Thompson each summer of the past few years to tour the state's most a-maze-ing cornfield. On 8 acres of her 1,200-acre dairy farm, Kristin Orr dreams up, plans, plants, *and* cuts an astonishing educational themed maze each year. One theme was Revolutionary history; another was Boston's Freedom Trail; 2007 was the Rivers of the United States, and, in 2008, the theme is the Appalachian Trail. Kristin creates the signage and the four-page game sheet of clues, questions, and activities that helps visitors navigate through all the stations within this immaculate maze. "That there is one maze of beauty," wrote one young visitor after a walk through this splendidly "corn-fusing" agricultural wonder. Kristin loves those fan letters, and she's had many in the past few years, as word of her exceptional maze has spread around New England and beyond. Scout troops, school groups, sports teams, and a ton of families have toured her maze and her pristine farmland, in cultivation since 1889. This is no Halloween-style free-for-all romp; it's a well-organized, mind-opening education in agriculture and whatever the year's theme may be. There's even a secret hero cut into each maze. Come find out who that might be this year.

Children's tours of the seventy English-style gardens are also offered from May through August; call to arrange one for your family. Thousands of organic lavender plants form three labyrinths as well, and you can walk those, too. Come here to pick and purchase your own organic blueberries—grown with no pesticides anywhere. Tours of the dairy can also be arranged. Four hundred Holstein, Jersey, and Guernsey cows and calves are on the property, and half of those are milked each day to contribute to the Farmer's Cow milk cooperative of Connecticut dairy farmers. This is a truly beautiful piece of sacred ground, as Kristin believes, and her philosophy, shared by her husband and children, is to ensure that it remains a pristine center for global well-being. Some folks drive miles in winter just to see the lighted message of peace that Kristin and her family create each December in their fields. It's a farm sanctuary, for sure, and visitors are lucky that the Orrs have opened it up for sharing.

Where to Eat

Buster's Restaurant. 274 Riverside Drive, at the junction of Routes 12 and 193; (860) 923-2908. Just about 8 feet from the gentle French River, this restaurant serves casual fare starting at 6:00 a.m. daily. Breakfast classics include eggs, pancakes, and Belgian waffles. For lunch and dinner, try burgers, salads, sandwiches, grill and barbecue specials, and thirty-six flavors of ice cream. Eat inside or outside on the deck overlooking the river in good weather. They close at 8:00 most evenings, and at 9:00 p.m. on Friday, leaving time for you to play their eighteen-hole miniature course. $–$$

Where to Stay

Lord Thompson Manor. Route 200, exit 99 off I-395, in Thompson; (860) 923-3886; www.lordthompsonmanor.com. Set off from the main thoroughfare, this thirty-six-acre estate, once a horse farm, is mostly booked for weddings or family reunion weekends. On occasion, however, you may rent a room nightly here or at its sister bed-and-breakfast inn (and spa), the **Cottage House,** a historic tavern on the Thompson green. Due to large numbers of summer weddings, availability may be better in the off-season. $$$$

Corttis Inn. 235 Corttis Road, North Grosvenordale; (860) 935-5652. These folks call their house spacious; I call it enormous. You'll be back in the eighteenth century among period furnishings, having hot cocoa in front of the kitchen fire, skating on the pond, bicycling the country lanes, hiking or cross-country skiing the trails through 900—yes, 900—acres of their private property, waking up to the delicious smells of homemade blackberry jam on warm, freshly baked muffins. Four rooms and a suite with private bath and private entrance are waiting for your family. No smoking. $$$–$$$$

Woodstock

Of all the Windham County towns, Woodstock may be the most gentrified, the most artsy, the most sophisticated. It is lovely, to be sure, and one can't blame the tourists for flocking here for the array of treats in store at every turn in the road.

Composed of several villages named North Woodstock, South Woodstock, and so on, the town center most noted for its picturesque qualities is Woodstock proper, a tasteful and sedate community located on beautiful Route 169. Atop the hill, its pretty town common beckons to the traveler with an eye for tranquil spaces. A leisurely stroll through Woodstock Center will reveal many lovely places in which to browse, buy country treasures, or pick up something tasty to eat.

Roseland Cottage (ages 4 and up)

556 Route 169; (860) 928-4074; www.historicnewengland.org/visit/homes/roseland. htm. Open June 1 through October 15, including July 4 and Columbus Day, Wednesday through Sunday 11:00 a.m. to 5:00 p.m., with tours on the hour until 4:00 p.m. Be sure

The Woodstock **Fair**

Held from 9:00 a.m. to 9:00 p.m. on Labor Day weekend, this fair (860-928-3246; www.woodstockfair.com) is one of the ten largest and one of the five oldest country fairs in the state. Each year since 1858 it has offered oxen pulls, horse shows, wood-chopping exhibitions, and hundreds of displays of premium livestock, prizewinning pies, gigantic vegetables, creative handiwork, and much more. These days you'll also find a midway, go-kart races, tons of food, and practically continuous stage entertainment to enhance your enjoyment of everything else. As many as 200,000 other fairgoers will be here with you at this four-day festivity that begins on Friday and rocks steady through Monday. $$, kids 10 and under free.

to call to inquire about the current calendar of special events planned throughout the year; the Web site lists events (and allows you to register/buy tickets) for the current month. $–$$

If you allow the children to wander awhile on the common, it shouldn't take them long to find Roseland Cottage just across the road. A candy-colored pink confection of a house, it is a most surprising attraction that may provide at least an afternoon's worth of entertainment. Built in 1846 in the newly fashionable Gothic revival style, this magnificent home was the summer retreat of Henry C. Bowen, native to Woodstock but long and successfully a New York dry-goods dealer.

Though he made and lost several fortunes in his lifetime, Bowen never lost the sense of stewardship and philanthropy that characterized his actions. Founder of churches, abolitionist and supporter of the Union cause in the Civil War, advocate of the beautification of common property, and a lifetime teetotaler, Bowen was also a mover and shaker in all kinds of social and political circles and liked nothing better than celebrations. Roseland Cottage was the site of many lawn parties, bowling contests in the indoor alley, and Fourth of July festivities that made all others look dull in comparison.

A visit to this house on one of its special festival days is everything but dull, an appropriate tribute to its former owner. In addition to tours of the luxurious "cottage," which retains most of its original furnishings, you can wander the labyrinthine pathways of the twenty-one formal gardens, have a picnic under one of the beautiful plantings on the lawn, and play nineteenth-century games with other visitors.

Regular tours of this magnificently restored estate focus on details of special interest to young people whenever a guide sees a child among the visitors. Even on an ordinary day here, children may explore such summer leisure activities as hoop rolling, graces, and bilboquet or play marbles or jacks. The staff serves pink lemonade every day, and families are encouraged to bring picnics and eat on the lawn. Hands-on history activities in the visitor center can occupy some time for children waiting for a tour. The most popular special events for families are the Fourth of July festivities, which include joyous celebrations and activities the Bowen family might have enjoyed decades ago, and the Civil War Encampment that spans a weekend in late August. At the latter event, which is completely **free** (unless you decide to take a house tour), children can interact with Union and Confederate reenactors, learning how to load a cannon, do codes and ciphers, march in a drill formation, and use signal flags. Skirmishes between the artillerymen and soldiers, cooking and other camplike demonstrations, and musical performances are all part of the event. Also here in summertime—and also **free**—are two or three Twilight Lawn Concerts, very popular with families. You might also want to come for the Fall Festival of Fine Arts and Crafts, which features tours, a food court, clowns and jugglers to entertain the children, and a juried show of nearly 200 artisans. Attendance at this fabulous celebration often reaches 10,000; it is held annually on the weekend after Columbus Day. Come back in December when the house is open at no charge during Woodstock's Winter Festival on the first weekend of the month.

Where to Eat

Java Jive. 283 Route 169; (860) 963-1241. This gourmet espresso cafe has an artsy, urban feel, but a down-to-earth motivation: Its profits are donated to Third World children in need of clean water and healthy food. Coffees, fruit smoothies, fine pastries, confections, and healthy, moderately priced breakfast and lunch. Open from 6:00 a.m. to 3:00 p.m. Monday through Friday, 7:30 a.m. to 4:00 p.m. Saturday, and 8:00 a.m. to noon on Sunday. $

Mrs. Bridge's Pantry. 292 Route 169 in South Woodstock, across from the Woodstock Fairgrounds; (860) 963-7040. Four acres of picnic grounds make this a great place to stop and smell the roses. British teas, hot cocoa, and traditional British favorites such as scones with clotted cream and jam, hot meat pies, salmon cakes, and tea sandwiches are the focus here. Open Wednesday through Monday year-round from 11:00 a.m. to 5:00 p.m. $

Stoggy Hollow General Store and Restaurant. 492 Route 198, Woodstock Valley; (860) 974-2889 This roadside wonder has omelets, house-made salad dressings, homemade soups, fresh-baked breads, muffins, turnovers and pies, grilled sandwiches, burgers, chicken pot pie, ham steaks, pizza, pasta, and seafood specials. Open daily year-round from 7:00 a.m. to 8:00 p.m. most nights, with shorter hours in winter. Eat on the deck in warm weather; shop in the general store for locally made goodies. $

Where to Stay

Beaver Pond B&B. 68 Cutler Hill Road, Woodstock; (860) 974-3312. 2 guest rooms with a shared bath make this a nice place for families who want a private getaway. Truly congenial hosts serve you a full country breakfast, then you can explore the options for hiking, fishing, and boating right on their twenty-three-acre property. $$

The Inn at Woodstock Hill. 94 Plaine Hill Road off Route 169, South Woodstock; (860) 928-0528; www.woodstockhill.net. This former Bowen Mansion has a wonderful cottage with 3 rooms, plus 19 rooms, all with private baths, in the main inn. Every inch of the house and fourteen-acre property is beautiful; the elegant atmosphere is enhanced by the friendly staff. Continental breakfast for guests; lunch, dinner, and Sunday brunch available in the restaurant, which enjoys its own major reputation. $$$$

Pomfret/Pomfret Center

First settled in about 1700, Pomfret was known in the 1890s as the "other Newport" as visitors from New York City began summering in these pretty woods and building three-story cottages to help them rough it here. Just 5 miles south of Woodstock on Route 169, it is home now to private secondary schoolers, several pretty inns and B&Bs, a great herb garden, a handful of antiques stores, and a new vineyard. Among its best attractions are the famed Wolf Den Trail in its state park and its early mill historic site, but be sure to stop also at the Connecticut Audubon Center at Pomfret if you treasure the outdoors.

Mashamoquet Brook State Park (all ages)

147 Wolf Den Drive, at the junction of Routes 44 and 101; park office: (860) 928-6121; www.nochildleftinside.org/parks/mashamoquet.php. Open year-round daily from 8:00 a.m. to sunset for day visitors. Free, except for parking fee ($$) only on weekends and holidays between April 15 and October 15. Camping reservations recommended especially for weekends and long stays; vacancies filled on first-come first-served basis. Campsites, $.

Nearly 1,000 acres are the combined area of the three sections that compose this large park: Wolf Den, Saptree Run, and Mashamoquet Brook. Seven miles of great trails link the areas and make this one of Connecticut's most popular state parks. In addition to hiking, fishing, and picnicking, Wolf Den offers camping, and Mashamoquet Brook offers swimming and camping. Wolf Den has thirty-five open sites with a flush toilet and drinking water from April 15 through October 15. Mashamoquet Brook has twenty wooded sites with a composting toilet and pump water.

The most famous of park attractions are the Table Rock and Indian Chair stone formations and the nearby Putnam Wolf Den Trail, accessible from Wolf Den Drive. Leave your car in the park's second parking area. The 4-mile loop trail leads past the campground to the Wolf Den area. Guided walks are offered from time to time; call for a schedule if you'd like to get the full story of Israel and the Wolf. You can also get the scoop by asking the rangers for a self-guided tour map. After you've seen the site of this sinister encounter, check out the natural formations of Indian Chair and Table Rock. They are just a little farther along the Wolf Den Trail, which also crosses Mashamoquet Brook and then returns to the parking area.

Brayton Grist Mill and the Marcy Blacksmith Shop Museum
(ages 6 and up)
At the entrance to Mashamoquet Brook State Park on Route 44. Open weekends from late May through September from 2:00 to 5:00 p.m. Free.

Maintained by the Pomfret Historical Society, Billy Brayton's four-story gristmill is the state's finest example of a one-man, water-powered mill operation of the 1890s. The equipment for generating power to grind grain and shell corn survives in the exact locations where Brayton used them. The turbine, the millstone, and a corn sheller are among the items you'll learn about on a tour of the museum.

An exhibit of handcrafted tools represents the labor of the Marcy family blacksmiths, who plied their trade from 1817 to 1946 in an area known as Marcy Hollow at the side of Mashamoquet Brook. Orin Marcy opened the shop in 1830, using a water-powered bellows and triphammer. A collection of tools made by the blacksmiths includes some used in the manufacture of wheels and horseshoes. In fact, Orin's son, Darius, earned first prize for his horseshoes at the Chicago World's Fair in 1893.

Connecticut Audubon Center at Pomfret (all ages)
189 Pomfret Street (Route 169); (860) 928-4948; www.ctaudubon.org/visit/pomfret .htm. Open year-round; sanctuary open daily dawn to dusk; center open Wednesday through Saturday, noon to 4:00 p.m. Free.

Folks who like birds are going to love this special refuge of nearly 700 acres of grassland and second-growth woodland that attracts many hard-to-find species year-round and seasonally. The Bafflin Sanctuary adjacent to the center is a beautiful area of meadows, forest, streams, and reclaimed farmland. The trails here offer many opportunities to enjoy the Quiet Corner's uniquely preserved habitats. Owls, hawks, songbirds, and ducks are abundant, as are wildflowers and butterflies.

Daytime and evening field walks are common, as are after-school and weekend workshops perfect for families. Preregistration is either required or strongly suggested. Changing natural history exhibits are inside the center, along with a classroom for special programs. Outside you may join a scheduled tour or walk the easy trails on your own. Even in this pristine environment, socks and water-resistant footgear are a great idea.

Israel and **the Wolf**

General Israel Putnam became famous for more than just his role in the Revolution and his famed ride against the British down the one hundred stone steps of his Greenwich hillside homestead. You see, he spent his young manhood in these parts, successfully pursuing the dual careers of innkeeper and farmer.

Legend has it that for several years young Israel and his neighbors were bothered by the killing instincts of a lone wolf that occasionally made a meal of the local livestock. One night in 1742 the wolf awakened Israel's protective instincts by making off with more than just a few of Israel's sheep. Israel vowed to bring down the killer and assembled a ragtag army of neighbors to help him do it. For days Israel, his neighbors, and their hounds tracked the wolf, finally finding her lair in the face of a high cliff. In went the hounds braying and barking, and out they came again, yelping and mewling. None of them would re-enter the cave.

Israel himself decided to go in after the beast. After a few almost comic attempts to apprehend the criminal, Israel was finally successful. He shot her and dragged her out by the ears. Some say she was the last wolf to live in Connecticut. Today you can hike to her den via the Mashamoquet State Park's Wolf Den Trail.

Where to Eat

Vanilla Bean Cafe. 450 Deerfield Road at the junction of Route 97 with Routes 169 and 44; (860) 928-1562; www.vanilla beancafe.com. Ideal for families, this cafe offers a huge breakfast/brunch on weekends and breakfast muffins and sandwiches the rest of the week. Lunch and dinner could be chili, quiches, stews, sandwiches, or soups. Entertainment on Saturday might be a folk artist or even an open mike—check the Web site for the lineup. Except for major holidays, it's open from 7:00 a.m. to 3:00 p.m. on Monday and Tuesday, to 8:00 p.m. on Wednesday, Thursday, and Sunday, and to 9:00 p.m. on Friday and Saturday. $

Where to Stay

Feather Hill Bed and Breakfast. 151 Mashamoquet Road, Pomfret; (866) 963-0522; www.featherhillbedandbreak fast.com. 4 spacious rooms and a suite, with private baths, in the main house (welcoming children over 12 only). Separate cottage, with bath and fireplace, that sleeps four can be rented by families with younger children (but no infants). Full breakfast. Swimming pool. $$$$

Eastford

West of Pomfret, taking Route 244 west from the center or going south on 169, then west on Route 44, take a side trip to Eastford, which is on Route 198. There's no doubt that Natchaug State Forest is the single biggest entity around here, and that's basically all that families might want to explore—at least after they stock up on all the wonderful agricultural goods produced in these parts by some of Connecticut's finest growers.

Buell's Orchard (all ages)

108 Crystal Pond Road, off Route 198, about 2 miles north of Phoenixville, via West-ford Road; (860) 974-1150; www.buellsorchard.com. Open Monday though Saturday from 8:00 a.m. to 5:00 p.m. and Sunday from 1:00 to 5:00 p.m. in September and October (except closed on the first Sunday of September); open in November and December, Monday through Friday 8:00 a.m. to 4:00 p.m. and Saturday 8:00 a.m. to 3:00 p.m. (closed Sunday).

If you'd like to pack some snacks for a day of hiking, start at Buell's, following the signs to the 100-acre farm from the center of Eastford on Route 198. Beginning with strawberries in June, blueberries in July, and going forward to apples and cider in the fall, you can pick your own fruit in season. They also sell pears, peaches, pumpkins, Vermont cheese, maple syrup, and more. After Labor Day, you can sink your teeth into one of Buell's Famous Caramel Apples. Come Columbus Day weekend for the annual Fall Festival and the opening of the pick-your-own pumpkin patch. Hayrides and **free** cider and doughnuts are part of the hoopla.

Natchaug State Forest (all ages)

Note: Usual entrance is 4 miles south of Phoenixville on Route 198, but the bridge there is under repair and is closed indefinitely; please use the secondary entrance off Pilfershire Road until further notice; DEP office: (860) 295-9523; park office: (860) 974-1562 or John Folsom, supervisor's office: (860) 928-6121; www.ct.gov/dep. Free.

Certainly the largest of the treasures families will find in Eastford, this forest has a name that means "land between the rivers," a reference to its position at the junction of the Still and Bigelow Rivers. Bounded by Routes 44, 6, 198, and 97, it lies adjacent to the beautiful Natchaug River, formed by the confluence of the two smaller rivers. Its 13,000 pristine acres offer elbow room to thousands of outdoor enthusiasts who use it for camping, fishing, picnicking, hiking, snowmobiling, cross-country skiing, and horseback riding.

Picnic sites overlook the river, and anglers of all ages enjoy the trout fishing allowed here from the third week in April to March 1. Besides its trails and picnic area, the State Forest Service provides outhouses and drinking water to day visitors as well as overnight visitors. Backpackers and horseback campers must pack in all supplies and register with the rangers. The Lost Silvermine Horse Camp is the site used by families with their own or rented horses. See Diamond A Ranch (earlier in this chapter) for a guided trip to this site.

Canoeing on the Natchaug is very popular. If you own a canoe, launch it just south of the junction of Routes 198 and 44 in Phoenixville, off General Lyons Road. A 7-mile run through a mix of flat water and quick water takes you past several dams and bridges to the take-out at England Road Bridge. This stretch is great for beginners; experienced canoeists might want to continue another 5.5 miles through several sets of rapids down to Mansfield Hollow State Park.

Town Line Sugarhouse (all ages)

96 Weeks Road; (860) 974-1618. Open Friday, Saturday, and Sunday during the last two weeks in March (but call ahead to confirm), from 10:00 a.m. to 4:00 p.m. Free **visits; maple sugar for sale.**

Steve Broderick, forester, conservationist, and codirector of the Green Valley Institute, owns this little maple sugarhouse in Eastford. He's a terrifically knowledgeable fellow in terms of these lovely Eastern Woodlands and lots more, and he really knows how to explain the sugaring process. He taps 250 to 300 sugar maple trees on this property and boils it all down for you to taste, purchase, and, for a taste of ye olde New England, to drizzle over some good vanilla ice cream when you get home. Typically maple-sugar season in Connecticut is in the neighborhood of the last two weeks or so in March, depending on the weather.

Family Camping on the **Natchaug River**

The state forest campground offers the basic necessities for primitive camping, but some families may enjoy the less limited amenities offered by two private campgrounds on the Natchaug's riverbanks. **Charlie Brown Campground** (860-974-0142 or 877-974-0142; www.charliebrowncamp ground.com) at 98 Chaplin Road (Route 198) has 123 grassy sites for tenters and RVers who need hookups, plus laundry, modern restrooms, and hot showers. Three covered camping pavilions, a limited camp store, a recreation hall with Saturday-night entertainment, and planned activities, plus on-site opportunities for hiking, swimming, tubing, and fishing. **Peppertree Camping** (860-974-1439) on Route 198 has fifty wooded sites along the river; it's a great place to launch canoes or tubes and a great spot for fishing the stocked river. It has all the amenities listed above, except for the rec hall and entertainment/activities. Make your own fun here. At both camps, site rates, $; weekly rates available.

Where to Eat

Still River Cafe. At North Ashford Farm, 134 Union Road (Route 171), Eastford; (860) 974-9988. Distinctly other than ordinary, this special-occasion, grown-up-centered restaurant offers gourmet-quality, truly locally grown (on this 27-acre farm) meals of particular note. Stunning—and pricey—but casual in mood. Nevertheless, dress nicely and bring good manners and a good appetite. You won't be disappointed. Dinner Friday and Saturday, from 5:30 to 9:00 p.m.; Sunday brunch, noon to 2:30 p.m.

Reservations encouraged. No children's menu. But, really—delicious. $$$$

Midway Restaurant & Pizza. 174 Ashford Center Road, Ashford; (860) 429-1932. For something completely different, not too far away: authentic and tasty Greek specialties, pizzas, salads. Family-owned and family-friendly. Open from 10:00 a.m. daily; closes at 9:30 to 10:00 p.m. on weekdays, 11:00 p.m. on Friday and Saturday. $–$$

Brooklyn

Windham County contains one of the top ten scenic highways in the United States, selected for that distinction by Scenic America, an environmental organization that works, in part, to identify and protect scenic American roads. In 1996 the National Department of Transportation designated the road a National Scenic Byway. Historically known as the Norwich–Woodstock Turnpike, the 32-mile section of Route 169 that lies between Lisbon, in New London County, and Woodstock is just about as pretty as pretty can get. Part of that route goes through Brooklyn, a quaint village with beautiful New England churches and a monument to Revolutionary War hero General Israel Putnam in its center.

Creamery Brook Bison (ages 2 to 12)

19 Purvis Road; (860) 779-0837; www.creamerybrookbison.com. Store open April through October, Monday through Friday from 2:00 to 6:00 p.m. and on Saturday from 10:00 a.m. to 2:00 p.m.; November to March, Wednesday through Friday from 2:00 to 6:00 p.m. and on weekends from 10:00 a.m. to 2:00 p.m. Call to schedule a farm tour or an ice-cream-making activity. Wagon tours July to September, Saturday at 1:30 p.m. (no reservations necessary), $–$$; children under 3 free; special rates (by reservation only) for groups of fifteen or more. Groups can also prearrange walking tours, ice-cream and butter-making activities, and wagon ride combinations.

Committed to educating the public about buffalo and dairy farming, this hundred-acre farm is also the home of seventy buffalo who roam its pastures and woodlands. Visit here year-round simply to see the bison; early evening, around 6:00, is the best viewing time, when the herd leaves the cool woods and comes down toward the open field. Come for a prescheduled tour of the farm; arrange an ice-cream-making outing in which you help make hand-cranked ice cream and butter; or come on out from July through September for a wagon ride out into those cool woods to see the herd. Along with Holstein and Jersey cows and the adult bison, you will more than likely see bison calves. You can't pet these magnificent creatures—except for Thunderbolt, a friendly female penned and amenable to gentle petting. Learn about the history, habitat, habits, and myths of these once nearly extinct animals; browse in the store for bison-related booty.

Birthday parties can also be arranged. These typically include a wagon tour, ice-cream-making activity, and a birthday cake for eight children and two adults. If you don't have the time or occasion for a whole party, just have gourmet ice cream in the ice cream shop, open from 2:00 to 9:00 p.m. in the summer.

Brooklyn Fair (all ages)

Route 169, Brooklyn Fairgrounds; (860) 779-0012; www.brooklynfair.org. Fourth weekend in August, Thursday 4:00 to 10:00 p.m., Friday and Saturday 8:00 a.m. to 10:00 p.m., and Sunday 8:00 a.m. to 6:00 p.m. $$, children 12 and under free. Parking, $.

Every year in late August, Brooklyn's population soars as visitors from all over come to the oldest continuously active agricultural fair in the United States. Held for four days the weekend before Labor Day, it is perhaps the best country fair in the state. I'll give you a partial list of what's in store for you: Oxen pull. Draft horse show. Skillet toss. Dog show. Circus. Midway. Pony pull. Cattle parade. Christmas tree show. Bingo. Barbecue. Tractor pull. Country dancing. Beekeeping exhibit. Children's games and contests. Art show. Stage entertainment for adults and children. I can assure you that your kids are going to love this event. Although the agricultural events are all free, you'll need a wad of currency for a day or evening here. That is, unless you and the kids don't eat any food, buy any crafts or gadgets, or ride any rides.

Allen Hill Farm (all ages)

542 Allen Hill Road, off Route 6; (860) 774-7064. Open in November and until December 24 from 10:00 a.m. to dusk Monday through Friday, and from 8:00 a.m. to dusk on the weekends. $

Owners Charles Langevin, Robert Langevin, and Roland Gibeault welcome visitors to their choose-and-cut hundred-acre tree farm, which may just be among the prettiest such enterprises in the whole state of Connecticut. You board one of their hay wagons, and they'll take you to their fields, where the views are just spectacular. They give you a saw, you choose, you cut, they wrap, and you go home with the most perfect Christmas tree ever, in the form of a Canaan, Douglas, Balsam, or Fraser fir, a blue or white spruce, or a white pine. You can also browse in the gift shop for locally made crafts, wreaths, and tree stands. Sample complimentary cookies and hot mulled cider, and visit with Santa and Mrs. Claus on weekends in December. This is the kind of place you'll be happy you drove quite a few miles to see.

Where to Eat

Hank's Restaurant. 416 Providence Road (Route 6); (860) 774-6071. Since 1972, this Brooklyn fixture has been serving up burgers, steaks, salads, soups, seafood, and pasta. A children's menu has typical favorites. Open Monday through Saturday at 11:00 a.m. and Sunday at noon. Kitchen closes at 9:00 p.m. Sunday through Thursday and at 10:00 p.m. Friday and Saturday. $

Where to Stay

Friendship Valley Inn B&B. 60 Pomfret Road (Route 169); (860) 779-9696. Children over age 7 are welcome in this 1795 Historic Register home with five bedrooms, private baths, and hearty, homestyle breakfasts. If the weather's cold, hunker down by one of the fireplaces and keep warm. $$$$

Canterbury

Famed for its own architectural style and for Crandall Academy, founded in 1832 by Prudence Crandall, Canterbury is an almost completely rural town that appears nearly the same as it did a century ago. Six miles south of Brooklyn on Route 169, its pretty Congregational Church on the Green was built in the 1960s as a replica of the original one built in 1804, and its public library resides in the building that was the Canterbury district's one-room schoolhouse until the 1940s. Enjoy the beauty and learn from the history you'll discover in quiet Canterbury.

Prudence Crandall Museum (ages 8 and up)

On the green at the corner of Routes 169 and 14; (860) 546-9916; www.ct.gov/cct. Open approximately April 2 through December 15, Wednesday through Sunday from 10:00 a.m. to 4:30 p.m. Closed major holidays, including Veterans Day. $, children under 5 free.

Site of the first New England academy for African-American girls, the Crandall Academy is now called the Prudence Crandall Museum. A National Historic Landmark, the 1805 structure is one of several houses in Canterbury with the distinctive "Canterbury style." Basically conforming to the Federal style, the house has twin chimneys and an elaborate two-story entrance ornamentation with a Palladian window on the second floor above the front doorway.

Far more famous than its architecture is the house's history and its mistress, Prudence Crandall. The story of Prudence's courage and the dignity of her students is told in tours of the museum. Exhibits explore topics such as local history, African-American history, the abolitionist movement, and women's rights. The museum also includes three period rooms, a gift shop, and a research library.

The Story of the **State Heroine**

In the summer of 1831, twenty-eight-year-old Prudence Crandall was asked by a group of Canterbury citizens to establish a private academy in which she would teach local children. Crandall purchased a large house on the Canterbury green and opened her academy in January 1832. All went well for several months. Crandall had the full support of the parents, who paid her $25 per quarter to teach their children reading, writing, arithmetic, grammar, geography, history, philosophy, chemistry, and astronomy.

Then, in the fall of 1832, Crandall accepted a new student. Sarah Harris, twenty years old, was black. Disapproval was immediate, and several families withdrew their children from the academy. Criticism was so harsh that Crandall dismissed the remaining students and reopened the school several months later as an academy for the instruction of "young ladies and little misses of color."

The first such school in all of New England, the academy added classes in French, drawing, painting, and piano. Outrage followed the earlier criticism as Crandall made it clear that no distinctions were to be made in the education of white and black children. In May 1833, Crandall was arrested and jailed for breaking the Connecticut General Assembly's new "Black Law," which prohibited the instruction of any "colored persons who are not inhabitants of this State."

Though her case was dismissed in July, Crandall and her students suffered greatly at the hands of the citizens of the Canterbury area. The house was pelted with rocks and eggs. An attempt was made to set it afire, and its windows were broken in an angry attack in September of 1834. Only then, fearing the physical safety of her students, did Crandall close the school.

Crandall and her husband left Canterbury and settled in Illinois, where they remained until his death in 1874. Crandall bought property in Kansas with her brother and lived there until her death in 1890 at the age of eighty-seven. She taught throughout her life.

Families might especially enjoy Prudence Crandall Day, typically held on the Saturday of Labor Day weekend. This special festivity offers nineteenth-century children's games, craft demonstrations, musical entertainment, and refreshments and crafts for sale. On the first Saturday in November from 1:00 to 4:00 p.m., the

museum usually hosts an annual Tea with Prudence Crandall. Local living-history per-
former Donna Dufresne portrays Prudence in a forty-five-minute dramatic monologue
and then interacts with the guests, who share tea and refreshments after the presentation. When the event is offered, advance registration is required.

Sterling/Oneco

If you enjoy taking the road less traveled, you might venture off I-395 and find the
township of Sterling and its village of Oneco off exit 88. Here Windham County feels
like a slice of life not so much from the 1850s but from the 1950s. If a time warp back
to simpler days and pleasures seems appealing, wander here awhile and enjoy the
country breezes and cool woods.

River Bend Campground and Mining Company (all ages)

**41 Pond Street (Route 14A), Oneco; (860) 564-3440; www.riverbendcamp.com. Open
mid-April through mid-October daily from 9:00 a.m. to 5:00 p.m. Day visitors should
call ahead in the off-season before Memorial Day and after Labor Day. Mining rates,
$$ for children; accompanying adults free. Gemstone panning, $$. Canoe rentals,
$$–$$$$. Mini-golf, $. Paddleboats and aquacycles, $$ per hour. Campsites and cabin
rentals, $–$$; weekly and seasonal rates available.**

This family campground, amusement center, and gem mine is an award-winning
compromise between the Great Outdoors and Great Adventure. Located on the
beautiful Moosup River and a thirty-five-acre pond, this center offers 160 campsites,
some with rental cabins, trailers, and campers. You can rent a canoe, tour the indoor
wildlife exhibit with diorama-style re-creations of life in the North American woodlands, or enter the walk-through gem mine re-creation to prospect for real gem-
stones from around the world or pan for gems and minerals in the outdoor sluice. A
kiddie train, aquacycles, paddleboats, kayaks, horseshoes, mini-golf, basketball, sand
volleyball, a moon bounce, outdoor movies, bingo, and other interactive areas, activities, and special events keep this place hopping. Luckily, there's plenty of room for
deciding whether you want to be in or out of the nearly continuous action.

Sterling Park Campground (all ages)

**177 Gibson Hill Road, Sterling; (860) 564-8777; www.sterlingcampground.com. Open
mid-April through mid-October. $, weekly rates available.**

The owners of Sterling Park Campground are proud of their commitment to providing wholesome family fun on the landscaped hills of their family campground. With
a staff of friendly faces, they offer guests two heated pools (one just for kiddies), a
rec hall, a children's playscape, mini-golf, a full-service snack shack (which also offers
three meals a day to noncamping visitors), a camp store, sports courts, and lots of

Hill Towns and **Mill Villages**

The first textile mill in Windham County was built in 1806 by Smith Wilkinson on the Quinebaug near present-day Putnam. It was a small cotton mill that depended on the fluctuating level of the river to drive its wheels and turbines. Soon the technology developed to control the water through the use of reservoirs, dams, and canals. It was only a matter of time before every town and village on the rivers had a textile mill. Thousands of immigrants poured into the region to work in the mills and make their homes in the towns. The Quinebaug Mill, built in Killingly in 1852, was one of the largest. It had 61,340 spindles and 1,656 looms, and produced 28 miles of cloth each day.

An excellent self-guided driving- or cycling-tour brochure, from which I have borrowed the title of this sidebar, of the principal mill sites remaining along Route 169 is available on the Web site of the Last Green Valley (www.thelastgreenvalley.org/brochures.html). Originally produced by the Northeast Connecticut Historical Societies and now reproduced and revised by the folks at the Last Green Valley, this three-part document provides a comprehensive look at the history hidden in these hills.

pretty wooded or open campsites. You can arrive with your own camper or tent (electrical and water hookups are available) or rent their cabin or trailer. **Free** hot showers and a laundry facility keep you comfortable throughout your stay.

Family movie nights, square dances, bingo games, hayrides, Kids' Olympics, and Christmas in July with a visit from Santa are among the events on the busy calendar. If you'd rather have quieter fun, you can fish in the two-acre stocked pond.

As if all this were not enough, the folks here decided a long time ago to set it all to music, at least once annually. Each year on the second weekend in June is the Sterling Bluegrass Festival, with foot-stomping, toe-tapping, knee-rocking music— the kind with banjos and guitars, mandolins and fiddles all singing sweetly in the great outdoors. A laid-back three-day affair that draws a moderate crowd, it features regional and local musicians. Call the campground for information, tickets, or camping reservations. For the festival, you're welcome whether or not you're campers.

Willimantic/Windham

Windham County has a sort of a little toe that pops westward from the lowest portion of its boundary with Tolland County. It is here in the toe that you'll find the small city of Willimantic and its sibling village of Windham. Situated on the banks of the

Shetucket River, Willimantic has a history that is tied firmly to the textile mills that dominated three centuries of Connecticut industry.

In fact, the history of many Windham County towns would have been totally altered were it not for the textile mills built along the Quinebaug and Shetucket Rivers in the eighteenth and nineteenth centuries. Today in Willimantic, families can visit one of these sites to learn more about life in Connecticut's mill villages.

Windham Textile and History Museum (ages 6 and up)

157 Union at Main Street, Route 66; (860) 456-2178; www.millmuseum.org. Open year-round on Friday, Saturday, and Sunday from 1:00 to 4:00 p.m. and by appointment. Closed major holidays. $

One of the most fascinating small museums in the state, the Windham Textile and History Museum examines the daily lives and culture of the people who labored in the mills, especially during the period from 1870 to 1920. It also explores the stories of those who developed the technology and collected the money earned from the labor of immigrants at the height of the Industrial Revolution. Through its creative exhibits, the museum provides an excellent overview of the cultural and economic changes brought about by both the development and demise of the Connecticut textile industry.

Located in two buildings of the former Willimantic Linen Company, the museum has an authenticity unsurpassed by any other re-creations in the region. Dugan Mill

Connecticut Eastern **Railroad Museum**

Train enthusiasts may enjoy knowing that the Connecticut Eastern Chapter of the National Railway Historical Society is building a railroad museum in Willimantic, with hopes of eventually creating an entire operating railroad village, off Bridge Street, on the site of the Columbia Junction Freight Yard. A turntable, a roundhouse, a freighthouse, a section house, an operator's shanty, and other village buildings are being constructed or restored here, and throughout 2007 track was repaired or laid to allow passengers to ride on the restored trains in the chapter's growing collection. Children are welcome to try a replica pump car along a section of track, and special excursions on the Providence and Worcester Railroad are planned. Open from May through October on weekends from 10:00 a.m. to 4:00 p.m., the museum is a work in progress. Admission $; children 12 and under free. Call ahead (860-456-9999) or check the Web site (www.cteastrrmuseum.org) to see what has developed here recently. The address is 55 Bridge Street (Route 32).

houses exhibits that bring the visitor right into the late nineteenth and early twenti-eth centuries, when tens of thousands of workers labored under difficult conditions and for very low pay. The exhibits include re-creations of an 1880s mill shop floor, equipped with a carding machine, a spinning frame, a loom, and a textile printer. At one end of the shop is the overseer's office, from which the workers were care-fully monitored.

The museum's main building houses the Company Store, a re-creation of the very shop that on this site once served employees' needs. It now doubles as the museum gift shop. A laborers' tenement, a mill agent's mansion from the Victorian era, and the 1877 Dunham Hall Library (a reading room open to visitors) are also housed here.

Special educational and social programs such as teas, sewing or needlework workshops, storytelling, and holiday events are scheduled regularly throughout the year for families, children, and adults. Check the Web site for listings of these offer-ings, some of which have fees.

Where to Eat

Willimantic Brewery and Main Street Cafe. 967 Main Street, Willimantic; (860) 423-6777. The dining room inside a historic post office is a dramatic setting for kid-friendly pub fare. Lunch and dinner, Tues-day through Sunday from 11:30 a.m. $–$$

General Information

Quinebaug and Shetucket Rivers Valley National Heritage Corridor Inc. (860) 963-7226; www.thelastgreenvalley.org or www.visitthelastgreenvalley.info. From the Web site, download various visitor guides, maps, and driving and cycling routes.

Mystic Country/Connecticut covers forty-two towns in the Eastern Regional Tourism District, including Windham County. Call (800) TO-ENJOY or (860) 444-2206 or visit 32 Hun-tington Street, New London 06320; www.mysticcountry.com; for brochures, maps, calen-dars of events, and information on attractions, dining, and accommodations.

Connecticut Department of Agriculture. 165 Capitol Avenue, Hartford 06106; (860) 566-4845. Produces pamphlets on pick-your-own farms, agricultural tours, farm activities, sugarhouses, and Christmas tree farms.

Connecticut Department of Environmental Protection. Office of State Parks and Recreation, 165 Capitol Avenue, Hartford 06106; Eastern District: (860) 295-9523. Pub-lishes booklet describing state parks and state forests, with day-use and camping informa-tion for each site.

New London County

Coastal Voyages and Country Sojourns

T he southeastern portion of Connecticut defies characterization. First, the county comprises a wide variety of habitats, so to speak. The hills and forests of its northern region are distinctly different from the meadows and marshes of its southern border along the Sound. Second, the population of the two areas is equally disparate. The peaceable hills to the north are much like Windham County in the state's so-called Quiet Corner, while the bustling towns of the shoreline reflect their long history of industry and commerce.

Both areas provide an abundance of attractions and activities for families. From fine art gallery to lighthouse museum, from woodland trail to fishing pier, with every level of sophistication and simplicity, New London's sights are as diverse as the county.

TopPicks for fun in New London County

1. Children's Museum of Southeastern Connecticut

2. *Sunbeam Express* Cruises

3. Project Oceanology

4. Mystic Seaport Museum

5. Mystic Aquarium and Institute for Exploration

6. Historic Ship *Nautilus* Memorial and Submarine Force Museum

7. Ocean Beach Park

8. Florence Griswold Museum

NEW LONDON COUNTY

Voluntown
Stonington
Hopeville
Preston City
Mystic
Mashantucket/
Ledyard
Noank
Groton
Uncasville
Norwich
Franklin
New London
Waterford
Montville
East Lyme
Niantic
Colchester
Old Lyme

Colchester

At the crossroads of Routes 11, 2, 16, and 85, Colchester is typical of the northern communities of New London County. Elegant houses surround its green; small shops, a few restaurants, and pretty public buildings provide the hub of a structure that is primarily rural in nature. Don't let it fool you that Colchester calls its main drag "Broadway." This really is a country town.

Day Pond State Park (all ages)
Route 149; (860) 295-9523. Free admission, except for day-use vehicle charge ($$) on weekends and holidays. Open daily, year-round, from 8:00 a.m. to sunset.

That country flavor is clearly apparent out at Day Pond. In fact, though the dirt road to the park is clearly marked now, the first time we visited here the sign was a paper plate nailed to a tree. Ain't no fancy city stuff here! Originally constructed by a pioneering family named Day, the pond is an antique mill pond, the water of which once turned an overshot waterwheel that powered the up-and-down saw of the family's sawmill. Now empty of all signs of industry, the pond is stocked regularly with trout and is popular with fishers, swimmers, and skaters. No boating is allowed on the seven-acre pond, which is also a spawning ground for migratory salmon.

As is typical at these parks, the state has provided telephones, restrooms, picnic tables, a large picnic shelter with fireplaces, and drinking water for your comfort. A small nature trail across from the parking areas has a fourteen-point trail guide booklet that also contains maps of the whole park and its various trails. Call the number above to obtain that guide in advance of your visit, or if you're here on the weekend, ask the parking attendant for a copy.

A loop trail that begins at Day Pond is an easy walk for families; it connects with a trail through the Salmon River Forest to the Comstock Bridge on the Salmon River. If there is a ranger around on the day you visit, ask for a map to these trails or come equipped with the wonderful *Connecticut Walk Book,* published in two volumes (East and West) by the Connecticut Forest and Park Association (860-346-2372; $24.95). You should also be able to find the trailhead yourselves by walking along Day Pond Road. The views of the Salmon River are beautiful; the trail actually hugs the river before reaching the 1873 covered bridge. The 4-mile combination of the two trails makes for a great day hike. Pack a lunch and eat at or on the bridge. Bring along a few night crawlers and a couple of poles and hooks, and you'll have the makings of a perfect country day.

Where to Eat

Harry's Place. (860) 537-2410. On Route 16 back near the center of town is about as classic a roadside stand as ever stood on an American highway. Open only from April 15 to Columbus Day, Harry's Place has been called "the ultimate

Country **Day-Tripping**

With a little planning, a good night's sleep, and a hearty breakfast packed in a picnic basket, you can tour the next four towns right smartly if you get an early start. Pick a weekend in late summer or early fall and have a brisk morning walk to the Salmon River from Day Pond in Colchester. Eat breakfast on the covered bridge, return to the pond, herd everyone back into the car, and head south on Route 149 and then east on Route 16 and grab an ice cream at Harry's. Ice cream for lunch is a great way to make your kids think that maybe you're still a lot of fun or maybe just half crazy so they'd better behave in case you do something really reckless. While you still have the kids raising their eyebrows in the backseat, take Route 16 northeastward until you can hang a right on Route 207. Travel that road to Lebanon and the junction with Route 87. Here's the perfect place to stop for a remedial dose of Revolutionary War history. This medicine goes down easy at the wonderful **Lebanon Historical Society Museum and Visitor Center** (856 Trumbull Highway; 860-642-6579; open Wednesday through Saturday, year-round noon to 4:00 p.m.), just north of Route 207. Take a left on Route 87 and travel just a smidgen up the road. You'll pass the town's remarkable mile-long green—the same green seen by George Washington, the Marquis de Lafayette, French general Rochambeau, General Israel Putnam, colonial governor Jonathan Trumbull, and other principal players in the Patriot cause. A hands-on history room in the museum, which has been designed with children in mind, explains it all. In addition to this family-centered museum, you can visit Governor Trumbull's house and the War Office, where Council of Safety meetings ensured the provisioning of the Continental Army. Taken all together, these Lebanon landmarks compose one of the nation's best Revolutionary War sites. When you have had your fill of history, continue on Route 207 to North Franklin. Chances are, things are sleepy at Blue Slope Farm (unless you choose the weekend after Independence Day or Columbus Day), so just continue on Route 207 to Route 138 to Route 201 to reach Hopeville Pond State Park. Take out the fishing gear you packed along with the picnic goods, and throw a line and rest awhile until the trout start jumpin'. Pack up around 3:00 or so and continue on to

Pachaug, where the cool woods in the late afternoon are just what you'll want to see. Skip the long hike—just drive up to near the top of Mount Misery and catch the breeze and the beauty of late afternoon. Now sweep southward on Route 165 and have a casual dinner at Village Pizza in Preston. When you can't eat another slice, mosey on up Route 164 and put up your feet at the Roseledge B&B, where a feather bed for you, a full-size trundle for the kids, and a fireplace at your feet await you. Zzzzzz . . .

burger joint" by the *Hartford Courant*. No waistline-trimming foods are served here—just burgers dripping with "juice," excellent onion rings, french fries, dogs, and sauerkraut. Wash these down with soft drinks and shakes while you sit at the picnic tables near the road. Harry's Place has been "proud to serve" since 1918, so maybe there's a secret to longevity in this greasy gastronomy. Check it out, daily from 11:00 a.m. to 9:45 p.m. (10:00 p.m. at the ice cream window). $

Franklin

With great affection I have to say that this little town is out in the middle of nowhere, a comment I can make safely because I know that most of its inhabitants like it just fine that way. There's not a lot here to make families jump in the car to get out this way, but one interesting site and a few events might make you tie in a visit with other plans elsewhere. Take Route 32 from Route 2 to reach the village. To reach Blue Slope Country Museum, take Route 2 to Exit 23 and follow the signs.

Blue Slope Country Museum (all ages)

138 Blue Hill Road; (860) 642–6413; www.blueslope.com. Open year-round by special arrangement for school, scout, senior, and other special groups. Open to the public just once yearly for a weekend festival in October (typically the weekend after Columbus Day) ($–$$, children under 4 free). Family groups can inquire about visits by appointment.

Once each year, Sandy and Ernie Staebner open their dairy farm to the public for a weekend of activities and wagon tours designed to let folks in on the bountiful history of farming and crafting that once flourished in these parts. Years ago there were more farms in New London County alone than there are in all of Connecticut today, and the Staebners have acquired an amazing collection of old-time tools, implements, and farm vehicles inside and outside of the 5,000-square-foot, two-story rustic museum building they constructed in 1990 to educate the public about that history.

Inside the museum and the authentic Amish-built barn are artifacts revealing interesting facts about the lives and labors of three centuries of farm families. Many objects are at least a century old, including woodworking tools, looms, spinning wheels, drills, wooden water pipes, butter churns, weapons, milk cans, rakes, axes, yokes, and toys. A library of vintage agricultural books and publications is also here.

If you come for the annual Fall Festival Tyme, the place is truly steeped in history as volunteers, many dressed in period clothing, demonstrate the skills that farmers and crafters used throughout New England in centuries past. Spinning, weaving, stone splitting, mowing, quilting, basketry, broom making, soap making, quilling, blacksmithing, woodworking, and whittling are among the activities you might see reenacted. Live bluegrass music, draft-horse demonstrations, horse-drawn wagon rides, barn tours, colonial games, and other special activities for children are part of the fun. Food and refreshments are available for purchase, as are books and hand-crafted gifts related to the country theme.

Visiting groups arriving throughout the year miss out on most of that, but they get a guided tour that shows the evolution of farming technology and demonstrations of some of the museum's 4,000 tools and implements.

Hopeville

One of the small village centers that compose the town of Griswold, Hopeville is just a bit more than a turn in the road. A rural and oddly reassuring enclave to those who live in hectic places, it's the home of one of northern New London County's most popular family parks.

Hopeville Pond State Park (all ages)

Route 201; main office: (860) 376-2920; campground: (860) 376-0313. Open year-round. Day use is 8:00 a.m. to sunset. Day use is free, except for parking fee ($$) on summer weekends and holidays; camping April through October ($). You can reserve sites by mail or hope for a site on a first come, first served basis.

Located just east of Hopeville, a tiny village in the northern township of Griswold, this park is noted for its glacial geology and its excellent trails and forest roads created by the Civilian Conservation Corps in the 1930s.

Freshwater fishing, swimming, and boating are possible uses of Hopeville Pond, an antique woolen millpond used in the early nineteenth century. The trails, of course, are perfect for hiking, and a sports field encourages use by families who like nothing better than an old-fashioned reunion-cum-ballgame. As usual, the state has provided drinking water and toilets, plus changing houses, a food concession (in summer), and a boat-launch ramp.

Best of all, however, is the Hopeville Pond campground. Eighty-one wooded sites are perfect for family campers, and you could easily spend a week here without getting bored. Call the campground directly to check availability; this is a very popular site.

Voluntown

As you know by now if you've read any parts of this book consecutively, Connecticut has a vast amount of acreage set aside as protected public land. A huge chunk of that land is Pachaug State Forest, spanning six towns in this region and accessible from Route 49 just a short distance north of its junction with Route 138/165 in Voluntown. Pachaug is an Indian word meaning "turn in the river," and it is the pretty Pachaug River and its tributary, Misery Brook, that meander through the forest. The 24,000 acres preserved here make this the largest protected site in the state and a great place for family camping and outdoor recreation.

Pachaug State Forest (all ages)

Route 49; (860) 295-9523. Open year-round. Campers don't need reservations, but they pay a nightly fee ($). Day use is free, except on weekends and holidays between Memorial Day weekend and Labor Day, when the per-vehicle charge is $$.

Entering the forest on Route 49, you will cross the Pachaug River and disappear for days into a veritable wilderness of greenery, 28,000 acres' worth. Most folks stay just long enough to soak up some of the beauty here and take it home with them in their souls.

Two separate campgrounds provide wooded sites for tenters who decide to soak overnight. You can haul in the motorhome, too, but no hookups are available. The park and forest service provides drinking water, toilets, canoe rentals, a boat ramp, and a horse camp. Once you're set up, you can hike, bike, canoe, bird-watch, swim, scuba dive, horseback ride, and picnic to your heart's content. You can also skate, snowmobile, snowshoe, or cross-country ski in winter.

Be sure to roam these rocky hills on the more than 30 miles of trails past interesting habitats such as a southern white cedar swamp, a rhododendron sanctuary, and the pond. A particularly great trail is the Nehantic Trail to the top of Mount Misery. From the east side of the parking area, it can be reached by beginning on a loop that will take you through the rhododendron grove (which blossoms abundantly in late spring, generally after the second week in June) and the cedar swamp, and then eventually hits the trail to the breezy, slightly balding top of the sorry-sounding mountain. If you don't feel like a moderate workout, you can also drive to within 200 yards of the summit. Most definitely, if you're looking for a little wilderness in this busy state, come here. You'll be amazed at how loud the quiet is.

Preston City

If you take Route 165 south from Voluntown, you'll end up in Preston, another rural enclave sought only by those travelers who reject the I-395 highway, which passes only a handful of miles to the west. At the junction of Routes 165 and 164, you should do yourselves a favor and take a right and drive north on 164 a few miles. Designated a scenic road for very good reasons, it leads past centuries-old farms and homesteads and the pretty Preston City Congregational Church—you won't be sorry you took a little detour before returning to head west again on Route 165 to the city of Norwich.

Maple Lane Farms (all ages)

57 Northwest Corner Road, off Route 164, south of Route 165 junction; (860) 889-3766; 24-hour pick-your-own information: (860) 887-8855; www.maplelane.com. Open daily in season from 8:00 a.m. to noon, plus on Tuesday and Thursday from 4:00 to 7:00 p.m. Call ahead for field conditions. They supply containers, saws, baling, and other necessary supplies. $-$$

Once 140 acres of overgrown pasture around an abandoned dairy farm, Maple Lane is now a thriving family farm with a marvelous spirit of confidence, abundance, and generosity fueled by hard work and determination. Share the positive energy by coming here to pick your own fresh blueberries, raspberries, cut flowers, and pumpkins, plus cut-your-own Christmas trees. Show up to pick your own, or call ahead and place an order for what you want them to pick for you.

Plucking sun-ripened raspberries on a clear summer day may inspire young gardeners to set down a few plants of their own. Who knows? It may well be you yourself who's struck with farm fever in this stunning country setting that kinda makes you want to trade in the Volvo for a John Deere.

Scenic hayrides are given on Saturday and Sunday from mid-September through October, from 9:00 a.m. to 4:00 p.m. ($). At holiday time, thirty-five acres of trees are available for cutting from Thanksgiving weekend through Christmas Eve. Hot cocoa and cookies are provided on the weekends. Call ahead to be sure of the crops and activities offered each season.

Where to Eat

Buttonwood Farm Ice Cream. 471 Shetucket Turnpike (Route 165), Griswold; (860) 376-4081; www.buttonwoodfarm icecream.com. Open March 1 to October 31, this cheerful, crystal-clean roadside establishment offers more than forty flavors of top-quality farm-fresh ice cream every day from 1:00 to 8:00 p.m. (and sometimes later). Try the Forbidden Silk Chocolate or the Purple Cow. From late September and most of October, take a tractor-drawn hayride ($) through their fields, 10:00 a.m. to dusk on weekends; 4:00 p.m. to dusk on weekdays. $

Village Pizza Family Restaurant. Route 165 in Fleming shopping center; (860) 887-1930. Spotless and perfect for families, this place is not just for pizza. Come also for Italian specialties, fresh sauces, chicken, veal, and seafood specials, salads, and a double helping of friendly service. Open for lunch and dinner Tuesday through Saturday 11:00 a.m. to 10:00 p.m. and Sunday until 8:00. $-$$

Where to Stay

Hidden Acres Family Campground. 47 River Road; (860) 887-9633. This is a clean, busy, family-friendly place with swimming, fishing, and hiking opportunities and showers, toilets, laundry, camp store, recreation hall, and rental units to help ensure your comfort. $

Roseledge Herb Farm B&B. 418 Route 164; (860) 892-4739 or (888) 996-7673; www.roseledge.com. Stop just for tea and fresh-baked goodies or stop for the night, the perfect endpoint of a country day. A 1720 farmhouse with fireplaces in every room, homemade soap in the baths, hearth-cooked foods (on occasional winter evenings), feather beds and trundle beds, goats and sheep, fresh-from-under-the-hen eggs, a charming tearoom for guests and visitors alike, and room galore for very welcome children. Join innkeepers Sandy and Gail Beecher for the morning chores—

goats have to be fed, eggs have to be collected—or explore the herb gardens and barn. Pull out an old sled if it's snowing, play in the sandbox if it's not. Take a ride on Black Cherry, the tire-swing horse who awaits you at the cherry tree. $$–$$$, ask about the midweek special.

Strawberry Park. Route 165; (860) 886-1944 or (888) 794-7944. This seventy-seven-acre family campground offers 440 campsites plus rental trailers that include kitchens, bedrooms, baths, and living areas. Some of the latter are positively luxurious; still, families provide their own linens, bedding, and cooking and eating equipment. Weekly and nightly rentals. Entertainment, swimming pools, game room. $$$

Norwich

A small city with the unfortunate distinction of being the birthplace of Benedict Arnold, Norwich has heretofore maintained a pretty low profile as far as tourism is concerned. But there's a new wind blowing on the Rose of New England these days. Pride in the city's active role in the Patriot cause, the production of woolens for Union uniforms in the Civil War, the importance of its shipping and manufacturing history, and its remarkable concentration of homes and public buildings of architectural importance have led to a deliberate attempt by city leaders to pull the city out of the doldrums.

Helped by a great number of forward-looking individuals plus a hefty bit of money garnered from the gaming done not far away on Indian lands, Norwich is making serious efforts to win the affection of travelers. The best of the family-fun stuff is listed below.

For further information on this very colorful and interesting city, contact the Norwich Tourism Office at (860) 886-4683 or (888) 4-NORWICH, or check the calendar of events and other details about parks and attractions on the Web site www.norwichct .org. Ask for two brochures: the *Kid's Guide* and *Norwich A–Z*. The Norwich Arts Council is also a great resource for visitors; call them at (860) 887-2789.

Slater Memorial Museum (ages 6 and up)
108 Crescent Street (Route 2), on the campus of the Norwich Free Academy; (860) 887-2505; www.norwichfreeacademy.com/museum. Open year-round Tuesday

through Friday from 9:00 a.m. to 4:00 p.m. and on Saturday and Sunday from 1:00 to 4:00 p.m. Closed Monday and holidays. $, children under 12 free.

Founded in 1888, the museum inside this Romanesque edifice is the place to take the children if you think it may be a while before you can take them to the Louvre, the Vatican, or any other of the world's finest sculpture galleries.

Slater Memorial has a notable and beautiful collection of 150 plaster cast statues of famed sculptures from around the world. Among these exact replicas of Greek, Roman, and Renaissance masterpieces are *Aphrodite* (the so-called Venus de Milo), Donatello's *David,* and Michelangelo's *Pieta.* Although it's true that the plaster casting doesn't do justice to the luminous and satiny quality of the marble originals, I still can't overstate the beauty of these magnificent pieces; truly, if you are at all interested in having your children see the unbelievable genius of Michelangelo, Donatello, Verrocchio, Luca della Robbia, and others, save yourself the airfare and come here.

The museum also houses a wonderful collection of American art from the seventeenth to twentieth centuries, plus American Indian artifacts and Oriental, African,

On the **Waterfront**

The waterfront/wharf area of Norwich continues to develop as a tourist area. Located at the head of the Thames River on Hollyhock Island, the **Chelsea Harbor Drive** (860-886-6363) and the **Marina at American Wharf** feature riverfront walkways, benches, picnic tables, barbecue grills, and flower beds. **Putts-up Dock Mini Golf** (860-886-7888) is touted as the most challenging course in New England; it has a volcano in its midst that fires every twenty minutes, to the delight of young visitors. Visitors can walk to this spot from the marina parking area, but its location across a good-size waterway also provides an opportunity to ride the free shuttle (weekends only) on a pontoon boat. The **Howard T. Brown Memorial Park** has a gazebo, picnic areas, fishing pier, and free concerts on selected Friday evenings in summer. **Cafe Kaydance Restaurant** (860-887-8555) is open only in summer, daily for lunch and dinner with seating inside and outside on the promenade; the **Harbor Bistro** serves breakfast and lunch year-round, and the ice cream bar at **Putts-up** is a best bet for something sweet in the summertime. In the cold months, come to this area to skate on the new ice rink installed each year on the promenade. Special events, including an annual Fourth of July celebration, a Taste of Italy Festival, and a Winter Festival Parade, have helped to encourage the continuing revitalization of this historic area. Entrance is on West Main Street.

and European art and textiles. The American Rooms are period rooms that trace American history from colonial to Victorian days. The Gualtieri Gallery is especially appealing to children; it contains dolls, circus figures, and sculpture you can touch.

Mohegan Park (all ages)

On Mohegan Park Road, but with access from four different points; in my opinion, best entrance is at corner of Judd and Rockwell Streets near the rose garden; (860) 886-2381. Open year-round from 9:00 a.m. to sunset. Free.

With its walkways, plantings, statuary, and fountain, the 385-acre woodland park can be a nice spot to spend an afternoon. Walking trails, a bicycle/stroller path, picnic areas with grills, and pavilions and gazebos help to make the park a family destination.

Near the park's fairly large pond is a good-size swimming area and a small beach perfect for young children; a play area with swings and such is also there. Popular with both families and area day camps, it can get crowded, but restrooms and a concession make it workable for families, and it is certainly a clean, safe place for an afternoon swim. It is open from June 1 to Labor Day and for skating, weather permitting, in winter.

The lovely roses in the park's formal gardens at the corner of Rockwell Street and Judd Street are award-winning and are in bloom from late May through October, peaking in June and early July. You'll enjoy grassy paths among patterned beds and trellises showcasing more than 2,500 bushes in 120 varieties. The picnic shelter at the side of the two-acre rose garden is a nice place to stop with a bag lunch. Accessible from sunrise to sunset at no charge.

Indian Leap and Upper Falls Heritage Walkway (all ages)

On the banks of the Yantic River off Sachem Street and Sherman Street. Open daily year-round. Free.

Beginning near a restored powerhouse that is no longer open to the public, this landscaped greenway is part of an ongoing attempt to preserve and restore the Yantic River and the various dams and mill buildings that contributed to Norwich's nineteenth- and twentieth-century history as a mill town.

The efforts to beautify and preserve the area included restoration of the dam, the falls, the 1910 powerhouse, and the sacred site known as Indian Leap, where a group of Mohegans jumped to their deaths to escape the Narragansetts in 1643. Once a camping and fishing spot of the Mohegans, the falls area includes the place where Uncas supposedly leapt the chasm with his enemies in pursuit. The 40-foot descent of the falls over large boulders and the natural chasm and surrounding waterways are very pretty; great blue herons, egrets, and beavers are among local species.

The 2-mile Heritage Walkway links the Upper Falls with Indian Leap, the Lower Falls, and the park and marina at Norwich Harbor. This signed walking path is part of the National Heritage Corridor, a protected green belt along the Quinebaug and Shetucket Rivers and their tributaries.

Indian **Burial Grounds**

On Sachem Street off Route 32 is the tiny parcel of land that is the final resting place of Uncas, the Mohegan warrior and statesman who befriended the European settlers and gave to them the land that became the city of Norwich. It lies on the left side of the street, very close to the corner as you enter from Route 32.

Dodd Stadium (ages 4 and up)

14 Stott Avenue in Norwich Industrial Park; (860) 887-7962; www.ctdefenders.com. April through September. Weekday and Saturday games typically at 6:35 p.m.; Sunday games at 1:05 p.m. Some variations. Call or check Web site for complete schedule and directions to stadium. $$

If you like baseball, come here for a taste of the great American pastime, with cheers led by the team mascot, the Connecticut Defenders' Eagle. The 6,000-seat stadium and lots of special events and promotional giveaways at nearly every game make this a fun, easy way to watch the sport, played by this AA affiliate of the San Francisco Giants.

Near-sellout crowds are attracted to these games played against affiliates of the Yankees, Red Sox, and Mets. Come early and have a casual supper here—the snack bar menu has the necessary hot dogs and popcorn, plus bratwurst, lobster rolls, soft pretzels, and ice cream. Special packages that offer some combination of meals and tickets make it easy to have a baseball birthday party. A happy-birthday message spoken by the public address announcer or posted on the scoreboard can be arranged.

Where to Eat

Old Tymes Restaurant. 360 West Main Street; (860) 887-6865. Casual ambience with old-time artifacts and good home-style American fare; children's specials; Southern-style favorites like fried catfish and crab cakes. Breakfast, lunch, and dinner daily year-round, 7:00 a.m. to 8:30 p.m. $–$$

Where to Stay

Comfort Suites. 275 Otrobando Avenue; (860) 892-9292 or (800) 847-7848. 119 suites with fridge, microwave; indoor pool, health club, game room; continental breakfast. $$$–$$$$

Courtyard by Marriott. 181 West Town Street; (860) 886-2600. 120 rooms, restaurant, indoor pool, health club. $$$–$$$$

Holiday Inn Norwich. 10 Laura Boulevard; (860) 889-5201 or (800) 272-6232. 127 deluxe units, restaurant and lounge with entertainment, indoor pool, exercise room. $$$

Montville/Uncasville

Just south of Norwich perched above the Thames River is the small town of Montville and its village of Uncasville, best known for their age-old connection to the Mohegan people. A visit here has a Native American focus.

Tantaquidgeon Indian Museum (ages 4 and up)

1819 Norwich–New London Turnpike (Route 32); (860) 862-6100. Generally open from May to October, the museum will open in other months for special requests from groups. Those interested should call the Tribe's cultural office at (860) 862-6390. Hours are Monday through Friday from 10:00 a.m. to 3:00 p.m. Donation.

Filled with stone, bone, and wooden objects used or made mostly by the Mohegan Indians, this museum, now operated by the Mohegan Tribal Office, is located in the heart of Mohegan territory. It also includes baskets, ladles, and bowls made by skilled Mohegan woodworker and basketmaker John Tantaquidgeon, a direct descendant of Uncas, a seventeenth-century sachem of the Mohegans, and the father of famed Mohegan Medicine Woman, anthropologist, and ethnobotanist Gladys Tantaquidgeon. Although the emphasis here is on the Mohegans and other Eastern Woodland tribes, the collection also includes artifacts from Native American peoples of the Southwest, the Southeast, and the Northern Plains. Pottery, rugs, dolls, tools, beaded bags, shoes, a beautiful canoe suspended from the ceiling, and other objects are among the items in this unique collection. The culture and history of each group are explained throughout the exhibits.

Fort Shantok (all ages)

450 Massapeag Side Road, off Route 32, Uncasville. Open 8:00 a.m. to sunset year-round.

The Montville area is rich in the history of the Mohegans. Drive north again from the Tantaquidgeon Museum on Route 32 to the area called Mohegan Hill (not actually clearly marked). In Fort Shantok (clearly marked), you will find the remains of the fortified village of the great Mohegan sachem, Uncas, and the 300-year-old sacred Mohegan burial ground. Here you can see the graves of the Tantaquidgeons and other descendants of Uncas. A stone monument marks the site of the seventeenth-century fort, and several small trails lead hikers along the banks of the Thames River, which flows past the edge of the park.

The park's large, open recreational areas are available to picnickers, anglers (there is a stocked pond here), and ballplayers, but the fort and burial ground area is a sacred site. Visitors are welcome to explore it respectfully. Please do not picnic in this shaded, peaceful area. Feel free to enjoy the riverside pathways as the Mohegans still do, as a place of quiet meditation. Annual events such as a three-day Wigwam Powwow in the third or fourth week of August are also open to the public.

The powwow features an elaborate Mohegan dance competition, Native American cultural exhibits, native foods such as succotash and clam and corn chowders, crafts and craft demonstrations, storytelling, and a theater production. Admission is **free.** Call (800) MOHEGAN for more information.

The Dinosaur Place (all ages)

1650 Route 85; (860) 443-GEMS; www.thedinosaurplace.com. **The outdoor areas are open daily, rain or shine, from 10:00 a.m. to 6:00 p.m. from mid-April through October; at 9:00 a.m. from Father's Day through Labor Day; and weekends only, 10:00 a.m. to 6:00 p.m., or dusk, in November, weather permitting. Last admission is one hour prior to closing. The Splashpad is open 10:00 a.m. to 5:00 p.m., weather permitting, daily from Father's Day through Labor Day. Outdoor admission is reduced after 4:00 p.m. Indoor activities are offered from 10:00 a.m. to 5:00 p.m. daily from Father's Day through Labor Day, and at the same hours on Saturday and Sunday only, year-round, as well as major Monday holidays and school vacation weeks. The gift shop is open from 10:00 a.m. to 6:00 p.m. daily, year-round, except when this whole operation is closed on Easter, Thanksgiving, December 25, and January 1. Admission fees are charged for visitors age 2 and older to the outdoor areas ($$ in the spring and fall seasons; $$$ in the summer season); separate fees are charged for each indoor activity area ($). No admission charge for the gift shop, the Fossil and Mineral Gallery, or the Fluorescent Room.**

What started as a retail/commercial establishment designed as much to produce income as it was to be an activity center motivated to educate and entertain young minds, this pairing of related entities has grown to be a true attraction. Families come here in droves to explore natural history and the beauties of the Earth—in particular, the great big beauties we call dinosaurs. Outside are nature trails around a pond called Raptor Bay; thirty life-size dinosaur replicas inhabit this space called Dinosaur Crossing, and you pay admission ($$) to it near the complex's expanded snack bar and picnic area. Outside now too are an expansive playground and an amazing 10,000-square-foot water-play area called Monty's Splashpad, where thirty dinosaur-themed water features sprinkle and splash young visitors in the summer months. Changing rooms and restrooms complete the outdoor area. Inside, the Fossil and Mineral Gallery includes fossils, petrified wood, real dinosaur eggs, crystals and other minerals, and life-size dinosaur skeleton casts. The Fluorescent Room, the largest such gallery in the state, features fluorescent minerals. In the activity areas, each of which has a separate fee and a take-home souvenir, visitors can dig for gems in the Jackpot Mine, pan for "gold" in Thunder Creek, or unearth a dinosaur skeleton in the Bone Zone. Combination packages are available in these activity areas, and birthday parties are very popular. The rest of the enormous indoor space is devoted to an amazing array of scientific toys, games, craft kits, fossils, rocks, and minerals for sale. You can even eat lunch or dessert in the store's Cobalt Cafe. This place has evolved greatly and is still growing. Check the Web site often for updates.

Old Lyme

A curious mix of authors, painters, and mariners inhabits Old Lyme, a lovely village that revels in its artsy reputation as well as its nautical one. It's no surprise that Old Lyme can employ the phrase "colony" to describe itself—it has long attracted residents who fall neatly into one or more of these three categories.

One of the earliest and most permanent of these groups was the artists who gathered at the home of Florence Griswold from 1899 until decades past the turn of the twentieth century. Known as the Lyme Art Colony, the folks who lived at Miss Florence's beautiful late-Georgian mansion played with light, color, and texture until they successfully settled upon characteristics later to become known as American Impressionism. J. Alden Weir, Childe Hassam, Henry Ward Ranger, William Chadwick, and many others perfected their brilliance here.

Florence Griswold Museum (ages 4 and up)
96 Lyme Street; (860) 434-5542; www.flogris.org. Open year-round. April through December, Tuesday through Saturday from 10:00 a.m. to 5:00 p.m. and Sunday from 1:00 to 5:00 p.m. January through March, Wednesday through Sunday, 1:00 to 5:00 p.m. Artist studio open April through October only. $–$$, children under 6 free.

Located on eleven acres next to the lovely Lieutenant River, this historic, soft-yellow mansion holds a magnificent collection of the works of the above-mentioned artists as well as related changing exhibitions throughout the year. You may wander the upper gallery rooms of the museum unescorted, but a guided tour of the downstairs period rooms, which are newly reinterpreted, is given first. If children are in the group, the gracious docents tell stories that capture young imaginations.

The museum also includes restored gardens, marvelous exhibition spaces and a wonderful museum shop in the Kreible Gallery at the riverside, and, in the mansion, several period rooms with Miss Griswold's furniture and personal effects. Especially wonderful are the original paintings on the panels in the dining room, the interpretation of an artist's bedroom at the height of the colony's popularity, and the restored studio of William Chadwick on the grounds. Visitors are encouraged to stroll and relax on the adjoining properties as the famed artists once did; you may even set up an easel and paint whichever of the lovely vistas catches your artist's eye.

The Hartman Education Center is the site of frequent programs for children as well as adults. On Sundays from 1:00 to 5:00 p.m., children can participate in hands-on Impromptu Encounters with Art, learning about some aspect of Impressionism or painting en plein air. A Midsummer Festival, which is a joyous and colorful collaboration of regional farmers and hand-crafters, includes varied activities and entertainments for children. Be sure to come for this very popular two-day festivity that includes activities and art shows at the Lyme Art Association gallery and the Lyme Academy of Fine Arts; it is typically the third Friday and Saturday in July.

Return in late November and December, when the mansion is decorated for Christmas. Story readings, special tours, art-making activities of interest to children, and holiday teas are offered throughout this low-key seasonal festivity.

McCulloch Farm (all ages)

100 Whippoorwill Road; (860) 434-7355; www.whippoorwillmorgans.com. Open daily from 10:00 a.m. to 4:00 p.m. but advance calls are required. Annual all-day events in spring and very early fall. Call or check Web site for dates. Free.

One of Connecticut's hidden treasures is the oldest continually operating and largest Morgan horse breeding farm in the state. Visitors are more than welcome, but a call ahead ensures that someone here is able to give you a tour. Half a dozen or more foals are born here each spring, and you can see and pet them and their elegant parents nearly any day year-round. The farm itself is a Connecticut pearl—450 acres here are protected under a Nature Conservancy easement, and—lucky you—are yours to explore. Although it's not maintained as a tourist attraction, its recently restored carriage paths lead through quiet corners where you may see wild turkeys, guinea hens,and many birds and butterflies of the Eastern Woodlands. The owners kindly ask that you enjoy the property respectfully. They prefer no pets or picnicking, and there is no hand-feeding of their magnificent Whippoorwill Morgans.

Come in May for Foals and Flowers, a three-day Open Barn event held every Memorial Day weekend, when visitors are welcomed into the barns for a close-up look at the newborn animals. Return in the fall for Foals and Foliage, also a three-day

Lyme **Art**

The **Lyme Academy of Fine Arts** (84 Lyme Street; 860-434-5232) and the **Lyme Art Association** (90 Lyme Street; 860-434-7802) have no articulated special focus for children and families, but both have ongoing exhibits in their galleries, plus classes, demonstrations, workshops, and lectures that may be of interest. Both are open year-round, but hours vary. Call for a schedule. Other shops and galleries on Lyme Street allow visitors the opportunity to see and purchase the work of local artists.

Ewe'll Love **This**

Sankow's Beaverbrook Farm in Lyme, at 139 Beaverbrook Road off Route 156 about 5.5 miles north of Route 1, opens to visitors seven days a week year-round so that families can enjoy their handmade woolens, farmstead sheep cheese, yogurt, and cottage cheese—and their 600 sheep and lambs. In spring, the 175-acre farm is fairly hopping with newborns; on the Saturday and Sunday after Thanksgiving, come for the annual Farm Day to see shearing demonstrations, take a horse-drawn hayride, buy freshly made gelato, browse their wool shop and buy country crafts from local artisans, and sample fresh meats and cheeses. Farm Day is held rain or shine. For more information, call (860) 434-2843 or (800) 501-WOOL, or check the Web site at www.beaver brookfarm.com.

Open Barn event, held every Columbus Day weekend, when you can see the weanlings just before they are ready to be separated from their mothers. Be sure to visit in September as well for Versatility Day (the first Saturday after Labor Day), a demonstration of the talents and tasks performed by the horses. Morgans from all over the country arrive for this eye-opening show. All three events are **free** to the public. No call ahead is required.

Sound View Beach (all ages)

Hartford Avenue off Shore Road (Route 156); Parks and Recreation, in summer only: (860) 434-2760. Open 8:00 a.m. to 9:00 p.m. Free street parking or parking fee ($–$$) at public and private off-street lots.

A wide, popular beach in the midst of a busy beach colony that looks like a throwback to earlier decades is great for playing or relaxing on a summer day or for strolling in autumn or winter. No coolers are allowed on the beach, there are no changing facilities or lifeguards, and the only restrooms are portable toilets. Even so, tons of families come here, and on summer weekends the joint is hopping as the delightfully summery and slightly seedy arcades, amusements, snack bars, and restaurants along Hartford Avenue are crowded with visitors. The Carousel Shop sells sunscreen, sunglasses, ice cream, beach chairs, floats, and beach toys. They also operate the brightly painted (but small) 1925 carousel, which runs nightly from 7:00 to 9:00 all summer. One ride is $1, 12 rides are $10, and so on up to 100 rides for $65 for parties or fanatics.

For food, try the beachy fare at whatever seasonal restaurants and snack bars may be open on Hartford Avenue. Be sure to have an Italian ice from Vecchitto's.

Where to Eat

HallMark Drive-in. Route 156; (860) 434-1998. An Old Lyme tradition, this classic shoreline shack specializes in fresh seafood, burgers, grinders, chicken, housemade ice cream and yogurt—even breakfast. Umbrella-shaded tables overlook the marsh so you can savor the salty air. Open March to November. $

Boom. 90 Halls Road (Route 1), in the Old Lyme Shopping Center; (860) 434-0075. The third in the very lively and successful trio of coastal Connecticut's Boom restaurants, this one is as welcoming and delicious as the others in Westbrook and Stonington. Seafood is a standout here; Angus beef dishes are popular too, and the sweet-potato ravioli is a favorite. Children's menu. Lunch Monday through Saturday from 11:30 a.m. to 2:30 p.m.; dinner, Monday through Saturday from 5:00 p.m.; Sunday brunch only, 11:00 a.m. to 3:00 p.m. $$–$$$. Be sure to stop next door at the **Turning Page Bookstore** (860-434-0380).

Where to Stay

Bayberry Motor Inn. 436 Shore Road (860-434-3024). 11 spacious rooms with 2 double beds and kitchenettes with microwave, toaster, and cookware, continental breakfast, and picnic area create a beachy getaway for families. Passes to private beach association. Children under 12 stay **free.** $$–$$$

Old Lyme Inn. 85 Lyme Street; (860) 434-2600 or (800) 434-5352. This lovely country inn located in the historic village area welcomes children and pets to the no-smoking establishment. Two of the 13 spacious rooms, all with private baths, have sofa beds, making them comfortable for families. Continental breakfast, inn restaurant and pub, entertainment, landscaped grounds. $$$$

East Lyme/Niantic

Though East Lyme actually extends northward several miles from I-95 (exit 72 northbound, exit 74 southbound), it is the activity in the southern part of town that attracts the most visitors. The village of Flanders centers on Route 1 where it bumps north of I-95. Though a nice reminder of how the Boston Post Road looked before gas stations and fast-food joints overtook most sections, Flanders itself offers no attractions for tourists. Niantic, East Lyme's second village, south of both Route 1 and the interstate, is the center of activity. Take Route 161 south and explore it and the east–west Route 156 to gain a perspective on this shoreline gem of private homes and beaches, marinas and fishing piers, and small shops and restaurants.

Rocky Neck State Park (all ages)

Route 156 or exit 72 from I-95; (860) 739-5471. Open year-round 8:00 a.m. to 8:30 p.m. From Memorial Day to Labor Day, parking fee is $$–$$$. Off-season visitors pay a weekends-only fee or no fee at all. The campground is open from April through September 30 ($).

Few better places exist for beachcombing and shore camping than Rocky Neck State Park. Its full mile of beach frontage on Long Island Sound provides swimming, saltwater fishing, and scuba diving opportunities; its 150-plus campsites provide a home away from home for professional beach bums, amateur naturalists, and the children thereof.

Interpretive programs, junior naturalist activities, and a full summer calendar of nature walks and slide shows are offered for campers as well as day visitors. Hiking and picnicking are also common pleasures for both campers and day visitors. An interpretive trail points out examples of shore flora and fauna. The state provides picnic shelters, bathhouses, food concessions, lifeguards, first aid, and telephones. Campers have drinking water and bathrooms with showers and toilets.

Like other state parks, Rocky Neck is safe and clean, but its windswept bluffs and gorgeous views of the Sound and offshore islands clearly create a special attraction. The park is one of the prettiest of public shoreline areas managed by the state. Its beautiful stone pavilion, constructed in the 1930s, has pillars cut from Connecticut's other state parks and forests. From dawn to dusk in winter, the park's trails and open spaces can be used for cross-country skiing, and there is no better place to simply enjoy a fall afternoon.

Children's Museum of Southeastern Connecticut
(ages 1 to 10)

409 Main Street; (860) 691-1111; www.childrensmuseumsect.org. Open year-round, Tuesday through Saturday, plus Monday in the summer and on most holiday Mondays when school is closed, from 9:30 a.m. to 5:00 p.m., except until 8:00 p.m. on Friday, and on Sunday from noon to 5:00 p.m. Closed Easter, Memorial Day, July 4, Labor Day, Thanksgiving, December 24 and 25, and January 1. $$; infants up to age 1 free.

Among the shops on Niantic's Main Street is a small museum for young children. Families from the far reaches of the state probably have a similar establishment closer to home, but if you happen to be in the area or you live nearby, come at once.

More a play area and experience center than a traditional museum, the popular Children's Museum provides a fantastic opportunity to develop young imaginations. See how creative your children can be in hands-on centers where the museum's staff has created activities and exhibits that explore the sciences, the arts, safety and health, and culture and history. The slides and building toys in the Nursery Rhyme Land play area are perfect for toddlers. The Discovery Room includes a crawl-in planetarium and a marine life aquarium. A wonderful model train exhibit depicts the real sights of the Connecticut shoreline and countryside, and a new exhibit celebrates the Niantic River watershed. Go outside to the renovated garden area and dig for fossils, play with the wondrous bubble table, or scale the climbing wall. Changing exhibitions keep folks coming to see what's new. This is a great rainy-day place if you are camping or vacationing in the area.

Niantic **Shoppers**

If your family is of a more strolling/browsing nature, cruise the shops and galleries of Niantic. Not to be missed just a ways along on Route 156, outside of the main village, is the **Book Barn** (41 West Main Street; 860-739-5715; www.bookbarnniantic.com), which has 75,000-plus used books (even more in their downtown satellite store at 269 Main Street). Both stores are open every day except Thanksgiving and December 25, from 9:00 a.m. to 9:00 p.m. Folks browse for so long here that the proprietors offer complimentary snacks, cocoa, and coffee.

Black Hawk II (ages 6 and up)

East Main Street (exit 72, left at Route 156, about 7 miles, under the bridge, into parking lot), Niantic Beach Marina; (860) 448-3662 or (800) 382-2824. Mid-May through October, daily sails at 6:00 a.m. and 1:00 p.m. $$$$, children under 12 half-price. No reservations necessary.

Fishing trips out on the Sound are the specialty of this boat. Use parental discretion as to whether your child is old enough to handle the excitement (and the equipment) necessary to hook a striped bass or a nice big bluefish. *Black Hawk II*'s crew and captain handle the driving, supply bait and setup, rent rod and reel ($) if you don't bring your own gear, and turn burgers and dogs at the snack bar on board if you don't bring your own picnic. **Free** instruction is available for beginners. They stay out five to six hours in the sun, wind, and even in light rain, so bring sweatshirts, caps, and sunscreen. It's first come, first served and quite popular. Arrive forty-five minutes before sail time on weekends and thirty-five minutes before on weekdays.

Where to Eat

Constantine's. 252 Main Street; (860) 739-2848. This clean, friendly, family-run establishment has great overstuffed sandwiches, house-made soups, salads, a children's menu, plus great seafood, chicken, veal, and steak dishes. Lunch and dinner, Tuesday through Sunday from noon. $$–$$$

Flanders Fish Market and Restaurant. 22 Chesterfield Road (Route 161), Flanders; (860) 739-8866. Cheerful, busy, and very casual, this place serves the best fish in town, plus lots of typical American fare appealing to kids. Open daily from 8:00 a.m. $–$$

Where to Stay

Best Western Hilltop Inn. 239 Flanders Road; (860) 739-3951. 90 units with refrigerator, some with microwave; outdoor pool, beach passes, continental breakfast. $$–$$$

Elms Hotel. 27–37 Ocean Avenue; (860) 739-5545 or (888) 437-1117. Just a stone's throw from Crescent Beach, this century-old restored waterfront classic offers 24 rooms with private baths, microwaves, and refrigerators; picnic area with outdoor games; beach with shore fishing and swimming; children under 12 **free.** Nonsmoking rooms available. $$–$$$$

Niantic Inn. 345 Main Street; (860) 739-5451. Great for families; 24 roomy studios with dining and living areas and in-room fridge, continental breakfast. Beach practically out the door. $$$–$$$$

Days Inn. 265 Flanders Road; (860) 739-6921 93 units, refrigerator, microwave, outdoor pool. $$–$$$

Waterford

Waterford offers lots of shopping, plenty of movie theaters, and an amazing complex called Sonalysts Studios. Unfortunately, the mall and movies won't add much to a family vacation, and, right now anyway, neither will Sonalysts, since they don't offer tours. From its setting right on the Sound, however, Waterford nonetheless offers a couple coastal attractions you might want to check out.

Sunbeam Express Cruises (ages 4 and up)

Captain John's Sport Fishing Center, 15 First Street; (860) 443-7259; www.sunbeam fleet.com. Lighthouse, fireworks, Sailfest, and harbor seal cruises, $$$$. Children 4 and under free. Groups of ten or more get a discount. Eagle cruises and whale watches can also be arranged for large groups, by charter only. Reservations are recommended so the captain can call you if a cancellation due to bad weather is necessary; no deposit is required. The boats leave promptly; please check traffic conditions and plan to arrive thirty to forty-five minutes before departure.

Down at the docks on the Niantic River between Niantic and Waterford at Captain John's Sport Fishing Center, you can take a public lighthouse or seal-watching cruise, or, if you collect a large enough group of friends and family, arrange another kind of nature cruise.

Captain John's boats leave from the First Street dock for seal-watching trips; harbor seals and harp seals have returned to these waters in increasing numbers recently. The boat cruises Fishers Island Sound and other areas of eastern Long Island Sound in search of seals, waterfowl, and other wildlife. These cruises are narrated by a naturalist; in 2007 just two public seal cruises were offered in mid- to late April. They departed at noon and returned around 3:00 p.m. Throughout the summer season are six to ten lighthouse cruises. Crossing the Sound through Plum Gut and across the Race, the boat departs Waterford at 10:00 a.m. and 3:00 p.m. Guided by lighthouse historian Captain Ben Rathbun, the cruise highlights eleven lighthouses on both the Connecticut and New York shores. Cruises to see the Saybrook Fireworks in late June or early July are also popular, as are cruises to the excitement of Sailfest on the Thames River in July. Check the Web site for current cruise information.

By private pre-arrangement, the boats can be hired in February through about mid-March for naturalist-guided bald eagle cruises that depart from Old Saybrook and head up the Connecticut River to see the birds that come from Canada to feed on white perch in unfrozen sections of the river south of Haddam. Call ahead to join your party of ten, for instance, to another party of twenty or such and create a large enough group to start the engines on this 100-foot boat. Each cruise highlights any wildlife you might see, from ospreys, herons, and other waterfowl to wild turkeys, fox, and deer on the riverbanks.

The crew typically brings lunches, snacks, and soft drinks aboard for sale in the galley, or you can pack a lunch (no alcoholic beverages). Pack a Dramamine, a ginger capsule, or a wristband if you get seasick and dress appropriately for the weather. Bring a sweatshirt even in summer, and winter gear at other times. The heated cabin helps to keep you toasty, but despite the large windows the best viewing is still outside at the rail, so be prepared. Restrooms are on board.

Harkness Memorial State Park (all ages)

275 Great Neck Road (Route 213); (860) 443-5725. Open year-round 8:00 a.m. to sunset. Daily parking fee ($$) in summer. Free from Labor Day to Memorial Day. Free mansion tours on weekends and holidays only from Memorial Day weekend until Labor Day; first tour, 10:00 a.m.; last tour 2:15 p.m.

On the gorgeous seaside site of a former private estate, the park itself is a feast for the eyes. Pack a basket of goodies and spread a picnic on the lovely grounds surrounding Eolia, a restored forty-two-room mansion once owned by oil tycoon and philanthropist Edward S. Harkness and his wife, Mary. Bequeathed to the State of Connecticut, the house is now open to the public in season for free guided tours. A picnic area and fishing area are offered for day visitors, but no swimming is allowed, due to a strong undertow.

Sand and **Song**

The **Waterford Town Beach** offers six free concerts on Wednesday evenings at 6:00 from late June through early August. The free concerts are open to the public in the recreation field, adjacent to the main parking lot and pavilions at 317 Great Neck Road, just about a mile down the road from Harkness State Park. It is possible to walk here directly from one park to the other, but I recommend hopping back in the car and taking the drive. If you come just for the evening (after 5:00), there is no charge at all for these family-friendly concerts. If you arrive earlier in the day, nonresidents pay a parking fee ($$–$$$). For a schedule of concerts, call the Waterford Parks and Recreation Department at (860) 444-5881.

Where to Eat

Sunset Rib Company. 378 Rope Ferry Road; (860) 443-7427. Sunset views of the Sound and river complete with great ribs, chicken, pastas, salads, burgers, and more. Indoor and outdoor seating. Open daily for lunch and dinner from mid-March to mid-September. Call for information on closings or reduced hours in the fall and winter. $$

Unk's on the Bay. 361 Rope Ferry Road (Route 156); (860) 443-2717. Close to the water and slightly more upscale than other family places, Unk's offers good food at fair prices. Open year-round Wednesday through Monday for lunch and dinner. $–$$$

Where to Stay

Oakdell Motel. 983 Hartford Turnpike, which is Route 85; (860) 442-9446. Immaculate roadside motel. 22 efficiencies; each room has a fridge, microwave, and private bath, and either one or two double beds. Outdoor pool and grills. Complimentary continental breakfast. $$$

SpringHill Suites by Marriott. 401 North Frontage Road; (860) 439-0151. Two queen-size beds and a pull-out sofa in most rooms make this hotel great for families. In-room refrigerator, microwave, coffeemaker; continental breakfast, indoor pool, whirlpool, exercise room. $$$$

New London

Like its sister city, Groton, across the Thames River, New London has a long maritime history that has influenced its development into a center of commerce and industry. Settled in 1646 as Pequot Plantation by John Winthrop Jr., it was by 1846 the second-largest whaling port in the world. Long a manufacturing and shipbuilding city, it offers an eclectic assortment of attractions of value to families. This guide touches just the highlights of New London. Be sure to contact the New London Visitors Information Service (860-444-7264) or New London Main Street (860-444-CITY) for maps, brochures, and walking guides to all of this 6-square-mile city's museums, historic sites, shopping areas, restaurants, and lodging choices. A look at the city's Web site (www.ci.new-london.ct.us) may be helpful, too.

U.S. Coast Guard Academy (ages 6 and up)

15 Mohegan Avenue off Route 31; Public Affairs Office: (860) 444-8270. Campus open year-round daily 9:00 a.m. to 5:00 p.m. A Visitors Pavilion, which is currently under repair, is typically open May through October 10:00 a.m. to 4:00 p.m. The separate museum operates year-round 9:00 a.m. to 4:30 p.m. on weekdays only. The *Eagle*, when in port, is open for guided tours Friday through Sunday 1:00 to 5:00 p.m. Free.

If you have someone in the family with an interest in the Coast Guard, you should know that New London is the home of its academy. The beautiful 100-acre campus overlooks the Thames River. The academy has a museum and a visitor center that features a multimedia show on cadet life. Tours of the bark USCG *Eagle* are offered

New London's **Historic Center**

You may also be interested in these important points of interest near or within New London's Historic District:

- **Fort Trumbull State Park.** 90 Walbach Street; (860) 444-7591. Built on the site of Revolutionary War fortifications, Connecticut's newest state park has spectacular views of the river and sea. Guided tours, fishing pier, visitor center. Park open year-round daily, 8:00 a.m. to sunset; fort and visitor center open Memorial Day through Columbus Day, Wednesday through Sunday, 9:00 a.m. to 4:00 p.m. Free to park and stroll; visitor center and fort tours, $.

- **Nathan Hale Schoolhouse.** Foot of State Street. One of the two Connecticut schools where Hale taught before losing his life in the American Revolution. Open May through October, Wednesday to Sunday, 11:00 a.m. to 4:00 p.m. Free.

- **Custom House Maritime Museum.** 150 Bank Street; (860) 447-2501. Oldest customs house in the United States, now restored with museum on the customs service. Open April through December, Tuesday through Sunday, 1:00 to 5:00 p.m. and by appointment. Free; donations welcome.

- **Whale Oil Row.** Huntington Street. Restored row of 1832 Greek revival houses owned by whaling tycoons.

- **Starr Street Restoration Area.** Another row of Greek revival homes laid out in 1835 on the site of a ropewalk.

- **Shaw Mansion.** 11 Blinman Street; (860) 443-1209. Built for wealthy Captain Nathaniel Shaw in 1756. Used as naval war office during Revolution. Open year-round Wednesday through Friday, 1:00 to 4:00 p.m.; Saturday from 10:00 a.m. to 4:00 p.m. $

- **Monte Cristo Cottage.** 325 Pequot Avenue; (860) 443-0051. Boyhood home of Pulitzer and Nobel Prize–winning playwright Eugene O'Neill. Great tour, but stories are sad and somewhat adult. Look for O'Neill's statue, sweetly portraying his boyhood, on rock overlooking the harbor on Eugene O'Neill Drive. Open Memorial Day to Labor Day; call for days and hours. $; children under 5 free.

whenever it is in port. Dress parades and concerts by the Coast Guard Band are held on a seasonal schedule, usually on Friday at 4:00 p.m. in the spring and fall.

Lyman Allyn Art Museum (ages 4 and up)

625 Williams Street; (860) 443-2545; www.lymanallyn.org. Open year-round, except Monday and major holidays. Tuesday through Saturday 10:00 a.m. to 5:00 p.m., Sunday 1:00 to 5:00 p.m. $, children under 8 free. The admission fee allows entrance to the doll exhibit in the adjacent Deshon-Allyn Mansion as well. Admission is free to all every Sunday; the first Sunday of each month includes free Family Day activities from 1:00 to 4:00 p.m.

Like the New Britain Museum of American Art, the Lyman Allyn owns one of Connecticut's little-known but exceptional small art collections. The fine and decorative arts from America, Europe, Asia, and the South Pacific make this a perfect introduction to art history for young children. Located in a pristine setting near Connecticut College and the Coast Guard Academy, this beautiful neoclassic museum contains 30,000 pieces; some holdings of special appeal to children are an Egyptian falcon mummy and Native American artifacts. The museum's American collection is excellent. Take the kids on an art history tour of American style from the late 1600s through the Impressionism of the twentieth century.

The museum also owns a notable collection of nineteenth- and twentieth-century dolls and dollhouses. A portion of that collection is exhibited in the 1827 Deshon-Allyn mansion adjacent to the main museum. If you would like to see those displays, just call ahead and ask for an appointment. A docent will be happy to take you to the Deshon-Allyn during your visit to the main museum. It is enchanting.

The museum arranges special changing exhibitions with children in mind at least twice yearly, usually in the summer and between Thanksgiving and New Year's Day. The first Sunday of each month features special Family Day activities, such as live music performances, storytellings, poetry readings, or gallery tours. Outside on the museum's front lawn is a sculpture garden designed to demonstrate the evolution of art. Children are welcome to climb on, play in, and ponder each object in the park. Back inside is a museum shop with gifts of appeal to children and young artists.

Hempsted Houses (ages 5 and up)

11 Hempstead Street; (860) 443-7949. Open mid-May to mid-October on Thursday through Sunday; tours from noon to 4:00 p.m. $

This "compound" in the historic downtown area includes one of the oldest documented houses in America; both homes are among the few New London structures to have survived the burning of the city in 1781 by the British troops under the command of Benedict Arnold.

The Joshua Hempsted House was built by Joshua Hempsted the elder in 1678 and is one of the oldest frame buildings in New England. Joshua Hempsted the

What's the Story at
Connecticut College?

The picturesque campus and liberal arts tradition at **Connecticut College** draw students from every corner of the nation. Families are also drawn here to the arboretum (www.arboretum.conncoll.edu), which is open daily year-round from dawn to dusk, and to the Connecticut Storytelling Festival, held annually in late April at the Connecticut Storytelling Center. For three days, professional and student storytellers gather for performances, workshops, and story swaps. Stories from traditions around the globe are told to audiences of adults and children. The opening story "concert" on Friday evening is often specially directed to families. Admission is charged. For information, call (860) 439-2764 or check the Web site at www.connstorycenter.org/festival.html. $$–$$$

younger, who was born the year his father constructed the house, kept diaries for more than forty of the years he lived in the house. A ropemaker and father of nine children, Joshua kept his diaries from 1711 to 1758, and these writings have contributed greatly both to the excellent interpretation of the house itself and to our knowledge of eighteenth-century colonial American life. The newer, 1759 Nathaniel Hempsted House is one of the most unusual historic homes in New England—it has 2-foot-thick stone walls, a gambrel roof, and an exterior projecting beehive oven. Its mysterious French connections, the subject of recent research, are revealed in the intriguing tours.

Hands-on activities for children are offered on special weekends once each month. On Labor Day weekend a special focus is made on women's work of the eighteenth century. A Hempsted Thanksgiving is celebrated the Saturday after Thanksgiving. Costumed docents, open-hearth cooking, and food samples are part of the celebration. In addition, an excellent colonial life summer camp is offered for children ages eight to twelve or so.

Garde Arts Center (ages 4 and up)
325 State Street. For a calendar of events or other information, call (860) 444-6766; www.gardearts.org. For tickets, call the box office (860) 444-7373 or (888) ON-GARDE. $$–$$$$

If you have never taken the kids to a real movie palace, the kind with gilded architecture and acoustics to spare, plush seats, and a giant movie screen, go to the Garde, downtown in the historic district.

In addition to its noteworthy new and classic film series, the 1,500-seat theater presents nationally and internationally known live performing artists throughout the year. Select from a Broadway series and a Family Theatre series, plus country music, dance, and comedy series. Tickets to single performances are available as well.

Look closely at the upcoming season's announcements. At far more affordable prices than Broadway, the family can enjoy wonderful theater, dance, and more. This 1926 theater, by the way, has enjoyed a $19 million restoration/expansion that has transformed this already grand lady into a state-of-the-art performing arts center. See the beautiful results in its marvelous grand entrance and circular marquee that usher audiences into three floors of new and restored Moroccan-style lobbies. It's a great place to see a holiday spectacular like *The Nutcracker,* or check out the Young and Fun series of dance, comedy, magic, and other youthfully exuberant productions.

Ocean Beach Park (all ages)

1225 Ocean Avenue; (860) 447-3031 or (800) 510-SAND; www.ocean-beach-park.com. Access to the beach and park free year-round, dawn to dusk. Entertainments and concessions open Memorial Day weekend through Labor Day weekend, 9:00 a.m. to 11:00 p.m. Admission collected through a parking fee ($$–$$$). Use of water slide, pool, lockers, and mini-golf involves extra per-person or per-family charges.

For the kind of family fun wherein everybody gets wet, come to a place that offers not one but three ways to get soaked. Right on the Sound, Ocean Beach Park is both old-fashioned public beach resort and newfangled party/conference/banquet facility.

A half-mile-long, very clean white-sand beach is the focal point of the park. Owned and maintained by the City of New London, Ocean Beach Park also has Connecticut's only wide wooden boardwalk down the length of the beach. It leads

New London **Waterfront Park**

A beautiful, wide, half-mile-long esplanade is the highlight of Waterfront Park, located along the Thames River in downtown New London (111 Union Street; 860-447-5201). See historic sites, enjoy the activities of the ferry terminals, or soak up the views of the river and waterfront. A good place to enter the area is behind the railroad station near the Fishers Island Ferry or at City Pier at the foot of State Street. Free live entertainment and special events are frequent on the stage at City Pier Plaza; the new Children's Discovery Pier has permanent displays about local marine wildlife; *Amistad* Pier offers fishing space; and the Custom House Pier hosts vessels of all sizes, including tall ships and luxury cruise liners.

New London **Sets Sail**

A variety of boats leave from New London docks. Check among these for the trips that best fit your family's interests and budget:

- **Block Island Express.** (860) 444-4624; www.goblockisland.com. 2 Ferry Street. High-speed passenger-only service (seventy minutes) to Block Island from New London. Bicycles and surfboards welcome, but no motorized vehicles. Late May to October.
- **Cross Sound Ferry Services.** (860) 443-5281; www.longislandferry .com. 2 Ferry Street. Seven vessels offer passenger and vehicle service (eighty minutes) to Orient Point, Long Island. An eighth vessel, the high-speed *Sea Jet 1*, offers passenger-only service (forty minutes) to Orient Point.
- **Viking Fleet.** Cross Sound Ferry dock at 2 Ferry Street; (631) 668-5700; www.vikingfleet.com. New London to Montauk, Long Island, May to September. Links to Martha's Vineyard and Block Island.

past food concessions, a pinball and electronic game arcade, a kiddie playground, volleyball nets, and an eighteen-hole miniature golf course ($) complete with life-size spouting sperm whale.

Lifeguards and a first-aid station help make this a popular destination for families. Entertainment on the boardwalk on Friday, Saturday, and Sunday is provided for all park visitors. An immaculate Olympic-size swimming pool and bathhouse with changing rooms, lockers, and showers are also available for individual fees ($).

Once home to several carnival-style kiddie rides, the park now has one remaining amusement park–style water slide. A triple-run tower of serpentine slides, this is a humdinger of a ride and, with the exception of the beach itself, is the most popular attraction here. A height requirement of 46 inches helps keep the ride safe for all visitors. Smaller children cannot ride double with a parent or sibling, and the folks in charge here are strict about the guidelines.

The three flumes begin about 50 feet up at the top of a challenging set of stairs, so depending on your speed and stamina in climbing those stairs, you'll get ten to fifteen runs down the flume of your choice in a half-hour time slot. Each person pays $12 for unlimited rides throughout a whole day. Our kids like the medium flume best; the fast one is fun, but small kids are tossed around a bit at the bottom of the run; we came home with a few elbows and knees rubbed raw. If you like quieter fun, take the nature walk to Alewife Cove and check out the birds from the observation deck.

Mystic Whaler **Cruises**

If you have the time and the money, these just may be the cream of the crop in terms of boat excursions along the entire Connecticut coastline. The cruise options are varied to suit nearly any desire; the schooner is an awe-inspiring 110-foot beauty carrying 3,000 square feet of sail, and, whether on a three-hour lobster cruise or a seven-day odyssey, the crew cheerfully invites both landlubbers and skilled show-offs to hoist the sails, plot the course, or take a turn at the wheel. If you can spring for an overnight sea trek, you can choose from five accommodations options, from the tiny Sloop to the Great Room, which gives you a taste of life belowdecks for the common sailor, to the Clipper cabins, which provide skylights, private head and shower en suite, a sink with hot and cold running water, and a double bed.

Three-hour lobster cruises include steamed lobster and fresh clam chowder served on-deck under sail. Six-hour day sails include a hearty barbecue fresh off the on-board grill served while cruising Fishers Island Sound; if the wind is right, it includes a swim in a sheltered cove before returning to Mystic. Overnight sails of one, two, three, five, and seven days include such ports of call as Mystic herself, Block Island, Shelter Island, Sag Harbor, Newport, Cuttyhunk, and Martha's Vineyard. Full-moon cruises, pirate-treasure adventure cruises, lighthouse cruises, and art cruises that encourage you to bring along your art supplies and camera are among the maritime mini-vacations that Captain John Eginton plans to tempt you aboard. It might be worth it to skip the crowds at Disney World and have the adventure of a lifetime on your own private getaway windjammer.

The *Mystic Whaler* sails out of New London's Waterfront Park. Cruises range from $80 to $890 per person. Children 10 and older are welcome on overnight voyages at full fare. Children ages 5 to 10 are welcome on day sails and evening cruises at half-fare, with the understanding that parents are wholly responsible for the child throughout the cruise. To obtain rates and reservations, check the Web site at www.mysticwhaler.com, or call (860) 536-4218 or (800) 697-8420.

Where to Eat

Fred's Shanty. Pequot Avenue, overlooking Thamesport Marina; (860) 447-1301. The quintessential seafood shack, immortalized in Mark Shasha's children's picture-book *Night of the Moonjellies*. Boats, gulls, "long dogs," fries, great seafood, burgers, outdoor-only seating. Open mid-March through late October for lunch and dinner. $–$$

Recovery Room. 445 Ocean Avenue; (860) 443-2619. Great family place, a cousin to the equally wonderful Pizzaworks in Mystic and Old Saybrook. Terrific menu and atmosphere for children. Open year-round for lunch Monday through Friday from 11:30 a.m., and daily for dinner from 4:00 p.m., except Christmas and New Year's Day. $

Zavala. 2 State Street; (860) 437-1891. Authentic—and deliciously gourmet-quality—Mexican cuisine near Waterfront Park. Tex-Mex choices may please younger diners. Open for lunch from 11:30 a.m. and dinner from 3:00 p.m. on weekdays, and for dinner only from 3:00 p.m. on Saturday and Sunday. $$–$$$

Little Havana. Rear of 114 Bank Street; (860) 440-3582. Southeastern Connecticut's only Cuban-American restaurant offers chicken and steak on skewers, coconut shrimp, citrus pulled pork, and much more. Eat inside or, in season, on the garden patio overlooking the Thames River. $–$$

Lobster on the River. 114 Bank Street; (860) 447-3873. The only year-round seafood restaurant on the Thames, this snappy place offers lobster rolls, steamers, catfish, lobster Alfredo—you name it. If it swims, it's probably served here. Burgers, chicken, fries, salads, and plenty of other kid-pleasers. Open-air deck overlooking the river, plus indoor dining room. $$–$$$

Where to Stay

Holiday Inn New London/Mystic. 269 North Frontage Road; (860) 442-0631 or (800) HOLIDAY. 136 units including 24 efficiencies, restaurant, outdoor pool, exercise room. $$$–$$$$

Lighthouse Inn Resort. 6 Guthrie Place; (860) 443-8411. This 1902 mansion is set back a short stretch from Long Island Sound and has access to the private Guthrie Beach Association down the lane. The main mansion has 27 nonsmoking rooms; 24 more rooms are in the carriage house. Complimentary continental breakfast; on-site restaurant. The inn also has a day spa and is popular for weddings and other gatherings, so inquire about the hustle and bustle if you are hoping for a quiet haven. $$$$

Radisson Hotel New London/Mystic. 35 Governor Winthrop Boulevard; (860) 443-7000. 120 deluxe units with 4 suites, restaurant, indoor pool, exercise room. $$$–$$$$

Groton

Back on an even keel since the U.S. Naval Reserve Station decided to stay in town, Groton remains a busy center of naval and defense-related industry. Its long history as such defines its attractions as well. Surrounded on three sides by the waters of

Long Island Sound, the Thames River, and the Mystic River, Groton has been a leading shipbuilding center since the eighteenth century. For much of the past century, it has been most famed as the home of the Electric Boat Division of General Dynamics, the leading designer and manufacturer of nuclear submarines.

Historic Ship *Nautilus* and Submarine Force Museum
(ages 3 and up)

Naval Submarine Base, Crystal Lake Road; (800) 343-0079 or (860) 694-3174; www.uss nautilus.org. Open year-round from May 15 to late October, Wednesday through Monday 9:00 a.m. to 5:00 p.m., Tuesday open at 1:00 p.m., and from November 1 to May 14 (but closed the first full week of May) Wednesday through Monday from 9:00 a.m. to 4:00 p.m. Also closed the last full week of October, plus Thanksgiving, Christmas, and New Year's Day. Handicapped access to the submarine is limited. Free.

A visit to Groton has to include a visit to the USS *Nautilus,* the world's first nuclear submarine. The USS *Nautilus* Memorial at the U.S. Naval Submarine Base on Route 12 includes tours of the *Nautilus* and an award-winning museum that explores the history and technology of submarines.

Excellently presented in a state-of-the-art facility, the museum exhibits celebrate the achievements of the human mind in devising this technology. Children can stand in the re-created sub attack center and hear the sounds of battle. They can operate three working periscopes. They can watch films of submarine history, and they can explore mini-subs outside and models inside. Other outstanding exhibits explain the important uses of the submarine both in defense and underwater exploration.

Aboard the *Nautilus* you will explore the sonar and torpedo rooms and the navigation and control room. You will visit the crew's living quarters, the galley, and the captain's quarters. The impact of the ship's huge size is somewhat lost due to the way it is moored to give visitors access, but, once inside, visitors will easily imagine life and work aboard this amazing vessel that explored beneath Arctic ice and the 20,000 leagues of the deep ocean.

Project Oceanology (ages 6 and up)

1084 Shennecossett Road, at foot of Benham Road, Avery Point Campus of UConn; (800) 364-8472 between 9:00 a.m. and 4:00 p.m.; www.oceanology.org. Public oceanography cruises from mid-June through August 31 at 10:00 a.m. and 1:00 p.m. Seal-watching cruises, Saturdays only in February; Saturday and Sunday in March. Lighthouse cruises, 4:00 p.m., June through August on Tuesday, Thursday, and Saturday and in September on Saturdays only. $$$. Reservations strongly recommended; a Visa or Mastercard number is required to hold your reservation. Note: No children under age 6 are allowed onboard for safety reasons.

The lure of the sea may capture you once again in Groton. If so, head to the Institute of Marine Science at the Avery Point campus of the University of Connecticut, where you can board *Enviro-Lab II* or *III* for a two-and-a-half-hour cruise called Project Oceanology Study Cruises. These summer expeditions are among the best family activities offered in the state, especially for those families that have a child interested in marine biology.

Enviro-Lab's instructors are marine scientists who accompany each group of about twenty-five passengers for an afternoon or morning of study. Using the same methods the scientists use in their work, you will measure and record data about the geology and biology you observe. You will learn the uses of nautical charts and navigation instruments. You will collect and test water, mud, and sand samples. You will pull trawl nets and examine the plants and animals you catch. All the while the crew and captain provide a wonderfully interesting narration about the islands, light-houses, and watercraft that surround your area of exploration.

Also available through Project Oceanology are cruises for observing gray and harbor seals in Fishers Island Sound. These weekends-only winter cruises are pre-ceded by a twenty-minute slide presentation. Inquire also about the lighthouse tour to New London Ledge; the fare is the same as for other cruises.

In summer, be sure to wear sunscreen, a hat, and sneakers. Bring a sweatshirt or a windbreaker. In winter, dress appropriately for cold weather, even though the boat has a heated cabin. Project Oceanology's headquarters are in a waterfront labora-tory building near its boat docks. A seawater aquarium system, classrooms, a library, several labs, and a hostel are housed there; a cafeteria where visitors can purchase snacks and lunches is available to day-trippers. You can also picnic on the campus before or after a cruise.

Bluff Point Coastal Reserve (all ages)

Depot Road off Route 1 (go to the very end of Depot Road under the railroad over-pass to reach the parking lot). Open year-round from 8:00 a.m. to sunset. For info, you can call the rangers at Fort Griswold. Free.

Thames River Fireworks and **Sailfest**

If you can get to Groton and New London in early July, coordinate your visit with the annual **Sailfest,** a three-day celebration of life on the water. Sailing regattas, musical entertainment, boat shows, craft shows, chil-dren's activities, and a parade through historic New London are on the schedule that touches both cities on the Thames. The crowning event has to be the absolutely fantastic Grucci Brothers Fireworks Show. Sponsored by the Mashantucket Pequot Tribal Nation, the fireworks are launched from three barges in the middle of the Thames River. This is a must-see show, but you have to like crowds. In my opinion, Fort Gris-wold State Park is the best viewing site. Get there by 7:00 p.m. to stake a good spot.

Those who prefer to explore the shore on foot may do so at this beautiful park. From the parking area on Depot Road, it might take up to a half hour to walk the 1.5-mile trail through its upland forest to the rocky bluff for which the park is named. Below the bluff lie the beach and tidal salt marsh. Saltwater fishing, beachcombing, and hiking are popular here, as is cross-country skiing in the wintertime.

You can also horseback-ride, bring in a boat or Jet Ski to launch from the sand ramp right into the water, and go shellfishing, scuba diving, snorkeling, and swimming. No lifeguards are here. This wonderfully wild place is a marvelous site from which to enjoy the sea and the sunset.

Fort Griswold Battlefield State Park and the Ebenezer Avery House (all ages) 🏛️ 👶

Monument Street and Park Avenue; (860) 445-1729. Battlefield and fort ruins open daily year-round 8:00 a.m. to sunset. The museum (860-449-6877) and monument are open from Memorial Day to Labor Day from 10:00 a.m. to 5:00 p.m. and from the weekend after Labor Day until Columbus Day on weekends only at the same hours. The Avery House (860-446-9257) is open only on weekends from June to Labor Day from 1:00 to 5:00 p.m. Free admission to all sites at all times. Free guided tours available.

Revolutionary War buffs might want to visit this site of the 1781 massacre of American defenders by British troops under the command of Benedict Arnold. The fort includes ramparts, battlements, and buildings dating from the Revolution, and the view of the river is wonderful. For a view to beat all, climb the 134-foot monument. When you descend, visit the museum, which tells the story of the battle and includes exhibits on other elements of southeastern Connecticut history from Native American times through colonial settlement, the Revolution, the Civil War, and whaling days. Ask for the dates of the Revolutionary War reenactment in early September. This Living History Weekend demonstrates camp lifeways and military drills.

Also on the park grounds is the 1750 Ebenezer Avery House, which, in its original site on Thames Street, was a repository for some of the wounded patriots. Moved to the park in 1971, the house features a kitchen and weaving room that are furnished as they might have been in the eighteenth century.

Noank Village (all ages)

From Route 1 heading east out of the city of Groton, take Route 215 (Groton Long Point Road) south to the village of Noank.

One of Connecticut's most picturesque shoreline enclaves, 300-year-old Noank has real beach-town flavor in its quiet, narrow streets, historic buildings, and shops and marinas. You could linger here all day if your idea of fun is wandering and wading at some low-key shoreline spots.

Esker Point Beach. Groton Long Point Road (Route 215) and Marsh Road; (860) 572-9702. One of the prettiest points on the Connecticut coast, with a perfect beach for children. Linger through a couple of meals to catch the sunset. Wednesday evening concerts in summer. Parking fee in summer only, $$ on weekdays, $$$ on weekends.

Noank Historical Society Museum. Sylvan Street; (860) 536-3021. Open July 4 through October 12 on Wednesday, Saturday, and Sunday from 2:00 to 5:00 p.m. $

Spicer Park. Spicer Avenue, off Route 215, overlooking Beebe Cove. Grills, picnic area. Great spot for bird-watching. **Free.**

Noank Play Area. In the village on Main Street. Playground and picnic area perfect for taking a break from a village stroll. **Free.**

Where to Eat

Abbott's Lobster in the Rough. 117 Pearl Street, Noank; (860) 536-7719. Fifty-plus years of extraordinary seaside ambience with beautiful views of bobbing boats and offshore islands. Eat out in the breeze and sun on picnic tables, under the striped tent, or inside the casual dining room. Lobsters, steamers, clams, oysters, shrimp, steamed corn, seafood sandwiches, barbecued chicken, hot dogs, and strawberry shortcake. Open May through Labor Day, noon to 9:00 p.m. daily, then Friday to Sunday through Columbus Day, from noon to 7:00 p.m. $$$

Mystic River Baking Company. 19 Pearl Street, Noank; (860) 536-0182. The best place for lunch, picnic and beach foods, delicious baked treats. Open daily March through December. $

Paul's Pasta. 223 Thames Street, Groton; (860) 445-5276. The best pasta for lunch and dinner from 11:00 a.m. to 9:00 p.m. Tuesday through Sunday. $–$$

Where to Stay

Best Western/Olympic Inn. 360 Route 12; (860) 445-8000 or (800) 622-7766. 140 rooms, restaurant, health club, sauna. $$$–$$$$

Mystic Marriott Hotel and Spa. 625 North Road; (860) 446-2600 or (866) 449-7390. Located on Route 117 close to the Noank area of Groton, this four-diamond AAA-rated establishment has 285 rooms, including 6 suites perfect for larger families. Cribs available. Indoor pool, health club, coffee bar; Elizabeth Arden Red Door Spa; Octagon restaurant serves three meals daily. $$$–$$$$

Thames Inn and Marina. 193 Thames Street; (860) 445-8111. 21 efficiencies, 4 semi-efficiencies, overnight boat dockage and fishing, right on the Thames River. $$$

Mystic

If I were to name the ten towns in Connecticut that most typify the essence of New England, I surely would mention Mystic. Rich in history that harks back to the earliest days of the Connecticut Colony, it is a town that has witnessed the first of the difficult compromises between settler and native, the glory days of whaling and shipbuilding,

Lantern Light Tours **at the Seaport**

During the month of December (check the seaport Web site or call 860-572-5331 for the exact schedule) the seaport offers seventy-minute lantern light tours ($$$–$$$$) that reenact the scenarios that may have enlivened a similar town of the eighteenth century at holiday time long ago. Costumed reenactors set the scenes in a dozen or more sites throughout the village; your family eavesdrops on the goings-on as your guide leads you by lamplight through the darkened streets. You'll enter parlors, taverns, and shops, and even go down to the crew's quarters on the whaler *Charles W. Morgan*. The wind may wail, rain may lash at your cheeks, or perhaps snow will fall lightly on your path, but all seem merely enhancements to the special effect of these marvelous portrayals. Reservations are a must; these tours are not recommended for children under age four.

If you have children over age seven, you might also consider the Nautical Nightmares tours in the second half of October. Decidedly spooky, the ghostly tour guides tell eerie tales throughout the village and aboard creaking ships.

the rise of industrialization, and the decline of agriculture. Throughout this history Mystic has remained a vital community composed of diverse citizens engaged in the simple craft of building an American tradition.

For many years Mystic has been a tourist destination, most notably because of Mystic Seaport, among the nation's most outstanding maritime history museums. Now home to other notable attractions, Mystic is a destination for more tourists than ever before in its history. Even its downtown, until somewhat recently unknown to out-of-towners, is now a thriving center enjoyed by tourists as well as townies. Not an official political entity itself, Mystic lies on the shoreline, half in the town of Groton and half in Stonington along both banks of the Mystic River.

Mystic Seaport, the Museum of America and the Sea (all ages)

75 Greenmanville Avenue (Route 27), off I-95 exit 90; (860) 572-5315; www.mystic seaport.org. The seaport is open year-round, daily, except Christmas Eve and Day. From April through October, the hours are 9:00 a.m. to 5:00 p.m.; from November through March, 10:00 a.m. to 4:00 p.m. $$–$$$; children 5 and younger free. Half-price admission after 4:00 p.m. Second consecutive day is free.

The first stop in Mystic for most visitors, the seaport's seventeen acres of historic buildings and re-creations represent a nineteenth-century New England whaling and shipbuilding village. An incredible array of educational and entertainment activities is offered here throughout the year. From rope-making to printing to oystering, from sailor to chandler to merchant, the arts, crafts, and occupations of an early American seaport are demonstrated for visitors of all ages.

Horse and buggy rides, planetarium shows, sea chantey sing-alongs, chowder festivals, lantern-light dramas at both Halloween and Christmas, tall-ship tours, fine arts exhibitions, hands-on activities, and outstanding special events are key to the seaport's success. Summer camps, living-history workshops, boat excursions, and concerts are among the opportunities for families.

If you haven't already visited here, plan to do so soon. You may find yourself riding an early-twentieth-century bicycle, stitching a sailor's log book, or sampling a hearty New England stew. After your adventures, shop in the seaport's outstanding art gallery and excellent five-part gift shop for a memento of your trip.

Sabino Mystic River Cruises (all ages)

From the Sabino Dock at Mystic Seaport; use south parking lot across from Seaport main entrance; (860) 572-5315. Check the Web site for rates; call for reservations after 10:00 a.m. on the day of the sail. Ninety-minute downriver cruises every Sunday through Thursday at 4:30 p.m., mid-May through Columbus Day; also every Friday and Saturday at 6:30 p.m. For these cruises, tickets are $$$; reservations are required, but no seaport admission is necessary. Daily half-hour cruises leave on the half hour, from 11:30 a.m. to 3:30 p.m. from mid-May to Columbus Day. Tickets are $, plus required seaport admission; children under 6 free.

The *Sabino* is the last coal-fired passenger steamboat in operation. Built in 1908 in East Boothbay, Maine, for passenger service on the Damariscotta River, it now carries passengers on its double decks for a cruise back in time. Watch the crew shovel the anthracite coal into the glowing maw of the boat's steam plant, then shift your gaze to the historic homes that grace the banks of the peaceful Mystic River. For the evening cruise, bring aboard a sweatshirt and a picnic dinner (or ask about their boxed dinner and beverage service) and settle in for the one-and-a-half-hour journey downriver and into Fishers Island Sound.

Mystic Aquarium and Institute for Exploration (all ages)

55 Coogan Boulevard, off I-95 exit 90; (860) 572-5955; www.mysticaquarium.org. Open daily (except Thanksgiving and Christmas); from March 1 through November 30, Sunday through Saturday from 9:00 a.m. to 6:00 p.m. (last entry at 5:00 p.m.); from December 1 through February 29, Monday through Friday, from 10:00 a.m. to 5:00 p.m. (last entry at 4:00 p.m.), and Saturday, Sunday, and major holidays from 9:00 a.m. to 6:00 p.m. (last entry 5:00 p.m.). $$$; children 2 and under free. Validated tickets good for three consecutive days. Family memberships offered.

During recent years the Mystic Aquarium has been transformed into a state-of-the-art facility. Continually refined and updated, the exhibit areas have been configured to represent the trio of "islands" of marine life found across the globe: the estuar-

Beluga **Encounter**

The Mystic Aquarium offers a program that allows the public to have contact with their whales. Adventurers 5 feet tall and over can make arrangements to spend time in the pool with the aquarium's beluga whales. An expensive adventure for most families, it may still be a once-in-a-lifetime experience worth the splurge to animal lovers. Call the aquarium or check the Web site for more details on this exciting program. A similar program allows contact with the aquarium's penguins. Children over age six may participate. Click on Penguin Contact Program on the Web site for more details.

ies, the coral reefs, and the upwelling zones. From a New England tidal marsh to a coral reef re-creation to a penguin paradise, the aquarium's indoor and outdoor exhibits focus on 4,500 mammals, fish, and invertebrates of the sunlit seas. With its focus on the vital importance of the essential elements of a healthy ocean ecosystem, the aquarium also continues its primary mission of education, research, and conservation.

The magic starts at the main entrance, with a 750,000-gallon beluga whale pool that features both the deepwater areas and shallow cobble beaches of the beluga's south-central Alaskan habitat. Other indoor and outdoor exhibits include sharks, seals, sea lions, hundreds of species of fish, and invertebrates of every sort. The outdoor seal, sea lion, and penguin exhibits are re-creations of the animals' natural habitats in the North Pacific and Africa. The skylit marine theater allows staff marine biologists to demonstrate the dramatic talents and capabilities of California sea lions. The Aquatic Animal Study Center concentrates on puzzling out the habits, behaviors, and needs of marine animals to help wildlife conservation efforts.

The aquarium has an exciting relationship with underwater explorer Robert Ballard in the Institute for Exploration, which introduces visitors to undersea technology, oceanographic exploration, and marine archaeology. Simulated deep-sea dives aboard a manned submersible include the sights and sounds that one might experience during a 12,000-foot descent; another exhibit shows the robotic and other technology being used to explore famed shipwrecks.

The aquarium also has an excellent gift shop/bookstore, which shoppers may browse without an admission ticket. Workshops, classes, and special events are held at the aquarium throughout the year.

Olde Mistick Village (all ages)

At the junction of Route 27 and Coogan Boulevard, immediately adjacent to the aquarium; (860) 536-4941. Open year-round daily, from Monday through Saturday from 10:00 a.m. to 6:00 p.m. and on Sunday from noon to 5:00 p.m. Summer and holiday hours are often extended.

A shopping center built as a re-creation of a circa-1720 New England village, its pretty paths, reproduction freestanding shops, and ponds, fences, stone walls, and waterwheels make for a very pleasant shopping experience. Restaurants, tea shops, jewelry stores, clothing and toy shops, gourmet coffee and chocolate shops, and much more are here.

Olde Mistick Village is especially pretty in summer, when its ponds are busy with waterfowl, its gazebo is the site of **free** concerts, and its flowers and trees are in bloom. During December the village and its pretty, white New England church replica are aglow with holiday light displays, and various complimentary festivities and promotions in individual shops lure cheerful holiday shoppers along the luminaria-lined pathways.

Denison Pequotsepos Nature Center and Peace Sanctuary
(all ages)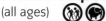

109 Pequotsepos Road; follow Coogan Boulevard to its eastern end, take right on Jerry Browne Road, then right on Pequotsepos; (860) 536-1216; www.dpnc.org. Open year-round Monday through Saturday from 9:00 a.m. to 5:00 p.m. and Sunday from 10:00 a.m. to 4:00 p.m. $–$$, children 5 and under free. Trails are open dawn to dusk; leave a donation in the box. Leashed pets are welcome. Picnicking is allowed.

If you need a break from the busyness and the marine and historical themes, visit this 200-acre preserve with 7 miles of trails through woods and meadows and past ponds. Wildflower and fern gardens are among the areas created to encourage homeowners to create their own similar backyard habitats. Here you may see otter, mink, and other mammals native to southeastern Connecticut, plus 150 species of birds, including bluebirds and scarlet tanagers.

The Pequotsepos natural history museum includes indoor native wildlife exhibits in woodland, wetland, and meadow habitats. Frogs, fish, birds, and reptiles are among the animals here. Be sure to stop in the Night in the Meadow Theater to experience a simulation of the sounds and sights in a meadow on a summer evening. Outdoor flight enclosures provide homes for nonreleasable owls. The Trading Post gift shop sells field guides, birding supplies, natural science materials for children, and locally made nature-related items. A full schedule of guided walks, summer camps for children ages three to sixteen, birding activities, and field trips can be found on the center's Web site.

The center's Peace Sanctuary on River Road is about a mile away on the western bank of the Mystic. Atop rocky ledges, this wooded, thirty-acre preserve offers trails overlooking the river. Ask for directions when you visit the main center. Open at no charge from dawn to dusk, it is well named and especially lovely to explore during the early morning and close to dusk when the birds are most active. If you come in May, you may witness the charm of the 400 pink lady-slipper plants that blossom here.

Downtown Mystic (all ages)
West and East Main Street (Route 1); Water Street; Bank Street; Pearl Street; and other nearby streets.

A few years back only the locals knew the secrets of the "real" historic center of Mystic. Now the whole downtown area rocks and rolls with the tourist crowd that has discovered the no-longer-neglected inner core of the village. If your appetite for the sea has simply been whetted by the sights upriver, head downtown to Route 1 via Route 27 and the famed counterweighted bascule drawbridge that leads you to picturesque Mystic center. Linger awhile on the bridge itself (park the car somewhere else first) and watch the jellyfish and other flotsam. Stay to see the hourly raising of the bridge and the passage of the yachts and sailboats as they cruise up- or downriver. Then stroll the boutiques, galleries, bookstores, candy shops, and restaurants. Discover your own favorite places, but be sure to take your time at the Mystic Army-Navy Store, the Mystic Art Association Gallery, Mystical Toys, the Mystic River Park, the Mystic Drawbridge Ice Cream Company, and the incomparable Sea Swirl seafood shack. You'll easily find them all in the 1-mile historic district. Return in mid-August for the Outdoor Art Festival, a two-day juried show of 300-plus artists who bring their wares to the sidewalks, parks, and riverbanks of downtown Mystic. Local vendors keep browsers on their feet with plenty of food and drink, and entertainment for all ages abounds throughout the festival scene. Downtown Mystic is serviced by a fun transportation option from Memorial Day to Labor Day: From 11:00 a.m. to 6:00 p.m. daily, Mystic Seaport's *Liberty* water-taxi leaves every thirty minutes from a dock behind the S&P Oyster House for rides ($) to or from the seaport (or just take a round-trip whirl, if you like).

Voyager Cruises (all ages)
15 Holmes Street; (860) 536-0416; www.voyagermystic.com. Public sails daily from mid-May to mid-October at 10:20 a.m., 2:20 p.m., and 5:30 p.m. $$$$, children under 2 free. Reservations recommended. Charters also available on this vessel and on the tall ship *Mystic*.

The *Argia,* a replica nineteenth-century gaff-rigged schooner, takes passengers on two- to three-hour day sails in scenic Fishers Island Sound. This beautiful white bird glides gracefully across these sheltered waters, providing a gentle ride that cannot fail to relax and refresh a weary day-tripping family. Beverages and light snacks are sold on board. You may also bring along a picnic lunch or dinner. If the majestic *Mystic Whaler* would break your bank, this more affordable option may be just right for a family cruise.

Into the **Mystic Cruises**

It seems there is no end to boating experiences out of Mystic, but the crowds are here to support them. Here are a few more options in case the others have failed to intrigue you:

Brilliant. Mystic Seaport, (860) 572-5315. Weeklong camps.

Resolute. Mystic Seaport, (860) 572-5315. Public sails.

Breck Marshall. Mystic Seaport, (860) 572-5315. Public sails.

Where to Eat

Pizzetta. 7 Water Street; (860) 536-4443. This snappy and savvy little place with admirable eco-conscious philosophies and practices was so popular when it first opened that it ran short on dough. Not anymore. Now the dough is locally made in great fresh batches so the owners can concentrate on their fresh house-made sauce. The Neapolitan-style thin-crust pie is very good and comes just about any way you want it. Locally farmed salads are offered as well. Even their cleaning products are green. Open Wednesday through Sunday for take-out and by-the-slice service from noon to 3:00 p.m. and for dining in from 4:00 to 10:00 p.m. $

Sea View Snack Bar. 145 Greenmanville Avenue; (860) 572-0096. Gulls circle the red-painted picnic tables, the sun glints on the river, the view of the *Charles W. Morgan* can be wonderful, and the food is typical summer seaside-shack cuisine: rings, wings, dogs, nuggets, fries, burgers, all sorts of seafood, and homemade chowder. $

Seaman's Inne. Greenmanville Avenue, near the north entrance to the seaport; (860) 536-9649. This tavernlike restaurant is great for New England-y dishes like seafood pot pie, crab cakes, and prime rib, plus soups, salads, and sandwiches. Dixieland Sunday brunch offers Southern-style fare and music. Open daily; lunch, $; dinner, $$–$$$$

Mystic Pizza. 56 West Main Street; (860) 536-6194. Who can resist? It's convenient, it's good, the menu has lots more than pizza, and it's famous, so be there, just for fun. Lunch and dinner, 10:00 a.m. to 11:00 p.m. every day of the year. $

Where to Stay

Best Western Mystic Hotel. 9 Whitehall Avenue; (860) 536-4281 or (800) 363-1622. 150 units, 4 suites, restaurant, sauna, fitness room, playground, indoor pool. $$$

Howard Johnson Inn. 253 Greenmanville Avenue; (860) 536-2654. Kid-friendly amenities make a stay here fun for families. Some rooms have fridges and microwaves. Indoor pool. Vacation packages starting at $199 include room, 4 tickets to the seaport, aquarium, or the Mashantucket Pequot Museum, plus full breakfast and discounts to other regional attractions. $$–$$$$

Seaport Campgrounds. Route 184, Old Mystic; (860) 536-4044. Spacious family campground for tenters and RVers. Swim-

Other Mystical **Attractions**

Denison Homestead Museum. Pequotsepos Road; (860) 536-9248. If the seaport fails to satisfy a history craving, this unusual 1717 house might do the trick. Its rooms represent periods from the 1720s to the 1940s.

Williams Beach Park at Mystic Community Center off Mason's Island Road; (860) 536-3575. There's a saltwater beach, playground, picnic and snack pavilions, and grills. **Free.** No lifeguards. Open June to Labor Day.

ming pool, fishing pond, playground, rec center, mini-golf, store, laundry, more. Open mid-March through late November. $

Whaler's Inn. 20 East Main Street; (860) 536-1506 or (800) 243-2588; www.whalers innmystic.com. 49 lovely rooms in the heart of downtown Mystic by the bridge. Homey ambience; children stay **free.** Complimentary continental breakfast. Three-diamond AAA rating. Four-star restaurant called Bravo Bravo. $$$–$$$$

Mashantucket/Ledyard

I'm not sure whether to call this Connecticut's oldest town or its newest, but it certainly is one getting an awful lot of attention. Inhabited by Europeans since early in the seventeenth century and for centuries before that by Native American people such as the Pequots, the Mohegans, and the Narragansetts, the mostly rural town of Ledyard now contains a village called Mashantucket. A federal reservation of the sacred tribal land of the Mashantucket Pequot Tribal Nation, it is the center of activity in this otherwise quiet, forested landscape.

Visitors arrive by the busload to Mashantucket's most famous attraction: the Foxwoods Resort Casino. I don't recommend this complex as a family attraction, but many folks might disagree. Billed as the largest gaming (read "gambling") facility in the world, Foxwoods rises upward from Route 2 as if it were Oz itself—not a bad comparison since it sure is about as far away from Kansas as one might travel, speaking both materially and spiritually. Besides the thousands of ways you can part with your shirt here, there are a score or more of restaurants, a four-diamond high-rise hotel with pool and spa, a retail concourse of specialty shops, and Cinetropolis, a so-called city of theaters including wraparound screens, a Turbo Ride with hydraulic action seats, and Virtual Adventures, in which theatergoers participate in the action on screen. The choice is yours, but I suggest a closer look at the simpler side of life in the Eastern Woodlands.

Ledyard's **Ups and Downs**

The northeastern part of Connecticut was famed in the nineteenth century for the number of water-powered mills that sprang up along the banks of the Quinebaug and Shetucket Rivers, and even along lower tidal rivers such as the Yantic and Thames. As a result, abandoned mill sites are not at all uncommon in these parts. Fully operational, restored sites are a rarity, however, and Ledyard has one to show off for you. Located near Lee's Brook in Sawmill Park on Iron Street, which is Route 214, the unusual Ledyard Water-Powered Up-Down Sawmill has been restored to the way it might have been when it was built by Israel Brown in 1869. Water levels on the mill's pond site are highest in spring and fall, so operation is seasonal, even though the park is open daily year-round and the public is welcome to enjoy its picnic tables and grills. If you visit during the operational seasons, you can see the vertical water wheel that turns the gears that move the up-down saw. This mill is still used to cut large logs into lumber. Demonstrations are given on Saturday from 1:00 to 4:00 p.m. during April and May and from mid-October through November. Also on this site are an operating shingle mill, an unrestored gristmill, and a blacksmith's forge. Admission is free. For further information on this National Historic Site or for information on the 1793 Nathan Lester House and Ledyard's Historic Districts, call (860) 464-2575.

Mashantucket Pequot Museum and Research Center
(all ages)

111 Pequot Trail, off Route 2; (860) 396-6800 or (800) 411-9671; www.mashantucket .com. Open year-round daily from 10:00 a.m. to 4:00 p.m. (last admission 3:00 p.m.). Closed Thanksgiving, Christmas, and New Year's Day and the eves of each of those days. $$–$$$, children under 6 free.

Established with the goal of preserving Pequot history and culture, the Mashantucket Pequot Museum and Research Center is a must-see experience for all travelers to Connecticut. Nearly $150 million went into the research, planning, and construction of this fabulous showcase—an astonishing sum that is apparent in every pore of this amazing complex. Pack the family up as soon as you can and plan to spend a full day here.

You'll enter the museum and purchase your tickets in a rather modest lobby of warm woods and polished granite floors imbedded with seashells, but don't let that subdued ambience fool you. From there onward, you will be totally absorbed in a glorious yet graceful celebration of the Mashantucket Pequot tribal history and the natural history of their beloved land. Steps from the entrance lobby is an enormous glass and steel Gathering Space, open to the woodlands and the sky and home to beautiful, life-size dioramas representing the native people who have inhabited that exterior landscape for more than 10,000 years. Above your heads on the second level of the Gathering Space is a full-service restaurant offering Native American and traditional American cuisine, and not far away is a 185-foot stone and glass tower that provides sweeping views of the Mashantucket Pequot reservation.

Don't hesitate too long in these spaces, however. Depending on the ages and interests of your group, you may need a good five or six hours to thoroughly explore the remarkable exhibits that await you. Your tour begins with an escalator ride through a simulated glacial crevasse complete with chilly temperatures and the sounds of howling winds. Traveling back to the Ice Age, learn how the movement of the glaciers shaped the land and how life began on the barren areas exposed when the ice caps melted. Time-traveling forward, see a life-size re-creation of an 11,000-year-old caribou kill; learn how the native people adjusted to the warming climate 8,000 to 3,000 years ago. Discover the ways the people adapted woodland resources for food and shelter. Traveling ever closer to our present time, walk through a 22,000-square-foot re-creation of a sixteenth-century coastal Pequot village, featuring dozens of realistic, life-size figures engaging in everyday activities that demonstrate the lifeways and beliefs of the Pequot civilization. Immersed in the light, sounds, and even the aromas of this village culture, you will be transported to a nearly lost but not forgotten time.

From there, explore the exhibit that re-creates a seventeenth-century Pequot fort discovered in 1992 just yards from the present-day museum. Stroll through an indoor and outdoor eighteenth-century Pequot farmstead, re-created on an acre of land right outside the museum walls. Step through the cabin door to an orchard and herb garden and learn about farming techniques and tools. Throughout the museum, watch films exploring such topics as food, wigwams, wampum, canoes, and Pequot history. (Note to parents: The excellent short film *The Witness*, recounting the story of the Pequot massacre at Mystic, is unflinching in its graphic portrayal of this brutal event. You, however, may flinch more than a few times, and youngsters under age ten may be disturbed by the violent nature of the film.)

You may be emotionally drained when you exit the theater if you have chosen to see the heartbreakingly honest *Witness*, but there is still much more to see. You can immerse yourself in exhibits describing the Reservation Period and the eighteenth-, nineteenth-, and twentieth-century struggles and lifestyles of the Mashantucket Pequots. The changing exhibition gallery usually features contemporary Native arts or traveling exhibitions from other collections and native cultures. Two excellent research libraries include an outstanding collection for children; a 400-seat auditorium offers live performances, films, and lectures. A regular calendar of activities and demonstrations for children is planned throughout the year. No matter what parts of the museum you see or what activities you try, a visit here promises to be unforgettable.

Where to Eat

The Mashantucket Pequot Museum has both a full-service restaurant and a snack bar. Elsewhere along Route 2 from Stonington north to Ledyard are a variety of eateries. Here's one local favorite.

Valentino's Italian Restaurant and Pizzaria. 725 Colonel Ledyard Highway; (860) 464-8584. With an emphasis on take-out New York–style pizza, this small restaurant also serves calzones, pasta dishes, salads, an array of appetizers, and seafood, veal, and chicken dishes for lunch and dinner daily. $$

Where to Stay

Abbey's Lantern Hill Inn. 214 Lantern Hill Road; (860) 572-0483; www.abbeys lanternhill.com. 7 rooms and a cottage in a contemporary country-style bed-and-breakfast in the countryside. Private baths (some with Jacuzzis); private decks or patios; complimentary full breakfasts on weekends; continental-style fixin's on weekdays. Children are warmly welcomed,

and well-behaved pets are welcome in the cottage. No smoking indoors. $$$–$$$$

Two Trees Inn. 240 Lantern Hill Road; (860) 312-3000 or (800) FOXWOODS. This is the self-billed "rustic" lodge-style alternative to the glitzy hotels of the Foxwoods complex, also owned and operated by the Mashantucket Pequots. 2-room suites, with sitting room and sleeper sofa adjoined to a bedroom with one king-size or two double beds. Standard rooms also available. Pool, gym, restaurant. Complimentary continental breakfast. $$$–$$$$

Mystic KOA. Route 49, North Stonington; (860) 599-5101 or (800) 624-0829; www .mystickoacampground.com. Tent sites, RV sites, and best of all, adorable and affordable rental cabins, all with multiple sorts of hookups, make this a best bet for families traveling anywhere in southeastern Connecticut. Pools, playground, recreation hall, mini-golf, shuffleboard, and much more. Daily, weekly, and seasonal rates. $

Stonington

Nestled between the coves near the easternmost boundary of the state, Stonington is my favorite Connecticut town. Someday I would like to live here in a tiny house overlooking the sea, with lupines below my balcony and kitchen herbs in my dooryard. One of my daughters loves this place, too, so much so that she doesn't like me to write about it. "I don't want anyone else to go there," she says.

Just about 5 miles east of downtown Mystic by way of Route 1, Stonington is very quaint, very New England, very evocative of the days of sea captains and West Indies

The Blessing **of the Fleet**

Perhaps the quaintest and most touching annual event in Connecticut is the blessing ceremony that offers spiritual protection to the fishermen who still ply these waters for the seaborne bounty that provides to them a living and to us a feast. Held usually near the end of July, the two-day event begins under a tent at the town dock with a traditional lobster/clambake that builds everyone's stamina for an evening of dancing on the dock until midnight. The next day the Fisherman's Mass is offered at 10:00 a.m. at St. Mary's Roman Catholic Church on Broad Street in the village, and then the street parade gets under way by 1:00 p.m., encircling the town before returning to the dock. A brief dockside ceremony precedes the bishop's boarding of the decorated fleet's lead vessel, which moves into the harbor for the bishop to bless each of the remaining boats as they pass in their own parade. Following the blessing, the vessels pass the breakwater and go out on the Sound, where the families of deceased fishermen toss into the sea floral tributes formed like broken anchors. When the boats return to the village, they are awarded prizes for the best decorations, and the dancing and eating resume until 6:00 p.m. Visitors of all faiths are welcome to join the celebration.

trading ships. Close your eyes and see the little girls playing hoops and graces, the little boys in knee pants shinnying their way up the flagpoles. Hear the clip-clopping of the horses, the whoosh of the gas lamps, the clanging of the bell buoys. It's easy to imagine in Stonington.

Once you have crossed the bridge to the borough, park anywhere and just stroll—it's a great walking town. Weave your way down Water Street, stopping at the shops and galleries as you wander. Rest awhile at a cafe or coffeehouse. Enjoy the marvelous model railroad in the Anguilla Gallery. Let the salty air lead you down to DuBois Beach right on the Point, and let the kiss of the sea breeze tease any stubborn knots from your work-worn shoulders. Hug one another and take a collective deep breath. Life doesn't get any better than this.

Old Lighthouse Museum (ages 4 and up)

7 Water Street; (860) 535-1440; www.stoningtonhistory.org. Open daily May through October from 10:00 a.m. to 5:00 p.m. Open by appointment November through April. $, children under 6 **free**. Includes admission to the Palmer House.

Inside the 1832 stone lighthouse at the foot of the village are displays of whaling and fishing equipment, swords and cannonballs and other instruments of defense,

Clyde's Cider Mill

On a crisp day in early fall when the apples are at their peak and the cider is at its sweetest, head to Clyde's (860-536-3354) on North Stonington Road in Old Mystic and watch this huge, steam-powered mill (the only such machine in the United States) press the amber juices from the apples that fill barrel after barrel to the brim. The whole place, in operation since 1881, is a National Historic Landmark. Sweet cider, hard cider, and the apples themselves are for sale, and on weekends especially there's always a crowd that adds to the aura of festivity here. Jams, jellies, honey, maple syrup, fudge, pies, breads, cornmeal, and local produce attract shoppers from near and far. Open daily 9:00 a.m. to 6:00 p.m. from early July through October and then closing at 5:00 p.m. until late December. Pressings are typically scheduled at 11:00 a.m. and 1:00 and 3:00 p.m. on weekends from September to Thanksgiving and at 1:00 and 3:00 p.m. on weekdays.

nineteenth-century portraits, and much more. One exhibit focuses on treasures brought back to Stonington by the captains of the China trade route. An antique dollhouse, decoys, toys, and model ships are often especially interesting to children.

You can learn about the history of Stonington and its role in the War of 1812. You can learn about the railroad that once transferred passengers from sailing ships to river steamboats. You can even climb the tower of the lighthouse itself for a marvelous view of the harbor and the fishing fleet that still works in these waters.

Captain Nathaniel B. Palmer House (ages 6 and up)

North Water and Palmer Streets; (860) 535-8445; www.stoningtonhistory.org. Open May through October on Tuesday through Sunday from 10:00 a.m. to 4:00 p.m. (last tour at 3:00 p.m.) and by appointment. $, children under 6 free. Includes admission to the Lighthouse Museum.

Home of the discoverer of Antarctica, this nineteenth-century mansion at the far north of the village has sixteen rooms filled with many examples of the clever architectural design work of the crafty captain himself. Better known for his success in the China trade and his discovery of the southernmost continent in 1820 in the relatively small sloop *Hero* while on a sealing expedition, the captain filled his elegant home with a variety of innovations and contraptions that intrigue young and old visitors. Lively one-hour tours relate the many adventures of Nat Palmer and his also-daring brother Alexander. Be sure to climb to the top of the cupola to have a look at the glorious view.

Barn Island State Wildlife Management Area (all ages)
🦆 ⛺ 👫

Palmer Neck Road off Green Haven Road off Route 1. Call area supervisor John Lincoln at (860) 445-1729. Free.

The easternmost village in the lower part of the county just before you cross the Rhode Island border on I-95, Pawcatuck is just a speck of a place officially in the town of Stonington. For centuries an agricultural enclave with fields lapped by the sea, it has within its boundaries the state's largest coastal property managed for conservation and wildlife purposes. Situated on Little Narragansett Bay between Wequetecock Cove and the Pawcatuck River, this pretty 1,000-acre refuge has 4 miles of trails and unpaved roads across the tidal marshes and upland oak forest. Because of the unusual population of native and migratory birds here, the area is popular for birdwatching. Hunting is allowed in the fall and spring, so in those seasons, wear brightly colored clothing.

To reach the refuge, take Green Haven Road south from the traffic light on Route 1 where the sign says Barn Island State-owned Boat Launching Area. A nearly immediate left on Palmer Neck Road takes you past Wequetecock Cove and down to the shore. Have a hike around this pretty site, where shorebirds nest and the marshes rustle. If you have a boat, launch it here and cruise the quiet inlets. Saltwater canoeing and kayaking are especially pleasant here and you can also fish, usually without too many other anglers to disturb your serenity. Be sure to tread lightly in this haven. Don't feed the wildlife or disturb their peace, and please pack out all your trash. This refuge is one of the state's best-kept treasures.

Where to Eat

Noah's. 113 Water Street; (860) 535-3925. Three solid meals a day at this warm and casual place with a down-home flair. Good cookin', served with a smile. The scrod melts in your mouth. Closed Monday. $–$$

Prime Time Cafe. 1 West Broad Street; (860) 599-3840. On the bridge overlooking the Pawcatuck River in downtown Pawcatuck, this brightly painted bistro-style restaurant serves breakfast from 7:00 a.m., lunch, and dinner from 5:00 p.m. daily. Everything is house-made and cooked to order. American cuisine. $–$$

The Yellow House. 149 Water Street; (860) 535-4986. Wonderful coffees and biscotti in a sunny space splashed with cheerful colors. Tasty sandwiches, tacos, quesadillas, soups, and other easy fare for children. Open daily from 6:30 a.m.; closes at 2:30 p.m. Monday through Friday, 3:00 p.m. Saturday, and noon Sunday. $

Where to Stay

Cove Ledge Inn and Marina. On Route 1 on Pawcatuck side of Stonington; (860) 599-4130; www.coveledgeinn.com. Right near the hub of a marina, this waterfront complex on five acres is both picturesque and convenient. 4 efficiency apartments, 2 guest houses, 2 suites in restored vintage main house, plus 16 motel rooms. Outdoor pool; playground; continental breakfast; kayak rentals. $$–$$$$

Inn at Stonington. 60 Water Street; (860) 535-2000. Top-drawer comforts are offered in this elegant 12-room inn in the center of Stonington Borough. Fireplaces, luxury baths. Exercise room, kayaks, and bicycles available. Complimentary continental breakfast. Midweek specials offered on occasion will get you a third night **free.** $$$$

Sea Breeze Inn. 812 Stonington Road (Route 1); (860) 535-2843. On a little arm of the sea, 30 units offer the basic necessities plus TV and air-conditioning. $$$

General Information

Mystic Country/Eastern Regional Tourism District. 32 Huntington Street, New London 06320; (860) 444-2206 or (800) TO-ENJOY; www.mysticcountry.com.

Mystic and Shoreline Visitor Information Center. Building 1D in Olde Mistick Village; Coogan Boulevard off Route 27, Mystic; (860) 536-1641. Open year-round daily; Memorial Day through Columbus Day from 9:00 a.m. to 6:00 p.m.; and during the rest of the year from 10:00 a.m. to 5:00 p.m. Monday through Saturday and until 4:00 p.m. on Sunday.

Mystic Chamber of Commerce. 14 Holmes Street, Mystic; (860) 572-9578. For Mystic and Stonington Borough and area information.

CT State Visitor Information Center. I-95 southbound, between Exits 92 and 91; (860) 599-2056. Open from 8:00 a.m. daily year-round; restrooms (open 24 hours daily); staff in summer. Maps, state tourism guides, brochures.

Norwich Tourism and Main Street Office. 77 Main Street, Norwich 06360; (860) 886-4683 or (888) 4-NORWICH; http://norwichct.org.

Visit **Mystic Web site:** www.visitconnecticut.com/mystic_eastern.html.

New London Visitor Center, at the Trolley Waiting Center. Eugene O'Neill Drive, New London; (860) 444-7264.

Mystic Coast & Country Travel Industry Association Inc. 12 Roosevelt Avenue, Mystic 06355; (860) 536-1205; www.mysticcountry.com. Destination marketing organization dedicated to promoting eastern Connecticut and southwestern Rhode Island.

Index